Mastering Azure Virtual Desktop

The ultimate guide to the implementation and management of Azure Virtual Desktop

Ryan Mangan

BIRMINGHAM—MUMBAI

Mastering Azure Virtual Desktop

Copyright © 2022 Packt Publishing

Group Product Manager: Rahul Nair

Publishing Product Manager: Preet Ahuja

Senior Editor: Athikho Sapuni Rishana

Content Development Editor: Nihar Kapadia

Technical Editor: Shruthi Shetty

Copy Editor: Safis Editing

Project Coordinator: Shagun Saini

Proofreader: Safis Editing

Indexer: Tejal Daruwale Soni

Production Designer: Prashant Ghare

Marketing Coordinator: Nimisha Dua

First published: March 2022

Production reference: 3290722

Published by Packt Publishing Ltd.
Livery Place
35 Livery Street
Birmingham
B3 2PB, UK.

ISBN 978-1-80107-502-2

www.packt.com

Technology made large populations possible; large populations now make technology indispensable.

— Joseph Wood Krutch

Just because something doesn't do what you planned it to do doesn't mean it's useless.

— Thomas Edison

Be passionate and bold. Always keep learning. You stop doing useful things if you don't learn.

— Satya Nadella

Foreword

I've long admired Ryan Mangan: over the years, I've read his enlightening books, attended his entertaining presentations, and occasionally had a beer with him. During all these activities I've come away with an impression of a highly technical individual who has that rarest of talents; the ability to make the complex simple. Whether it's his deep focus on the underlying platform or application delivery methods, Ryan is my go-to for many desktop virtualization topics. He has given a huge amount of time to the community, sharing knowledge on his blog and in person. Ryan has again and again given his time generously and in doing so has benefitted all of us in the industry.

Desktop virtualization has been around for a while, a long while. From its early on-premises inception to the current cloud-focused architectures, it's been an area of technology that's had times of stagnation and times of rapid changes. We are currently in the middle of one of those phases of accelerated evolution. I can think of no-one better than Ryan Mangan to be your guide through this time of transformation.

With this book you'll learn how to deploy, manage, monitor, and operate Azure Virtual Desktop. It will guide you from the high-level concepts right down to the detail of automating the environment, with clear steps for you to follow. You'll understand not just Azure Virtual Desktop, but the necessary surrounding technologies and how to implement them together.

In this Azure Virtual Desktop book, Ryan brings to bear a depth of knowledge gained through years of field experience working with some of the largest and most complex deployments. Whether this is your first exposure to desktop virtualization, or you are an old hand, you'll find something here to enhance your skills and become a technical thought leader in your organization. You will love the step-by-step instructions, screenshots, source-code snippets, examples, and links to additional sources of information provided in these pages.

Jim Moyle

Senior Program Manager, Azure Virtual Desktop, Microsoft

Contributors

About the author

Ryan Mangan is an end user computing specialist. He is a speaker, presenter, and author who has helped customers and technical communities with end user computing solutions, ranging from small to global, 30,000-user enterprise deployments in various fields. Ryan is the owner and author of `ryanmangansitblog`, and has over 3 million visitors and over 200+ articles. Some of Ryan's community and technical awards include Microsoft **Most Valuable Professional (MVP)**, VMware vExpert 2014, 2015, 2016, 2017, 2018, 2019, 2020, & 2021, VMware vExpert EUC 2021, VMware vExpert Desktop Hypervisor 2021, **Very Important Parallels professional program (VIPP)** 2019, 20, & 21, and LoginVSI Technology Advocate 19, and 20.

> *Writing a book does require lots of time, energy, and dedication, especially in the midst of a pandemic where the customer demand for technology and services increased significantly. I'd like to thank my wife, Alexandra, for supporting me and providing continued motivation as well as the private time to get the book finished. Also, my daughter, Sienna, who continues to this day to ask "what are you doing on the computer, Daddy?"*

About the reviewers

Marcel Meurer is responsible for the professional IT services business unit at sepago GmbH in Cologne and is the founder of the development company ITProCloud GmbH. In this role, he leads a team of consultants who provide their expertise in Microsoft and Citrix technologies for customers and partners. His technical focuses are Microsoft Azure platform services, and he has been a Microsoft Azure MVP since 2016.

He loves working in the community. Besides his blog, he publishes tools that simplify working with the Azure cloud – especially in the context of Azure Virtual Desktop. His well-known tools include WVDAdmin and Hydra for Azure Virtual Desktop.

Marcel Meurer graduated as an engineer in electrical engineering from the University of Applied Science, Aachen.

Marco Moioli is a cloud solution architect working for Microsoft's Italian subsidiary.

His goal is to enable Microsoft partners in understanding and to propose solutions based on the Azure cloud and Microsoft 365.

He spent the first part of his career as a consultant/presales engineer at Microsoft specializing in Windows deployment and security.

In 2019, he joined the Microsoft Partner division in West Europe with the role of cloud solution architect, dedicated to Azure Virtual Desktop.

In 2021, he took care of the infrastructure, identity, security, and compliance streams for the Microsoft Partner division in Italy.

He's also the author of the free ebook *Azure Virtual Desktop (Succinctly)*, which will be published in 2022 by Synchfusion.

I'd like to thank Michel Roth and Christiaan Brinkhoff for helping me to become an Azure Virtual Desktop expert.

Neil McLoughlin is based in Manchester in the UK. He has worked in the IT industry for over 20 years, working across many different sectors and roles. He spent around 10 years providing Citrix consultancy for large enterprise customers. Around 5 years ago, Neil discovered the cloud and DaaS and since then has specialized in cloud-based desktop solutions, mainly Azure Virtual Desktop and M365.

Neil is very passionate about community work and runs the UK Azure Virtual Desktop User Group and the Virtual Desktops Community, which is a worldwide community of people interested in Azure Virtual Desktop.

He is currently employed as the UK Field CTO for Nerdio but has previously worked for New Signature, Computacenter, and Cap Gemini as a senior consultant and architect specializing in end user computing.

You can find Neil on Twitter @virtualmanc.

Toby Skerritt is an experienced end user architect and engineer. He currently works as technology director for Foundation IT. He has been with Foundation IT for over 10 years, working mainly in the professional service and presales functions. Toby helped the organization to achieve multiple Microsoft accreditations and competencies, including Microsoft Gold Competency status for Cloud Platforms. Toby has been working in the technology space for the past 20 years, working predominantly with Windows OS deployment and virtual desktop technologies. He holds both Azure Administrator Associate and Azure Virtual Desktop Specialty accreditations and has written a number of blogs and opinion pieces on the cloud, Windows Desktop, and cloud desktop solutions.

Table of Contents

Preface

Section 1: Introduction

1

Introduction to Azure Virtual Desktop

Section 2: Planning an Azure Virtual Desktop Architecture

2

Designing the Azure Virtual Desktop Architecture

3
Designing for User Identities and Profiles

4

Implementing and Managing Networking for Azure Virtual Desktop

5
Implementing and Managing Storage for Azure Virtual Desktop

Section 3: Implementing an Azure Virtual Desktop Infrastructure

6
Creating Host Pools and Session Hosts

7

Configure Azure Virtual Desktop Host Pools

8

Azure AD Join for Azure Virtual Desktop

9

Creating and Managing Session Host Images

Section 4: Managing Access and Security

10

Managing Access

11

Managing Security

Section 5: Managing User Environments and Apps

12

Implementing and Managing FSLogix

13

Configuring User Experience Settings

14

MSIX App Attach

15
Configuring Apps on a Session Host

Section 6: Monitoring and Maintaining an Azure Virtual Desktop Infrastructure

16
Planning and Implementing Business Continuity and Disaster Recovery

17

Automate Azure Virtual Desktop Management Tasks

18

Monitoring and Managing Performance and Health

19

Azure Virtual Desktop's Getting Started Feature

Appendix

Microsoft Resources and Microsoft Learn

Final Assessment

Index

Other Books You May Enjoy

Preface

Mastering Azure Virtual Desktop offers complete coverage of Azure Virtual Desktop as well as up-to-date coverage of the AZ-140 exam so that you can take it with confidence. With this book, you will learn the steps for planning, implementing, and managing an Azure Virtual Desktop environment. You will also find hints, tips, and advice on common issues you may face with configuration and day-to-day management.

Who this book is for

This book is for IT professionals who wish to attain the Microsoft Certified: Windows Virtual Desktop Specialty certification and those who work in the end user computing field, whether as an administrator, consultant, or architect. Readers should already be familiar and comfortable with cloud computing and Microsoft Azure principles. You should also have experience administering core features and services within a Microsoft 365 tenant.

What this book covers

Chapter 1, Introduction to Azure Virtual Desktop, provides an introduction to Azure Virtual Desktop providing a high-level overview of the service offering and the associated benefits.

Chapter 2, Designing the Azure Virtual Desktop Architecture, provides guidance and the requirements to plan and design an Azure Virtual Desktop environment. You will also learn about sizing, network guidelines, and understanding Azure Virtual Desktop connectivity.

Chapter 3, Designing for User Identities and Profiles, covers everything you need to know for designing user identities and profiles.

Chapter 4, Implementing and Managing Networking for Azure Virtual Desktop, looks at the considerations and techniques for implementing and managing networking for Azure Virtual Desktop.

Chapter 5, Implementing and Managing Storage for Azure Virtual Desktop, details the requirements and storage options required for FSLogix components as well as teaching you how to create storage accounts and configure disks and Azure file shares.

Chapter 6, Creating and Configuring Host Pools and Session Hosts, teaches you how to create and configure Azure Virtual Desktop host pools and session hosts.

Chapter 7, Configure Azure Virtual Desktop Host Pools, guides you through the configuration of host pools, the use of a **Remote Desktop** (**RD**) license server for those using server-based session hosts, custom **Remote Desktop Protocol** (**RDP**) properties, and applying security and compliance settings to a session host.

Chapter 8, Azure AD Join for Azure Virtual Desktop, teaches you how to join session hosts to Azure Active Directory and how to carry out basic troubleshooting.

Chapter 9, Creating and Managing Session Host Images, looks at the configuration of host pools including the configuration of a gold image, Azure Compute Gallery optimization, and basic performance troubleshooting.

Chapter 10, Managing Access, discusses how to plan and implement Azure roles and **role-based access control** (**RBAC**) and how to manage local roles, groups, and rights assignments for Azure Virtual Desktop session hosts.

Chapter 11, Managing Security, provides a clear understanding of Azure multi-factor authentication and its benefits, how to configure conditional access policies, the use of Azure Defender for Cloud, and the configuration of Microsoft Defender Antivirus for Azure Virtual Desktop.

Chapter 12, Implementing and Managing FSLogix, shows how to install, configure, and manage FSLogix profile containers and Cloud Cache.

Chapter 13, Configuring User Experience Settings, looks at some of the features and functions you can configure with Azure Virtual Desktop, including Universal Print, Start Virtual Machine connect, Screen Capture Protection, FSLogix troubleshooting, and Remote Desktop client troubleshooting.

Chapter 14, MSIX App Attach, teaches you how to implement and manage MSIX app attach for Azure Virtual Desktop.

Chapter 15, Configuring Apps on a Session Host, teaches you how to configure app masking, deploy RemoteApp applications, configure Microsoft Teams AV Redirect, Multimedia redirect, and manage internet access for Azure Virtual Desktop.

Chapter 16, Planning and Implementing Business Continuity and Disaster Recovery, discusses the options available to you when planning and designing business continuity and disaster recovery for Azure Virtual Desktop.

Chapter 17, *Automate Azure Virtual Desktop Management Tasks*, teaches you how to automate repeated maintenance tasks, implement custom autoscaling scripts, and configure and deploy scaling plans.

Chapter 18, *Monitoring and Managing Performance and Health*, teaches you how to configure Azure Virtual Desktop insights to monitor user experience and overall environment performance. This chapter also discusses setting up alerts and an introduction to Kusto.

Chapter 19, *Azure Virtual Desktop's Getting Started Feature*, teaches you how to use the getting started feature to deploy an Azure Virtual Desktop environment.

Appendix, *Microsoft Resources and Microsoft Learn*, contains useful information and other interesting content from Microsoft, communities, and MVPs on Azure Virtual Desktop.

To get the most out of this book

If you are an IT professional, an end user computing administrator, architect, or consultant looking to learn about implementing and managing Azure Virtual Desktop, this book is for you.

Download the color images

We also provide a PDF file that has color images of the screenshots and diagrams used in this book. You can download it here: `https://static.packt-cdn.com/downloads/9781801075022_ColorImages.pdf`.

Conventions used

There are a number of text conventions used throughout this book.

`Code in text`: Indicates code words in text, database table names, folder names, filenames, file extensions, pathnames, dummy URLs, user input, and Twitter handles. Here is an example: "The client stores the connection configuration for each available resource in a set of `.rdp` files."

A block of code is set as follows:

```
{ "joeclbldhdmoijbaagobkhlpfjglcihd": { "installation_mode":
"force_installed", "runtime_allowed_hosts": [ "*://*.youtube.
com" ], "runtime_blocked_hosts": [ "*://*" ], "update_url":
"https://edge.microsoft.com/extensionwebstorebase/v1/crx" } }
```

Any command-line input or output is written as follows:

```
Install-Module -Name Az.DesktopVirtualization
```

Bold: Indicates a new term, an important word, or words that you see onscreen. For instance, words in menus or dialog boxes appear in **bold**. Here is an example: "You will then see the **Sign in to your account** popup."

Tips or important notes
Appear like this.

Get in touch

Feedback from our readers is always welcome.

General feedback: If you have questions about any aspect of this book, email us at customercare@packtpub.com and mention the book title in the subject of your message.

Errata: Although we have taken every care to ensure the accuracy of our content, mistakes do happen. If you have found a mistake in this book, we would be grateful if you would report this to us. Please visit www.packtpub.com/support/errata and fill in the form.

Piracy: If you come across any illegal copies of our works in any form on the internet, we would be grateful if you would provide us with the location address or website name. Please contact us at copyright@packt.com with a link to the material.

If you are interested in becoming an author: If there is a topic that you have expertise in and you are interested in either writing or contributing to a book, please visit authors.packtpub.com.

Share Your Thoughts

Once you've read *Mastering Azure Virtual Desktop*, we'd love to hear your thoughts! Scan the QR code below to go straight to the Amazon review page for this book and share your feedback.

https://packt.link/r/1801075026

Your review is important to us and the tech community and will help us make sure we're delivering excellent quality content.

Section 1: Introduction

This section offers an introduction to Azure Virtual Desktop with a view to providing a high-level overview of the subject before we start to delve into the details of the core functions and features of the product.

This part of the book comprises the following chapter:

- *Chapter 1, Introduction to Azure Virtual Desktop*

1

Introduction to Azure Virtual Desktop

In today's post-COVID 19 world, it has become crucial for businesses to enable remote work strategies for their teams while enhancing security, reducing infrastructure costs, and simplifying overall IT management. Azure Virtual Desktop allows users to continue to work in any location using Microsoft's latest desktop and application virtualization cloud technology, enabling companies to provide a secure, productive experience in this ever-changing world.

This book provides a complete guide to Azure Virtual Desktop. We will start with the essentials for understanding desktop virtualization, as well as planning, designing, implementing, and supporting an Azure Virtual Desktop environment.

Desktop virtualization

Virtual Desktop Infrastructure (**VDI**), also known as **Desktop Virtualization**, refers to virtualization and virtual machines that provide and manage virtual desktops. Users access these virtual machines remotely from any supported device, including remote locations, and the compute processing is completed on the host server. Users connect to their virtual desktop sessions through a **connection broker**. This broker is essentially a software layer that acts as the intermediary between the user and server, enabling the orchestration of user sessions to virtual desktops or published applications.

VDI is usually deployed in an organization's data center and managed by its IT department. Typical on-premises providers include Citrix, VMware, and Remote Desktop Services. VDI can be hosted on-premises or in the cloud. Some organizations use the cloud to scale virtual desktop environments, enabling a hybrid capability that allows IT admins to meet changing organizational demands quickly.

Azure Virtual Desktop – what is it?

Azure Virtual Desktop is a desktop and app virtualization service that runs on Microsoft Azure. Azure Virtual Desktop works across devices, including Windows, Mac, iOS, Android, and Linux, with apps that you can use to access remote desktops and apps. You can also use modern browsers to access Azure Virtual Desktop.

Providing the best user experience

Users have the freedom to connect to Azure Virtual Desktop from any capable device over the internet. You can use an Azure Virtual Desktop client to connect to published Windows desktops and applications. There are three flavors of client that you can use to connect: a native application on the device, a mobile app, or the Azure Virtual Desktop HTML5 web client.

You can improve application performance on session host **virtual machines** (**VMs**) by running apps near services by connecting to your data center or the cloud. This will reduce the risk of long loading times and keep your users productive.

User sign-in to Azure Virtual Desktop is much faster because user profiles are containerized using FSLogix profile containers. The user profile container is dynamically attached to the session host or VM in question at user sign-in. The user profile is made available and appears in the system exactly as a local user profile would.

You can provide individual ownership to session desktops using personal (persistent) desktops for those specific use cases. For example, you may want to offer personal remote desktops for members of a web development team. They would be able to add or remove programs without impacting other users on that virtual desktop.

Enhanced security

Azure Virtual Desktop provides centralized security for users' desktops with **Azure Active Directory** (**Azure AD**). You can further enhance security by enabling **multi-factor authentication** (**MFA**) to provide secure user access. You can also secure access to data by using Azure's granular **role-based access control** (**RBAC**) for users.

Azure Virtual Desktop separates the data and apps from the local hardware and runs both resource types on a remote server. The risk of confidential data being left on a personal device is significantly reduced when using Azure Virtual Desktop.

User sessions can be isolated in both single and multi-session virtual desktop deployments.

Azure Virtual Desktop improves security by using reverse connect technology, a more secure connection type than the **Remote Desktop Protocol** (**RDP**). However, the session hosts do open inbound ports to the session host VMs.

Simplify management

Azure Virtual Desktop is a Microsoft Azure service that's familiar to Azure admins. You use Azure Active Directory and RBAC to manage access to resources. With Microsoft Azure, you are provided with the tools to automate VM deployments, manage VM updates, and provide disaster recovery.

As with other Microsoft Azure services, Azure Virtual Desktop uses Azure Monitor for monitoring and alerts. This allows IT admins to identify issues through a single interface.

Managing Azure Virtual Desktop performance

Azure Virtual Desktop provides you with options to load balance users on your VM **host pools**. Host pools are collections of VMs with the same configuration assigned to multiple users.

You can configure session load balancing to occur as users sign in to session hosts, also known as breadth mode. Breadth mode essentially means that users are sequentially allocated across the host pool for your workload. You also have the option to configure your VMs for depth mode load balancing to save costs, where users are fully allocated on one VM before moving to the next. In addition, Azure Virtual Desktop provides the tools and the capability to automatically provision additional VMs when incoming demand exceeds a specified threshold.

Multi-session Windows 10/11

Azure Virtual Desktop enables and headlines Windows 11 and 10 Enterprise multi-session since they are the only Windows operating systems (client-based) that enable multiple concurrent users on a single Windows 11/10 VM.

Azure Virtual Desktop also provides a familiar experience with broader application support than the traditional Windows Server-based remote desktop solutions.

What licenses do I need?

Azure Virtual Desktop is available at no additional cost if you have an eligible Microsoft 365 license. However, it is important to note that you pay for the Microsoft Azure resources that are consumed by Azure Virtual Desktop:

- You must have a Windows or Microsoft 365 license to be able to use Windows 11 Enterprise and Windows 10 Enterprise desktops and apps (eligible).

- You must have a Microsoft **Remote Desktop Services** (**RDS**) **Client Access License** (**CAL**) for Windows Server Remote Desktop Services desktops and apps (eligible).

How does Azure Virtual Desktop work?

Azure Virtual Desktop is easier to deploy and manage than traditional RDS or VDI environments. You don't have to provision and manage servers and server roles such as the gateway, connection broker, diagnostics, load balancing, and licensing.

What's managed by Microsoft and what you manage

The following diagram shows what services Microsoft manages and what you manage:

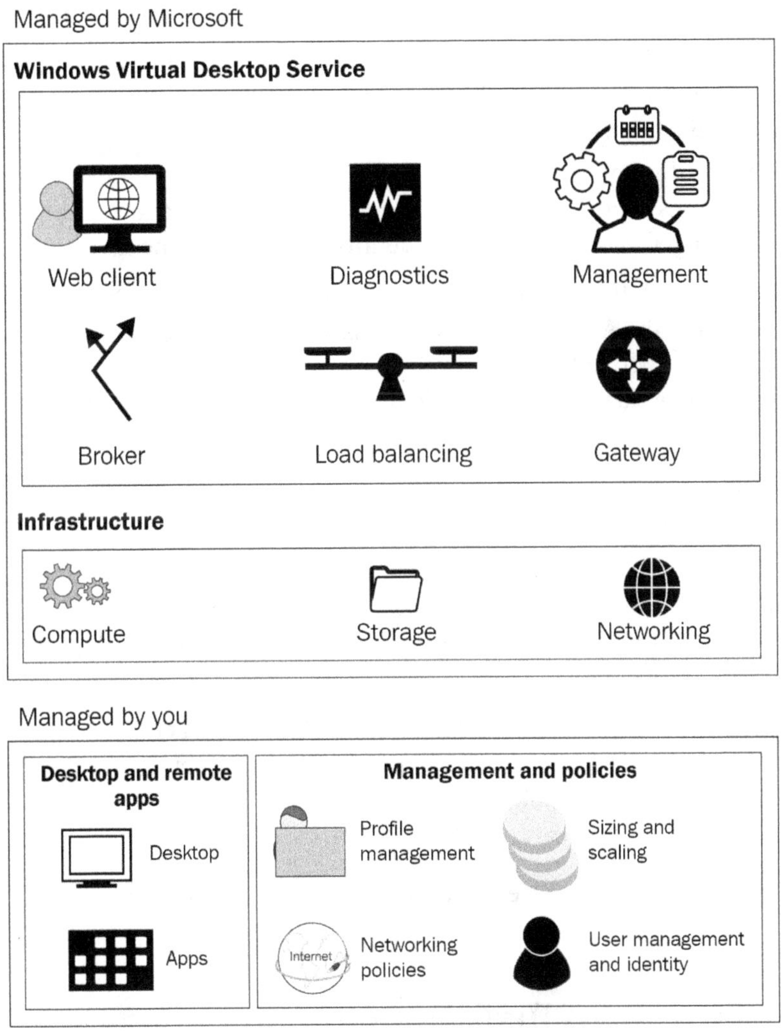

Figure 1.1 – Services managed by Microsoft and you

What Microsoft manages

Azure Virtual Desktop provides a virtualization infrastructure as a managed service. Azure Virtual Desktop's core components are as follows:

- **Web client**: The Web Access service within Azure Virtual Desktop management enables users to access virtual desktops and remote apps through the HTML5-compatible web browser, as they would with a local PC – from anywhere and on any device. In addition, you can secure Web Access by using MFA in Azure AD.

- **Diagnostics**: Remote Desktop Diagnostics is an event-based aggregator service that's provided through Azure Virtual Desktop management that marks each user or administrator's action on the deployment as a success or failure. Administrators can query the aggregation of events to identify failing components.

- **Management**: With this option, you can manage Azure Virtual Desktop configurations in the Azure portal, as well as manage and publish host pool resources. Azure Virtual Desktop also includes several extensibility components. You can manage Azure Virtual Desktop by using Windows PowerShell or with the provided REST APIs, enabling support from third-party tools.

- **Broker**: The Connection Broker service manages user connections to virtual desktops and remote apps. This also handles load balancing and reconnecting to existing sessions.

- **Load balancing**: This option provides session host load balancing by depth-first or breadth-first. The broker controls how new incoming sessions are distributed across the VMs in a host pool.

- **Gateway**: The Remote Connection Gateway service connects remote users to Azure Virtual Desktop remote apps and desktops from any internet-connected device that can run an Azure Virtual Desktop client. The client connects to a gateway that then orchestrates a connection from the VM back to the same gateway.

Windows Virtual Desktop uses Azure infrastructure services for compute, storage, and networking.

What does the customer manage?

Now, let's look at what you, as the customer, manage. First, we'll look at the desktop and remote apps part of Azure Virtual Desktop.

Desktop and remote apps

With this option, you can create application groups to group, publish, and assign access to remote apps or desktops:

- **Desktop**: Remote Desktop application groups give users access to a full desktop. You can provide a desktop where the session host's VM resources are shared or pooled. You can give dedicated personal desktops to those users who need to add or remove programs without impacting other users.

- **Apps**: RemoteApp applications groups provide users access to the applications you individually publish to the application group. You can create multiple RemoteApp app groups to accommodate different user scenarios. For example, you can use RemoteApp to virtualize an app that runs on a legacy OS or needs secured access to corporate resources.

- **Images**: When you configure session hosts for application groups, you have a choice of images. You should use a recommended image such as Windows 10 Enterprise multi-session and Office 365. Alternatively, you can choose an image in your gallery or an image provided by Microsoft or other publishers.

Management and policies

Now, let's look at the customer responsibilities for management and policies:

- **Profile management**: Configure FSLogix profile containers with a storage solution such as Azure Files to containerize user profiles and provide users with a fast and stateful experience.

- **Sizing and scaling**: Here, you can specify session host VM sizes, including GPU-enabled VMs, as well as specify depth or breath load balancing when you create a host pool. Finally, you can configure automation policies for scaling.

- **Networking policies**: Define a network topology to access the virtual desktop and virtual apps from the intranet or internet based on the organizational policy.

- Connect your Azure Virtual Network to your on-premises network by using a virtual private network. Alternatively, you can use Azure ExpressRoute to extend your on-premises networks into the Microsoft cloud platform over a private connection.

- **User management and identity**: Use Azure AD and RBAC to manage user access to resources. Take advantage of Azure AD security features such as conditional access, MFA, and Intelligent Security Graph. Azure Virtual Desktop requires **Active Directory Domain Services** (**AD DS**). Domain-joined sessions host VMs on this service. You can also sync AD DS with Azure AD so that users are associated between the two. Once you've done this, you can use Azure AD Join to deliver virtual desktops to your users.

Summary

This chapter provided an introduction to Azure Virtual Desktop, some of the key benefits of the service, and an overview of its components and capabilities. In the next chapter, we will look at designing an Azure Virtual Desktop architecture.

Section 2:
Planning an Azure Virtual Desktop Architecture

This section takes a look at the planning and design of Azure Virtual Desktop's architecture, which covers both the core architecture and the design of user identities and profiles.

This part of the book comprises the following chapters:

2
Designing the Azure Virtual Desktop Architecture

We will start this book by looking at the design of **Azure Virtual Desktop**. Design is an integral part of any suitable technology solution, and in this chapter, we will look at the areas you should consider when designing Azure Virtual Desktop.

In this chapter, we'll cover the following topics:

- Assessing existing physical and Virtual Desktop environments
- Assessing the network capacity and speed requirements for Azure Virtual Desktop
- Identifying an operating system for an Azure Virtual Desktop implementation
- Planning and configuring name resolution for Active Directory and Azure Active Directory Domain Services
- Planning a host pools architecture
- Recommended resource groups, subscriptions, and management groups

- Configuring the location for the Azure Virtual Desktop metadata
- Calculating and recommending a configuration for capacity and performance requirements

Assessing existing physical and Virtual Desktop environments

Before we can look at the components of Azure Virtual Desktop, we need to understand the current environment, the requirements, and other information that would be useful.

Assessing Azure Virtual Desktop deployments

When tackling the design of Azure Virtual Desktop, the first thing we must do is look at the current desktop estate within the organization's environment. The desktop estate could be purely physical, virtual, or a mixture of both physical and virtual. Suppose your organization is deploying a virtual desktop environment for the first time (**greenfield deployment**). In this case, you should still assess your physical desktop estate to understand the applications, data, and profile usage within your organization.

The desktop assessment should evaluate areas including the user's persona, consistent host pool types of virtual machines, applications, and user profiles. The data that's gathered from this assessment can be used to scope the deployment of new infrastructure and Azure Virtual Desktop migration.

When preparing your planning methodology, you can use Microsoft's best practices on cloud adoption. They will help you document your technology strategy and current desktop state:

- Inventory and rationalize your desktop estate based on assumptions that align with motivations and business outcomes with the digital estate guidance from Microsoft: `https://docs.microsoft.com/en-us/azure/cloud-adoption-framework/digital-estate/rationalize`.

- Establish a plan for initial organizational alignment to support the proposed adoption plan using the organizational alignment plan: `https://docs.microsoft.com/en-us/azure/cloud-adoption-framework/plan/initial-org-alignment`.

- Create a readiness plan for addressing any skills gaps that may be present. You can find this in the skills readiness plan: `https://docs.microsoft.com/en-us/azure/cloud-adoption-framework/plan/adapt-roles-skills-processes`.

- Develop a cloud adoption plan to manage change across the digital estate, operational and technical skills, and overall organization using the cloud adoption plan: `https://docs.microsoft.com/en-us/azure/cloud-adoption-framework/plan/plan-intro`.

Another helpful tool that can be used to plan is a digital estate assessment, which enables you to measure your desktop estate changes based on the organization's desired outcomes:

- **Infrastructure**: For organizations that are inward-facing and seek to optimize costs, operational processes, agility, or other aspects of their operations, the digital estate focuses on VMs, servers, and workloads.

- **Applications**: It is recommended that you focus on applications, APIs, and transactional data that supports the customers.

- **Data**: It is somewhat challenging to launch new products/services without some data. You should also focus on the silos of data across the organization.

- **Operational**: Businesses require stable technologies to operate efficiently and effectively. Where possible, businesses need to aim to be as close as possible to zero downtime. Service reliability is critical in today's competitive markets. When stability is a priority, the digital estate should be measured on the positive or negative impact on stable operations. The reliability of workloads, disaster recovery, and business continuity are good measures you can use for operational stability per asset.

Using the data you have collected and analyzed will help you create the migration plan. You may need to carry out workload assessments to capture specific requirements. For an Azure Virtual Desktop migration deployment plan, you will require data about the desktops, users, and workloads used by each user.

Let's look at some tools available to you.

Movere

Movere is a product designed to help you migrate resources to Microsoft cloud services. It improves business intelligence by reporting on entire IT environments within a single day. As organizations grow, change, and digitally optimize, Movere helps IT admins to see and control their IT environment.

You can access Movere through Microsoft Solution Assessment and Microsoft Cloud Economics Program. You can use these tools when you're planning and deploying an Azure Virtual Desktop environment. You can find out more about Movere at `https://www.movere.io/`.

Azure Migrate

Azure Migrate is used to discover, assess, and migrate on-premises servers, apps, and data to Microsoft Azure:

- Azure Migrate's appliance is used to discover installed applications (software inventory).

- Agentless VMware migration supports concurrent replication of 500 VMs per vCenter.

- Azure Migrate installs the Azure VM agent automatically on the VMware VMs while migrating them to Azure using the agentless VMware migration method.

Lakeside is also integrated with Azure Migrate within the virtual desktop infrastructure migration goals section to assess your current state. This vendor can help you map out an Azure Virtual Desktop deployment plan, including personas, host pools, applications, and user profiles specific to a Virtual Desktop environment.

User personas

User personas are the specifications for a particular group of users within a physical or virtual desktop environment with common characteristics or working methods. You may have multiple user personas in an Azure Virtual Desktop environment.

Once you have completed the required data capture, you will see the resources and workloads being used within your environment. You can then use this data to group user personas based on the following criteria:

- **Personal pools**: Some users may require dedicated desktops (personal pools). For example, security, compliance, high-performance, or noisy-neighbor requirements might lead to some users running on dedicated desktops that aren't part of a pooling desktop strategy. You can use one-to-one here, though one of the biggest benefits of using personal pools is the ability to give local administrator rights and solve the challenge of those apps that do not support pooled multi-session deployments. You would enter this information by specifying a personal host pool type during the Azure Virtual Desktop host pool deployment (`https://docs.microsoft.com/en-us/azure/virtual-desktop/create-host-pools-azure-marketplace#begin-the-host-pool-setup-process`).

- **Density**: Power users may benefit from fewer users per session host for the more intensive workloads. For example, heavier density (applications/users/load) may require two users per **virtual central processing unit (vCPU)** instead of the typical six users' light-user assumption per vCPU. You must enter the required density information in the pool settings of the Azure Virtual Desktop host pool deployment (`https://docs.microsoft.com/en-us/azure/virtual-desktop/create-host-pools-azure-marketplace#begin-the-host-pool-setup-process`).

- **Performance**: High-performance desktop requirements for workloads or specific user scenarios. Some users may need more memory per vCPU than the assumed 4 GB of RAM per vCPU. You must enter the VM sizing in the Azure Virtual Desktop host pool deployment in the virtual machine details section (`https://docs.microsoft.com/en-us/azure/virtual-desktop/create-host-pools-azure-marketplace#virtual-machine-details`).

- **Graphical processing**: Some users may require a **graphic processing unit (GPU)** for CAD or other graphical applications/workloads. Some users may require vGPU-based VMs in Azure, as demonstrated in this guide for configuring GPU VMs: `https://docs.microsoft.com/en-us/azure/virtual-desktop/configure-vm-gpu`.

- **Azure region**: Localized regional requirements to mitigate any **latency** and connectivity issues. Before configuring the host pool, it is recommended that a user from each region should test latency to Azure by using the Azure Experience estimation tool: `https://azure.microsoft.com/services/virtual-desktop/assessment/#estimation-tool`. The test user should provide details for the lowest-latency Azure region and the latency in milliseconds for the top three Azure regions. Additionally, if a local backend is needed for the applications that are served via AVD, the latency between the application and the backend can be more important than the latency between the user and the session.

- **Business functions**: Department grouping for billing or specific operational requirements. This type of grouping will help you align corporate costs in later stages of operations. You can use different subscriptions per department or use tagging to allocate costs to different business cost centers.

- **User count**: One question you should consider is, *How many users will be in each distinct persona?*

- **Max session counts**: Based on the geography and hours of operation, how many concurrent users are expected for each persona during maximum load? These are factors you should consider.

The following table shows responses to populating a completed assessment or design document:

Example User Groupings			
Criterion	**User Group 1**	**User Group 2**	**User Group 3**
Pool Type	Shared	Shared	Personal (security concerns)
Density	Light (6 users/vCPU)	Heavy (2 users/vCPU)	Dedicated (1 user/vCPU)
Performance	Low	High memory	Low
GPU	N/A	Required	N/A
Azure Region	UK West	Western Europe	UK South
User Count	1,000	50	20
Session Count	200	50	10

Each persona/grouping, or each group of users with distinct business functions and technical requirements, would require a specific host pool configuration.

The end user assessment helps you realize the required data: pool type, density, size, CPU/GPU, Landing Zone region, and so on.

> **Important Note**
>
> You can read more about Azure Landing Zones here: `https://docs.microsoft.com/en-us/azure/cloud-adoption-framework/ready/landing-zone/`.

The host pool configuration assessment maps that data to a deployment plan. Aligning the technical requirements, business requirements, and cost will help determine the host pools' proper number and configuration.

Pricing examples are available for Microsoft Azure in the East US (`https://azure.com/e/448606254c9a44f88798892bb8e0ef3c`), West Europe (`https://azure.com/e/61a376d5f5a641e8ac31d1884ade9e55`), and Southeast Asia (`https://azure.com/e/7cf555068922461587d0aa99a476f926`) regions.

Application groups

Both Movere and Lakeside assess the current on-premises environment and provide data about the applications that are run on end user desktops. Using the data you have collected, you should create a list of all the applications that are required for each persona. For each required application, the answers to the following questions will help shape deployment iterations:

- Which applications need to be installed for the persona to use this desktop? (group/departmental applications)

  Unless the persona uses 100 percent web-based software as a service application, you will most likely need to create and configure a custom master VHD image (`https://docs.microsoft.com/en-us/azure/virtual-desktop/set-up-customize-master-image`) for each persona. You will then need to work out which applications are typical applications and group/departmental applications. Common applications should be installed on the master image.

  > **Tip**
  > You can create custom images within the Azure portal or use Hyper-V, as suggested in the preceding paragraph.

- Is this application compatible with a Windows 10 Enterprise multi-session (W10EMU)?

  If an application isn't compatible, a personal pool (`https://docs.microsoft.com/en-us/azure/virtual-desktop/configure-host-pool-personal-desktop-assignment-type`) may be required to run the custom VHD image.

- Will mission-critical applications suffer from latency between the Azure Virtual Desktop instance and any backend systems?

  If this is the case – and it is likely to be the case – you may want to consider migrating the backend systems that support the application to Azure.

These answers may require the plan to include remediation to the desktop images or support application components before desktop migration or deployment.

In this section, we looked at application groups and some of the tools available, as well as some questions to help you gather the requirements for your future Azure Virtual Desktop solution.

Now, let's look at the network capacity and speed requirements for Azure Virtual Desktop.

Assessing the network capacity and speed requirements for Azure Virtual Desktop

In this section, we will look at assessing the network requirements for Azure Virtual Desktop and some of the considerations you should factor into your design.

A **remote desktop protocol** (**RDP**) session relies on network bandwidth. Problems with bandwidth will impact your user experience within a Windows session. Depending on the applications and display resolutions, you may require different network configurations for specific groups within your organization. Incorrectly configuring your network to meet your remote desktop needs and requirements can lead to project failure and users not being able to carry out their required tasks within Azure Virtual Desktop.

Applications

Before we understand how applications affect bandwidth, let's look at what user-specific bandwidth recommendations are available:

Application Recommended Minimum Bandwidths	
Workload	**Bandwidth Recommendation**
Light User	1.5 Mbps
Medium User	3 Mbps
Heavy User	5 Mbps
Power User	15 Mbps

The preceding table provides guidance on the minimum recommended bandwidths for an acceptable user experience. The listed recommendations are based on the guidelines in Microsoft's guide to Remote Desktop workloads (https://docs.microsoft.com/en-us/windows-server/remote/remote-desktop-services/remote-desktop-workloads).

> **Important Note**
> The recommendations in the table apply to networks with less than 0.1% loss. These recommendations apply regardless of how many user sessions you are hosting on your virtual machines.

Remember, application workload outputs, frame rate, or display resolutions will apply stress to your network. As framerates increase, your bandwidth requirement will change.

A good example is when you add Microsoft Teams video conferences without any audio/visual redirection to a typical light workload with a high-resolution display – your bandwidth requirement will increase. We will look at how to improve user experience and performance using Teams AV redirect in *Chapter 13*, *Implementing and Managing Microsoft Teams AV Redirect*.

Some of the other typical use cases that have changing bandwidth requirements are as follows:

- Voice

- Real-time communication

- Streaming 4K video

Load testing the applicable use cases and scenarios in your deployment using tools such as Login VSI and PC Mark, which simulate load, is recommended. When load testing or benchmarking, it's important to vary the load sizes and run specific stress tests to simulate your future environment. It is also recommended that you test typical user scenarios in remote sessions to understand your network's requirements and capabilities.

Display resolutions

Your required display resolution will determine the required bandwidth. The following table provides an example of the required bandwidths Microsoft recommends you have for a display resolution with a frame rate of 30 **frames per second** (**FPS**). Following these guidelines will help you provide a smooth user experience. The same recommendations apply to both single and multiple user scenarios. Remember, scenarios involving a frame rate under 30 FPS, such as reading static text, will require less available bandwidth than any graphically intensive applications:

Typical Display Resolutions at 30 FPS	Recommended Bandwidth
About 1,024 × 768 px	1.5 Mbps
About 1,280 × 720 px	3 Mbps
About 1,920 × 1,080 px	5 Mbps
About 3,840 × 2,160 px (4K)	15 Mbps

We now move on to looking at the experience estimate for Azure Virtual Desktop.

Azure Virtual Desktop experience estimator

Latency can be defined as *the delay before data transfer begins after following an instruction for its transfer*. Latency does not have to be geographic – it can also be based on your company's network topology. The distance you are from a Microsoft Azure data center can have an impact on the user experience. You can check the **round trip time** (**RTT**) of each Azure region using Windows Virtual Desktop Experience Estimator (`https://azure.microsoft.com/services/virtual-desktop/assessment/`):

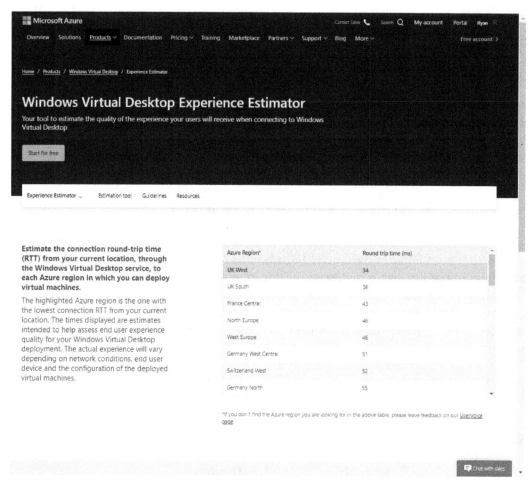

Figure 2.1 – Windows Virtual Desktop Experience Estimator

Windows Virtual Desktop Experience Estimator is a great tool to help you pick the appropriate Azure regions in terms of the closest region to deploy your Azure Virtual Desktop environment in. You can also use this tool to understand the best location for a possible Azure Virtual Desktop disaster recovery solution.

> **Assistive Technologies**
>
> The phrase **assistive technology** is used to describe products or systems that support and assist individuals with disabilities, restricted mobility, or other impairments.
>
> It is important to note that, when using assistive technology workloads, you will need to ensure that the round trip time is less than 20 **milliseconds (ms)** to achieve a good user experience.

Remote Desktop Protocol bandwidth requirements

Azure Virtual Desktop uses RDP as the connection method to provide remote display and input capabilities over network connections. RDP was initially released with **Windows NT 4.0 Terminal Server Edition** and has continuously evolved with every future Microsoft Windows and Windows Server release.

From the very beginning, RDP was developed to be independent of its underlying transport stack, and today, it supports multiple types of transport.

RDP is a complex technology that uses different techniques to deliver the server's remote graphics to the client device. Depending on the use case, scenario, availability of the compute resources, and network bandwidth, RDP dynamically adjusts various parameters to deliver the best remote user experience.

RDP multiplexes (multiple messages) multiply **Dynamic Virtual Channels (DVCs)** into a single data channel sent over different network transports. Did you know that there are separate DVCs for remote graphics, input, device redirection, printing, and others? The total amount of data that's sent over RDP depends on the user's activity – for example, a typical user working with basic textual content for most of the user's session. The bandwidth is low until the user generates a printout of a 100-page document to a printer. The print job will use more network bandwidth compared to the typical textual content that's used within the session.

A network's available bandwidth impacts the remote session's quality of experience. It is important to note that each application and display resolution can require different network configurations. It is essential to ensure that your network configuration meets your needs. It is recommended that you profile your network requirements based on user activity.

Estimating bandwidth utilization

RDP uses various compression algorithms for different types of data. The following table details some estimates for the data transfers:

Data type	Direction	How to Estimate
Remote Graphics	Session host to client	See the detailed guidelines (`https://docs.microsoft.com/en-us/azure/virtual-desktop/rdp-bandwidth?WT.mc_id=modinfra-17152-thmaure#estimating-bandwidth-used-by-remote-graphics`).
Heartbeats	Both directions	~ 20 bytes every 5 seconds.
Input	Client to session host	The amount of data is based on the user activity, which is less than 100 bytes for most operations.
File transfers	Both directions	File transfers use bulk compression. Use `.zip` compression for approximation.
Printing	Session host to client	Print job transfers depend on the driver and use bulk compression. Use `.zip` compression for approximation.

This table has been taken from Microsoft (`https://docs.microsoft.com/azure/virtual-desktop/rdp-bandwidth#estimating-bandwidth-utilization`).

As discussed in the previous section, *Assessing the network capacity and speed requirements for Azure Virtual Desktop*, you need to consider bandwidth changes when you're doing the following:

- Streaming 4K video
- Voice or video conferencing
- Real-time communication

Now, let's look at estimating bandwidth for users who require remote graphics.

Estimating the bandwidth that's used by remote graphics

It is difficult to predict remote desktop bandwidth usage. The bandwidth usage depends on the user's activities and those activities that generate the most remote desktop traffic. Every individual user is different, and differences in their work patterns may change network usage.

One of the recommended ways to assess network bandwidth requirements is to monitor real user session connections. You can monitor connections using the built-in performance counters, network equipment, or third-party tooling.

In most cases, you would estimate network utilization by understanding how RDP works by analyzing your organization's user work patterns.

The remote protocol delivers the remote server's graphics to be displayed on a local client monitor. This process's technical definition is *the remote protocol provides the desktop bitmap entirely composed on the server*. Sending a desktop bitmap may seem like a simple task. However, it does require a significant amount of resources to achieve. For example, a 1,080p desktop image in an uncompressed format is circa 8 MB in size. Displaying this image on a locally connected monitor with a screen refresh rate of 30 Hz requires approximately 240 MB/s of bandwidth.

RDP uses a combination of different techniques to reduce the amount of data that's transferred over a network, including, but not limited to, those mentioned in this table:

SN	Different RDP Techniques
1.0	Framerate optimization
2.0	Screen content classification
3.0	Content-specific codecs
4.0	Progressive image encoding
5.0	Client-side caching

To understand remote graphics, you should consider the following:

- The more complex/richer the graphics, the more bandwidth it will take:

  - Text, window UI elements, and solid color consume less bandwidth than anything else.

  - Natural images are the more significant contributors to bandwidth use. Client-side caching can help with reducing the natural image bandwidth.

- It is important to note that RDP only transmits changed parts of the screen. When there are no visible updates on the session screen, no updates are sent.

- Image slideshows are also known as video playbacks and other high-framerate content. RDP dynamically uses the required video codecs to deliver content close to the original frame rate. However, graphics are the most significant contributors to bandwidth utilization.

- An idle remote desktop uses minimal bandwidth during idle times.

- When the Remote Desktop Client window is minimized, no graphical updates are sent from the session host.

Please note that the stress you apply to your network depends on both the application workload's output, framerate, and display resolution. If the framerate or display resolution increases, the bandwidth requirement increases. One example is a light workload with a high-resolution display requiring more available bandwidth than a light workload with regular or low resolution. When using high display resolutions, expect to see the bandwidth requirements increase.

The following table provides examples of the data that's used by different graphic scenarios. These figures apply to a single monitor configuration with a 1,920 x 1,080 resolution and with both default graphics and H.264/AVC 444 graphics modes:

Scenario	Default Mode	H.264/AVC 444 Mode	Description of the Scenario
Idle	0.3 Kbps	0.3 Kbps	The user has paused their work, and there are no active screen updates.
Microsoft Word	100-150 Kbps	200-300 Kbps	The user is actively working with Microsoft Word, typing, pasting graphics, and switching between documents.
Microsoft Excel	150-200 Kbps	400-500 Kbps	The user is actively working with Microsoft Excel. Multiple cells with formulas and charts are updated simultaneously.
Microsoft PowerPoint	4-4.5 Mbps	1.6-1.8 Mbps	The user is actively working with Microsoft PowerPoint, typing, and pasting. The user is also modifying rich graphics and using slide transition effects.
Web Browsing	6-6.5 Mbps	0.9-1 Mbps	The user is actively working with a graphically rich website that contains multiple static and animated images. The user scrolls the pages both horizontally and vertically.
Image Gallery	3.3-3.6 Mbps	0.7-0.8 Mbps	The user is actively working with the image gallery application, browsing, zooming, resizing, and rotating images.
Video Playback	8.5-9.5 Mbps	2.5-2.8 Mbps	The user is watching a 30 FPS video that consumes half of the screen.
Fullscreen Video playback	7.5-8.5 Mbps	2.5-3.1 Mbps	The user is watching a fullscreen, 30 FPS video.

This table has been taken from Microsoft (`https://docs.microsoft.com/en-us/azure/virtual-desktop/rdp-bandwidth#estimating-bandwidth-used-by-remote-graphics`).

Dynamic bandwidth allocation

RDP is designed to dynamically adapt to the changing network conditions. Instead of using the hard limits on bandwidth utilization, RDP uses a capability called **continuous network detection**, which actively monitors the available network bandwidth and packet round-trip time.

Based on what's been detected, RDP dynamically selects the graphic encoding options and allocates bandwidth for device redirection and other virtual channels.

This technology allows RDP to use the entire network pipe, when available, and can quickly back off when the network is required for other services. RDP can detect this and adjust the image quality, frame rate, or compression algorithms if other applications request the network bandwidth.

Limit network bandwidth use with throttle rate limiting

There's no need to limit bandwidth utilization as limiting may affect the overall user experience in most scenarios. However, in constrained networks, you may want to restrict or limit network utilization to prevent service degradation. Another good example is leased networks (mobile hotspots or pay as you consume connectivity), which charge for the amount of traffic/bandwidth used.

In these cases, the advice is to limit RDP outbound network traffic by specifying a throttle rate in a **Quality of Service (QoS)** policy.

> **Important Note**
> Throttle rate limiting is not supported for reverse connect transport with Azure Virtual Desktop. Microsoft details how to enable this here: `https://docs.microsoft.com/en-us/azure/virtual-desktop/shortpath`.

Reverse connect transport

Azure Virtual Desktop uses reverse connect transport to establish the remote session and carries RDP traffic from the session host to the broker. The client then connects to the broker. Unlike the traditional on-premises Remote Desktop Services deployments, reverse connect transport doesn't use a TCP listener to receive incoming RDP connections. Instead, it uses outbound connectivity to the Azure Virtual Desktop infrastructure over the HTTPS connection, hence the term reverse connect.

Session host communication channel

Upon starting the Azure Virtual Desktop session host, the installed Remote Desktop Agent service establishes a connection to the AVD broker's persistent communication channel. This communication uses a secure **Transport Layer Security (TLS)** connection. This serves as a bus for service message exchange between the session host and Azure Virtual Desktop infrastructure. Essentially, this allows Azure Virtual Desktop to know when a session host is available, offline, or has any issues.

Client connection sequence

The following client connection sequence is used for Azure Virtual Desktop:

1. Using a supported Remote Desktop Client, the user *subscribes* to the Azure Virtual Desktop workspace or workspaces. We will cover this in *Chapter 3, Designing for User Identities and Profiles*, and *Chapter 6, Creating Host Pools and Session Hosts*.

2. Azure Active Directory authenticates the user and returns the token that's used to enumerate resources available to authenticate the user.

3. The client passes the token to the Azure Virtual Desktop feed subscription service.

4. The Azure Virtual Desktop feed subscription service then validates the token.

5. The Azure Virtual Desktop feed subscription service then passes the list of available desktops and remote apps back to the client in a digitally signed connection configuration.

6. The client stores the connection configuration for each available resource in a set of .rdp files.

7. When a user selects the resource that they want to connect to, the client uses the associated .rdp file, which establishes a secure TLS 1.2 connection to the closest Azure Virtual Desktop gateway instance and passes the connection information.

8. The Azure Virtual Desktop gateway validates the request and asks the Azure Virtual Desktop broker to orchestrate the connection.

9. The AVD broker service identifies the session host and uses the previously established persistent communication channel to initialize the connection.

10. The Remote Desktop stack initiates the TLS 1.2 connection to the same Azure Virtual Desktop gateway instance that's used by the client.

11. Once both the client and session host are connected to the AVD gateway, the gateway can then start relaying the raw data between both endpoints; this establishes the base reverse connect transport for the RDP connection.

12. Once the base transport has been set, the client initiates the RDP handshake.

You can read more here: `https://docs.microsoft.com/en-us/azure/virtual-desktop/network-connectivity#client-connection-sequence`.

Connection security

Azure Virtual Desktop Infrastructure, session hosts, and clients all use TLS 1.2 to initiate connections.

Azure Virtual Desktop uses the same TLS 1.2 ciphers, just like Azure Front Door (`https://docs.microsoft.com/en-us/azure/frontdoor/front-door-faq#what-are-the-current-cipher-suites-supported-by-azure-front-door`).

> **Important Note**
> Make sure both the client computers and session host the required TLS 1.2 ciphers; otherwise, you will have connection issues.

For reverse connect transport, both the client and session host connect to the Azure Virtual Desktop gateway. After establishing the TCP connection, the client or session host validates the Azure Virtual Desktop gateway's certificate. Once the base transport has been established, RDP establishes a nested TLS connection between the client and session host using the session host's certificates. By default, the certificate that's used for RDP encryption is self-generated by the OS during the deployment. If desired, customers may deploy centrally managed certificates that have been issued by the enterprise certification authority.

You can also read more about the concept of the Fish tank here: `https://ryanmangansitblog.com/2020/01/24/wvd-reverse-connect-the-fish-tank-analogy/`.

For more information about configuring certificates, see Microsoft's Windows Server documentation: `https://docs.microsoft.com/en-us/troubleshoot/windows-server/remote/remote-desktop-listener-certificate-configurations`.

This section covered how to assess and plan for the required network bandwidth. This could be in main offices and home workers. Ensuring you have the correct bandwidth is important to ensure your users have a good user experience when using Azure Virtual Desktop.

Now, let's look at the operating system images you can use for an Azure Virtual Desktop implementation.

Identifying an operating system for an Azure Virtual Desktop implementation

In this section, we will cover the different operating systems available to you.

Supported Azure OS images

Azure Virtual Desktop supports the following operating system images:

- Microsoft Windows 11 Enterprise multi-session
- Microsoft Windows 11 Enterprise
- Microsoft Windows 10 Enterprise multi-session, version 1809 or later
- Microsoft Windows 10 Enterprise, version 1809 or later (Semi-Annual Channel only)
- Microsoft Windows 7 Enterprise
- Microsoft Windows Server 2019
- Microsoft Windows Server 2016
- Microsoft Windows Server 2012 R2

Importantly, *Azure Virtual Desktop does not support x86 (32-bit) operating systems or any of the following*:

- Microsoft Windows 10 Enterprise N.
- Microsoft Windows 10 Pro.
- Microsoft Windows 10 Enterprise KN operating system.
- Microsoft Windows 7 also does not support virtual disk VHD/VHDX-based profile solutions due to a sector size limitation on managed Azure Storage.

Depending on the OS and version you choose, different OSes and versions have different automation and deployment options, as shown in the following table:

Supported Virtual Machine OS Images				
Operating System	**Azure Image Gallery**	**Manual VM deployment**	**Azure Resource Manager template integration**	**Provision host pools on Azure Marketplace**
Windows 11 Enterprise Multi-Session	Yes	Yes	Yes	Yes
Windows 10 Enterprise (multi-session), version 21H2	Yes	Yes	Yes	Yes
Windows 10 Enterprise (multi-session), version 20H2	Yes	Yes	Yes	Yes
Windows 10 Enterprise (multi-session), version 2004	Yes	Yes	Yes	Yes
Windows 10 Enterprise (multi-session), version 1909	Yes	Yes	Yes	Yes
Windows 10 Enterprise (multi-session), version 1903	Yes	Yes	No	No
Windows 10 Enterprise (multi-session), version 1809	Yes	Yes	No	No
Windows 7 Enterprise	Yes	Yes	No	No
Windows Server 2019	Yes	Yes	No	No
Windows Server 2016	Yes	Yes	Yes	Yes
Windows Server 2012 R2	Yes	Yes	No	No

This support table has been taken from Microsoft (https://docs.microsoft.com/azure/virtual-desktop/overview#supported-virtual-machine-os-images).

What is Windows 10 multi-session?

Windows 10 multi-session, also known as Windows 10 Enterprise Multi-Session and Microsoft Windows 10 **Enterprise for Virtual Desktops** (**EVDs**), is a new Remote Desktop Session host offering that allows multiple concurrent remote user sessions. Previously, you had no option but to use multi-session using Windows Server operating systems.

> **Important Note**
>
> Windows 11 multi-session support for Azure Virtual Desktop was announced on October 5, 2021. You can read more here: `https://techcommunity.microsoft.com/t5/azure-virtual-desktop/windows-11-is-now-generally-available-on-azure-virtual-desktop/ba-p/2810545`.

This new version gives users the same Windows 10 desktop experience rather than a server desktop UI. Organizations can also benefit from multi-session cost benefits and use existing per-user Windows licensing rather than the traditional **RDS Client Access Licenses** (**CALs**). For more information about licenses and pricing, see the Azure Virtual Desktop pricing page at `https://azure.microsoft.com/pricing/details/virtual-desktop/`.

Windows 10 multi-session is a virtual edition of Windows 10 Enterprise for use only on Microsoft Azure. The key difference when using Windows 10 multi-session compared to traditional Windows 10 is that this OS reports ProductType as having a value of 3. This is the same value that's used by the Windows Server OS. This property allows the OS to be compatible with existing host management tools, host multi-session-aware applications, and performance optimizations for session hosts.

It is important to note that some application installers can block the installation on Windows 10 multi-session through the installer. If your app doesn't install, contact your application vendor for an updated version or packaging company to repack it into a suitable format.

Windows 10 Enterprise Multi-Session is not to be used with on-premises production environments. This is because it has been optimized for Azure Virtual Desktop using Microsoft Azure.

> **Important Note**
>
> It's against the Microsoft licensing agreement to run Windows 10 Enterprise Multi-Session outside of Azure for production purposes. Furthermore, Windows 10 Enterprise Multi-Session will not activate against on-premises **Key Management Services (KMSes).**
>
> It is currently impossible to upgrade an existing VM running Windows 10 Professional or Enterprise to Windows 10 Enterprise Multi-Session. When using Windows 10 Enterprise Multi-Session, you may decide to update the product key to another edition. You will not be able to switch back to Windows 10 Enterprise Multi-Session. You will need to redeploy the VM.

Customizing the Windows 10 multi-session image for your organization

You would customize the image just like any image outside of Azure Virtual Desktop. You would deploy the VM in Azure with Windows 10 multi-session and customize it with the required **line of business (LOB)** applications, settings, and customizations, including optimizations. You can then proceed with Sysprep/generalize, ready to create an image template.

You can find the Windows 10 multi-session images in the Azure gallery. To find the available image templates, navigate to the Azure portal and search for Windows 10 Enterprise for Virtual Desktops. There are two options for integration with Microsoft 365 Apps for enterprise and a plain image, and Microsoft Windows 10 + Microsoft 365 Apps for enterprise and Microsoft Windows 10.

Windows 10 multi-session supported versions

These Windows 10 releases follow the same support life cycle policy as the traditional Windows 10 Enterprise operating system. This means that the March release is supported for 18 months and that the September release is supported for 30 months.

> **Important Note**
>
> Windows 10 Enterprise Multi-Session versions 1809 and later are supported. You can find the supported versions in the Azure gallery. The end of support for Windows 10 can be found here: `https://docs.microsoft.com/en-us/lifecycle/products/windows-10-enterprise-and-education`.

Profile management solution for Windows 10/11 multi-session

You should consider using **FSLogix** profile containers when deploying Azure Virtual Desktop environments, especially on non-persistent deployments or other specific use cases requiring a centrally stored profile.

One of the key benefits of using FSLogix is that you can centralize your user profiles and provide a seamless experience for users accessing Azure Virtual Desktop resources.

Azure Virtual Desktop entitled users can use FSLogix at no additional cost. FSLogix comes pre-installed on all Windows 10 Enterprise multi-session images. However, you still need to configure the FSLogix profile container via the registry or group policy for a storage share location and any customizations required specifically for your environment.

We will cover FSLogix profile containers in more detail in *Chapter 12, Implementing and Managing FSLogix.*

Check out the Azure Virtual Desktop pricing page for a complete list of applicable licenses: `https://azure.microsoft.com/pricing/details/virtual-desktop/`.

Planning and configuring name resolution for Active Directory and Azure Active Directory Domain Services

Azure Virtual Desktop can be used in a cloud-only organization or a hybrid environment. Hybrid is an approach that's used within IT where some of your IT resources are in-house and others are cloud-based services. You need to ensure that the following is configured/set up before proceeding with an Azure Virtual Desktop project.

For hybrid environments that use Azure AD and Active Directory services, you'll need the following:

- An Azure Active Directory domain.
- A domain controller that is configured and synced with Azure Active Directory. You can configure this with one of the following:
  - Azure AD Connect
  - **Azure Active Directory Domain Services (Azure AD DS)**
- An Azure subscription that contains a virtual network connected to Windows Server **Active Directory (AD)** or **Active Directory Domain Services (AD DS)**.

For cloud-only organizations, you'll need the following:

- An Azure Active Directory organization
- Azure AD DS setup and configured
- An Azure subscription that contains a virtual network connected to the Active Directory Domain Services

The Azure VMs you create for Azure Virtual Desktop must be as follows:

- Standard domain-joined or hybrid AD-joined. VMs can also be Azure AD-joined
- Run a supported OS image.

We will cover Active Directory and the various deployment configurations in more detail in *Chapter 3, Designing for User Identities and Profiles*, and *Chapter 8, Azure AD Join for Azure Virtual Desktop*.

Planning a host pools architecture

A host pool is one or multiple virtual machines within Azure using the same image. These are registered as AVD session hosts that have a configured Azure Virtual Desktop agent. It is recommended that all session host virtual machines be deployed from the same template image for optimal user experience in a host pool.

There are two types of host pools:

- The Personal host pool type is used for individual desktop user assignments.
- A Pooled host pool type is where session hosts can have multiple users connecting to multiple session hosts, sharing the compute resources of hosts within that host pool.

There are several additional properties available for configuration for host pools. You can also configure the host pool's load balancing behavior, which includes how many sessions each session host can handle and what the user can do while connected to session hosts in the host pool. You control the resources that have been published to users through app groups, as mentioned previously.

> **Important:**
> Please see the link for Azure Virtual Desktop service limits to help when planning and designing your environment: `https://docs.microsoft.com/en-us/azure/azure-resource-manager/management/azure-subscription-service-limits#azure-virtual-desktop-service-limits`

App groups

The best way to describe an app group is that it's a logical grouping of applications configured for use with a session host pool. There are two app group types:

| RemoteApp | This is used to provide user access to RemoteApps you individually select and publish to the app group. |
| Desktop | This option provides users with access to a full desktop. |

The host pool deployment automatically creates a desktop app group (named **Desktop Application Group**). App groups can be removed at any time. It is important to note that you cannot have multiple desktop app groups in a host pool.

When publishing a RemoteApp, first, you need to create a RemoteApp app group. Once created, you can create multiple RemoteApp app groups to cater to the possible different user scenarios required. You can have multiple RemoteApp app groups with overlapping RemoteApps.

When publishing remote resources to users, you should assign the users to specified app groups. When assigning users to app groups, you should consider the following things:

- You can assign users to both a desktop app group and a RemoteApp app group in the same host pool. It is important to note that users can only launch one type of app group per user session from the same host pool. It is not possible to launch both types of app groups within a single session simultaneously.

- Users can be assigned to one or many app groups within the same host pool. The user workspace feed will show a mixture of both app group types.

> **Important Note**
> A workspace is described as *a logical grouping of application groups* in Azure Virtual Desktop. Each AVD app group must be associated with a workspace to see the remote apps and desktops published to users.

End users

Once you've assigned users to the required app groups, they can connect to an Azure Virtual Desktop deployment with any supported Azure Virtual Desktop clients.

Registering the DesktopVirtualization resource provider

Before you can provision Azure Virtual Desktop resources, you need to register the required subscription(s) with the **Microsoft.DesktopVirtualization** resource provider once. Follow these steps to complete this process:

1. Open the Azure **Subscriptions** services menu:

Figure 2.2 – Various subscriptions

2. Select the subscription you would like to register:

Figure 2.3 – Selecting the required subscription

3. Search for the **Microsoft.DesktopVirtualization** provider and click **Register**:

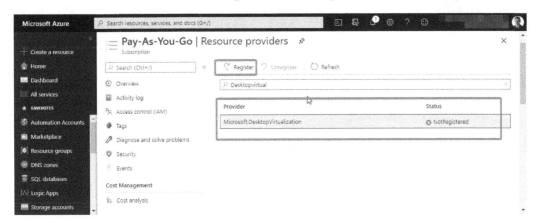

Figure 2.4 – Registering the chosen subscription with the Microsoft.DesktopVirtualization provider

4. Once registered, the status will change to **Registered**, as shown in the following screenshot:

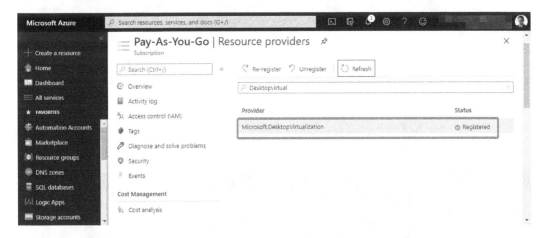

Figure 2.5 – The Microsoft.DesktopVirtalization provider showing as Registered

Once the registration has been completed and shows as **Registered**, you can deploy Azure Virtual Desktop components within your subscription.

Registering the provider using Azure PowerShell (optional)

The following steps detail the process of registering the provider using PowerShell:

1. Check the registration status of the provider:

    ```
    Get-AzResourceProvider -ProviderNamespace "Microsoft.
    DesktopVirtualization"
    ```

2. Register the `Microsoft.DesktopVirtualization` provider:

    ```
    Register-AzResourceProvider -ProviderNamespace
    "Microsoft.DesktopVirtualization"
    ```

    You'll see the following output:

    ```
    PowerShell  ∨   ⏻  ?  ⚙  ⤓  ⤒  {}  ⬀

    PS /home/ryan> Register-AzResourceProvider -ProviderNamespace "Microsoft.DesktopVirtualization"

    ProviderNamespace : Microsoft.DesktopVirtualization
    RegistrationState : Registering
    ResourceTypes     : {workspaces, applicationgroups, applicationgroups/applications, applicationgroups/desktops…}
    Locations         : {East US, East US 2, West US, West US 2…}
    ```

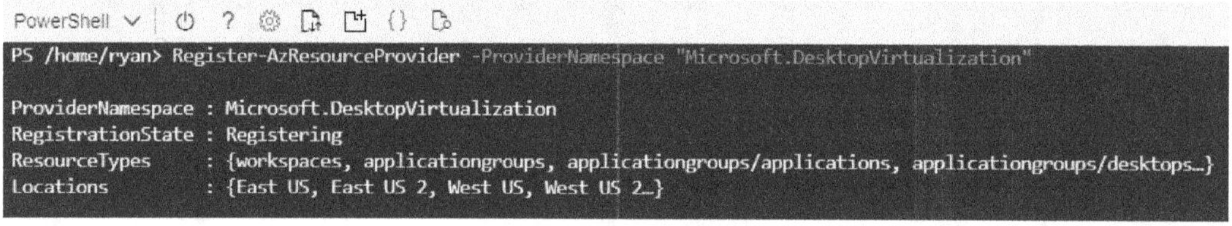

    Figure 2.6 – Powershell cmdlet to register the Desktop Virtualization provider

3. Rerunning the same PowerShell cmdlet will confirm the status of the registration:

    ```
    Register-AzResourceProvider -ProviderNamespace
    "Microsoft.DesktopVirtualization"
    ```

    You'll see the following output:

    ```
    PS /home/ryan> Register-AzResourceProvider -ProviderNamespace "Microsoft.DesktopVirtualization"

    ProviderNamespace : Microsoft.DesktopVirtualization
    RegistrationState : Registered
    ResourceTypes     : {workspaces, applicationgroups, applicationgroups/applications, applicationgroups/desktops…}
    Locations         : {East US, East US 2, West US, West US 2…}
    ```

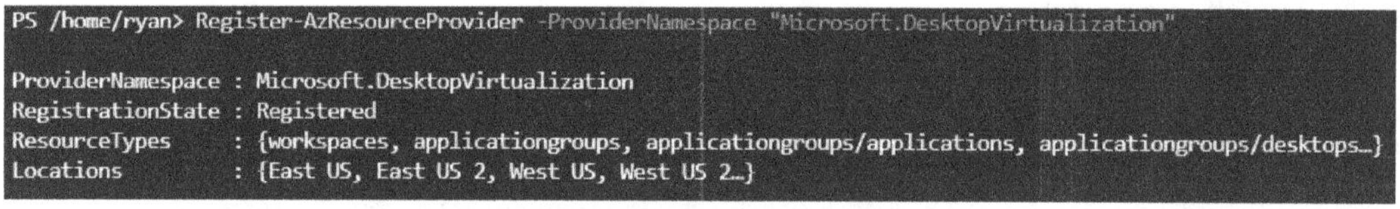

    Figure 2.7 – The output of running the register-AZResourceProvider cmdlet

In this section, we showed you how to register the `Microsoft.DesktopVirtualization` provider using both the GUI within the Azure portal and using Powershell. In the next section, we will look at the resource groups, subscriptions, and management groups limits.

Resource groups, subscriptions, and management groups limits

You can scale an Azure Virtual Desktop environment to over 10,000 sessions hosted per workspace.

It is advised that you consider the Azure Virtual Desktop control plane limitations during the initial design to limit any changes that may be required later:

- Microsoft recommends that you do not deploy 5,000+ VMs per Azure subscription per region. This recommendation is for both host pool types – personal and pooled – for a Windows 10 Enterprise single and multi-session deployment. It is suggested that most organizations will want to use Windows 10 multi-session, which allows multiple users to log on to a session host VM. You can increase the resources (compute and storage) of an individual session host VM to facilitate additional remote sessions.

- There are limits of circa 1,200 VMs per Azure subscription per region for automated session host scaling tools.

- You should create multiple Azure subscriptions in a hub and spoke architecture and connect them via virtual network peering to manage environments with more than 5,000 VMs per Azure subscription in the same region. You can also deploy VMs in different regions within the same subscription to increase your total number of VMs.

- The API throttling limit prevents you from exceeding 600 Azure VM reboots per hour via the Azure portal when using the **Azure Resource Manager** (**ARM**) subscription.

> **Tip**
> You can reboot all your virtual machines via the operating system by using scripting or third-party products that do not consume any Azure Resource Manager subscription API calls.

- You can deploy 399 virtual machines per Azure Virtual Desktop (ARM) template deployment without using availability sets at the time of writing. Alternatively, you can deploy 200 VMs per availability set.

> **Tip**
>
> You can increase the number of virtual machines per deployment by turning off availability sets in the ARM template or the Azure portal host pool enrolment.

- VM session hostname prefixes within Azure cannot exceed 11 characters due to auto-assigning instance names. It is also important to note that the NetBIOS limit of 15 characters per computer account still applies.

- You can deploy 800 instances of resource types within a resource group.

> **Important Note**
>
> For more information about Azure subscription limitations, see Azure subscription and service limits, quotas, and constraints at `https://docs.microsoft.com/en-us/azure/azure-resource-manager/management/azure-subscription-service-limits`.

Configuring the location for the Azure Virtual Desktop metadata

Azure Virtual Desktop is currently available for deployment in all Azure regions. IT admins can select the geographical location to store metadata in when creating their host pool virtual machines and associated services. You would want to store the metadata locally to your organizations for data soverancy purposes.

You can find out more about Azure geographies using the Azure data center map: `https://azuredatacentermap.azurewebsites.net/`. There is no region restriction or limit to where you can access user- and app-specific data.

Azure Virtual Desktop metadata is collected, and the information that's captured includes host pool names, app group names, workspace names, and user principal names in a data center.

When an admin creates a service object, they will be asked to select a location for the service object. The location that's selected essentially determines where the metadata for the object will be stored. As part of its design, you will need to decide where you would like to store your metadata.

For a list of all Azure-associated regions and geographies, see Azure geographies: `https://azure.microsoft.com/global-infrastructure/geographies/`.

Microsoft currently only supports storing metadata in the following locations:

- **United States** (**US**) (generally available)
- **Europe** (**EU**) (generally available)
- **United Kingdom** (**UK**) (generally available)
- **Canada** (**CA**) (generally available)

> **Important Note**
>
> When you select a region to create Azure Virtual Desktop service objects in, you will see regions under both US and EU geographies. It is recommended that you understand which region would work best for your deployment. To find out more, take a look at Microsoft's Azure global infrastructure map: `https://azure.microsoft.com/global-infrastructure/geographies/#geographies`.

Metadata is encrypted and stored at rest, and georedundant mirrors are kept within the geography.

It is understood that Microsoft is working on more geographies that will become available as the service grows.

> **Important Note**
>
> Microsoft replicates service metadata within the Azure geography for disaster recovery purposes.

Calculating and recommending a configuration for capacity and performance requirements

This section provides a high-level set of recommendations for sizing Azure Virtual Desktop. This will help you to plan and also calculate the costs of what the compute resource may look like. It is advised that you load test all the workloads, even when following guided recommendations.

Multi-session recommendations

The following examples should be used as guidance for initial performance estimates. As you build out your Azure Virtual Desktop environment, you will need to tweak and adjust these configurations to meet the requirements of your user base.

The following table shows the number of users per vCPU and the suggested VM hardware configuration for each workload. It also provides an example of session host sizing recommendations based on the number of users per vCPU and workload type. This example is suitable for 20 users or less:

Multi-Session Recommendations – Less than 20 Users per Host				
Workload Type	**Maximum users per vCPU**	**vCPU/RAM/OS storage minimum**	**Example Azure instances**	**Profile container storage minimum**
Light User	4	4 vCPUs, 16 GB RAM, 32 GB storage	D4s_v3, F4s_v2, D4as_v4	30 GB
Medium User	2	4 vCPUs, 16 GB RAM, 32 GB storage	D4s_v3, F4s_v2, D4as_v4	30 GB
Heavy User	2	4 vCPUs, 16 GB RAM, 32 GB storage	D8s_v3, F8s_v2, D8as_v4, D16s_v3, F16s_v2, D16as_v4	30 GB
Power User	1	6 vCPUs, 56 GB RAM, 340 GB storage	D4s_v3, F4s_v2, D4as_v4, NV12, NVv4	30 GB

This table was taken from the Microsoft document *Remote Desktop workloads*: https://docs.microsoft.com/en-us/windows-server/remote/remote-desktop-services/remote-desktop-workloads.

The following article shows some real-life examples of different performance results from testing different Azure Virtual machine sizes for use with Azure Virtual Desktop: https://ryanmangansitblog.com/2021/09/20/results-from-benchmark-tests-completed-on-avd-and-cloud-pc-virtual-machines/.

The following table provides an example of session host sizing recommendations based on the number of users per vCPU and workload type. The following table shows that this example would be suitable for more than 20 users:

Multi-Session Recommendations – +20 Users per Host				
Workload type	**Maximum users per vCPU**	**vCPU/RAM/OS storage minimum**	**Example Azure instances**	**Profile container storage minimum**
Light User	6	8 vCPUs, 16 GB RAM, 16 GB storage	D8s_v3, F8s_v2, D8as_v4, D16s_v3, F16s_v2, D16as_v4	30 GB
Medium User	4	8 vCPUs, 16 GB RAM, 32 GB storage	D8s_v3, F8s_v2, D8as_v4, D16s_v3, F16s_v2, D16as_v4	30 GB
Heavy User	2	8 vCPUs, 16 GB RAM, 32 GB storage	D8s_v3, F8s_v2, D8as_v4, D16s_v3, F16s_v2, D16as_v4	30 GB
Power User	1	6 vCPUs, 56 GB RAM, 340 GB storage	D8s_v3, F8s_v2, D8as_v4, D16s_v3, F16s_v2, D16as_v4, NV12, NVv4	30 GB

This table was taken from the Microsoft document *Remote Desktop workloads*: https://docs.microsoft.com/en-us/windows-server/remote/remote-desktop-services/remote-desktop-workloads.

Microsoft recommends using VM sizes between 4 vCPUs and 24 vCPUs. It is not recommended to use less than two cores or more than 32 or more cores per session host.

> **Tip**
>
> Windows 10 require a minimum of two parallel threads for the heavier rendering operations. Having multiple users on a two-core or fewer VM could lead to a poor user experience. It's advised for stability that you use four or more cores when using a multi-user VM.

Recommendations on sizing VMs

When increasing the number of virtual machine cores, it's important to note that the overhead of the VM will increase (system synchronization). For most workloads, it's advised that you stick to no more than 16 cores per session host. As the CPU number increases, the lower the return on investment. The additional capacity is negated by the synchronization overhead.

Microsoft, as per their best practices, states that you should stay in the range of 4 to 24 vCPU cores per session host.

> **Tip**
>
> It is suggested that a 1.75 ratio scenario offers improved burst capacity for applications that have short-term CPU demands.
>
> When you have 20 or more user session connections on a single VM, it is advised that multiple smaller VMs would show better results than one or two larger VMs. It is also recommended that you have used smaller VMs instead of larger ones so that shutdown management is simpler. This is particularly useful for update management. From my testing and field experience, I have always found AMD Azure Virtual Machine skews to offer better performance and user experience compared to the Intel equivalent skews.

A common resource that is sometimes forgotten when sizing resources is the session host virtual disk and associated **input/output operations per second** (**IOPS**, pronounced *eye-ops*). Poor performing storage can result in a degraded user experience.

For persistent VMs (single user/single session), it is recommended that you use VMs with a minimum of two CPU cores per VM. However, for the best results, Microsoft recommends four vCPUs with hyperthreading enabled.

General recommendations for VMs

Microsoft recommends using premium storage (SSD) for Azure Virtual Desktop Session hosts as they offer high-performance and low-latency disk support for the session host virtual machine.

> **Tip**
>
> For a production workload requiring a **service-level agreement** (**SLA**), you will need to assign your VM's premium storage (SSD). For more details, see the SLA for virtual machines: https://azure.microsoft.com/support/legal/sla/virtual-machines/v1_8/.

You can enhance the user session experience even further using **graphics processing units (GPU)**, which lets you use graphic-intensive programs such as 3D design, video rendering, and simulation software. You can read more about graphics acceleration by going to the *Remote Desktop Services – GPU acceleration* guide: `https://docs. microsoft.com/en-us/windows-server/remote/remote-desktop- services/rds-graphics-virtualization`.

You can read more about the Microsoft Azure graphics acceleration deployment options that are available, as well as the GPU VM sizes offered, by going to the *GPU optimized virtual machine sizes* page: `https://docs.microsoft.com/en-us/azure/ virtual-machines/windows/sizes-gpu`.

> **Tip**
> B-series burstable VMs are helpful for users who don't always need maximum CPU performance. However, these are not so good if you use all the burstable resources. These are also useful for older applications that are delivered via RemoteApp. Just remember to benchmark usage before using it as burstable storage has a very limited use case.

You can find out more about VM types and sizes by going to the *Sizes for Windows virtual machines in Azure* document: `https://docs.microsoft.com/en-us/azure/ virtual-machines/windows/sizes`.

You can find the pricing information on Microsoft's *Virtual Machine Series* page: `https://azure.microsoft.com/pricing/details/virtual-machines/ series/`.

Testing workloads

Before rolling out any new desktop virtualization project to production, it is recommended that you run several tests, including simulation tests, to stress test for real-life usage. This will help provide a baseline and ensure that the environment you plan to release offers the resilience and responsive performance required to meet the current and future needs.

Load testing is a really good way to understand the limitations of the desktop environment, which helps with capacity planning as well as managing and maintaining a good user experience.

> **Tip**
> You can use tools such as LoginVSI, which can automate load tests for your Azure Virtual Desktop Environment, to help you understand performance, capacity management, and potential user experience issues. You can read more about LoginVSI here: `https://www.loginvsi.com/`.

Summary

In this chapter, we discussed assessing your current desktop estate to understand current baselines for performance, data, and user experience. We then looked at the considerations for Azure Virtual Desktop, including network bandwidth planning, sizing, and Windows 10 multi-session. Throughout this chapter, tips and recommendations were provided for you to get the most out of your Azure Virtual Desktop environment.

The next chapter will look at the design for user identities and profiles, where we will look at selecting an appropriate licensing model for Azure Virtual Desktop based on our requirements. Here, we will recommend an appropriate storage solution, plan for Azure Virtual Desktop client deployments and user profiles, and recommend a solution for network connectivity and planning for Azure AD Connect for user identities.

Questions

Here are a few questions to test your understanding of this chapter:

1. Which tools can you use for assessing your requirements for Azure Virtual Desktop?

2. Before you can start to deploy Azure Virtual Desktop, what do you need to register for the subscription?

3. What is the name of the tool that's used to gauge the round trip time (latency) of Azure Virtual Desktop?

4. What is the benefit of Windows 10 multi-session over other operating system types?

Answers

1. *Lakeside systrack, Movere, and Azure Migrate.*

2. *Register the Microsoft.DesktopVirtualization provider.*

3. *Windows Virtual Desktop Experience Estimator.*

4. *Windows 10 multi-session offers a familiar Windows 10 experience that's exclusively offered to Microsoft Azure.*

Further reading

You can refer to the following links for more information regarding the topics that were covered in this chapter:

- Azure Virtual Desktop for the enterprise – Azure Example Scenarios | Microsoft Docs (`https://docs.microsoft.com/en-us/azure/architecture/example-scenario/wvd/windows-virtual-desktop`).

- Microsoft Cloud Adoption Framework for Azure – Cloud Adoption Framework | Microsoft Docs (`https://docs.microsoft.com/en-us/azure/cloud-adoption-framework/`).

- For more information on the Azure subscription limitations, see the following links for management groups (`https://docs.microsoft.com/en-us/azure/governance/management-groups/overview`) and general limits (`https://docs.microsoft.com/en-us/azure/azure-resource-manager/management/azure-subscription-service-limits`).

- Deliver remote desktops and apps from Azure with Azure Virtual Desktop – Learn | Microsoft Docs (`https://docs.microsoft.com/en-us/learn/paths/m365-wvd/`).

3
Designing for User Identities and Profiles

In this chapter, we will look at designing for user identities and profiles. This is important as a poor design can impact the user experience and, in turn, affect other components such as applications, as well as the overall functionality of Azure Virtual Desktop.

In this chapter, we'll cover the following topics:

- Selecting a licensing model for your Azure Virtual Desktop deployment
- Planning for user profiles
- Planning for Azure Virtual Desktop client deployment
- Summarizing the prerequisites for Azure Virtual Desktop

Selecting a licensing model for your Azure Virtual Desktop deployment

This section will introduce Azure Virtual Desktop licensing and the entitlements associated with it. You need to make sure that you are properly licensed.

> **Important Note**
>
> Before getting started, please note that the previously named Microsoft 365 for Business is now known as Microsoft 365 Business Premium. Users can use Azure Virtual Desktop from their non-Windows pro devices if they have a Microsoft 365 E3/F3/E5/Business/A3/Student user or a Windows 10 VDA per-user license.

The following table details the licenses and their eligibility for Azure Virtual Desktop:

Type	Description	Eligibility
Virtualize Windows 11, 10, and Windows 7	Windows 11 Enterprise, Windows 10 Enterprise, and Windows 7 Enterprise desktops and apps are included if you have an eligible Windows or Microsoft 365 license. You can also get free extended security updates until January 2023 for your Windows 7 virtual desktop, offering more options that support legacy apps while you transition to Windows 10.	You are eligible to access Windows 11, Windows 10, and Windows 7 with Azure Virtual Desktop if you have one of the following per-user licenses*: Microsoft 365 E3/E5 Microsoft 365 A3/A5/Student Use Benefits Microsoft 365 F3 Microsoft 365 Business Premium** Windows 10 Enterprise E3/E5 Windows 10 Education A3/A5 Windows 10 VDA per user
Virtualize Windows Server	Access desktops powered by Windows Server Remote Desktop Services desktops and apps at no additional cost if you are an eligible Microsoft **Remote Desktop Services (RDS) Client Access License (CAL)** customer.	You are eligible to access Windows Server 2012 R2 and newer desktops and apps if you have a per-user or per-device RDS CAL license with active **Software Assurance (SA)**.

The preceding table was taken from the Microsoft licensing page at: `https://azure.microsoft.com/en-gb/pricing/details/virtual-desktop/`.

You will also need an Azure subscription to be able to deploy and manage your desktop virtualization environment. The following Azure components are key areas when you're looking at Azure Virtual Desktop deployment costs:

- Networking and any third-party **Network Virtual Appliances** (**NVAs**)
- **Virtual machines** (**VMs**) and **operating system** (**OS**) storage
- Data disk (optional)
- Storage for user profiles

> **Important Note**
>
> Session host VMs on Azure deployments are billed at Linux compute rates for the following OS versions: Windows 10 single, Windows 10 multi-session, and Windows Server. You can read more on this here: `https://azure.microsoft.com/en-us/pricing/details/virtual-desktop/`.

Applying the Azure Virtual Desktop licensing to VMs

This section covers how to check if your Azure Virtual Desktop session hosts have the correct licensing applied.

> **Important Note**
>
> This process is typically taken care of for you when creating VMs from the wizard. However, it's worth checking to ensure the license type is set correctly. It's also advised that you check this when you deploy from a custom or imported image.

One way you can apply a license to a VM is by using the following PowerShell cmdlet:

```
$vm = Get-AzVM -ResourceGroup <resourceGroupName> -Name
<vmName>
$vm.LicenseType = "Windows_Client"
Update-AzVM -ResourceGroupName <resourceGroupName> -VM $vm
```

Here's what the output looks like:

```
PS /home/ryan> $vm = Get-AzVM -ResourceGroup MSIXAA -Name MSWVD-1
PS /home/ryan> $vm.LicenseType = "Windows_Client"
PS /home/ryan> Update-AzVM -ResourceGroupName MSIXAA -VM $vm

RequestId IsSuccessStatusCode StatusCode ReasonPhrase
--------- ------------------- ---------- ------------
                         True         OK OK


PS /home/ryan>
PS /home/ryan>
```

Figure 3.1 – PowerShell script showing how to apply Azure Virtual Desktop licensing to VMs

Once you have set the license type, you can check it using the following cmdlet:

```
Get-AzVM -ResourceGroupName <resourceGroupName> -Name <vmName>
```

Here's what it looks like:

```
PS /home/ryan> Get-AzVM -ResourceGroupName MSIXAA -Name MSWVD-1


ResourceGroupName  : MSIXAA
Id                 :
/subscriptions/d96471f8-340c-42d6-92df-eba6fccca8e4/resourceGroups/MSIXAA/providers/Microsoft.Compute/virtualMachines/MSWVD-1
VmId               : c5684ea9-2ada-43b2-819e-2df39ad8538f
Name               : MSWVD-1
Type               : Microsoft.Compute/virtualMachines
Location           : uksouth
LicenseType        : Windows_Client
Tags               : {}
DiagnosticsProfile : {BootDiagnostics}
Extensions         : {dscextension, joindomain}
HardwareProfile    : {VmSize}
NetworkProfile     : {NetworkInterfaces}
OSProfile          : {ComputerName, AdminUsername, WindowsConfiguration, Secrets, AllowExtensionOperations,
RequireGuestProvisionSignal}
ProvisioningState  : Succeeded
StorageProfile     : {ImageReference, OsDisk, DataDisks}


PS /home/ryan>
```

Figure 3.2 – The output of running the get-AZVM cmdlet

If you run the following cmdlet, this will provide you with a list of all the VMs licensed under `Windows_client`:

```
$vms = Get-AzVM
$vms | Where-Object {$_.LicenseType -like "Windows_Client"} |
Select-Object ResourceGroupName, Name, LicenseType
```

Here's what the output looks like:

```
PS /home/ryan> $vms = Get-AzVM
PS /home/ryan> $vms | Where-Object {$_.LicenseType -like "Windows_Client"} | Select-Object ResourceGroupName, Name, LicenseType

ResourceGroupName Name       LicenseType
----------------- ----       -----------
MSIXAA            MSWVD-1 Windows_Client
```

Figure 3.3 – The licensed VMs

In the next section, we look at the recommended storage solutions for Azure Virtual Desktop.

Recommended storage solution

FSLogix is a profile container technology that is included with Azure Virtual Desktop at no extra cost. FSLogix lets you roam profiles in desktop virtualization environments such as Azure Virtual Desktop.

There are multiple storage options available to use for storing your FSLogix Profile Containers. The most common option organizations use is Azure Files.

> **Important Note**
>
> Microsoft recommends Azure Files for typical FSLogix profile container deployments, though it's recommended that you use Azure NetApp Files for enterprise environments.

When a user signs into an Azure Virtual Desktop session, the container (container FSLogix (profile container)) is attached (dynamically) to the allocated session host using a natively supported virtual disk, known as **Virtual Hard Disk/Hyper-V Hard disk (VHD/VHDX)**.

The user's profile is made available and provides the same user experience, just like a native user profile would.

The following table provides a comparison between the three common storage solutions available for FSLogix Profile Containers with Azure Virtual Desktop:

Azure Storage platform comparison

Features	Azure Files	Azure NetApp Files	Storage Spaces Direct
Use Case	General-purpose Storage	Ultra performance (Enterprise) or migration from NetApp on-premises Storage solutions	Cross-platform.
Platform Service Type	Azure solution	Azure solution	No, self-managed.
Azure Regional Availability	All Azure regions	Selective regions (`https://azure.microsoft.com/en-us/global-infrastructure/services/?products=netapp&regions=all`)	All Azure regions.
Redundancy	Locally redundant/ zone-redundant/ geo-redundant/ geo-zone-redundant	Locally redundant/cross-region replication	Locally redundant/ zone-redundant/ geo-redundant.
Storage Tiers and Performance	Standard (transaction optimized) or Premium up to a maximum of 100K IOPS per share with 10 GBps per share at about 3 ms latency	Standard, Premium, and Ultra up to 320k (16K) IOPS with 4.5 GBps per volume at about 1 ms latency	Standard HDD: Up to 500 IOPS per-disk limits Standard SSD: Up to 4k IOPS per-disk limits Premium SSD: Up to 20k IOPS per-disk limits It is recommended that premium disks are used for Storage Spaces Direct.

Capacity Capability	100 TiB per share, up to 5 PiB per general-purpose account	100 TiB per volume, up to 12.5 PiB per subscription	Maximum 32 TiB per disk.
Required Infrastructure	Minimum share size 1 GiB	Minimum capacity pool 4 TiB, minimum volume size 100 GiB	Two VMs on Azure IaaS (plus Cloud Witness) or at least three VMs without any costs for disks.
Protocols	SMB 3.0/2.1, NFSv4.1 (preview), REST	NFSv3, NFSv4.1 (preview), SMB 3.x/2.x	NFSv3, NFSv4.1, SMB 3.1

The following table provides a comparison between the features of these three storage solutions available for FSLogix Profile Containers with Azure Virtual Desktop:

Azure Storage feature comparison

Features	Azure Files	Azure NetApp Files	Storage Spaces Direct
Type	Cloud, on-premises, and hybrid (Azure file sync)	Cloud, on-premises (via ExpressRoute)	Cloud, on-premises
Backup Capabilities	Azure backup snapshot integration	Azure NetApp Files snapshots	Azure backup snapshot integration
Security and Compliance	All Azure supported certificates	ISO completed	All Azure supported certificates
Azure Active Directory Integration	Azure Active Directory Domain Services and Native Active Directory	Azure Active Directory Domain Services and Native Active Directory	Active Directory or Azure Active Directory Domain Services support only

You can review the pricing for each storage method using the Azure pricing calculator: https://azure.microsoft.com/pricing/details/virtual-desktop/.

Azure Files tiers

In this section, we will look at the different Azure Files tiers and the benefits of each.

There are two types of storage when it comes to Azure Files: standard and premium. These two tiers offer different performance requirements and costs. The following is to help you weigh up which is more suited to your needs.

The key differences between the two tiers are the type of disks in use. Premium uses **solid-state drives (SSDs)**, while standard uses traditional **hard disk drives (HDDs)**:

- Premium file shares provide high performance and low latency for **input and output (I/O)**-intensive workloads. This is useful for the larger organizations or user profiles that require higher I/O.

- Standard file shares are suitable for the less intensive I/O workloads, such as general-purpose file shares and dev/test environments. These are more suitable for the smaller Azure Virtual Desktop environments.

The following table provides guidance when it comes to choosing a recommended file tier:

Workload	Recommended File Tier
Light (less than 200 users)	Use standard file shares.
Light (more than 200 users)	Use premium file shares or standard with multiple file shares split between user groups/departments.
Medium Workloads	Use premium.
Heavy Workloads	Use premium.
Power Workloads	Use premium.

This section provided an overview of the storage options available to you when using FSLogix Profile Containers with Azure Virtual Desktop. Next, we will look at the installation and configuration of the Azure Virtual Desktop client.

Planning for user profiles

In this section, we will discuss user profiles and some of the considerations for Azure Virtual Desktop.

User profiles

A user profile comprises several data elements of a user. This can include desktop settings, persistent network connections, and application configuration settings. On the first login, Windows creates a (local) user profile from the default template. The user profile is tightly integrated within the Windows OS and is required for the user session to function correctly.

When comparing a remote user profile to a local profile, the key difference is that the remote profile allows the Windows OS to be replaced without impacting the user data. This means you can log into another session host and will still have the same settings that you did previously. Remote profiles are typically used in a pooled (non-persistent) desktop virtualization environment.

Microsoft has several products available for delivering remote user profiles, including the following:

- **User profile disks (UPD)**
- **Enterprise state roaming (ESR)**
- **Roaming user profiles (RUP)**

UPDs were previously the most widely used profile technology for desktop virtualization. There has been a significant shift toward FSLogix Profile Containers after their acquisition in 2019.

Challenges with previous user profile technologies

Traditional user profile solutions present a few challenges. For example, a lot of organizations that wanted to migrate to **Microsoft 365** struggled with UPDs. Some of the issues with traditional profile disks were related to caching mailboxes problems and other applications not functioning correctly as the redirection was not seamless.

When using the **Azure Virtual Desktop service**, it is recommended that user profiles are configured using FSLogix Profile Containers. FSLogix has been designed to enable roaming profiles for desktop virtualization environments such as Azure Virtual Desktop. It stores the user profile in a single VHD/VHDX container. When a user initiates the connection to a virtual desktop, the user profile is made available and appears exactly like a local user profile would.

Now, let's take a deeper look into FSLogix and build on the information that we've covered within this and the previous chapter.

An introduction to FSLogix Profile Containers

Microsoft acquired the vendor FSLogix on November 19, 2018, which came with a set of products and solutions to improve desktop virtualization products. One of the main driving forces for the acquisition was so that Microsoft could replace UPDs with FSLogix Profile Containers. This was due to the limitations within the UPD, which had an impact on those who wanted to use Microsoft 365.

The FSLogix product portfolio includes the following:

- Profile Container
- Office Container
- Application Masking
- Java Version Control

Some of the key benefits when using FSLogix include the following:

- The ability to minimize sign-in times for pooled virtual desktop environments, also known as non-persistent desktops.
- Using FSLogix's filter driver enables a much better profile experience and removes many of the traditional compatibilities with UPD relating to what some describe as visible redirection.
- One of the features that can be sometimes forgotten is Java Version Control. This is a very useful tool that lets you specify the version of Java for a specific URL or/and application.
- Application masking enables you to hide applications on a central desktop image from users who have not been assigned permission via a security group.

FSLogix capabilities

This section provides an introduction to some of FSLogix's capabilities and the benefits associated with them:

- Redirecting user profiles to a network storage location. Profile Containers can be stored as VHD or VHDX files. As the profiles are accessed via a network share, this eliminates delays that are typically seen with profile solutions that copy files from the share to the target device.
- FSLogix can also maintain the Windows Index and the result is a smoother login on new VMs (there is no requirement to recreate the index).

- FSLogix offers Office containers. These types of containers allow you to solve Office issues within a non-persistent desktop virtualization environment. One common use case is how to handle Outlook .ost files or the Microsoft Teams cache, which we cover in *Chapter 12, Implementing and Managing FSLogix*.

- FSLogix's filter driver architecture redirects the profile so that applications and the Windows OS do not recognize that the user profile is stored outside the host. Typically, most applications won't work on user profiles stored on remote storage.

- FSLogix Cloud Cache enables you to create a highly available desktop virtualization environment. The technology works by placing a portion of the user profile on the host's local disk. With Cloud Cache, you can also configure multiple remote profile locations, which protect users from network and storage issues/failures.

- Application masking enables you to control access to applications and other items, such as fonts. Application masking helps you segregate apps and other items via user groups or other IP addresses to provide better segregation on a central gold image.

FSLogix requirements

To be entitled to use Profile Containers and the other suite of tools by FSLogix, you will need to ensure you have one of the following licenses:

- Microsoft 365 E3/E5
- Microsoft 365 A3/A5/Student Use Benefits
- Microsoft 365 F1/F3
- Microsoft 365 Business
- Windows 10 Enterprise E3/E5
- Windows 10 Education A3/A5
- Windows 10 VDA per user
- RDS CAL
- RDS SAL

You can use the FSLogix products on any public or private data center with the correct license. The following link goes to the Microsoft official documentation on the eligibility requirements: https://docs.microsoft.com/en-us/fslogix/overview.

FSLogix filter driver architecture

Traditional profile technologies copy the user profile to and from the network during sign-in and sign-out. The problem is that this can cause delays and, if profiles are larger, which can often be the case, the sign-in and sign-out times could reach unacceptable time frames. One of the key differences with FSLogix is that the user profile is stored centrally on a network share rather than being copied. The profile is essentially redirected when the profile disks are mounted when the user logs in. As the profile is being mounted, this reduces the traditional delays associated with the copy.

The following diagram depicts the architecture of how FSLogix works within a Windows OS. Two filter drivers are injected into the OS, which are then installed when you run the FSLogix installer. We will learn how to install FSLogix in *Chapter 12, Implementing and Managing FSLogix*. The diagram depicts Azure Storage. Using the OS registry or group policies (ADMX), you can specify the location of where to store your VHD or VHDX container:

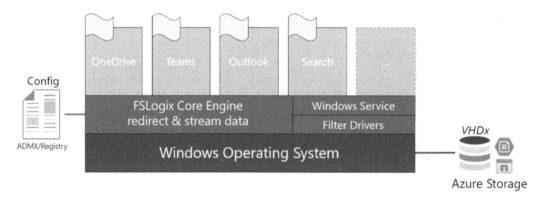

Figure 3.4 – FSLogix architecture

Exploring the differences between Profile Containers and office containers

FSLogix offers two types of containers for profiles – Profile Containers and office containers. You should note that the office container is essentially a subset of the profile container. There are use cases of when you should use these together, particularly in larger organizations where you want to split the profile from the Office data. It is important to fully understand the process of configuring them together to avoid impacting user profiles.

The key differences between the two containers are that the office container is specifically for improving the performance of Microsoft Office within a non-persistent desktop virtualization environment. The benefit of using both allows you to segment office profile components on one office container disk and everything else on a profile container disk.

> **Important Note**
>
> When using FSLogix in an Azure Virtual Desktop environment, it is recommended that you only use Profile Containers unless there is a specific requirement for **Business Continuity and Disaster Recovery (BCDR)**.

Let's briefly take a look at the concept of multiple profile connections.

Multiple profile connections

This refers to a user connected to multiple desktop virtualization sessions. This could be multiple hosts or one concurrently using the same profile. It's important to not get confused with the term multi-session.

> **Important Note**
>
> Concurrent or multiple connections are not recommended when using Azure Virtual Desktop. Microsoft suggests that you should create a different profile location for each host pool.

Some of the limitations associated with multiple connection deployments are as follows:

- Microsoft OneDrive is not supported with multiple connection environments.
- You could experience data loss when attempting to use OneDrive with multiple profile connections.
- There is limited support with Microsoft Outlook for multiple connections.
- End user training would be required as the user experience changes. Using a read, the only container changes how they should use the virtual desktop session. Without training or proper context, users could experience data loss.

FSLogix performance requirements

When you're planning for an FSLogix profile container deployment, you need to consider a few things. The overall profile size and limitations will depend on the storage type you use, as well as the chosen disk format type – VHD or VHDX.

It is recommended that you plan for 5 – 30 IOPS per user profile as profile requirements can widely vary, depending on the exact usage. The performance requirements are most likely different for each organization. Each user is different, and it is suggested that you review a subset of users, their applications, and their activity to gain an understanding of true profile performance needs.

It is also recommended that you conduct profile assessments to establish your current profile utilization, which will help you scope more accurate storage requirements. There are several community tools available to help you assess your current profile size state and these tools can also shrink the profiles reducing the overall storage size.

> **Tip**
> Jim Moyle created a community tool that can be used to shrink FSLogix and O365 dynamically expanding disks. You can read more here: `https://github.com/FSLogix/Invoke-FslShrinkDisk`.

The following table provides an example of the typical resources a profile needs to have to support each user:

Performance Requirements	
Resource	Requirement
Steady state IOPS	10
Sign-in/sign-out IOPS	50

For example, you have 100 users within an organization. Using the preceding table as a baseline, you may require around 1,000 IOPS. You would also need a suggested 5,000 IOPS at login or sign up. You should also factor in login storms. If any users log in at the same time, it would likely create a login storm. To avoid this, you should factor in any additional IOPS to reduce the likelihood of a login storm.

Now, let's recap the storage options from the previous chapter.

Storage options for FSLogix Profile Containers

There are multiple storage solutions available to you for use with FSLogix Profile Containers. Azure Files is recommended for most scenarios; however, there are multiple storage options available for FSLogix Profile Containers. It is recommended that enterprises use Azure NetApp Files to benefit from high-performance storage in larger deployments.

> **Tip**
> It is not recommended for production use, but you can use **Storage Spaces Direct (S2D)** with FSLogix and Azure Virtual Desktop.

FSLogix storage best practices

This section will specify the best practices you should remember when deploying and configuring FSLogix Profile Containers:

- Ensure that your chosen storage and host VMs are within the same data center location for optimal performance.

- Ensure you set exclusions for antivirus scanning on VHD and VHDX disks to prevent antivirus-induced performance bottlenecks.

- Exclude the VHD(X) files for Profile Containers from antivirus scanning to avoid performance bottlenecks.

- Use separate Profile Containers per host pool when you want to use multiple active sessions.

The following table details the recommended Azure Storage permissions for use with an FSLogix profile container:

User Account	Folder	Permissions
Users	This Folder Only	Modify
Creator/Owner	Subfolders and Files Only	Modify
Administrator (optional)	This Folder, Subfolders, and Files	Full Control

The following table shows the required permissions you should set for Azure Files:

Role	Group
Storage file Data SMB Share contributor	Domain users or AVD users
Storage file Data SMB Share Elevated contributor	Storage admin

Azure Files integration with Active Directory Domain Services

Microsoft announced the general availability of Azure Files authentication with **Active Directory Domain Services** (**ADDS**) on August 7, 2019. This lets you use NTFS permissions with Azure Files.

The following diagram details the steps of on-premises AD DS authentication to Azure Files using **Server Message Block** (**SMB**). The AD DS environment must be synced with **Azure Active Directory** (**Azure AD**) using Azure AD Connect Sync. Only configured hybrid users in Azure AD and Active Directory Domain Services can access and be authorized to use Azure File shares. This is because the share-level permissions are configured against the identity represented in Azure AD, while the directory or file is enforced with AD DS. Therefore, you need to ensure that you configure the permissions correctly for hybrid users.

The following diagram shows the process of using AD credentials for Azure Files:

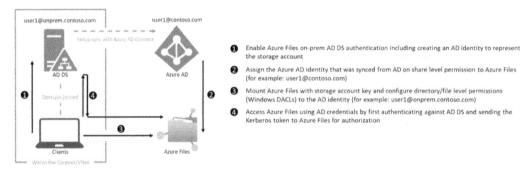

Figure 3.5 –Azure Files integration with ADDS

This provides seamless integration for those who want to integrate Azure Files into Active Directory, including the use of FSLogix and MSIX app attach. It is also important to note that using Azure Files with integration with Active Directory Domain Services offers improved security as it allows you to configure **access control lists** (**ACLs**), similar to a traditional Windows File Server. Without ADDS integration, you will only have basic security features, which may not be suitable for the organization you are deploying Azure Files to.

> **Important Note**
>
> You can use **Azure Active Directory Domain Services** (**AADDS**) for domain joins. The best practice would be to use Active Directory Domain Services where possible as AADDS does have limitations.

This section discussed the topic of planning for user profiles; this included using Azure Files storage, FSLogix Profile Containers, recommendations, and best practices.

Planning for user identities

Before you can get started with Azure Virtual Desktop, you need to choose an identity strategy. The following identity strategies could apply to your Azure Virtual Desktop and Azure infrastructure:

Option	Pros	Cons
Deploy a Domain Controller in your Azure subscription.	You can sync with on-premises domain controllers using a VPN or ExpressRoute. All familiar AD Group Policies experience.	An added layer of management through the use of VMs and Active Directory in Azure.
Cloud-only organizations, use Azure AD DS.	Great for testing or lab/isolated environments that do not require connectivity to on-premises resources.	AADDS is a service that is always running, resulting in a fixed charge per month. AAD DS doesn't provide all the functions that native AD does. It's been known that a lot of organizations that have deployed Azure AD DS have been removed due to some of the limitations they have experienced.
Hybrid organizations can use VPN or ExpressRoute and make sure your on-premises Domain Controllers can communicate in Azure.	No requirement for AD DS or a Domain Controller in Azure.	Increased latency could add delays during user authentication to VMs.
Azure AD Join for Azure Virtual Desktop.	No requirement for AD DS or a Domain Controller in Azure.	Azure AD-joined VMs don't currently support external users and only support local user profiles at this time. The Windows Store client is not currently supported at the time of writing and you cannot access Azure Files file shares for FSLogix or MSIX app attach unless you're using third-party solutions.

> **Important Note**
> Most organizations choose option one or three when choosing an identity strategy.

If you're using native Active Directory, identities must be synchronized with Azure AD. Azure AD Connect is used to link on-premises Active Directory to Microsoft Azure, providing a seamless single sign-on experience between cloud and on-premises services.

Some of the key benefits of using AD Connect are as follows:

- You can use a single identity to access cloud services, such as Microsoft 365, and on-premises applications.
- A simple tool that takes care of the deployment, sign in, and synchronization.
- Replaces older versions of identity synchronization such as Azure AD Sync and DirSync.
- Azure AD Connect is included in your Azure subscription at no cost.

The following diagram depicts how Azure AD Connect works logically:

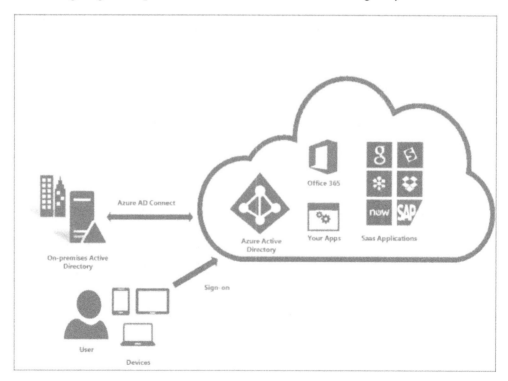

Figure 3.6 – A logical diagram showing how Azure AD Connect works

Domain join VMs

Azure Virtual Desktop does not support the use of workgroups. Here, you need an Active Directory domain.

To domain join the VMs you create, you need to specify the full Active Directory domain name to join, such as `RMITBLOG.com`. If you've set up a test environment with Azure AD DS, use the DNS domain name that's on the properties page for Azure AD DS; for example, `RMITBLOG.onmicrosoft.com`.

You will also need to specify an administrator account so that the provisioning process can join the VMs to the domain. This account should be delegated with the correct permissions so that you can join session hosts to the domain.

Firewall and other network requirements

Azure Virtual Desktop requires a specific set of firewall rules to function correctly. Failing to ensure these rules are applied to the VM, Azure Firewall, or a third-party firewall could result in networking communication issues with Azure Virtual Desktop. One example of this is Windows activation failing as the outbound `1688` TPC port for `kms.core.windows.net` being blocked.

There are mandatory firewall rules for Azure VMs:

Address	Outbound TCP Port	Purpose	Service Tag
`*.wvd.microsoft.com`	443	Service Traffic	Azure Virtual Desktop
`mrsglobalsteus2prod.blob.core.windows.net`	443	Agent and SXS stack updates	Azure Cloud
`*.core.windows.net`	443	Agent Traffic	Azure Cloud
`*.servicebus.windows.net`	443	Agent Traffic	Azure Cloud
`prod.warmpath.msftcloudes.com`	443	Agent Traffic	Azure Cloud
`catalogartifact.azureedge.net`	443	Azure Marketplace	Azure Cloud
`kms.core.windows.net`	1688	Windows activation	Internet
`avdportalstorageblob.blob.core.windows.net`	443	Azure portal support	Azure Cloud
`*.prod.warm.ingest.monitor.core.windows.net`	443	Agent traffic	Azure Cloud

It may be worth checking the following: `https://docs.microsoft.com/en-us/azure/virtual-desktop/safe-url-list#virtual-machines`

The following are not mandatory; however, it advised that these URLs be added:

Address	Outbound TCP Port	Purpose	Service Tag
`*.microsoftonline.com`	443	Authentication to Microsoft Online Services	None
`*.events.data.microsoft.com`	443	Telemetry Service	None
`www.msftconnecttest.com`	443	Detects if the OS is connected to the internet	None
`*.prod.do.dsp.mp.microsoft.com`	443	Windows Update	None
`login.windows.net`	443	Sign in to Microsoft Online Services, Microsoft 365	None
`*.sfx.ms`	443	Updates for OneDrive client software	None
`*.digicert.com`	443	Certificate revocation check	None

The mandatory Remote Desktop client URLs are as follows:

Address	Outbound TCP Port	Purpose	Client(s)
`*.wvd.microsoft.com`	443	Service traffic	All
`*.servicebus.windows.net`	443	Troubleshooting data	All
`go.microsoft.com`	443	Microsoft FWLinks	All
`aka.ms`	443	Microsoft URL shortener	All
`docs.microsoft.com`	443	Documentation	All
`privacy.microsoft.com`	443	Privacy statement	All
`query.prod.cms.rt.microsoft.com`	443	Client updates	Windows Desktop

In this section, we looked at planning for user profiles comprised of licensing, storage, profile options, and Azure AD. In the next section, we look at the Azure Virtual Desktop Client.

Planning for Azure Virtual Desktop client deployment

The **Windows Remote Desktop client** can access Azure Virtual Desktop on devices within **Windows 10**, **Windows 10 IoT Enterprise**, and **Windows 7**.

In this example, we will deploy a Windows Remote Desktop client.

> **Important Note**
> The Windows Desktop client does not support Windows 8 or Windows 8.1.

Installing the Windows Desktop client

In this section, we will cover how to install and set up Windows Desktop Client:

1. Open the **Remote Desktop Setup** client and click **Next**:

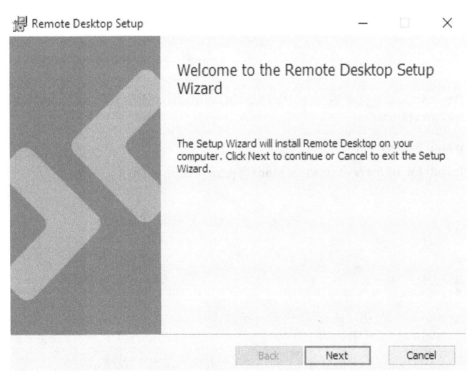

Figure 3.7 – Remote Desktop Setup wizard

2. Select **I accept the terms in the License Agreement** and click **Next**:

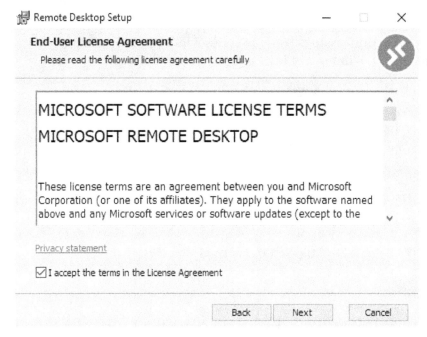

Figure 3.8 – Licence agreement

3. After downloading the Remote Desktop client installer, when you run it, you will have two options:

- **Install just for you**
- **Install for all users of this machine** (requires admin rights):

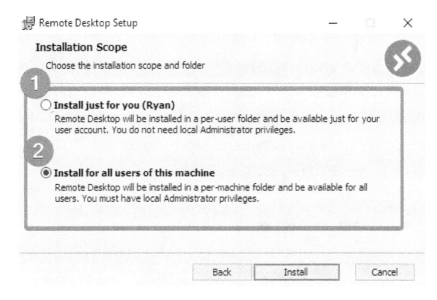

Figure 3.9 – Installation scope

4. If more than one user uses the client device, make sure option 2 is selected and click **Install**.

5. When the installation is completed, click **Finish**:

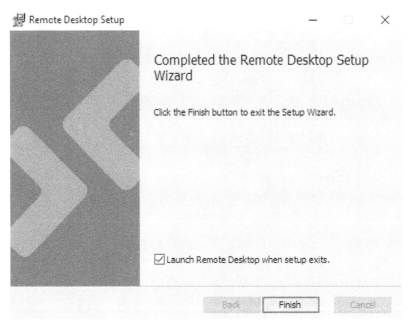

Figure 3.10 – Remote Desktop Setup wizard completed

With that, we are done with installing the Remote Desktop client.

Subscribing to a workspace

When you subscribe to a workspace or multiple workspaces, you will be provided with a list of managed resources you can access that the admin has provided you with. When subscribing, the resources become available on your supported device. The Windows Desktop client supports Azure Virtual Desktop published resources.

There are two options for subscribing to a workspace. One way is that the client can discover the resources available to you using a work or school account. The second is by directly specifying the URL where the resources are. The second option is typically used when the client cannot find the resources.

Once subscribed to a workspace, you will be able to launch resources using one of the following two methods:

- Using the Start menu, navigate to the workspace's name or enter the resource name in the search bar.
- Within Connection Center, double-click the required resource to launch it.

The following URLs are used for subscribing to a workspace:

Available Resources	URL
Azure Virtual Desktop (classic)	`https://rdweb.wvd.microsoft.com/api/feeddiscovery/webfeeddiscovery.aspx`
Azure Virtual Desktop	`https://rdweb.wvd.microsoft.com/api/arm/feeddiscovery`
Azure Virtual Desktop (US Gov)	`https://rdweb.wvd.azure.us/api/arm/feeddiscovery`

Access client logs

If you do experience issues with the Remote Desktop client, you can investigate a problem using the client logs.

To collect the client logs, follow these steps:

1. Close all the sessions on the client's device first.

2. Also, ensure that the client process isn't running in the background. You can complete this by right-clicking on the **Remote Desktop** icon in the system tray and selecting **Disconnect all sessions**.

3. Open **File Explorer**.

4. Navigate to the `%temp%\DiagOutputDir\RdClientAutoTrace` path:

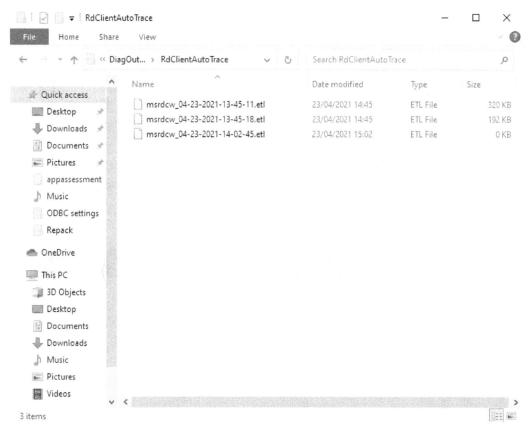

Figure 3.11 – Remote Desktop client log files

You will then see the **Event Trace Log** (**ETL**) files for the Remote Desktop client.

Connecting to Azure Virtual Desktop using the Web Client

Azure Virtual Desktop lets users connect to resources using a supported browser.

> **Important Note**
> At the time of writing, the Web Client does not support mobile OS support.

The following table details the supported web browsers for accessing Azure Virtual Desktop:

Browser	Supported OS	Notes
Microsoft Edge	Windows	
Apple Safari	macOS	
Mozilla Firefox	Windows, macOS, Linux	Version 55 or later
Google Chrome	Windows, macOS, Linux, Chrome OS	

To access the Web Client, you must navigate to `https://rdweb.wvd.microsoft.com/arm/webclient` using one of the supported browsers, as shown here:

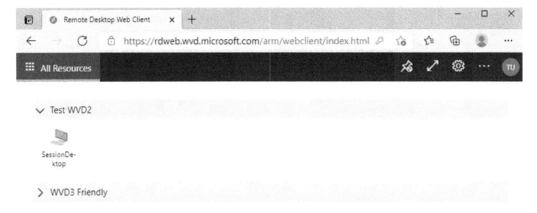

Figure 3.12 – Remote Desktop Web Client – All Resources page

> **Important Note**
> As of 18th April, 2022, the URL for accessing the web client is changed to:
> `https://docs.microsoft.com/en-us/azure/virtual-desktop/user-documentation/connect-web`

In this section, we covered the Azure Virtual Desktop client and Web Client. Microsoft does offer mobile client support and a Microsoft Store client version. You can find out more here: `https://docs.microsoft.com/en-us/azure/virtual-desktop/user-documentation/connect-web`.

Setting up email discovery to subscribe to the Azure Virtual Desktop feed

This section will show you how to set up a DNS record to enable email discovery to subscribe to an Azure Virtual Desktop feed.

You can improve the user experience when connecting to a workspace by configuring a DNS record so that users can use their email address to discover the subscription. This makes it very easy for users to access their desktops and RemoteApps.

Important Note

Azure Virtual Desktop (ARM) requires the following URL: `https://rdweb.wvd.microsoft.com/api/arm/feeddiscovery`.

To set up email discovery, you need to configure a few things.

Within your domain registrar or DNS, you will need to enter a new DNS record with the following properties:

- **Host:** `_msradc`
- **Text**: `<RD Web Feed URL>`
- **TTL:** `300 seconds`
- **TXT**: `https://rdweb.wvd.microsoft.com/api/arm/feeddiscovery`

The names of the DNS records fields can vary, depending on the domain name registrar. The generic process will result in a TXT record named `_msradc.<domain_name>` (`like as _msradc.rmitblog.com`) that has the value of the full Remote Desktop web feed.

The following screenshot depicts the steps within Azure DNS:

Figure 3.13 – Adding a DNS record for email discovery

In this section, we showed you how to configure DNS to enable email discovery within workspaces. Next, we'll summarize the prerequisites for Azure Virtual Desktop.

Summarizing the prerequisites for Azure Virtual Desktop

The following table summarizes the prerequisites for deploying an Azure Virtual Desktop environment:

Infrastructure:	Azure Virtual Desktop can only be used in a cloud-only organization or a hybrid environment. Your infrastructure needs the following components to support Azure Virtual Desktop:

Hybrid Active Directory environments/Cloud Organizations:	• An Azure Active Directory organization.
	
	• A domain controller that's synced with Azure Active Directory. You can configure this with one of the following:
	
	  ▪ Azure AD Connect.
	
	  ▪ Azure Active Directory Domain Services (Azure AD DS).
	
	  ▪ A virtual machine in Azure acting as a domain controller.
	
	  ▪ An Azure subscription that contains a virtual network that either contains or is connected to Windows Server Active Directory or Active Directory Domain Services.
	
	  ▪ Azure AD DS.

The Azure VMs you create for Azure Virtual Desktop must be as follows:	• Standard domain-joined or hybrid AD-joined. • Running one of the supported OS images.
Supported Remote Desktop clients:	The following Remote Desktop clients support Azure Virtual Desktop: • Windows Desktop • Web • macOS • iOS • Android • Linux thin clients that are connecting using the official SDK

Supported VM OS images:	Azure Virtual Desktop supports the following x64 operating system images: • Windows 11 • Windows 10 Enterprise multi-session, version 1809 or later • Windows 10 Enterprise, version 1809 or later • Windows 7 Enterprise • Windows Server 2019 • Windows Server 2016 • Windows Server 2012 R2 Azure Virtual Desktop doesn't support x86 (32-bit), Windows 10 Enterprise N, or Windows 10 Enterprise KN operating system images. Windows 7 also doesn't support any VHD or VHDX-based profile solutions hosted on managed Azure Storage due to a sector size limitation.

Summary

In this chapter, we covered the requirements for designing user identities and profiles. This included the licensing options available for Azure Virtual Desktop, the available storage solutions, and the recommended solutions, such as Azure Files, Azure Virtual Desktop client deployments, planning for user profiles, identity strategies, firewalls, and other network requirements.

In the next chapter, we will look at implementing and managing networking for Azure Virtual Desktop.

Questions

Here are a few questions to test your understanding of this chapter:

1. What is the recommended profile container technology for Azurc Virtual Desktop?

    A. FSLogix Profile Containers

    B. User profile disks

    C. Local profiles

2. Is there a license you should apply to an Azure Virtual Desktop VM?

    A. Yes

    B. No

3. What types of storage can you use for Azure Virtual Desktop?

    A. Azure Files, Azure NetApp Files, and Storage Spaces Direct

    B. Local storage

4. When configuring an Azure Storage account for FSLogix, which two privileges do you need to assign administrators (storage admins)?

    A. Storage File Data SMB Share Contributor role, Full Control NTFS permissions

    B. Blob Data Contributor role, Modify NTFS permissions

Answers

1. A

2. A

3. A

4. A

4
Implementing and Managing Networking for Azure Virtual Desktop

In this chapter, we will take a look at the implementation and management of networking for Azure Virtual Desktop (AVD). First, we will look at an overview of designing an Azure Virtual Desktop environment and the differences and requirements between a single and multi-region deployment. We will then look at the AVD networking considerations and understand Virtual Machine (VM) sizing and scale. Then we will understand the Active Directory (AD) considerations with AVD, maintenance, and how to support AVD.

The following topics will be covered in this chapter:

- Implementing Azure Virtual Network connectivity
- Managing connectivity to the internet and on-premises networks
- Implementing and managing network security
- Managing AVD session hosts by using Azure Bastion
- Monitoring and troubleshooting network connectivity

Implementing Azure Virtual Network connectivity

Before we start building out an AVD environment, we need to look at the network requirements and some of the different components and configuration options available to you.

Azure Virtual Network

When deploying an AVD environment, one of the first things you need to ensure that you have configured correctly is the **Virtual Network** (**VNet**).

The VNet is essential for enabling Azure resources such as Azure **Virtual Machines** to communicate and access the internet and on-premises networks.

The VNet is similar to a traditional network you would operate within your environment; however, you get to take advantage of Microsoft Azure's infrastructure, including availability, scaling, and isolation.

Azure VNets

Azure VNets allow resources to communicate securely, connect to services and communicate, and access on-premises resources. VNets have several features and configurable options to filter and route traffic and integration to Azure services. These next couple of sections detail some of the features and what they do specifically.

Communication between Azure resources

Azure resources communicate with each other through a virtual network, using network interfaces or service endpoints. Different VNets can be connected via VNet peering.

The following is a table listing the various Azure resources and their descriptions:

Type	Description
Virtual Network	Deploy VMs, and other types of Azure resources, to a virtual network, such as Azure App Service, **Azure Kubernetes Service** (**AKS**), and Azure Virtual Machine Scale Sets.
Virtual Network Service Endpoint	Virtual Network Service Endpoints allow you to connect your virtual network's private address space to Azure service resources. These resources include Azure storage accounts and Azure SQL databases. Service endpoints essentially enable you to securely connect to Azure service resources directly without passing through the public internet. The use of private endpoints can offer potential performance benefits also.
VNet Peering	Using virtual network peering, you can connect virtual networks to one another. Virtual networks can connect in the same or different Azure regions, thereby providing flexibility. When peering between two or more subscriptions, you can associate against the same or different AD tenants.

Communication with on-premises networks

The following table shows you the options available when you want to connect your on-premises computers and networks to an Azure virtual network:

Type	Description
Point-to-site **Virtual private network (VPN)**	Point-to-site connections are similar to a typical client VPN. They allow a client device to connect to an Azure network. The communication between the client and a virtual network is sent through an encrypted tunnel over the internet.
Site-to-Site VPN	A Site-to-Site VPN connects the VPN device and an Azure VPN gateway that has been deployed on a virtual network. This type of connection allows you to connect your Azure network to on-premises resources (for example, the local data center). The connection between your on-premises VPN device and an Azure VPN gateway communicates through an encrypted tunnel over the internet.
Azure ExpressRoute	An ExpressRoute is a connection between your network and Azure using an ExpressRoute ISP partner. The ExpressRoute connection is private, and traffic does not communicate over the internet. This type of connectivity allows you to connect your Azure network to on-premises resources (for example, the local data center). You can share ExpressRoute connections across multiple subscriptions.

Filtering and routing Azure network traffic

You can filter network traffic between subnets using one or both of the following two features within Azure:

Filtering network traffic	
Network security groups (NSGs)	NSGs and application security groups can be configured with multiple inbound and outbound security rules. These enable the filtering of traffic to and from resources by source and destination IP address, port, and protocol. An NSG can be applied to a network interface or a subnet.
Network Virtual Appliance (NVA)	An NVA is a VM that performs a network function, such as a firewall, WAN optimization, or other network function. You can deploy these from the Azure Marketplace. Vendors include Check Point, Watchguard, and SonicWALL, to name a few.
Azure Firewall	Azure Firewall enables the ability to centrally create allow and deny network filtering rules by source and destination IP address, port, and protocol.

By default, you can route Azure traffic between subnets, connected virtual networks, on-premises networks, and the internet. You can configure both options shown in the following table:

Routing network traffic	
Route tables	Create and configure custom route tables with routes that control the routing of traffic for each subnet.
Border Gateway Protocol (BGP) routes	Virtual networks connected to an on-premises network using an Azure VPN gateway or ExpressRoute connection can propagate on-premises BGP routes to the Azure virtual networks.

Understanding what virtual network integration is for Azure services

One of the features you are most likely to use within AVD is the integration of Azure services with an Azure virtual network. This is because of the requirement for Azure Files and the ability to create a private endpoint. This allows traffic from the service to communicate on the VNet rather than publicly.

The following options are available to you when integrating Azure services into your virtual network:

- You can deploy a dedicated instance of a service into a virtual network. The services can then be accessed within the virtual network and from on-premises networks that are connected to Microsoft Azure.

- A private link is used to access a specific instance of a service privately from your virtual network and from on-premises networks.

- You can also access services using public endpoints by extending a virtual network to the service. This is done through service endpoints. Service endpoints allow service resources to be secured through a virtual network.

> **Important Note**
>
> There are limits regarding the number of Azure resources you can deploy. Check out `https://docs.microsoft.com/en-us/azure/azure-resource-manager/management/azure-subscription-service-limits#networking-limits`, which shows the Azure networking limits and maximum values.

In this section, I provided an introduction to the chapter, why there is a requirement to use Azure virtual networks, communication between Azure and on-premises, and an overview of filtering and routing. In the next section, we will see how to manage connectivity to the internet and on-premises networks.

Managing connectivity to the internet and on-premises networks

In this section, we look at the different options available to you for **VPN** gateway design. This should enable you to make an informed choice that best suits your deployment needs. Please note that the VPN is only required for connecting resources between on-premises and cloud platforms. For client connectivity to the AVD platform, you would use the reverse connect feature built into the AVD Management plane.

Types of VPN available to you

The following sections cover several different configurations available for VPN connections. In the following sections, I have provided a summary of each type and a diagram to help you decide on which topology meets your requirements.

Site-to-Site

Site-to-Site, also known as an **S2S** VPN gateway connection, is an IPsec/IKE (IKEv1 or IKEv2) VPN tunnel. This type of connection can be used for cross-premises and hybrid connectivity. A S2S connection does require an on-premises VPN device with an assigned public IP address.

Figure 4.1 shows a S2S VPN:

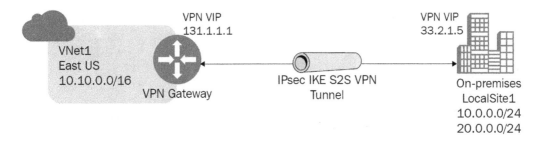

Figure 4.1 – S2S connection

You can configure a VPN gateway in active-standby mode using one public IP address, or alternatively, you can configure an active-active connection using two public IP addresses. Further details regarding these follow here:

- **Active-standby**: This enables the switch-over of traffic to the standby tunnel in the event of an issue.

- **Active-active**: This is the recommended option in which both tunnels are active, which allows higher throughputs as well as the active-active mode to prevent noticeable failure. Throughput may be constrained in a partial failure scenario.

Multi-site

A multi-site VPN connection allows you to have more than one VPN connection from a virtual network gateway. This allows you to connect to multiple sites, which are typically on-premises. Note that you must use a route-based VPN (`https://docs.microsoft.com/en-us/azure/vpn-gateway/vpn-gateway-connect-multiple-policybased-rm-ps#about`) type when using multiple connections, also known as a **dynamic gateway**. This is because each virtual network can only have one VPN gateway and all connections through a gateway share the bandwidth.

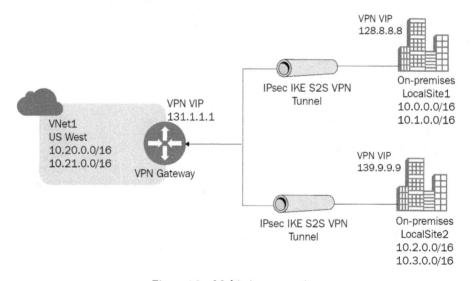

Figure 4.2 – Multi-site connection

Point-to-Site VPN

Point-to-Site (P2S) VPN connections are established from a client computer. This solution is helpful for telecommuters who need to connect to an Azure VNet from a remote location such as a home office or a conference center. P2S connections do not require a public-facing IP address or a VPN device:

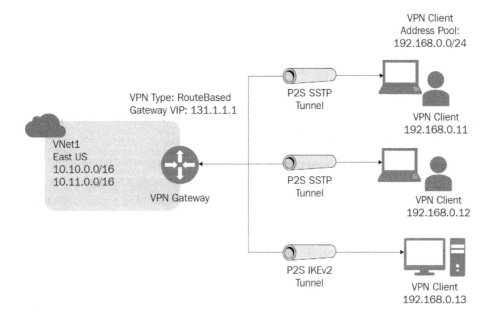

Figure 4.3 – P2S connection

VNet-to-VNet connections (IPsec/IKE VPN tunnel)

VNet-to-VNet connections are essentially a connection from one virtual network to another. This type uses IPsec/IKE (`https://docs.microsoft.com/en-us/azure/vpn-gateway/vpn-gateway-ipsecikepolicy-rm-powershell`) to provide a secure tunnel between the same or different regions/subscriptions/deployment models. You can also combine VNet-to-VNet communication with multi-site connection configurations.

Figure 4.4 – VNet-to-VNet connection

VNet peering

VNet peering is a way of connecting two VNets without using a virtual network gateway. You can connect VNets in the same and different subscriptions. Traffic is essentially routed through Microsoft's backbone infrastructure, meaning there is no public network involved.

Figure 4.5 – VNet peering

ExpressRoute (private connection)

ExpressRoute is a typical deployment option within an enterprise. This connection type enables you to extend your on-premises network to Microsoft Azure over a private connection. This is something that an **Internet Service Provider** (**ISP**), also known as a network service provider, can facilitate.

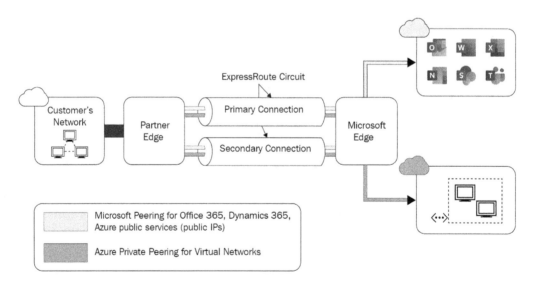

Figure 4.6 – ExpressRoute connection

ExpressRoute allows connections to Microsoft Cloud services such as Microsoft Azure, Microsoft 365, and CRM Online. There are several connectivity options available, including any-to-any, point-to-point, or virtual cross-connection options.

ExpressRoute is a private connection that is slightly different compared to other connection types that use the public internet. This provides better reliability, faster speeds, lower latency, and higher security than the traditional connection types that use the internet. It's also important to note that ExpressRoute offers a 99.95% uptime SLA for each ExpressRoute deployed. You can read more about the ExpressRoute SLA here: `https://azure.microsoft.com/en-gb/support/legal/sla/expressroute/`.

> **Important Note**
> You can have multiple VNets in different subscriptions that connect using the same ExpressRoute. This offers a benefit compared to using VPN connections. You can read more on this here: `https://docs.microsoft.com/en-us/azure/expressroute/expressroute-howto-linkvnet-portal-resource-manager#connect-a-vnet-to-a-circuit---same-subscription`.

When configuring an ExpressRoute, you need to select the gateway type as **ExpressRoute** instead of **VPN**.

> **Important Note**
> ExpressRoute traffic is not encrypted by default; however, it is possible to send encrypted traffic over an ExpressRoute circuit.

S2S and ExpressRoute coexisting connections

As well as an ExpressRoute, you can configure a S2S VPN as a secure failover path for the ExpressRoute. The capability of being able to configure both S2S VPN and ExpressRoute connections for a virtual network has benefits.

You can connect to sites that are not part of your ExpressRoute network as well as add a failover path using the S2S VPN:

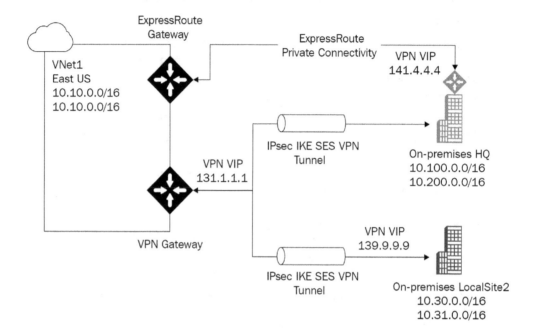

Figure 4.7 – S2S and ExpressRoute connections

This section provided an overview of the different connectivity options available to you within Azure to connect on-premises infrastructure. In the next section, we take a look at network security for AVD.

Implementing and managing network security

In this section, we cover some of the network security features available for AVD.

Azure network security overview

Microsoft Azure offers a wide range of protecting resources to prevent unauthorized access or attacks by applying network controls to the Azure VNet. These are as follows:

- Azure networking
- Network access control

- Azure Firewall
- Secure remote access and cross-premises connectivity
- Availability
- Name resolution
- Perimeter network (DMZ) architecture
- Azure DDoS protection
- Monitoring and threat detection

This section provides a high-level overview and we will now look at specific network connectivity requirements for AVD.

Understanding AVD network connectivity

AVD uses the **Remote Desktop Protocol** (**RDP**) to connect to an AVD deployment. The RDP connection is responsible for providing display and input functions over a network connection.

When we look at the connection data flow for AVD, the client starts with a **Domain Name Server** (**DNS**) lookup for the nearest Azure data center. The lookup uses **round trip time** (**RTT**) to identify the nearest data center. The gateway is used as an intelligent reverse proxy that manages all session connectivity, with nothing but the RDP bitmap (pixels) reaching the client.

The following are the five connection flow process steps for AVD:

1. The user first authenticates in Azure **AD**; a token is returned to the Remote Desktop Services client.
2. The AVD gateway checks the token with the AVD connection broker.
3. The broker queries the AVD Azure SQL database for resources assigned to the user.
4. The AVD gateway and the AVD broker select the session host for the connected client.

5. The session host creates a reverse connection to the client by using the
    AVD gateway.

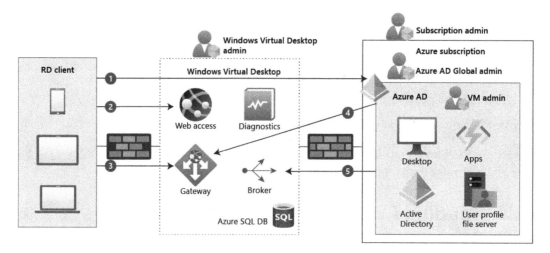

Figure 4.8 – Connection flow process

> **Important Note**
>
> AVD uses the same TLS 1.2 ciphers as Azure Front Door. You would need to
> make sure that the client computers and session hosts can use these ciphers.

Reverse connect

Reverse connect is a technology that removes the requirement for a session host within
AVD to have any inbound ports opened. By default, the RDP port, TCP/3389, doesn't
have to be open. Instead, the agent on the session host creates an outbound connection
using TCP/443 to the **Azure Virtual Desktop Management** plane. This is essentially a
reverse proxy for RDP traffic.

Virtual machines in AVD are not publicly exposed to the internet directly. They use a
private IP address within an Azure VNet and run isolated from other workloads or even
the internet if required.

> **Important Note**
>
> Where possible, avoid direct access to session hosts in your environment.
> Suppose you need direct access for troubleshooting or administration. In that
> case, you should connect from an internal network or by enabling just-in-time
> access to reduce the attack surface on a session host or by using a bastion host.

Network security groups and service tags

Network security groups (**NSGs**) are an excellent way to control/limit AVD traffic. You can configure network security on both a VM and an Azure Virtual Network, making it easy to restrict network access.

You can also use service tags within NSG rules to allow or deny traffic to a specific Azure service per Azure region or globally.

An NSG is essentially a collection of rules for inbound/outbound traffic, allowing you to control network traffic flow in and out of Azure resources.

Each rule can be configured with the following properties: name, priority, source or destination, protocol, direction, port range, and action.

> **Important Note**
>
> NSGs are a layer 3 and layer 4 network security service. An NSG consists of several security rules (allow or deny). This is achieved using a 5-tuple hash. A 5 tuple-hash is based on the source and destination IPs, the protocol, and destination ports.

When you create an Azure VM for AVD, you must configure security network filtering using NSGs or another chosen configuration to grant access to the following URLs:

Address	Outbound TCP port	Purpose	Service tag
`*.wvd.microsoft.com`	443	Service traffic	WindowsVirtual Desktop
`gcs.prod.monitoring.core.windows.net`	443	Agent traffic	AzureCloud
`production.diagnostics.monitoring.core.windows.net`	443	Agent traffic	AzureCloud
`*xt.blob.core.windows.net`	443	Agent traffic	AzureCloud
`*eh.servicebus.windows.net`	443	Agent traffic	AzureCloud
`*xt.table.core.windows.net`	443	Agent traffic	AzureCloud
`*xt.queue.core.windows.net`	443	Agent traffic	AzureCloud
`catalogartifact.azureedge.net`	443	Azure Marketplace	AzureCloud
`kms.core.windows.net`	1688	Windows activation	Internet

Address	Outbound TCP port	Purpose	Service tag
`mrsglobalsteus2prod.blob.core.windows.net`	443	Agent and SXS stack updates	AzureCloud
`wvdportalstorageblob.blob.core.windows.net`	443	Azure portal support	AzureCloud
`169.254.169.254`	80	Azure Instance Metadata service endpoint	N/A
`168.63.129.16`	80	Session host health monitoring	N/A

What is Azure Firewall?

Azure Firewall is a Microsoft-managed network security service that protects your Azure virtual network resources. This is a fully stateful firewall with the added benefits of cloud high availability and scalability.

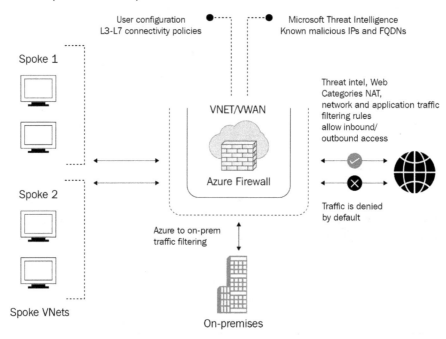

Figure 4.9 – Azure Firewall standard

It is also important to note that there is also an Azure Firewall Premium version that offers advanced capabilities, including signature-based IDPs.

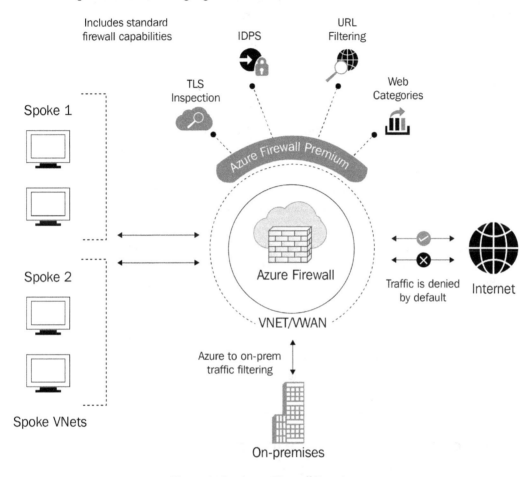

Figure 4.10 – Azure Firewall Premium

Azure Firewall allows you to create, configure, and log network and application connectivity policies across Azure subscriptions and virtual networks. You can even integrate with the Azure Monitor service for logs and analytics.

> **Important Note**
> Azure Firewall uses a static public IP address for virtual network resources for external network devices to identify traffic originating from your Azure virtual network.

Azure Firewall for application-level protection

Azure Firewall provides an AVD **Fully Qualified Domain Name** (**FQDN**) tag to simplify the deployment and configuration of allowed URLs.

The following four steps will guide you through allowing outbound AVD traffic using Azure Firewall:

1. Deploy Azure Firewall and configure your AVD host pool subnet **User Defined Route** (**UDR**) to route all traffic via Azure Firewall.

2. Create an application rule collection and add a rule to enable the AVD FQDN tag.

3. As the set of required storage and service bus accounts for your AVD host pool is unique to your deployment, this information will not be captured in the AVD FQDN tag by default. You can resolve this by allowing HTTP access from your host pool subnet to the specific service using wildcard FQDNs, for example, `*app.blob.core.windows.net`.

4. Create a network rule collection and allow traffic from your **Active Directory Domain Services** (**ADDS**) private IP address to `*` for TCP and UDP port `53` and allow traffic from your AVD VMs to Windows Activation Service TCP port `1688`.

> Tip
>
> Under *step 3*, you can also use a log analytics query to list the exact required FQDNs and then allow them explicitly in your firewall application rule. This provides more granular control over access.
>
> These wildcard FQDNs enable the required access but are less restrictive.

Host pool outbound access to the internet

There may be a need to enable secure outbound internet access for users. In scenarios where the list of allowed destinations is defined, you can use the Azure Firewall application and network rules to control the required access granularly. You may also want to include whitelists for required destinations such as web services that the organization's users may use.

> Important Note
>
> You can configure AVD host pools using an explicit proxy configuration using an existing on-premises secure web gateway. However, this may impact performance. You may want to consider using Azure **Network Virtual Appliances** (NVAs) to offer content filtering/proxy-based filtering services. You can also use Microsoft Defender for endpoints and Azure Firewall using the web categories feature.

Network Virtual Appliances

To benefit from standardization and comply with any organizational technology policies, you can deploy An NVA to your Azure Virtual Network. These NVAs can be firewalls deployed as VMs on Azure. Routing would be configured so that the NVA controls inbound and outbound traffic flow as well as the publishing of network services through the use of public IP addresses.

NVAs can be used with AVD, which can add benefits such as advanced network security to your VNet and content filtering and threat detection capabilities.

In this section, we looked at the implementation of network security for AVD, NSGs, Reverse Proxy, Azure Firewall, and NVAs. We will now look at how to manage session hosts using Azure Bastion.

Managing AVD session hosts by using Azure Bastion

In this section, we look at Azure Bastion as an additional layer of security for accessing VMs securely through an HTML5 browser within the Azure portal.

What is Azure Bastion?

Azure Bastion is a platform-managed service that enables admins to connect to VMs in Azure using your web browser. The service makes it easy to connect securely to your VMs directly from the Azure portal over a **Transport Layer Security** (**TLS**) connection. Azure Bastion also removes the need for public IPs or Remote Desktop Services ports to open on your NSGs for the internet.

When using Azure Bastion, you use the Azure portal to connect the VM, which is essentially an HTML5 TLS connection. The Bastion deployment then connects to the resources securely inside the virtual network using RDP or **Secure Shell** (**SSH**) protocol, depending on the VM remote protocol requirement.

> **Important Note**
> Azure Bastion uses port 443; ensure that you configure the NSG for this port when using Bastion deployments.

Azure Bastion is deployed per virtual network, which means that if you use multiple virtual networks for AVD, you will need multiple Bastion deployments.

The benefit of Bastion is that standard RDP/SSH ports are not exposed over the internet, providing a secure connection to Azure resources. This also reduces the threat surface for an attacker.

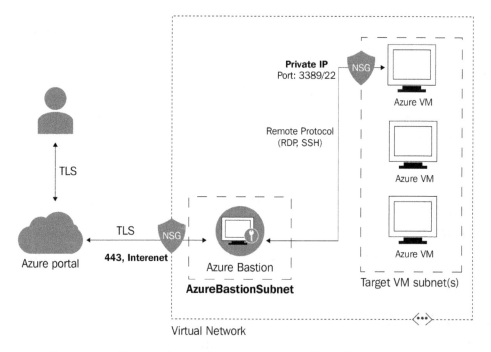

Figure 4.11 – Diagram showing the communication followed for Azure Bastion

Setting up Azure Bastion

This section provides a high-level deployment guide for setting up your first Bastion object within the Azure portal.

> **Important Note**
> You will need to deploy a Bastion instance for each virtual network you wish to connect to.

The steps are as follows:

1.   From the Azure portal **Home** page, select **+ Create a resource**.

2.   On the **New** page, in the **Search** box, type `Bastion`, and then click **Enter** to get to the search results. On the result for `Bastion`, verify that the publisher is Microsoft.

3.   Select **Create**.

4. On the **Create a Bastion** page, configure a new Bastion resource, as shown in the following screenshot:

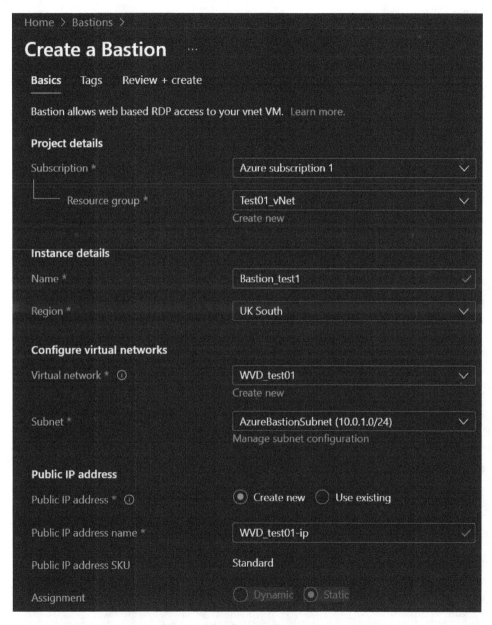

Figure 4.12 – Create a Bastion page

You will then be presented with the **Create a Bastion** page. Ensure that you fill out the following:

a) Select the required Azure subscription.

b) Choose the resource group in which you will deploy the Bastion resource.

c) Give the Bastion resource a name.

d) Select the required Azure region.

e) Select the virtual network where the Bastion will be created. You can create a new virtual network or use an existing one.

f) The Bastion host is deployed to its own dedicated subnet.

g) Use an existing public IP address or a new one.

h) You cannot change the public IP address SKU.

i) Assignment should be the default setting of **Static**.

5. Once you have finished specifying the required settings, select **Review + create**.

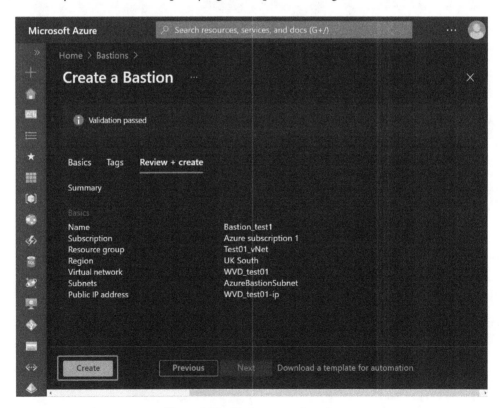

Figure 4.13 – Review + create page

6. Review the settings and then click **Next** at the bottom, as shown in the preceding screenshot.

Connecting to a VM using Azure Bastion

The steps for this are as follows:

1. Navigate to the VM you wish to connect to using Bastion. Click on **Connect** and then click **Bastion**.

Figure 4.14 – Connecting to a VM using Bastion

2. You should see the **Connect using Azure Bastion** page. Enter the username and password for the VM and then click **Connect**.

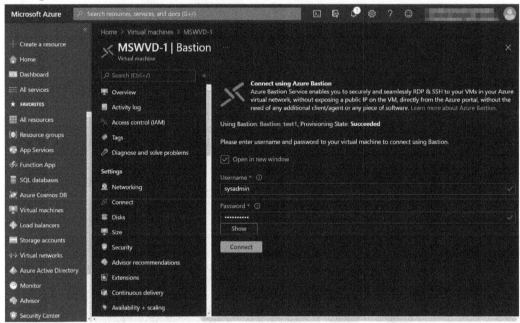

Figure 4.15 – Connecting using the Azure Bastion page

3. The administrative RDP connection to the VM will be completed using Bastion, and then the session will be streamed over HTML5 using port 443. The following screenshot shows a session using the Bastion service:

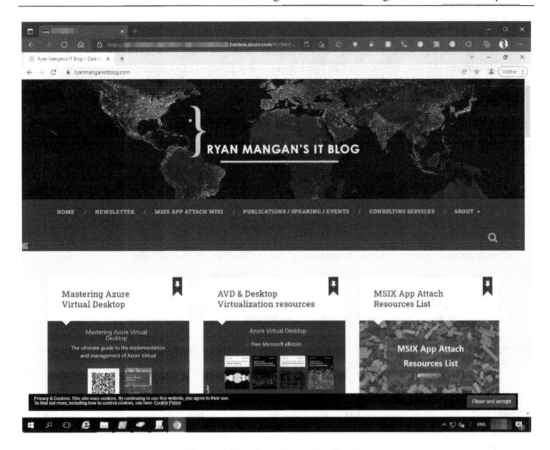

Figure 4.16 – A session using Bastion

In this section, we took a look at what Azure Bastion is and how to configure/deploy Azure Bastion for AVD. In the next and final section, we will provide an overview of monitoring and troubleshooting network connectivity.

Monitoring and troubleshooting network connectivity

This section briefly covers some of the tools you can use to monitor and troubleshoot network connectivity issues for AVD. This section provides a high-level overview as we cover both Log Analytics and Azure Monitor in *Chapter 18, Monitoring and Managing Performance and Health*.

> **Important Note**
>
> Ensure that you have configured DNS correctly since, if the session hosts cannot see the domain controller, the provisioning process may fail on the next step. You should ensure that the VNet is configured with AD as a DNS server.

Using Azure Monitor to diagnose network issues

Azure Monitor Logs is a collection of features that collects and organizes log and performance data from Azure resources (monitored).

The data is collected from different sources, such as Azure services and VM agents, which are then consolidated into a single Log Analytics workspace to be analyzed. You can perform simple queries that retrieve specific datasets or perform sophisticated data analysis to identify any critical patterns within your monitored data.

You work with log queries using Log Analytics and create alert rules to notify you about issues or visualize results in a dashboard or workbook.

The following diagram depicts the log collection and output capabilities of Azure Monitor, which is using Azure Log Analytics:

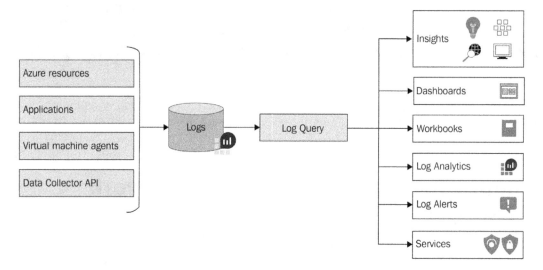

Figure 4.17 – Log collection and output capabilities

Some of the examples when working with AVD are as follows:

- The following screenshot shows the Azure Monitor dashboard for AVD. This dashboard comprises several Azure log sources reported centrally in a single dashboard:

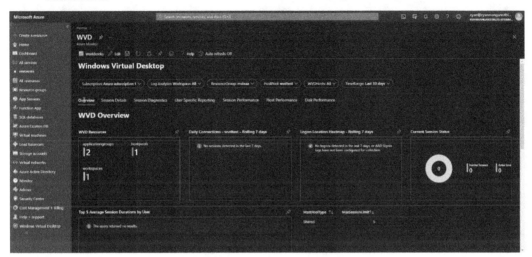

Figure 4.18 – Azure Monitor dashboard for AVD

- The following screenshot shows **Connections Overview** from a VM using Log Insights:

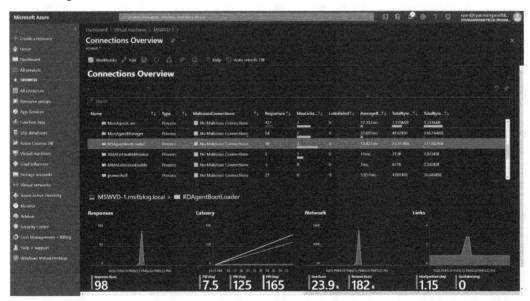

Figure 4.19 – Connections Overview page

- The following screenshot shows the Insights workspace for AVD, allowing you to explore different tabs from **Overview** to **Alerts**:

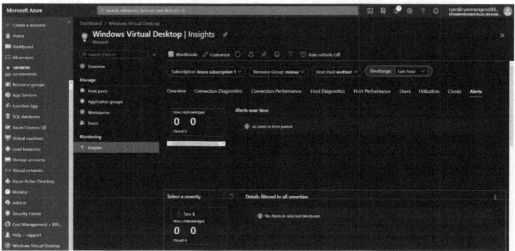

Figure 4.20 – AVD Insights page

You need to enable Log Analytics and the collection of logs on the various components for AVD before reviewing and monitoring log data for AVD.

> **Important Note**
>
> I will show you how to enable monitoring for AVD in *Chapter 18, Monitoring and Managing Performance and Health*. The key takeaway is that you can use Azure Monitor and Log Analytics to diagnose network issues.

Confirming all required URLs are not blocked

To confirm that you have set up your Azure virtual network correctly and allowed the required URLs, you can run a built-in tool called `WVDAgentURLTool.exe`. You can find this command-line tool within the RD agent folder on the session host.

> **Tool Requirements**
>
> The RD agent needs to be version 1.0.2944.400 or higher. See the link here for the latest version: `https://docs.microsoft.com/en-us/azure/virtual-desktop/safe-url-list`.

You can find your agent version from the host pool within the Azure portal, as shown in the following screenshot:

Figure 4.21 – AVD Session hosts page

Using the URL check tool

Before starting, please check your agent version as the folder may vary depending on the AVD agent version.

To use the tool, perform the following steps:

1. On the session host, open a command prompt as an administrator.

2. Run the following command to change the directory to the same folder as the AVD build agent:

```
cd C:\Program Files\Microsoft RDInfra\
RDAgent_1.0.2944.1400
```

3. Then, run the tool:

```
WVDAgentUrlTool.exe
```

4. Once you run the command-line app, you'll see a list of accessible and inaccessible URLs for AVD, as shown in the following screenshot:

```
C:\Program Files\Microsoft RDInfra\RDAgent_1.0.2944.1400>WVDAgentUrlTool.exe
WVD
================================================================
Accessible URLs:
================================================================
gcs.prod.monitoring.core.windows.net
production.diagnostics.monitoring.core.windows.net
gsm1044859968eh.servicebus.windows.net
gsm265134562eh.servicebus.windows.net
gsm473136880eh.servicebus.windows.net
gsm1463510419eh.servicebus.windows.net
gsm900951011eh.servicebus.windows.net
gsm1044859968xt.blob.core.windows.net
gsm1044859968xt.queue.core.windows.net
gsm1044859968xt.table.core.windows.net
gsm265134562xt.blob.core.windows.net
gsm265134562xt.queue.core.windows.net
gsm265134562xt.table.core.windows.net
gsm473136880xt.blob.core.windows.net
gsm473136880xt.queue.core.windows.net
gsm473136880xt.table.core.windows.net
gsm1463510419xt.blob.core.windows.net
gsm1463510419xt.queue.core.windows.net
gsm1463510419xt.table.core.windows.net
gsm900951011xt.blob.core.windows.net
gsm900951011xt.queue.core.windows.net
gsm900951011xt.table.core.windows.net
gsm900951011xt.table.core.windows.net
rdbroker-g-us-r0.wvd.microsoft.com
rdbroker-g-us-r1.wvd.microsoft.com
rddiagnostics-g-us-r0.wvd.microsoft.com
rddiagnostics-g-us-r1.wvd.microsoft.com
rdweb-g-us-r0.wvd.microsoft.com
rdweb-g-us-r1.wvd.microsoft.com
rdgateway-g-us-r0.wvd.microsoft.com
rdgateway-g-us-r1.wvd.microsoft.com
mrsglobalsteus2prod.blob.core.windows.net
catalogartifact.azureedge.net
wvdportalstorageblob.blob.core.windows.net
maupdateaccount.blob.core.windows.net
www.wvd.microsoft.com
rdbroker.wvd.microsoft.com
rddiagnostics.wvd.microsoft.com
rdweb.wvd.microsoft.com
rdgateway.wvd.microsoft.com
rdbroker-r0.wvd.microsoft.com
rdbroker-r1.wvd.microsoft.com
rddiagnostics-r0.wvd.microsoft.com
rddiagnostics-r1.wvd.microsoft.com
rdweb-r0.wvd.microsoft.com
rdweb-r1.wvd.microsoft.com
rdgateway-r0.wvd.microsoft.com

C:\Program Files\Microsoft RDInfra\RDAgent_1.0.2944.1400>
```

Figure 4.22 – List of accessible and inaccessible URLs for AVD

As shown in the preceding screenshot, you can see that the tool has output all the accessible URLs, meaning the network configuration is correct.

In this section, we looked at how to test to ensure that the URLs for AVD are accessible using the **WVDAgentURL** tool. Based on the results, this will confirm whether everything is working correctly or guide you to the missing URLs that you need to add, check, and possibly configure.

Summary

Networking is the core of how AVD functions and it is essential that you design and configure the appropriate connectivity to ensure you can communicate with your Azure Virtual Desktop environment.

In this chapter, we took a look at Azure virtual network connectivity for AVD. We covered implementing Azure virtual network connectivity, managing connectivity between on-premises and the internet, implementing network security, Azure Bastion, and monitoring and troubleshooting network connectivity within Azure.

In the next chapter, we will look at implementing and managing storage for Azure Virtual Desktop.

Questions

1. What tool can you use to check the AVD URLs?
2. Is Azure Bastion configured per subnet or virtual network?
3. What can you use to secure the networking of Azure Virtual Desktop?
4. What Azure feature can you use to monitor and diagnose AVD networking issues?

Answers

1. *WVDAgentURLTool.exe*
2. *Virtual network*
3. *Azure Firewall*
4. *Azure Monitor*

5
Implementing and Managing Storage for Azure Virtual Desktop

In this chapter, we'll learn how to implement and manage storage for AVD. We'll create a storage account and configure Azure Files for FSLogix Profile Containers.

The following topics will be covered in this chapter:

- Configuring storage for FSLogix components
- Configuring storage accounts
- Creating file shares
- Configuring disks

Configuring storage for FSLogix components

This chapter looks at the storage options that are available for FSLogix Profile Containers when preparing and configuring AVD. We will focus on Azure Files as the storage option of choice as this is the most commonly used storage option for AVD.

FSLogix Profile container storage options

There are three common storage options available for **Azure Virtual Desktop** (**AVD**). This section provides a comparison of the options available to you.

> **Important Note**
>
> Microsoft recommends storing FSLogix Profile Containers in Azure Files unless there is a specific requirement not to. However, this may not meet all organization's requirements.

FSLogix is a profile solution that was acquired by Microsoft to provide Azure Virtual Desktop with roaming profiles by dynamically attaching a virtual hard disk at sign-in. The user profile that's stored on the virtual disk becomes immediately available and appears in the system like a typical user profile.

> **Important Note**
>
> You can use the FSLogix Profile solution outside of AVD.

The following table provides a comparison of the different storage options and features:

Features	Azure Files	Azure NetApp Files	Storage Spaces Direct
Use case	General-purpose.	Ultra performance or migration from NetApp on-premises.	Cross-platform.
Platform service	Yes; Azure-native solution.	Yes; Azure-native solution.	No, self-managed.
Regional availability	All regions.	Select regions.	All regions.
Redundancy	Locally redundant/ zone-redundant/ geo-redundant/ geo-zone-redundant.	Locally redundant/ cross-region replication.	Locally redundant/zone-redundant/geo-redundant.
Tiers and performance	Standard (transaction optimized). Premium. Up to a maximum of 100K IOPS per share with 10 GBps per share at about 3 ms latency.	Standard. Premium. Ultra. Up to 4.5GBps per volume at about 1 ms latency. For IOPS and performance details, see the Azure NetApp Files performance considerations and the FAQ.	Standard HDD: Up to 500 IOPS per-disk limits. Standard SSD: Up to 4K IOPS per disk limits. Premium SSD: Up to 20K IOPS per-disk limits. We recommend Premium disks for Storage Spaces Direct.
Max capacity	100 TiB per share, up to 5 PiB per general-purpose account.	100 TiB per volume, up to 12.5 PiB per subscription.	Maximum 32 TiB per disk.
Required infrastructure	Minimum share size 1 GiB.	Minimum capacity pool 4 TiB, minimum volume size 100 GiB.	Two VMs on Azure IaaS (plus Cloud Witness) or at least three VMs without and costs for disks.
Protocols	SMB 3.0/2.1, NFSv4.1 (preview), REST.	NFSv3, NFSv4.1 (preview), SMB 3.x/2.x.	NFSv3, NFSv4.1, SMB 3.1.

This table was taken from the following site: `https://docs.microsoft.com/en-us/azure/virtual-desktop/store-fslogix-profile?WT.mc_id=modinfra-17152-thmaure#azure-platform-details`.

As shown in the preceding table, Azure Files is the likely candidate for AVD deployments, while Azure NetApp Files offers high performance. There is also an Azure **Virtual Machine (VM)** option for using Storage Spaces Direct.

The following table details the features available for Azure Files, Azure NetApp Files, and Storage Spaces Direct:

Features	Azure Files	Azure NetApp Files	Storage Spaces Direct
Access	Cloud, on-premises, and hybrid (Azure File Sync)	Cloud, on-premises (via ExpressRoute)	Cloud, on-premises
Backup	Azure backup snapshot integration	Azure NetApp Files snapshots	Azure backup snapshot integration
Security and compliance	All Azure supported certificates	ISO completed	All Azure supported certificates
Azure Active Directory integration	Native Active Directory and Azure Active Directory Domain Services	Azure Active Directory Domain Services and Native Active Directory	Native Active Directory or Azure Active Directory Domain Services support only

This table was taken from the following site: `https://docs.microsoft.com/en-us/azure/virtual-desktop/store-fslogix-profile?WT.mc_id=modinfra-17152-thmaure#azure-management-details`.

The preceding table shows the features that are available for each service, including Azure Files, Azure NetApp Files, and Storage Spaces Direct.

This section looked at the three storage options that are available when you're planning to configure FSLogix Profile Containers. In the next section, we will look at the two different Azure Files tiers.

The different Azure Files tiers

Azure Files has two different tier types of file storage: standard and premium. The key difference between the two is performance, as premium uses **solid-state drives (SSDs)** and are deployed in the file storage account type. Premium file share types are helpful in larger organizations where the requirement for higher performance and low latency is required due to the number of users accessing the file share storage.

Standard file shares use **hard disk drives (HDDs)** and are deployed as **general-purpose version 2 (GPv2)** storage account types. Therefore, you should expect to use standard file shares in small environments or organizations with low I/O needs.

> **Important Note**
> Standard file shares are only available in pay-as-you-go billing models. This means that billing is based on the total storage used, whereas when you're using premium file shares storage, you pay for the configured capacity.

The following table provides examples of when you should use standard file shares versus premium file shares:

Deployment Type	Recommended Storage Tier
Fewer than 200 users	Standard file shares
Greater than 200 users	Premium file shares or standard with multiple file shares
Medium	Premium file shares
Heavy	Premium file shares
Power	Premium file shares

This section explored the two different Azure files storage tiers and when to use each type. The next section looks at Azure Files integration with Azure Active Directory Domain Service.

Best practices for Azure Files with AVD

The following are some of the best practices associated with Azure Files when you're configuring it for use with AVD:

- It is advised that you create your storage accounts in the same region as the session host VMs. This is to ensure that latency is kept to a minimum. This also applies to optimal performance when you're using FSLogix Profile Containers.

- It is recommended that you should be using Active Directory integrated file shares for security and that the following permissions should be set:

User Account	Folder	Permissions
Users	This Folder Only	Modify
Creator/Owner	Subfolders and Files Only	Modify
Administrator (optional)	This Folder, Subfolders, and Files	Full Control

- When you're storing images in Azure Files, it is advised that you store the master image in the same region as where the VMs are being provisioned.

This section looked at the different storage options available to you, including Azure Files, Azure NetApp Files, and Storage Spaces Direct. We also looked at the different storage tiers for Azure Files, Active Directory Domain Services integration, and storage best practices when configuring FSLogix Profile Containers.

Now, let's learn how to configure a storage account.

Configure storage accounts

This section will look at creating a storage account and configuring data protection.

To create a storage account, you need to follow the stepwise procedure detailed in the following subsections.

Step 1 – create a new storage account

From the left menu within the Azure portal, select **Storage accounts** to display a list of your storage accounts. You can also search for `storage accounts` in the top search bar. This is shown in the following screenshot:

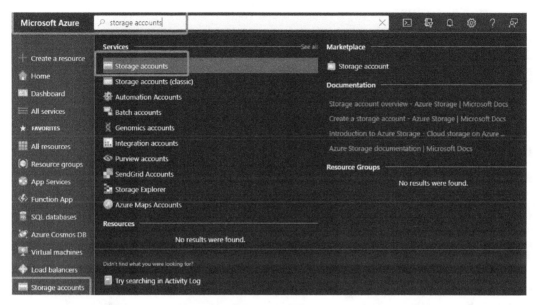

Figure 5.1 – Using the search bar to show the Storage accounts service in the Azure portal

Once on the **Storage accounts** page, you will see all the storage accounts and an icon to create one in the page's navigation bar. To create a new storage account, click **Create**:

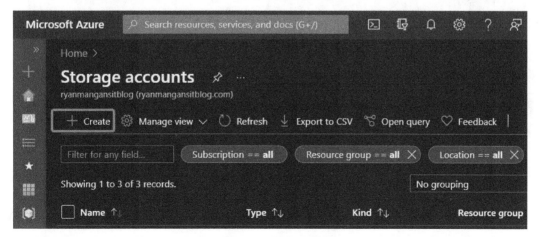

Figure 5.2 – Storage accounts

Once you have clicked **Create**, we can move on to the next section.

Step 2 – configure the basics

Once you have selected **Storage accounts** and clicked **Create**, you will see the basic **Create a storage account** page:

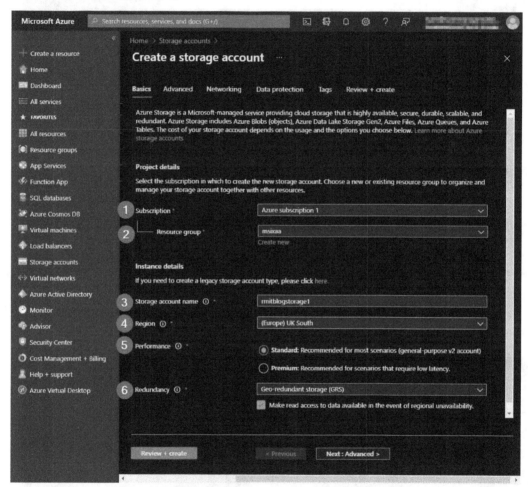

Figure 5.3 – Creating a storage account

The following table details the steps shown in the preceding screenshot. You are required to complete these steps before progressing to the **Advanced** tab:

SN	Name	Required or Optional	Description
1	Subscription	Required	Select the subscription that's required for the storage account.
2	Resource group	Required	Select an existing resource group for this storage account, or create a new one.
3	Storage account name	Required	Choose a name for your storage account; this must be unique. Storage account name must be between 3 and 24 characters in length and contain numbers and lowercase letters only.
4	Region	Required	Select the region for your storage account.
5	Performance	Required	Select Standard performance for general-purpose v2 storage accounts; this is the default. Microsoft recommends this type of account for most scenarios. Use Premium storage for low latency.
6	Redundancy	Required	Select the required redundancy configuration. Remember, not all redundancy options are available in all regions. By selecting geo-redundant configuration (GRS or GZRS), your data is replicated to a data center in a different region. For read access to data in the secondary region, ensure you select Make read access to data available in the event of regional unavailability.

Once you have configured the **Basics** section of creating a new storage account, we can look at configuring advanced settings.

> **Important Note**
>
> Not all regions are supported for all types of storage accounts or redundancy configurations. The choice of region can also have a billing impact.

Step 3 – configure advanced settings

Once you're in the **Advanced** tab, you will see several security and storage configuration options. You can leave these as-is or customize them as required:

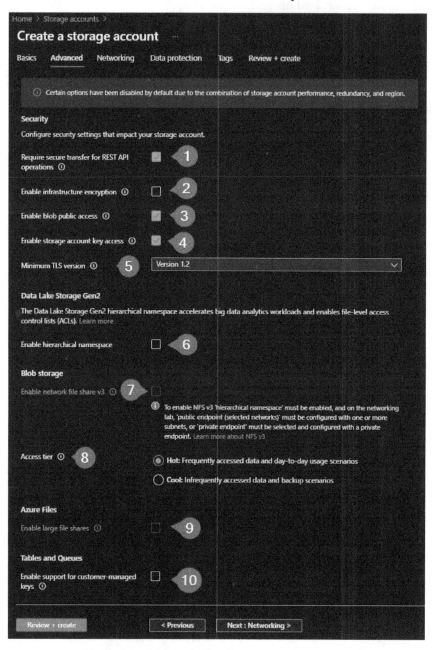

Figure 5.4 – Advanced tab – Create a storage account

The following table details the 10 configuration options. Eight are optional, while two are mandatory. These configuration settings are cross-referenced in the preceding screenshot:

SN	Name	Required or Optional	Description
1	Enable secure transfer	Optional	Enabling secure transfer requires that incoming requests to this storage account are made only via HTTPS (default). This is recommended for optimal security.
2	Enable infrastructure encryption	Optional	Infrastructure encryption is not enabled by default. You can enable infrastructure encryption to encrypt your data at both the service level and the infrastructure level.
3	Enable blob public access	Optional	Users with the appropriate permissions can enable anonymous public access to a container in the storage account when enabling this setting. If you disable this setting, it prevents all anonymous public access to the storage account, making it private.
4	Enable storage account key access	Optional	When enabled, this setting allows clients to authorize requests to the storage account using either the account access keys or an **Azure Active Directory** (**Azure AD**) account. Disabling this setting prevents authorization with the account access keys.

SN	Name	Required or Optional	Description
5	Minimum TLS version	Required	Select the minimum version of **Transport Layer Security** (**TLS**) for incoming requests to the storage account. The default value is TLS version 1.2. When set to the default value, incoming requests made using TLS 1.0 or TLS 1.1 are rejected.
6	Enable hierarchical namespace	Optional	You need to configure a hierarchical namespace to use this storage account for Azure Data Lake Storage Gen2 workloads.
7	Enable **network file system** (**NFS**) v3 (preview)	Optional	NFS v3 provides Linux filesystem compatibility at object storage scale and enables Linux clients to mount a container in Blob storage from an Azure VM or a computer on-premises.
8	Access tier	Required	Blob access tiers enable you to store blob data cost-effectively, based on usage.
9	Enable large file shares	Optional	This is only available for premium storage accounts for file shares.
10	Enable support for customer-managed keys	Optional	To enable support for customer-managed keys for tables and queues, it is advised that you ensure this setting is enabled while creating the storage account.

Once you have chosen the required advanced settings, you can start configuring the **Networking** section.

Step 4 – configure networking

This step is where you configure specific network connectivity requirements, including public and private endpoints. You can also specify the required routing option:

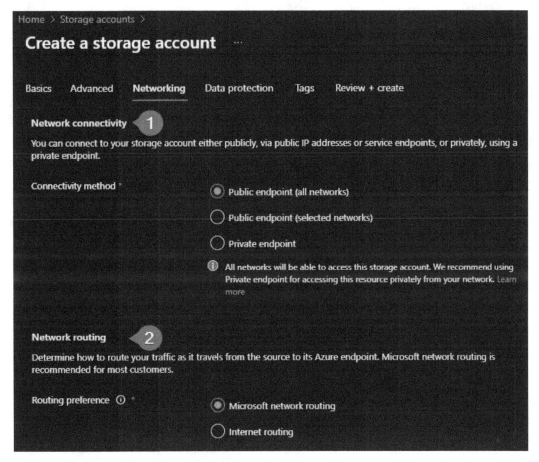

Figure 5.5 – The Networking tab

The preceding screenshot is numbered to reference the **Connectivity method** and **Routing preference** areas shown in the following table:

SN	Name	Required or Optional	Description
1	Connectivity method	Required	Incoming network traffic is routed to the public endpoint for your storage account by default. You can specify that traffic must be routed to the public endpoint through an Azure virtual network. You can also configure private endpoints for private network communication to the storage account.
2	Routing preference	Required	This setting specifies how network traffic is routed to the public endpoint of your storage account from clients over the internet. A new storage account uses Microsoft network routing by default. However, you can also configure how network traffic is routed through the **point of presence** (**POP**) closest to the storage account, which may lower networking costs.

Now that you have configured the networking section of the *Creating a storage account*, we can move on to step five, where we will configure the data protection settings for the storage account.

Step 5 – configure data protection

Within this tab, you can configure the various recovery and tracking options for your storage account. The following screenshot, whose numbers are referenced in the following table, shows several options that are available to you:

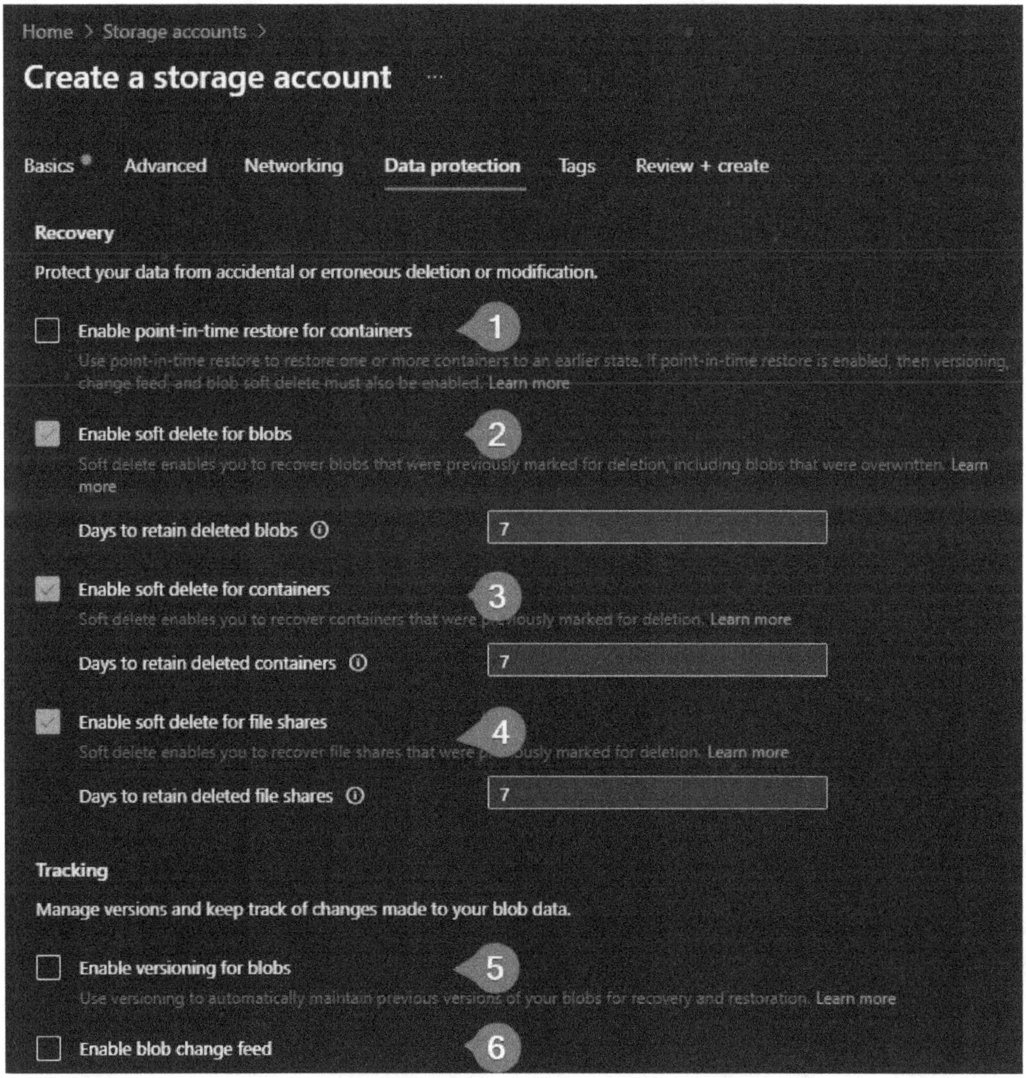

Figure 5.6 – The Data protection tab

The preceding screenshot is annotated with numbers one to six; this correlates with the following table, which shows the options for configuring data protection for the new storage account:

SN	Name	Required or Optional	Description
1	Enable point-in-time restore for containers	Optional	Point-in-time restore protects against accidental deletion or corruption by enabling you to restore block blob data to an earlier state. Enabling point-in-time restore enables blob versioning, blob soft delete, and blob change feed. These prerequisite features have a cost impact, so be sure to check their pricing first.
2	Enable soft delete for blobs	Optional	Blob soft delete protects an individual blob, snapshot, or version from accidental deletes or overwrites by maintaining the deleted data in the system for a specified retention period. During the retention period, you can restore a soft-deleted object to its state when it was deleted.
3	Enable soft delete for containers	Optional	Container soft delete protects a container and its contents from accidental deletes by maintaining the deleted data in the system for a specified retention period. During the retention period, you can restore a soft-deleted container to its state at the time it was deleted.
4	Enable soft delete for file shares	Optional	Soft delete for file shares protects a file share and its contents from accidental deletion by maintaining the deleted data in the system for a specified retention period. During the retention period, you can restore a soft-deleted file share to its state at the time it was deleted.

SN	Name	Required or Optional	Description
5	Enable versioning for blobs	Optional	Blob versioning automatically saves the state of a blob in a previous version when the blob is overwritten. It is recommended that you enable blob versioning for optimal data protection for the storage account.
6	Enable blob change feed	Optional	The blob change feed provides transaction logs of all the changes that have been made to all the blobs in your storage account, as well as their metadata.

Once you have selected the required options for data protection, you can set **Tags** or proceed to the **Review + create** tab.

Within the **Review + create** tab, check if all the settings are as you require, then proceed to create the storage account:

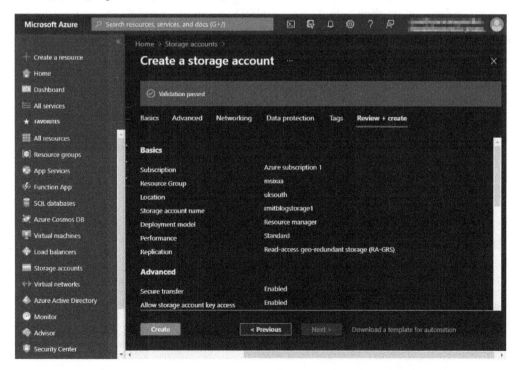

Figure 5.7 – The Review + create tab

Once the storage account has been created, you will see it appear on the **Storage accounts** page. In the next section, we will look at configuring an Azure file share.

Configuring file shares

Once you have created your storage account, you need to create a file share for FSLogix Profile Containers. This section will look at configuring a file share in a storage account ready for use with FSLogix.

Before we get started with Azure file shares, let's have a look at the different tiers that are available per share:

- **Premium** file shares use SSDs, which provide higher constant performance and lower latency than standard storage. This file share tier type is beneficial for larger shares or high I/O workload requirements.

- **Transaction** optimized file shares, similar to standard storage, use HDDs. This is suitable for heavy workloads but does not provide the required latency that premium file shares offer.

- **Hot** file shares provide storage optimized for general-purpose file sharing for items such as department shares. Hot files use HDDs.

- **Cool** file shares provide cost-effective storage for archive storage requirements. This type of storage tier uses HDDs.

> Important Note
>
> For larger organizations and high I/O workloads, it is recommended that you use the premium storage tier for Azure file shares.

Creating an azure file share is quite simple. You need to make sure you have created a storage account before proceeding. Within the storage account, you need to navigate to the **File Shares** icon within the table of contents for the storage account:

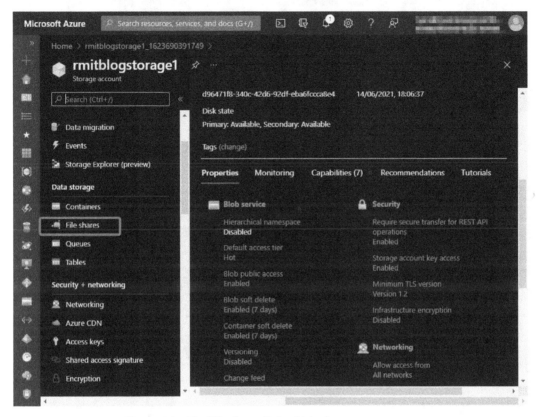

Figure 5.8 – The File shares link within the storage account

On the **File shares** page, click the **File share** button, as shown in the following screenshot:

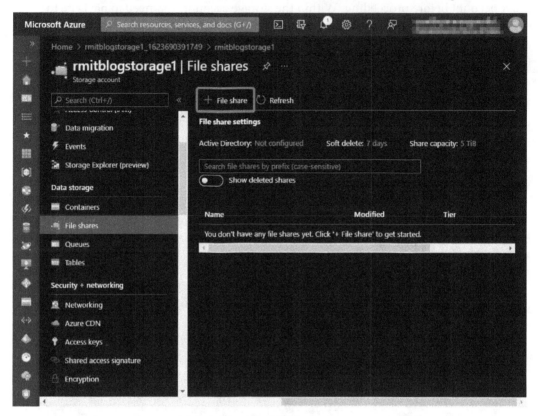

Figure 5.9 – The File share button

Once you have clicked the **File share** button, you will see the **New file share** blade appear. Fill in the following fields in this blade to create a new file share:

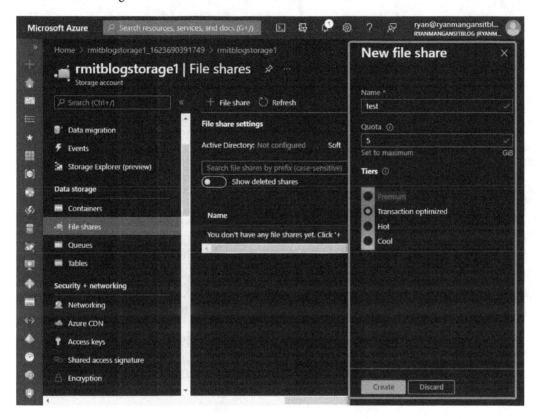

Figure 5.10 – The New file share blade

You will need to enter a **Name** for the share, a **Quota** size, and choose the tier you would like.

Once you have entered the required details, click **Create** to finish creating the new share:

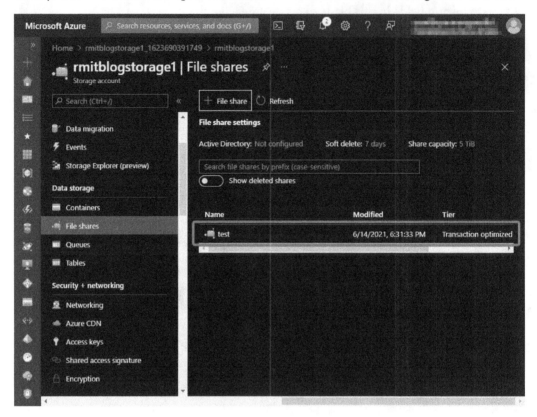

Figure 5.11 – The newly created file share

Note that the experience within a storage account using premium storage for file storage has a slightly different UI experience, as shown in the following screenshot:

Figure 5.12 – Configuring premium file shares

This section summarized the different Azure file share storage tier options and how to create a new Azure file share. In the next section, we will look at Azure Managed Disks, ephemeral OS disks, and learn how to prepare a custom image.

Configuring disks

This section will look at Azure Managed Disks, the different available options, and how to prepare a custom VHD image.

An Azure managed disk is essentially a virtual disk (block-level storage volume) in conjunction with Azure VMs. Managed disks are designed to provide an availability of 99.999%. This is achieved by providing three replica copies of your data, which provides high durability.

The following table details the different types of managed disks that are available:

Detail	Ultra Disk	Premium SSD	Standard SSD	Standard HDD
Disk type	SSD	SSD	SSD	HDD
Scenario	I/O-intensive workloads such as SAP HANA, top tier databases (for example, SQL, Oracle), and other transaction-heavy workloads	Production and performance-sensitive workloads	Web servers, lightly used enterprise applications, and dev/test	Backup, non-critical, and infrequent access
Max disk size	65,536 gibibytes (GiB)	32,767 GiB	32,767 GiB	32,767 GiB
Max throughput	2,000 MB/s	900 MB/s	750 MB/s	500 MB/s
Max IOPS	160,000	20,000	6,000	2,000

This table was taken from the following site: `https://docs.microsoft.com/en-us/azure/virtual-machines/disks-types`.

As shown in the preceding table, each type of disk has a specific use case. For AVD multi-session deployments, it is recommended that you use premium SSDs to avoid any IOPs bottlenecks. You can use standard SSDs for personal desktop deployments. It is not recommended to use standard HDD disks for AVD deployments as performance could be degraded:

> **Important Note**
> It is recommended that premium SSDs be used for session hosts.

Premium SSD Sizes	P10	P15	P20	P30	P40	P50	P60	P70	P80
Disk size in GiB	128	256	512	1,024	2,048	4,096	8,192	16,384	32,767
Provisioned IOPS per disk	500	1,100	2,300	5,000	7,500	7,500	16,000	18,000	20,000
Provisioned Throughput per disk	100 MB/sec	125 MB/sec	150 MB/sec	200 MB/sec	250 MB/sec	250 MB/sec	500 MB/sec	750 MB/sec	900 MB/sec
Max burst IOPS per disk	3,500	3,500	3,500	30,000*	30,000*	30,000*	30,000*	30,000*	30,000*
Max burst throughput per disk	170 MB/sec	170 MB/sec	170 MB/sec	1,000 MB/sec*	1,000 MB/sec*	1,000 MB/sec*	1,000 MB/sec*	1,000 MB/sec*	1,000 MB/sec*
Max burst duration	30 min	30 min	30 min	Unlimited*	Unlimited*	Unlimited*	Unlimited*	Unlimited*	Unlimited*
Eligible for reservation	No	No	No	Yes, up to 1 year	Yes, up to 1 year	Yes, up to 1 year	Yes, up to 1 year	Yes, up to 1 year	Yes, up to 1 year

This table was taken from Microsoft's documentation site: `https://docs.microsoft.com/en-us/azure/virtual-machines/disks-types#premium-ssd-size`.

Typically, Azure Managed Disks are **locally redundant storage** (**LRS**). This means that the storage is replicated three times within a single data center in the region where you deployed the VM.

You can also configure **zone-redundant storage** (**ZRS**) for managed disks. ZRS replicates Azure Managed Disks synchronously across three Azure availability zones within a selected Azure region. Each zone is a separate physical location with independent networking, cooling, and power.

There is no difference in latency or performance; the only improvement when using ZRS is the improved data protection.

Ephemeral OS disks

Ephemeral OS disks, also known as stateless disk storage, are created on the Azure Hypervisor's local storage as part of the VM cache. One benefit of using ephemeral disks over Azure Managed Disks is that ephemeral disks are free. This allows the stateless disk storage to provide lower latency and faster reads and writes.

The following table details the differences between Azure Managed Disks and ephemeral disks:

	Azure Managed Disks	Ephemeral OS Disks
Size limit for OS disk	2 TiB.	Cache size for the VM size or 2 TiB, whichever is smaller. For the cache size in GiB, see DS, ES, M, FS, and GS.
VM sizes supported	All.	VM sizes that support (cache disk) premium storage such as DSv1, DSv2, DSv3, Esv3, Fs, FsV2, GS, and M.
Disk type support	Managed and unmanaged OS disk.	Managed OS disk only.
Region support	All regions.	All regions.
Data persistence	OS disk data that's written to OS disks is stored in Azure Storage.	Data written to OS disk is stored in the local Hypervisor storage and is not persisted to Azure Storage.
Stop-deallocated state	VMs and scale set instances can be stop-deallocated and restarted from the stop-deallocated state.	VMs and scale set instances cannot be stop-deallocated.
Specialized OS disk support	Yes.	No.
OS disk resize	Supported during VM creation and after the VM is stop-deallocated	Supported during VM creation only.
Resizing to a new VM size	OS disk data is preserved.	Data on the OS disk is deleted, OS is re-provisioned.
Page file placement	For Windows, the page file is stored on the resource disk.	For Windows, the page file is stored on the OS disk.

This table was taken from the following Microsoft site: `https://docs.microsoft.com/en-us/azure/virtual-machines/ephemeral-os-disks`.

Note that you cannot start and stop/deallocate an Azure VM that's been configured with an ephemeral OS disk (OS cache). The only options that are available to you are to restart or reimage.

> **Important Note**
>
> If you want to use ephemeral disks, you need to use a custom ARM template or third-party tooling and PowerShell.

In this section, we looked at what ephemeral disks are, the pros and cons, and the differences between Azure Managed Disks and ephemeral disks. In the next section, we will create a custom master VHD image.

Creating a VHD image

In this section, you will learn how to prepare a master **virtual hard disk** (**VHD**) image for Azure. Note that Microsoft recommends that you use an image from the Azure image gallery. However, this section covers both options, giving you the ability to customize an image offline and upload it to Azure when you're finished. You can also use Microsoft Deployment Toolkit and SCCM to create images for AVD. To upload these images, you can use the following tools:

- **Azure portal**: Use the upload feature within the storage account.
- **Azure Storage Explorer**: `https://azure.microsoft.com/features/storage-explorer/`
- **Az copy**: `https://docs.microsoft.com/azure/storage/common/storage-ref-azcopy`

> **Important Note**
>
> Ensure your image does not have the AVD agent installed on the VM. The agent can cause issues, including blocking registration and preventing user session connections.

Creating a VM

There are two options for creating a VM. First, you can provision the VM in Azure, and then customize and install the required software. Alternatively, you can create an image locally using Hyper-V and customize it to your requirements.

First, let's look at deploying a VM in Azure:

1. Within the Azure search bar, type `virtual`; the **Virtual machines** page link will be shown. Click on **Virtual machines**:

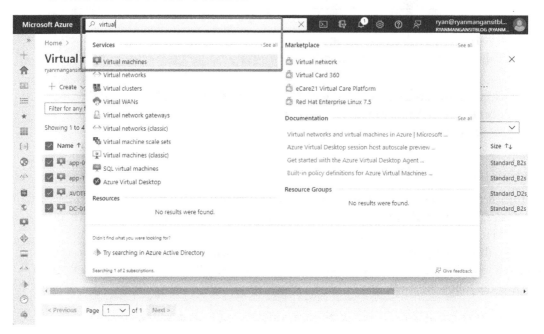

Figure 5.13 – Search bar displaying the Virtual machines page link in the Azure portal

2. Within the **Virtual machines** page, click **Create** and select **Virtual Machine**. This will open the **Create a virtual machine** page:

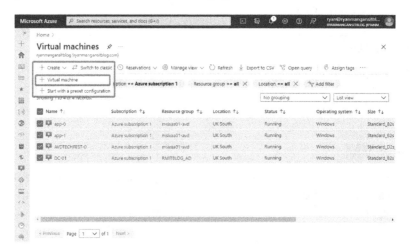

Figure 5.14 – Creating a VM within the Virtual machines page in the Azure portal

3. Within the **Create a virtual machine** page, you will need to fill in all the required fields:

    ▪ Under the **Subscription** section, select the required subscription and select an existing **Resource group** or create a new one.

    ▪ Under the **Instance details** section, provide a **Virtual machine name**, select a **Region**, select an **Image**, and specify a **Size**. This will be a VM skew:

Create a virtual machine   ⋯

Basics	Disks	Networking	Management	Advanced	Tags	Review + create

Create a virtual machine that runs Linux or Windows. Select an image from Azure marketplace or use your own customized image. Complete the Basics tab then Review + create to provision a virtual machine with default parameters or review each tab for full customization. Learn more ☐'

Project details

Select the subscription to manage deployed resources and costs. Use resource groups like folders to organize and manage all your resources.

Subscription * ⓘ	Azure subscription 1 ∨
⌐ Resource group * ⓘ	(New) image-example ∨
	Create new

Instance details

Virtual machine name * ⓘ	TestImage ✓
Region * ⓘ	(Europe) UK South ∨
Availability options ⓘ	No infrastructure redundancy required ∨
Security type ⓘ	Standard ∨
Image * ⓘ	⊞ Windows 10 Enterprise multi-session, version 21H1 + Microsoft 365 App ∨
	See all images	Configure VM generation
Azure Spot instance ⓘ	☐
Size * ⓘ	Standard_B2s - 2 vcpus, 4 GiB memory (£25.68/month) ∨
	See all sizes

Figure 5.15 – The Basics tab within the Create a virtual machine page

4. Within the same tab, provide an administrator username and password.

5. Set the inbound port rules if required.

6. Check the **Licensing** check box to confirm that you have the correct licensing rights:

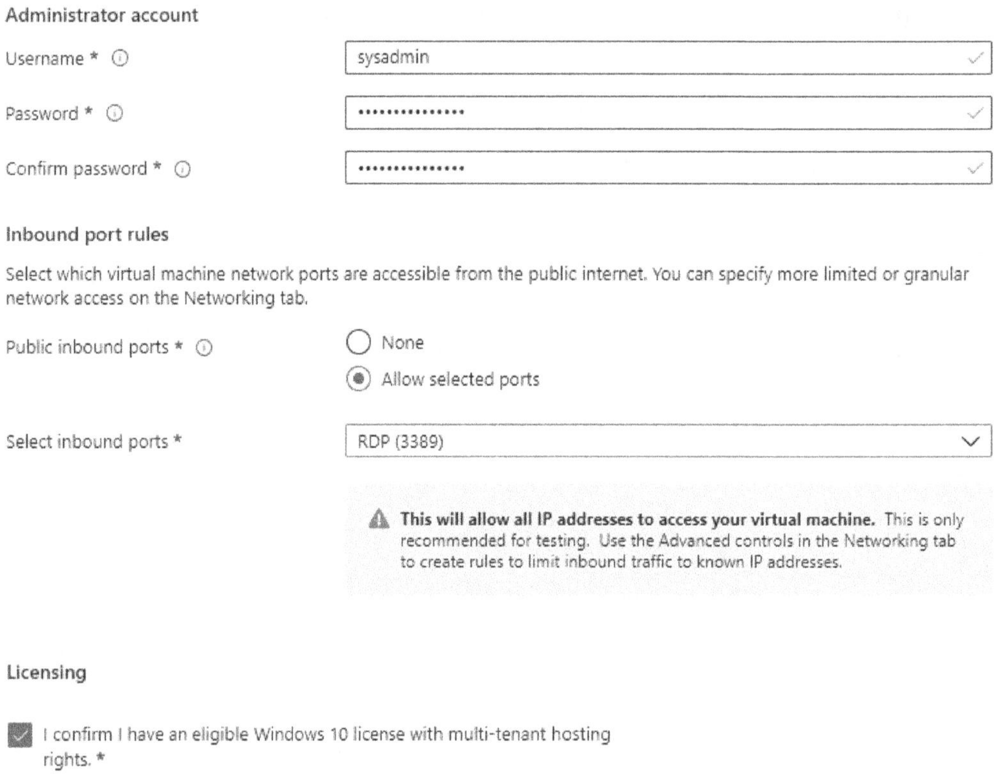

Administrator account

Username * ⓘ   sysadmin

Password * ⓘ   ················

Confirm password * ⓘ   ················

Inbound port rules

Select which virtual machine network ports are accessible from the public internet. You can specify more limited or granular network access on the Networking tab.

Public inbound ports * ⓘ   ○ None
                              ◉ Allow selected ports

Select inbound ports *   RDP (3389)

⚠ **This will allow all IP addresses to access your virtual machine.** This is only recommended for testing. Use the Advanced controls in the Networking tab to create rules to limit inbound traffic to known IP addresses.

Licensing

☑ I confirm I have an eligible Windows 10 license with multi-tenant hosting rights. *

Figure 5.16 – The Administrator account section within the Basics tab of the Create a virtual machine page within the Azure portal

7. On the **Disks** tab, select the required disk. As we mentioned previously, a premium SSD is recommended:

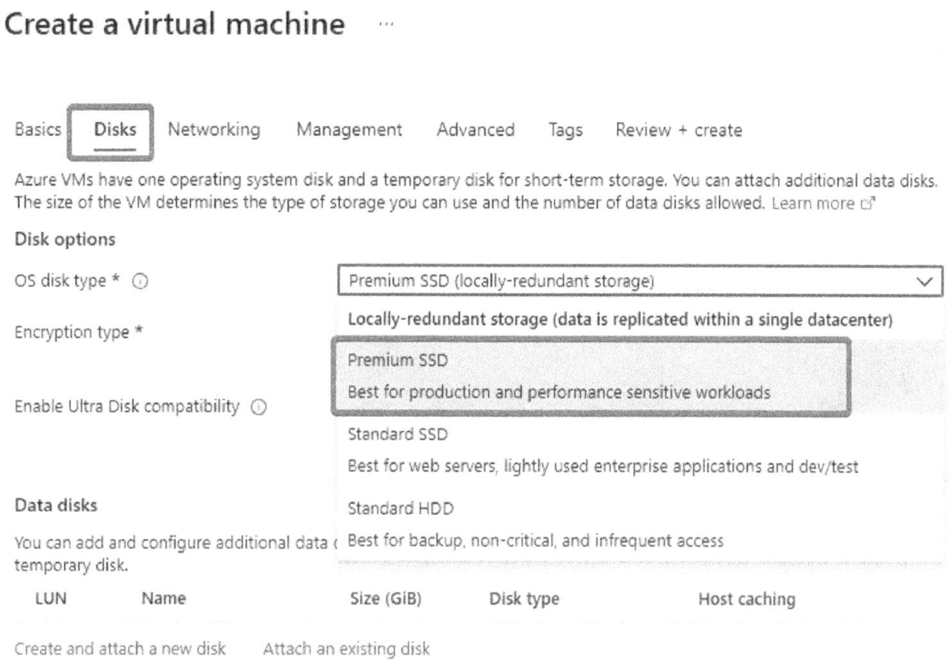

Create a virtual machine   ...

| Basics | **Disks** | Networking | Management | Advanced | Tags | Review + create |

Azure VMs have one operating system disk and a temporary disk for short-term storage. You can attach additional data disks. The size of the VM determines the type of storage you can use and the number of data disks allowed. Learn more ⏷

Disk options

OS disk type * ⓘ | Premium SSD (locally-redundant storage)   ⌄ |

Encryption type *

Locally-redundant storage (data is replicated within a single datacenter)

Enable Ultra Disk compatibility ⓘ

Premium SSD
Best for production and performance sensitive workloads

Standard SSD
Best for web servers, lightly used enterprise applications and dev/test

Data disks   Standard HDD

You can add and configure additional data (Best for backup, non-critical, and infrequent access
temporary disk.

| LUN | Name | Size (GiB) | Disk type | Host caching |

Create and attach a new disk   Attach an existing disk

Figure 5.17 – The Disks tab within the Create a virtual machine page of the Azure portal

8. Once you have finished choosing the required disk and settings within the **Disks** tab, click the **Networking** tab and configure the required networking.

9.   Under the **Networking** tab, configure the following:

- Select the required **Virtual network**.

- Select the required **Subnet**.

- Set a public VM, if required.

- Set the network security groups, if required:

Basics	Disks	Networking	Management	Advanced	Tags	Review + create

Define network connectivity for your virtual machine by configuring network interface card (NIC) settings. You can control ports, inbound and outbound connectivity with security group rules, or place behind an existing load balancing solution. Learn more ☐

Network interface

When creating a virtual machine, a network interface will be created for you.

Virtual network * ⓘ	WVD_test01	⌄
	Create new	
Subnet * ⓘ	default (10.0.0.0/24)	⌄
	Manage subnet configuration	
Public IP ⓘ	None	⌄
	Create new	

NIC network security group ⓘ	⦿ None
	◯ Basic
	◯ Advanced

ⓘ The selected subnet 'default (10.0.0.0/24)' is already associated to a network security group 'Network'. We recommend managing connectivity to this virtual machine via the existing network security group instead of creating a new one here.

Accelerated networking ⓘ	☐
	The selected VM size does not support accelerated networking.

Load balancing

You can place this virtual machine in the backend pool of an existing Azure load balancing solution. Learn more ☐

Place this virtual machine behind an existing load balancing solution?	☐

Figure 5.18 – The Networking tab within the Create a virtual machine page of the Azure portal

10. If you require specific settings under the **Management**, **Advanced**, and **Tags** tabs, complete the required settings and progress to the **Review + create** tab. If you do not require specific settings under these tabs, skip to the **Review + create** tab:

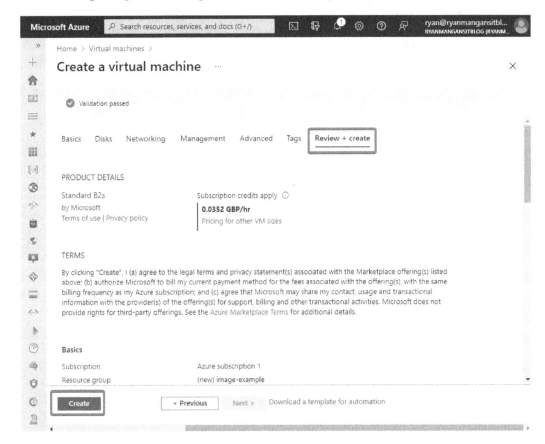

Figure 5.19 – The Review + create tab of the Create a virtual machine page within the Azure portal

This section showed you how to deploy a VM image template for AVD in the Azure portal. Next, we will learn how to create a local image on Hyper-V.

Creating a local image

First, you will need to download the required OS image. Then, using Hyper-V, you must create a VM using the downloaded VHD. You need to ensure that you complete the following steps:

1. Specify the generation as **Generation 1**:

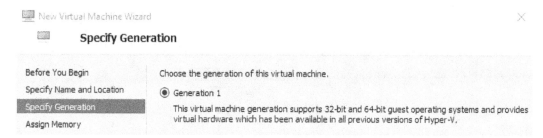

Figure 5.20 – Choosing Generation 1 in Hyper-V

2. Disable the checkpoints for the VM:

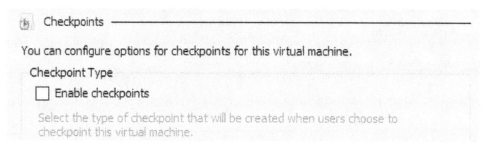

Figure 5.21 – Disabling the Enable checkpoints box

The following PowerShell cmdlet allows you to disable checkpoints:

```
Set-VM -Name <VMNAME> -CheckpointType Disabled
```

Now, let's look at the difference between dynamic and fixed disks since Azure only supports the fixed disk format.

Dynamic disks versus fixed disks

When creating a VM from an existing VHD, it creates a dynamic disk by default. However, you can change this by selecting the **Edit Disk…** option within Hyper-V.

You can also use PowerShell to change a dynamic disk to a fixed disk, as follows:

```
Convert-VHD -Path c:\test\MY-VM.vhdx -DestinationPath c:\test\
MY-NEW-VM.vhd -VHDType Fixed
```

This section detailed the options available to you when creating an image. We also covered some of the requirements for if you decide to customize an image outside of AVD using Hyper-V.

Summary

In this chapter, we looked at implementing and managing storage for AVD. First, we explored the requirements for storing FSLogix Profile Containers, storage account tiers, Azure Files storage tiers, and Azure Files integration with Active Directory Domain Services. Next, we looked at creating a new storage account and configuring Azure File Shares. Then, we reviewed the differences between Azure Managed Disks and ephemeral Operating System disks and finished by looking at the options available for creating a VM with Azure.

In the next chapter, we will look at creating and configuring host pools and session hosts.

Questions

Here are a few questions to test your understanding of this chapter:

1. What is the recommended storage solution for FSLogix Profile Containers?
2. Do all regions support all types of storage accounts and redundancy configurations?
3. When it comes to storage accounts for larger organizations and high I/O workloads, what is the recommended storage tier?
4. What is the recommended disk type for session hosts?
5. What disk format does a virtual hard disk need to be to upload and function correctly within Azure?

Answers

1. *Azure Files*

2. *No*

3. *Premium tier*

4. *Premium SSD*

5. *Fixed disk*

Further reading

Please refer to the following links for more information regarding the topics that were covered in this chapter:

- Using Azure NetApp Files for FSLogix: `https://docs.microsoft.com/en-us/azure/architecture/example-scenario/wvd/windows-virtual-desktop-fslogix#storage-options-for-fslogix-profile-containers`

- Settig up an Azure NetApp Files account for FSLogix: `https://docs.microsoft.com/azure/virtual-desktop/create-fslogix-profile-container`

Section 3: Implementing an Azure Virtual Desktop Infrastructure

In this section, we look at how you would implement an Azure Virtual Desktop environment, including the creation of Azure host pools, Azure AD Join, customization, and managing session host images.

This part of the book comprises the following chapters:

- *Chapter 6, Creating Host Pools and Session Hosts*
- *Chapter 7, Customizing Azure Virtual Desktop Host Pools*
- *Chapter 8, Azure AD Join for Azure Virtual Desktop*
- *Chapter 9, Creating and Managing Session Host Images*

6
Creating Host Pools and Session Hosts

This chapter takes a look at creating host pools and deploying session hosts. We will cover the creation process first using the Azure portal in the web browser and then using PowerShell, which is great for automation and repeat processes.

The following topics are covered in this chapter:

- Creating a host pool by using the Azure portal
- Automating the creation of AVD hosts and host pools

Creating a host pool by using the Azure portal

In this section, we'll look at creating and configuring host pools and session hosts. Host pools are essentially a collection of one or more **virtual machines** (**VMs**) within **Azure Virtual Desktop** (**AVD**) environments. These are typically identical and are created from a central image or the Azure Gallery, or a custom image. We'll also take a look at Azure Compute Galleries for template deployment in *Chapter 9, Creating and Managing Session Host Images*. In addition, each host pool can contain app groups that are used for user assignments. This section looks at creating a host pool for AVD through the Azure portal.

Before we get started, you need to ensure you have the following host pool prerequisites ready:

- The VM image name
- VM configuration
- Domain and network properties
- AVD host pool properties

> **Important Note**
>
> You need to ensure that a virtual network exists in the Azure region of your choice and that it has a "line of sight" with the domain.

You also need to consider the following:

- Are you using an operating system image from the Azure Gallery or a custom image?
- Domain join credentials to connect your session hosts to your domain.

> **Tip**
>
> Make sure you have registered the Microsoft.DesktopVirtualization resource provider before attempting to deploy a host pool. When using an account with Global Administrator admin rights, the registration is automatically done during the host pool creation.

Host pool creation

In this section, we will create our first host pool using the Azure portal:

1. First, sign in to the Azure portal at `https://portal.azure.com`.

> **Important Note**
>
> If you're signing in to the US government portal, go to `https://portal.azure.us/` instead.

2. Enter `Azure Virtual Desktop` into the search bar; from the results, select **Azure Virtual Desktop** under **Services**.

3. On the **Azure Virtual Desktop** overview page, select **Create a host pool**.

4. You will then be presented with the **Basics** tab. Select the correct subscription under **Project details**.

5. Select **Create new** to create a new resource group or select an existing resource group you may have created previously in the drop-down menu.

6. Enter a unique name for your new host pool.

7. Select the Azure region to create the host pool using the drop-down menu in the **Location** field.

    The Azure geography associated with the Azure region you selected is where the metadata for this host pool and related objects will be stored. Make sure you choose the region inside the geography you want the service metadata to be stored in:

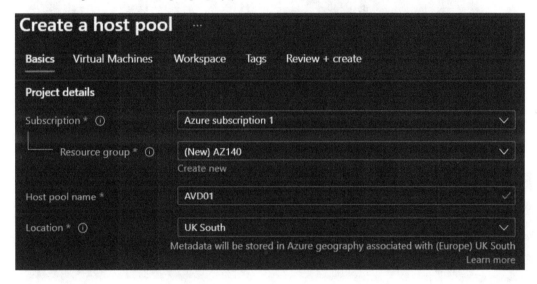

Figure 6.1 – Screenshot showing the Create a host pool page

Important Note

The AVD service metadata is independent of the VM location. It is also important to understand that the metadata locations are not available for all Azure regions.

8. Under **Host pool type**, select whether you want to create a **Personal** or **Pooled** host pool. If you choose **Personal**, you will need to select **Automatic** or **Direct** in the **Assignment type** field:

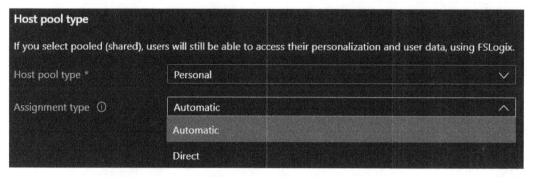

Figure 6.2 – Screenshot showing Personal host pool type options

If you choose **Pooled**, you need to specify the following information:

- For **Max session limit**, enter the maximum number of users you want load-balanced on a single session host.

- For **Load balancing algorithm**, choose either **Breadth-first** or **Depth-first**, depending on your usage pattern.

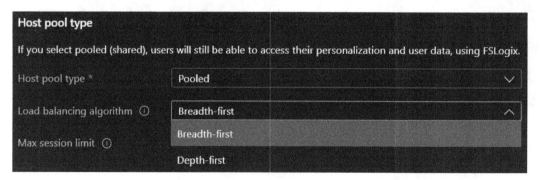

Figure 6.3 – Screenshot showing pooled host pool options

Load balancing algorithm has the following two options:

- **Breadth-first**: The breadth-first load balancing mechanism is essentially a method that uses an algorithm to determine the fewest sessions on a session host for the placement of new sessions. For example, say a user connects to an AVD host pool with **Breadth-first** configured. During the login process, a query is run against the available session hosts within the host pool. The load balancing method selects the session host with the fewest sessions. If there are two or more session hosts with the same number of sessions active, then the method selects the first session host identified in the query:

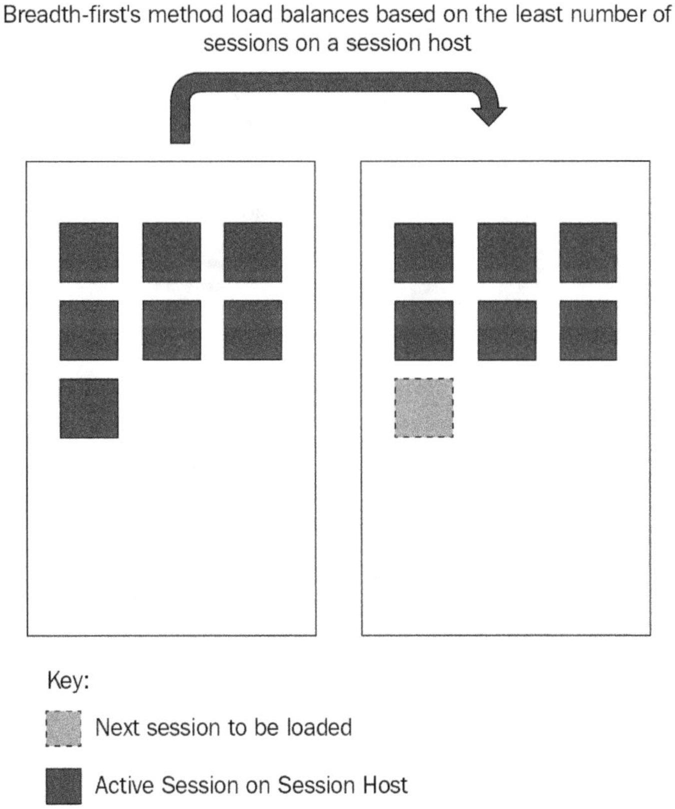

Breadth-first's method load balances based on the least number of sessions on a session host

Key:

Next session to be loaded

Active Session on Session Host

Figure 6.4 – Diagram showing an example of how breadth-first load balancing works

- **Depth-first**: The depth-first load balancing method maximizes session utilization of a session host before loading sessions onto the next available session host. It is suggested that this algorithm is for organizations who want to operate an active/passive AVD deployment or reduce costs. The depth-first method queries the available session hosts to establish where to place new sessions. If a session host has exceeded the maximum session limit specified against the host pool, new sessions will be loaded onto the next available session host. Again, if there are two session hosts with the same number of sessions, then the first is selected in the query. This process is depicted in the following diagram. Using depth-first load balancing in conjunction with scaling plans enables you to power on session hosts when a session host reaches near session capacity, thus enabling cost management based on compute resource utilization. This means additional session hosts are powered on when needed and powered off outside peak times:

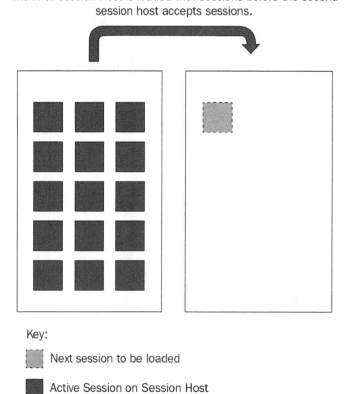

Figure 6.5 – Diagram showing an example of depth-first load balancing

9. Select **Next: Virtual Machines**. If you have already created VMs and want to use them with this new host pool, select **No** then **Next: Workspace** and move on to the **Workspace information** section. However, if you want to create new VMs and register them to the new host pool, click **Yes**, as highlighted in the screenshot in *Figure 6.6*:

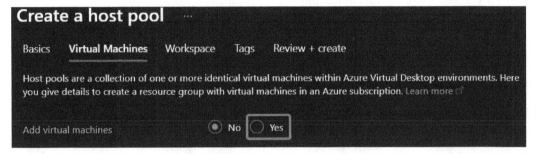

Figure 6.6 – Screenshot showing the tab to create VMs in the host pool

> **Important Note**
>
> A workspace is a logical grouping of application groups within AVD. Each AVD application group must be associated with a workspace for users to see the remote apps and desktops published to the workgroup.

We now take a look at creating VMs within the **Create a host pool** tab.

Creating VMs within the Create a host pool tab

When setting up your VM within the host pool setup process, you need to complete the following:

1. In the **Resource group** section, choose the resource group where you want to create the VMs (session hosts). This can be a different resource group than the one you used for the host pool or the same.

2. After that, you will need to provide a name prefix, which is used to assign names to the VMs during the creation process. The suffix will be – with numbers starting from 0.

3. Choose the location where you want to create the VMs. The location can be the same as your host pool or different. It is advised that you deploy VMs in the same region unless there is a specific reason.

4. Next, choose the availability option that best suits your needs.

> **Important Note**
>
> **Availability sets** offer a 99.95% Azure **Service Level Agreement (SLA)** and essentially provide a logical grouping of VMs. Microsoft recommends that you use two or more VMs within an availability set to provide high availability.
>
> **Availability zones** allow you to control where in the Azure region your VMs are stored. There are three availability zones per supported Azure region. Each zone has what Microsoft describes as a distinct power source, network, and cooling. This enables you to split session host deployments between different zones.

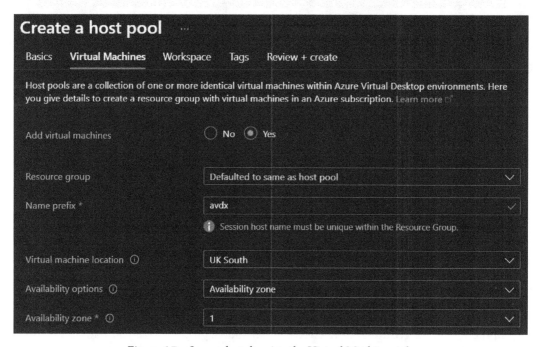

Figure 6.7 – Screenshot showing the Virtual Machines tab

5. Next, choose the VM image that needs to be used to create the VM. You can choose either **Gallery** or **Storage blob**.

If you choose **Gallery**, select one of the images from the drop-down menu:

> **Important Note**
>
> The Gallery images created by Microsoft include the FSLogix agent. Microsoft maintains these and keeps them updated with the latest patches and updates.

- Windows 11 Enterprise multi-session

- Windows 11 Enterprise

- Windows 10 Enterprise multi-session, Version 1909

- Windows 10 Enterprise multi-session, Version 1909 + Microsoft 365 Apps

- Windows Server 2019 Datacenter

- Windows 10 Enterprise multi-session, Version 2004

- Windows 10 Enterprise multi-session, Version 2004 + Microsoft 365 Apps

- Windows 10 Enterprise multi-session, Version 20H2

- Windows 10 Enterprise multi-session, Version 20H2 + Microsoft 365 Apps

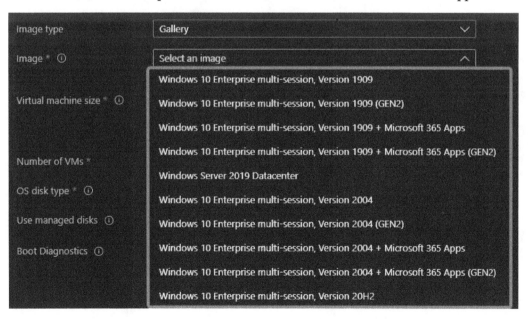

Figure 6.8 – Screenshot showing images within the Gallery

6. If you do not see the image you require, select **See all images** and browse to another image in your Gallery or an image provided by Microsoft or other third-party publishers. Make sure that the image you choose is one of the supported images shown in the following table:

Operating system	Azure Image Gallery	Manual VM deployment	Azure Resource Manager template integration	Provision host pools on Azure Marketplace
Windows 11 Enterprise multi-session	Yes	Yes	Yes	Yes
Windows 11 Enterprise	Yes	Yes	Yes	Yes
Windows 10 Enterprise multi-session, version 1909 and later	Yes	Yes	Yes	Yes
Windows 10 Enterprise, version 1909 and later	Yes	Yes	Yes	Yes
Windows 7 Enterprise	Yes	Yes	No	No
Windows Server 2019	Yes	Yes	No	No
Windows Server 2016	Yes	Yes	Yes	Yes
Windows Server 2012 R2	Yes	Yes	No	No

This table was taken from `https://docs.microsoft.com/azure/virtual-desktop/overview#supported-virtual-machine-os-image`.

The following screenshot in *Figure 6.9* shows you some of the images available within the Azure Marketplace:

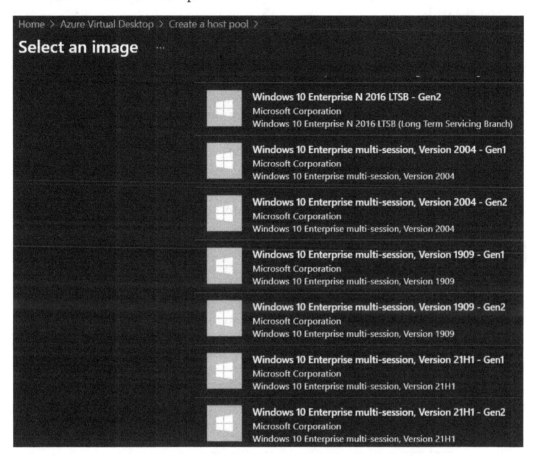

Figure 6.9 – Screenshot showing images in the Marketplace

7. You can also navigate to **My Items** and choose a custom image you may have already uploaded:

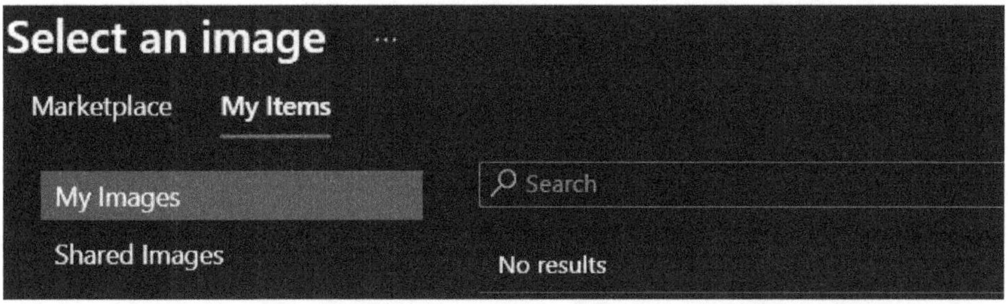

Figure 6.10 – Screenshot showing selecting an image from My Images

If you choose **Storage Blob**, you can use your image build through Hyper-V or an Azure VM. To do this, you need to enter the location of the image in the storage blob as a URI.

> **Tip**
>
> The image's location is independent of the availability option, but the image's zone resiliency determines whether that image can be used with the availability zone. Therefore, if you select an availability zone while creating your image, make sure you are using an image from the Gallery with zone resiliency enabled.

8. After that, choose the **Virtual machine size** value you want to use. You can keep the default size as is or select **Change size** to change the size. If you select **Change size**, choose the size of the VM suitable for your workload in the window that appears.

9. Under **Number of VMs**, provide the number of VMs you want to create for your host pool.

> **Important Note**
>
> The deployment process can create up to 400 VMs while setting up your host pool, and each VM setup process creates four objects in your resource group. The creation process doesn't check your subscription quota, so you need to ensure the number of VMs you enter within the Azure VM and the API limits for your resource group and subscription do not exceed the maximums. You can add more VMs after you finish creating your host pool.

10. Choose the type of operating system disks you want your VMs to use: **Standard SSD**, **Premium SSD**, or **Standard HDD**.

> **Tip**
>
> Microsoft recommends using **Premium SSD** for AVD session hosts. See *Chapter 5, Implementing and Manage Storage for Azure Virtual Desktop.*

11. Under the **Network and Security** section, select the virtual network and subnet where you want the VMs to reside.

> **Tip**
> Ensure the virtual network can connect to the domain controller as the VMs need to join the domain. You should configure the virtual network DNS to be configured with the IP address of your domain controller.

The following screenshot shows where you would configure the virtual network DNS to point to the domain controller:

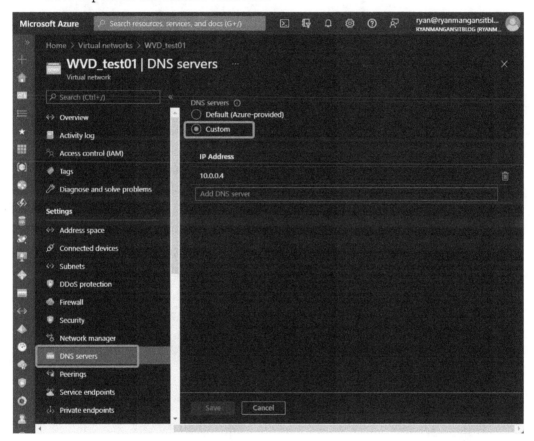

Figure 6.11 – Screenshot showing the domain controller added as a custom DNS entry on the Azure virtual network

12. Select the security group type you want: **Basic**, **Advanced**, or **None**. If you select **Basic**, you will need to select whether you want any inbound ports open. If you select **Yes**, choose from the list of standard ports to allow inbound connections to:

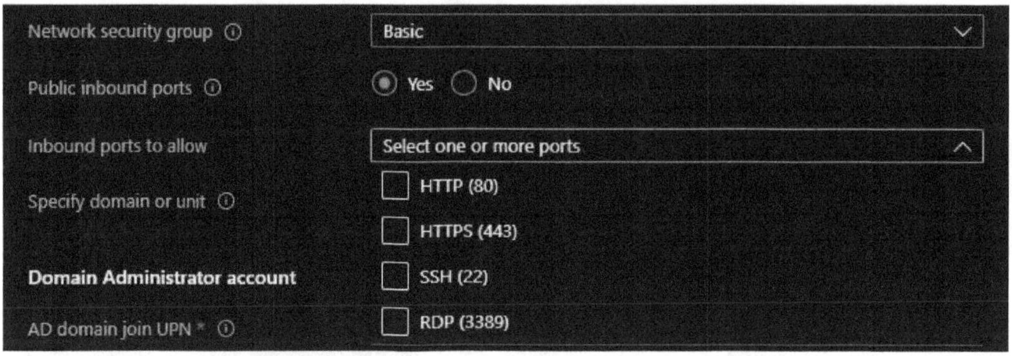

Figure 6.12 – Screenshot showing network security options

If you choose the **Advanced** option, select an existing network security group that you have already configured.

> **Important Note**
>
> For enhanced security, Microsoft recommends that you don't open public inbound ports.

13. Once selected, you will need to select whether you want the VMs to be joined to a specific domain and organizational unit. If you choose **Yes**, make sure to specify the domain to join. You can optionally add a specific organizational unit you want the VMs to be in. If you choose **No**, the VMs will be joined to the domain matching the suffix of the AD domain join UPN.

> **Tip**
>
> When you specify an organizational unit, make sure you use the full path known as the **distinguished name** (**DN**). You can find a DN by enabling advanced settings within Active Directory and navigating to the **Attributes** section of an organizational unit.

14. In the **Domain Administrator account** section, enter the credentials for the Active Directory domain admin account of the virtual network you selected. This admin account can't have **multi-factor authentication** (**MFA**) enabled as this will cause the deployment to fail. It is recommended that you use a service account with specific permissions on the target organizational unit.

When joining an **Azure Active Directory Domain Services** (**Azure AD DS**) domain, the account must be part of the Azure AD DS Administrators group. Additionally, the account password must also work in Azure AD DS.

15. Provide a VM administrator account. The password needs to be at least 12 characters long.

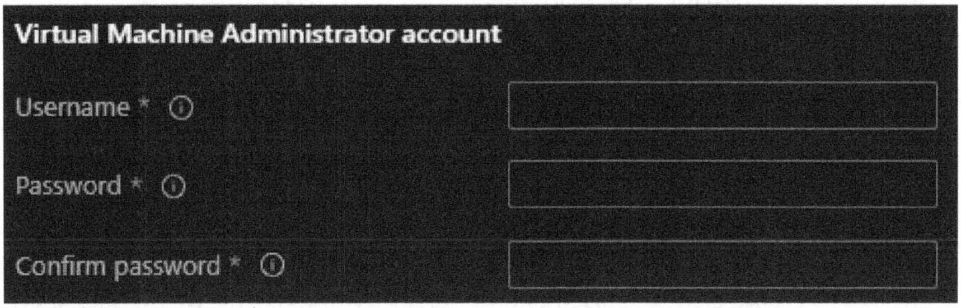

Figure 6.13 – Screenshot showing the Virtual Machine Administrator account section

> **Important Note**
> It is now possible to join session hosts directly to Azure Active Directory.

16. As an optional setting, you can set post-update custom configurations using **Azure Resource Manager** (**ARM**) templates.

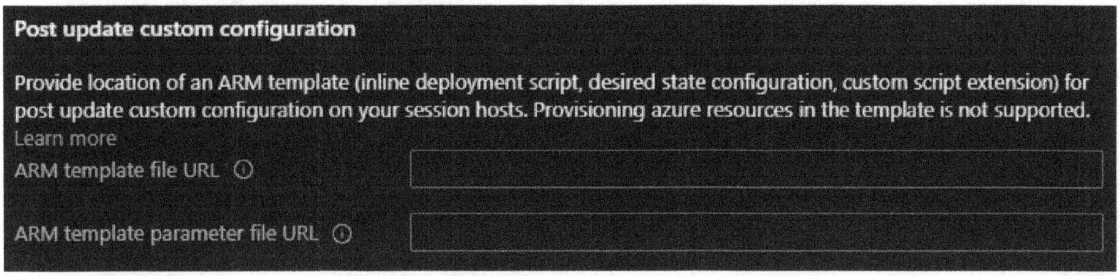

Figure 6.14 – Screenshot showing the option to add post-update custom configurations

17. Select the **Next: to the Workspace** tab.

We'll now move on to setting up your new host pool: registering an app group to a workspace.

Workspace information

The host pool deployment process creates a desktop application group by default. This is the default app group of a host pool. For the host pool to function correctly, you'll need to publish this app group to users or user groups, and you must also register the app group to a workspace.

To register the desktop app group to a workspace, you need to complete the following steps:

1. Select **Yes** under **Register desktop app group**.

   If you select **No**, you can register the app group later. However, Microsoft recommends you complete the workspace registration during the host pool deployment.

2. Next, choose to create a new workspace or select from existing workspaces. Only workspaces created in the same location as the host pool will register the app group:

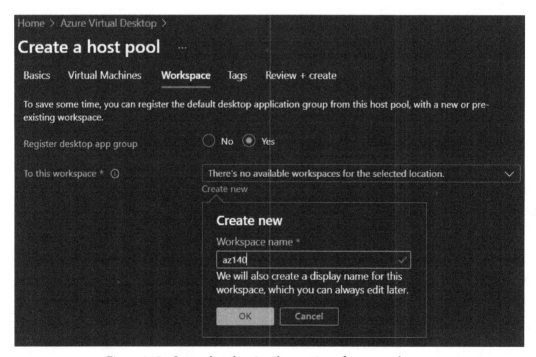

Figure 6.15 – Screenshot showing the creation of a new workspace

3. Optionally, you can select **Next: Tags**.

> **Tip**
> Adding tags to group the objects with metadata is helpful for IT admins.

4. When you have finished, select **Review + create**.

> **Important Note**
> The **Review + create** validation process doesn't check whether your admin password meets security standards or your architecture is correct. You must check your deployment before continuing.

5. Before proceeding with the deployment, you should review the information about your deployment to make sure everything looks correct. When you have finished, select **Create**.

   This starts the deployment process, which creates the following Azure objects:

   - The new host pool.
   - The desktop app group.
   - A workspace if you choose to create it.
   - Registration of the desktop app group; the registration will be completed.
   - If you choose to create VMs, they are joined to the domain and registered with the new host pool.

- A download link for an ARM template based on your configuration:

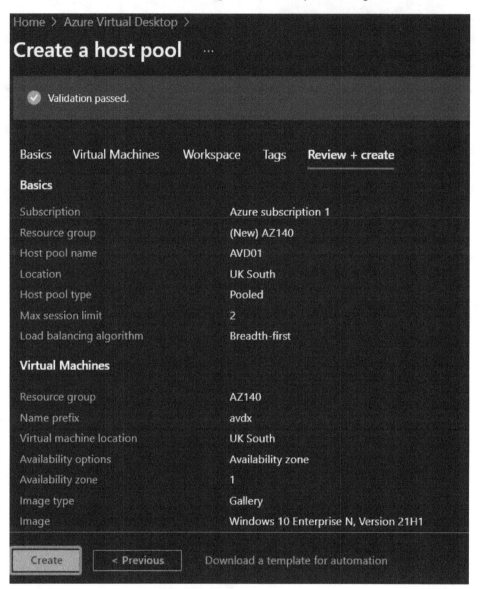

Figure 6.16 – Screenshot showing the Review + create page

After that, you just need to wait for your deployment to finish:

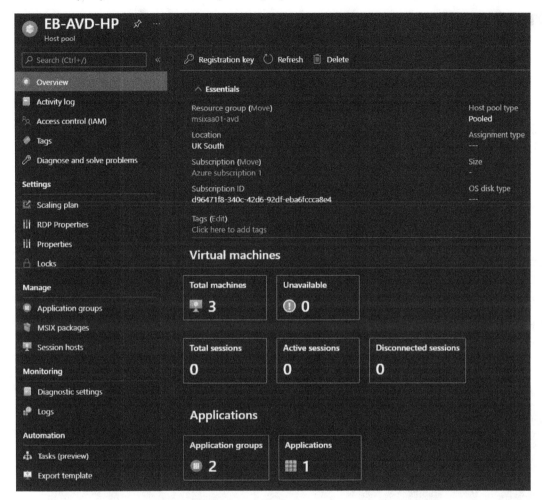

Figure 6.17 – Screenshot showing an example of the created host pool

This section looked at creating a host pool and deploying VMs into the new host pool. We will now take a look at an automated approach to creating AVD host pools using PowerShell.

Automating the creation of AVD hosts and host pools

This section looks at setting up PowerShell for AVD and deploying a new host pool using PowerShell.

Setting up PowerShell for AVD

Before we can get started, you first need to install the PowerShell module for AVD. You can do this by opening PowerShell in elevated mode.

> **Tip**
>
> Make sure you install the Az module. If you haven't already done so, run the `Install-Module -Name Az -Force` command.

Once you have opened PowerShell in elevated mode, run the following cmdlet:

```
Install-Module -Name Az.DesktopVirtualization
```

The following screenshot shows you how to install the `Az.DesktopVirtualization` PowerShell module:

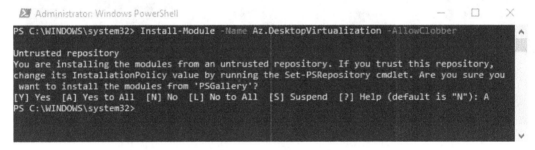

Figure 6.18 – Screenshot showing the installation of the PowerShell module for
Az.DesktopVirtualization

As shown in *Figure 6.18*, you may be asked to confirm whether you trust the repository.

Next, you will need to connect to Microsoft Azure using the following cmdlet:

```
Connect-AzAccount
```

Once you have run the cmdlet, you will then see the **Sign in to your account** popup:

Figure 6.19 – Screenshot showing the Sign in to your account popup

Enter your username/password and any MFA details that may be requested.

The output from completing this process is shown in *Figure 6.20*:

Figure 6.20 – Screenshot showing cmdlet to connect to Azure

As shown in *Figure 6.20*, once you have connected to Azure, you should see the details of any subscriptions in the tenant.

The final step is to select the required subscription you plan to deploy AVD resources into.

Select the subscription you want to use; you can use the `out-gridview` cmdlet to select the one you want:

```
Get-AzSubscription | Out-GridView -PassThru | Select-
AzSubscription
```

Once you have selected the subscription you require, click **OK**. In this example, there is only one subscription available:

Figure 6.21 – Screenshot showing the grid view for selecting an available Azure subscription

In this section, we looked at setting up PowerShell for AVD. It is important to ensure you have the correct PowerShell modules and Azure connectivity via PowerShell working before continuing. We will now move on to deploying a host pool using PowerShell.

Creating an AVD host pool with PowerShell

In this section, we'll look at creating some resources for AVD using PowerShell.

We will use PowerShell to do the following:

- Create a resource group.
- Create a host pool.
- Create a registration token.
- Assign users to a host pool application group.
- Assign groups to a host pool application group.

Once connected to Azure via PowerShell following the instructions set out in the *Setting up PowerShell for AVD* section, you can start to deploy your AVD host pool using PowerShell.

First, we need to create a resource group.

To do this, you can use the following cmdlets:

```
New-AzResourceGroup -Name <Resource Group Name> -Location
<Region>
Example:
#Create Resource Group
New-AzResourceGroup -Name az140pw -Location "UK South"
```

Once we have created the resource group, we can then proceed with creating the host pool:

```
New-AzWvdHostPool -ResourceGroupName "<Resource Group Name>`
-Name <Host Pool Name> -WorkspaceName <Workspace Name>
-HostPoolType <Host Pool Type>
-LoadBalancerType <Load balancer method> -Location <Region>
-DesktopAppGroupName <App group Name> -PreferredAppGroupType
<App group type>
```

Example cmdlets used to deploy a host pool using PowerShell are as follows:

```
#Create Host Pool
New-AzWvdHostPool -ResourceGroupName "az140pw"`
-Name "pwdeployment" -WorkspaceName "workspacename1"
-HostPoolType "Pooled"`
-LoadBalancerType "BreadthFirst" -Location "UK South"-
DesktopAppGroupName "az140pw" -PreferredAppGroupType "Desktop"
```

Figure 6.22 shows the output from running the creation of both a resource group and host pool:

```
PS C:\WINDOWS\system32> #Create Resource Group
PS C:\WINDOWS\system32> New-AzResourceGroup -Name az140pw -Location "UK South"


ResourceGroupName : az140pw
Location          : uksouth
ProvisioningState : Succeeded
Tags              :
ResourceId        : /subscriptions/d96471f8-340c-42d6-92df-eba6fccca8e4/resourceGroups/az140pw



PS C:\WINDOWS\system32>
PS C:\WINDOWS\system32> #Create Host Pool
PS C:\WINDOWS\system32> New-AzWvdHostPool -ResourceGroupName "az140pw"
>> -Name "pwdeployment" -WorkspaceName "workspacename1" -HostPoolType "Pooled"
>> -LoadBalancerType "BreadthFirst" -Location "UK South" -DesktopAppGroupName "az140pw" -PreferredAppGroupType "Desktop"

Location Name         Type
-------- ----         ----
uksouth  pwdeployment Microsoft.DesktopVirtualization/hostpools



PS C:\WINDOWS\system32>
PS C:\WINDOWS\system32>
```

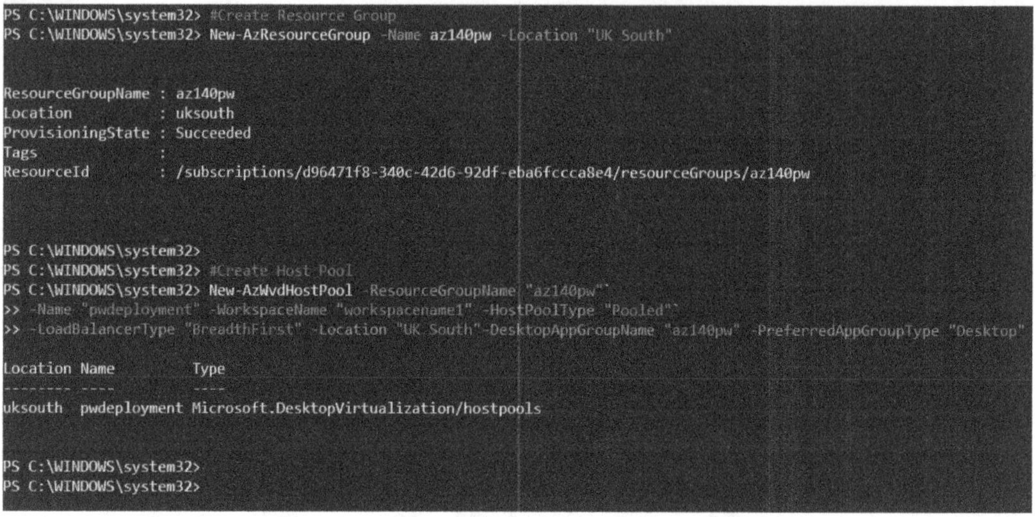

Figure 6.22 – Screenshot showing creating a resource group and creating a host pool

As shown in *Figure 6.22* we have now deployed our host pool using PowerShell. You can find out more about the cmdlets for creating a host pool at https://docs.microsoft.com/en-us/powershell/module/az.desktopvirtualization/new-azwvdhostpool?view=azps-6.1.0.

You can check that the resource group and host pool have been created by navigating to the path in the Azure portal. As shown in the following screenshot, you can see the AVD resources have been deployed into the resource group:

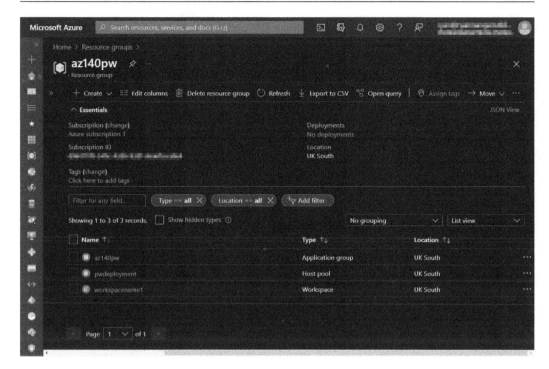

Figure 6.23 – Screenshot showing resources created using PowerShell for AVD

The next step would be to create a registration token for the deployment of session hosts into a host pool. This can be done by using the following cmdlets:

```
New-AzWvdRegistrationInfo -ResourceGroupName <Resource
group name> -HostPoolName <Host pool name> -ExpirationTime
$((get-date).ToUniversalTime().AddHours(<hours eg (2)>).
ToString('yyyy-MM-ddTHH:mm:ss.fffffffZ'))
```

The following provides an example of what the cmdlet should look like:

```
# create a registration token
New-AzWvdRegistrationInfo -ResourceGroupName az140pw
-HostPoolName pwdeployment -ExpirationTime $((get-date).
ToUniversalTime().AddHours(2).ToString('yyyy-MM-ddTHH:mm:ss.
fffffffZ'))
```

The following screenshot, *Figure 6.24*, shows the output of generating a new registration token:

Figure 6.24 – Screenshot showing the creation of a registration token

As shown in *Figure 6.24*, you can see that the new token has been generated ready for deploying VMs in a custom deployment. Token generation is taken care of natively.

Before we recap on deploying session hosts into a host pool, let's look at adding users and groups to a host pool via app groups.

To assign a user to an app group, you would use the following cmdlets:

```
New-AzRoleAssignment -SignInName <User UPN name@company.
com> -RoleDefinitionName "Desktop Virtualization User"
-ResourceName <App group Name> -ResourceGroupName <Resource
Group Name> -ResourceType 'Microsoft.DesktopVirtualization/
applicationGroups'
```

The following example shows the assignment of a user to an app group within a host pool:

```
New-AzRoleAssignment -SignInName testuser@ryanmangansitblog.com
-RoleDefinitionName "Desktop Virtualization User" -ResourceName
az140pw -ResourceGroupName az140pw -ResourceType 'Microsoft.
DesktopVirtualization/applicationGroups'
```

The following screenshot, *Figure 6.25*, shows the output of running the New-AzRoleAssignment cmdlet:

```
PS C:\WINDOWS\system32> New-AzRoleAssignment -SignInName testuser@ryanmangansitblog.com -RoleDe
finitionName "Desktop Virtualization User" -ResourceName az140pw -ResourceGroupName az140pw -Re
sourceType 'Microsoft.DesktopVirtualization/applicationGroups'


RoleAssignmentId     : /subscriptions/d96471f8-340c-42d6-92df-eba6fccca8e4/resourceGroups/az140p
                       w/providers/Microsoft.DesktopVirtualization/applicationGroups/az140pw/pro
                       viders/Microsoft.Authorization/roleAssignments/a37a482b-ff41-4a27-aa4c-1a
                       469ce03627
Scope                : /subscriptions/d96471f8-340c-42d6-92df-eba6fccca8e4/resourceGroups/az140p
                       w/providers/Microsoft.DesktopVirtualization/applicationGroups/az140pw
DisplayName          : test user
SignInName           : testuser@ryanmangansitblog.com
RoleDefinitionName   : Desktop Virtualization User
RoleDefinitionId     : 1d18fff3-a72a-46b5-b4a9-0b38a3cd7e63
ObjectId             : b4a25de1-014a-41a8-89de-10f82ba41ad3
ObjectType           : User
CanDelegate          : False
Description          :
ConditionVersion     :
Condition            :


PS C:\WINDOWS\system32>
```

Figure 6.25 – Screenshot showing user assignment to AVD resource group

Figure 6.25 shows the assignment of a user to the app group for the newly created host pool.

You can also assign a group rather than a user using the object ID of the group. You would use the following cmdlets to add a group to an app group:

```
New-AzRoleAssignment -ObjectId <Group Object ID>
-RoleDefinitionName "Desktop Virtualization User"
-ResourceName <App Group Name> -ResourceGroupName <Resource
Group Name> -ResourceType 'Microsoft.DesktopVirtualization/
applicationGroups'
```

An example showing the cmdlets to add a group to an app group is as follows:

```
New-AzRoleAssignment -ObjectId c203d0fa-a05a-40be-acd5-
d203b252435a -RoleDefinitionName "Desktop Virtualization User"
-ResourceName az140pw -ResourceGroupName az140pw -ResourceType
'Microsoft.DesktopVirtualization/applicationGroups'
```

The screenshot in *Figure 6.26* shows the use of the `New-AzRoleAssignment` cmdlet to assign a group via object ID:

```
PS C:\WINDOWS\system32> New-AzRoleAssignment -ObjectId c203d0fa-a05a-40be-acd5-d203b252435a -Ro
leDefinitionName "Desktop Virtualization User" -ResourceName az140pw -ResourceGroupName az140pw
-ResourceType 'Microsoft.DesktopVirtualization/applicationGroups'

RoleAssignmentId    : /subscriptions/d96471f8-340c-42d6-92df-eba6fccca8e4/resourceGroups/az140p
                      w/providers/Microsoft.DesktopVirtualization/applicationGroups/az140pw/pro
                      viders/Microsoft.Authorization/roleAssignments/776b331f-787d-4185-b967-1e
                      1372b29bc3
Scope               : /subscriptions/d96471f8-340c-42d6-92df-eba6fccca8e4/resourceGroups/az140p
                      w/providers/Microsoft.DesktopVirtualization/applicationGroups/az140pw
DisplayName         : AVD Users
SignInName          :
RoleDefinitionName  : Desktop Virtualization User
RoleDefinitionId    : 1d18fff3-a72a-46b5-b4a9-0b38a3cd7e63
ObjectId            : c203d0fa-a05a-40be-acd5-d203b252435a
ObjectType          : Group
CanDelegate         : False
Description         :
ConditionVersion    :
Condition           :


PS C:\WINDOWS\system32> _
```

Figure 6.26 – Screenshot showing group assignment to AVD resource group

As shown in *Figure 6.26*, the group has been assigned to the app group.

Once we have finished setting up the host pool and assigning users and groups, we can add session hosts to the host pool. This is typically done using the UI. You can follow the steps detailed in the *Creating VMs within the Create a host pool tab* section.

To add VMs, you need to make sure that you have created a registration token and the previous one has not expired. If it has expired, you will need to run the **Create registration token cmdlets** script again to enable the ability to add VMs to the host pool.

The following details the process to add or expand a host pool by adding VMs:

1. Sign in to the Azure portal.

2. Search for and select **Azure Virtual Desktop**.

3. In the menu on the left side of the screen, select **Host pools**, then select the name of the host pool you want to add VMs to.

4. Select **Session hosts** from the menu on the left side of the screen.

5. Select **+ Add** to start creating your host pool, as shown in *Figure 6.27*.

   The screenshot in *Figure 6.27* shows the button to add session hosts to a host pool:

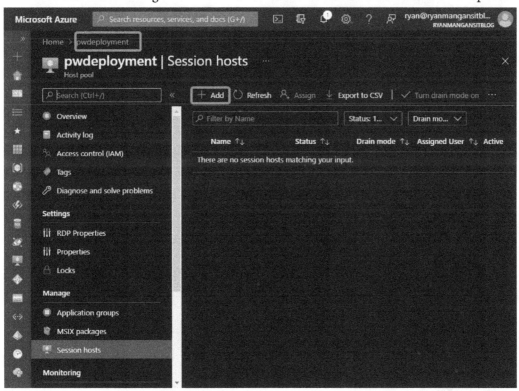

Figure 6.27 – Adding session hosts to the new deployment

Figure 6.28 shows the **Add virtual machines to a host pool** page within the Azure portal for deploying VMs into a host pool:

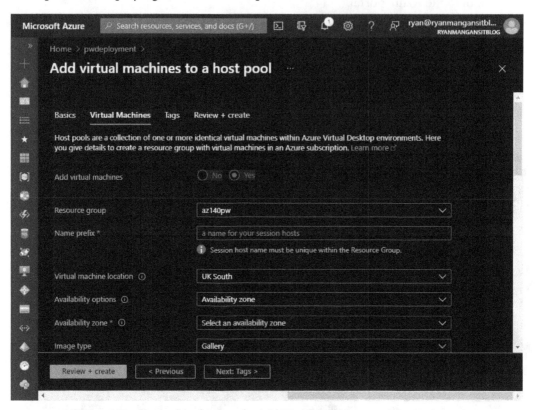

Figure 6.28 – Screenshot showing the Add virtual machines to a host pool page

6. Ignore the **Basics** tab as this is not required; instead, select the **Virtual Machines** tab. On this tab, you can view and edit the details of the VM you want to add to the host pool.

7. Select the resource group you want to create the VMs under, then select the Azure region. You can also choose the current Azure region you're using or a new Azure region.

8. Enter the required number of session hosts you want to add to your host pool. For example, if you're expanding your host pool by two hosts, enter 2.

> **Important Note**
>
> Although it's possible to edit the image and prefix of the VMs, Microsoft does not recommend editing them if you have VMs with different images in the same host pool. Edit the image and prefix only if you plan on removing VMs with older images from the affected host pool.

9. For **virtual network information**, select the virtual network and subnet to which you want the VMs to join. You can select the same virtual network your existing machines currently use or choose a different one that's more suitable to the Azure region you should have selected in *step 7*.

10. For **Administrator account**, enter the username and password associated with ADDS or AADDS on the virtual network you selected. These credentials will be used to join the VMs to the virtual network. Ensure you check the password as the deployment will fail if incorrect.

> **Tip**
>
> Ensure your admin names comply with the information given onscreen and MFA is not enabled on the account.

11. Select the **Tag** tab or skip if not required.

12. Select the **Review + create** tab. Review your configuration and if everything looks fine, select **Create** to start the deployment.

13. Once the deployment has finished, check your VMs and you should be ready to test.

> **Tip**
>
> You can also deploy the host pool and create session host VMs using an ARM template. You can download an example from `https://github.com/Azure/RDS-Templates/tree/master/ARM-wvd-templates`.
>
> It is also important to note that if you are using an automated process to build your AVD environment, you will need to use the latest configuration JSON file available. You can download this from `https://wvdportalstorageblob.blob.core.windows.net/galleryartifacts/armtemplates/Hostpool_10-13-2021/CreateHostpoolTemplate.json`.

You are now skilled with configuring PowerShell, then creating a resource group, deploying a host pool, generating a registration token, and configuring users/groups.

Summary

In this chapter, we looked a creating a host pool using the Azure portal and using PowerShell. We looked at some of the requirements and gotchas associated with creating a host pool and how to overcome them. We also deployed a host pool using PowerShell and assigned users access to the host pool via app groups.

In the next chapter, we will continue our journey through AVD and take a look at configuring host pools and session hosts. This includes creating Windows Server session hosts, configuring host pool settings, assigning users to host pools, and finally, applying updates and security and compliance settings to session hosts.

Questions

1. Before creating a host pool, what is the first thing you should check?

2. Which load balancing method is used to consolidate sessions onto a session host before allocating sessions to a new session host?

3. You plan to deploy your first AVD host pool. What do you need to configure on the virtual network before you deploy your first host pool?

Answers

1. That the Microsoft.DesktopVirtualization resource provider is registered.

2. The depth-first load balancing method.

3. Modify the DNS settings of the virtual network ("line of sight" with the Active Directory domain).

7

Configure Azure Virtual Desktop Host Pools

In this chapter, we look at configuring Azure Virtual desktop host pools. This includes license configuration for server-based multi-session deployments, configuring host pool settings, using PowerShell to customize Remote Desktop Protocol (RDP) properties, configuring host pool load balancing methods, personal desktop assignment, and security for host pools and session hosts.

We start this chapter by looking at deploying Windows Server licensing for those who want to move existing Server session hosts from on-premises to Azure Virtual Desktop. This may not be a common use case for Azure Virtual Desktop deployments, however, it's important that we cover this concept for those who require the use of Server session hosts within Azure Virtual Desktop.

We will cover the following topics in this chapter:

- Windows Server session host licensing
- Configuring host pool settings
- Configuring Azure Virtual Desktop load balancing methods

- Assigning users to host pools
- Applying OS and application updates to a running Azure Virtual Desktop host
- Applying security and compliance settings to session hosts

> **Important Note**
>
> It is important to note that Windows 10 and Windows 11 including multi-session do not require a licensing server.

Windows Server session host licensing

This section looks at installing the **Remote Desktop** (**RD**) licensing role and activating the licensing server to use server operating systems in Azure Virtual Desktop. To use a server operating system in Azure Virtual Desktop, you will need to deploy a server with the RD licensing role installed and configured on the Azure virtual network. The following steps summarize the installation and configuration of the RD licensing rol:.

1. Sign in to the server with an administrator account.

2. In the **Server Manager** console, click **Roles Summary**, and then click **Add Roles**. Click **Next** on the first page of the roles wizard.

3. Select **Remote Desktop Services**, click **Next**, and then **Next** on the **Remote Desktop Services** page.

4. Select **Remote Desktop Licensing**, and then click **Next**:

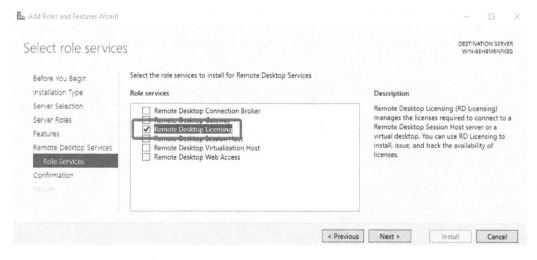

Figure 7.1 – The Add Roles and Features Wizard for the server OS

5. To configure the domain, select **Configure a discovery scope for this license server**, click **This domain**, and then click **Next**.

6. Then click **Install**:

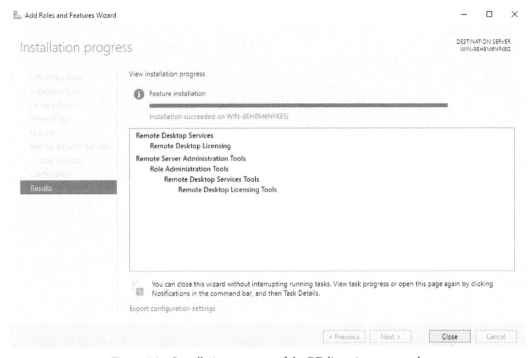

Figure 7.2 – Installation progress of the RD licensing server role

Once installed, the **Remote Desktop Licensing Manager** app will appear in the Start menu.

To activate the licensing server, please see the following steps:

1. Open the **Remote Desktop Licensing Manager** app, and go to **Start | Administrative Tools | Remote Desktop Services | Remote Desktop Licensing Manager**:

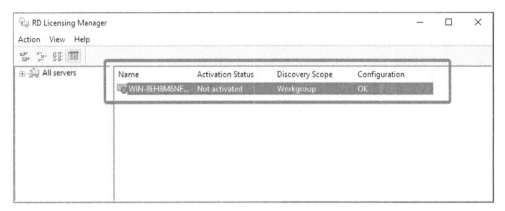

Figure 7.3 – License server role installed but not activated

2. Right-click the license server, and then click the **Activate Server** option.

3. Click **Next** on the welcome page.

4. For the connection method, select **Automatic connection** as recommended by Microsoft, and then click **Next**:

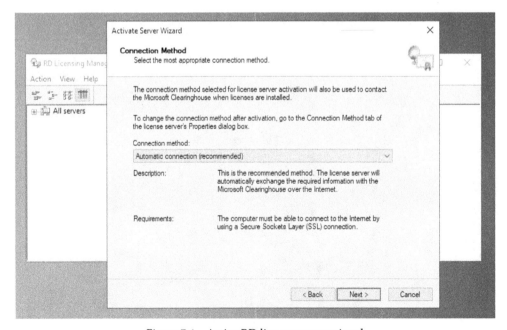

Figure 7.4 – Active RD license server wizard

5. Enter your company details (your name, the company name, and the geographic region), and then click **Next**.

6. You can also enter optional information (for example, email and company addresses) and then click **Next**.

7. Ensure that **Start Install Licenses Wizard** is not selected as this is done later, and then click **Next**. Your license server is ready to start issuing and managing licenses:

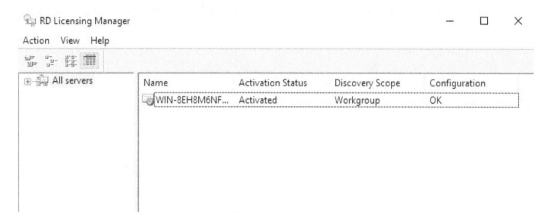

Figure 7.5 – RD license server activated

For information on installing the RDS client access license, please see the following link to the Microsoft article: `https://docs.microsoft.com/windows-server/remote/remote-desktop-services/rds-install-cals`.

There you have it; we have now configured an RD licensing server for use when using server operating systems as session hosts on our Azure Virtual Desktop environment. In the next section, we take a look at configuring host pool settings.

Configuring host pool settings

This section looks at customizing a host pool, including RD properties, load balancing methods, and configuring personal host pool assignment types.

Customizing RDP properties

Azure Virtual Desktop allows you to configure and customize host pool settings using the RDP properties. This allows you to configure things such as audio redirection, video playback, and drive redirections.

The supported RDP settings are split into five different areas:

- Connection information
- Session behavior
- Device redirection
- Display settings
- RemoteApp

These different categories contain a wide range of settings you can apply to your host pool configuration.

You can find a complete list of settings that can be applied or changed here: `https://docs.microsoft.com/windows-server/remote/remote-desktop-services/clients/rdp-files`.

You can change the RDP settings by navigating to the host pool within the Azure portal and selecting **RDP Properties**. You will then see five tabs:

- **Connection information**
- **Session behaviour**
- **Device redirection**
- **Display settings**
- **Advanced**

Important Note

You can read more about redirection support for each different client type here:
`https://docs.microsoft.com/en-us/windows-server/`
`remote/remote-desktop-services/clients/remote-`
`desktop-app-compare#redirection-support`.

The tabs are shown in the following screenshot:

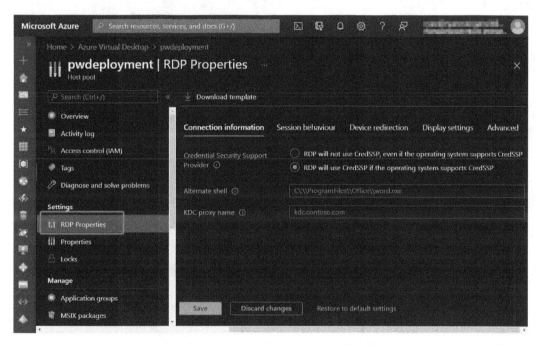

Figure 7.6 – RDP properties within a host pool

The Azure portal makes it easy for IT admins to make changes to the RDP properties as you can set parameters in the **Advanced** section or use the specific tabs that have radio buttons and drop-down boxes. You can see in the following screenshot an example of what to expect in the tabs:

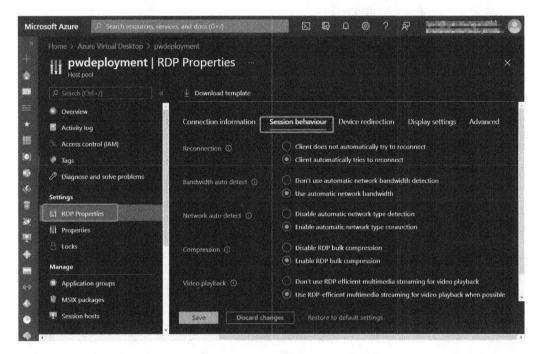

Figure 7.7 – The Session behaviour tab for RDP properties with a host pool

If you are looking to make more specific changes and customizations to the host pool's RDP properties, you can make changes within the **Advanced** tab as shown in *Figure 7.8*. It is also important to note that there are three buttons at the bottom of this Azure blade: **Save**, **Discard changes**, and **Restore to default settings**:

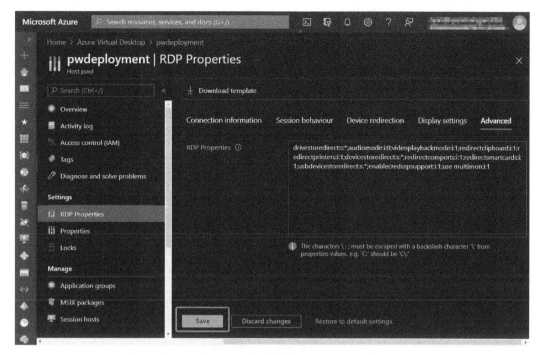

Figure 7.8 – Advanced tab of RDP properties of a host pool

Remember to click **Save** to apply customized settings and **Discard changes** if you want to revert before choosing customizations. It's also important to note that you can also use the **Restore to default settings** link to revert the custom RDP properties back to the defaults.

The step-by-step process of configuring RDP properties for a host pool is as follows:

1. Sign in to the Azure portal using `https://portal.azure.com`.

2. Enter `Azure Virtual Desktop` into the search bar located at the top of the page.

3. Under **Services**, select **Azure Virtual Desktop**.

4. Within the **Azure Virtual Desktop** page, select host pools on the left-hand side of the screen.

5. Choose the host pool you want to update.

6. Select **RDP Properties** in the menu on the left-hand side of the screen.

7. Set the property you want.

8. As mentioned, you can also use the **Advanced** tab to add/customize RDP properties in a semicolon-separated format.

9. Select **Save** to save changes when you have finished.

In the next section, we examine using PowerShell to configure RDP properties for a host pool.

Using PowerShell to customize RDP properties

Before you can use PowerShell to customize your host pool RDP properties, you will need to configure the PowerShell module for Azure Virtual Desktop as a prerequisite. I showed you how to do this in *Chapter 5, Implementing and Managing Storage for Azure Virtual Desktop.*

Adding or editing a single RDP property

In this subsection, we look at adding and editing a single/multiple RDP properties.

The following shows you the cmdlet parameters for updating an RDP property. This is useful for when you want to change an existing configuration:

```
Update-AzWvdHostPool -ResourceGroupName <resourcegroupname>
 -Name <hostpoolname> -CustomRdpProperty <property>
```

In this example, I apply the redirect clipboard custom RDP property by specifying the `redirectclipboard:i:1` custom RDP property. This property enables the clipboard feature when copying and pasting files between the remote session and the local desktop:

```
Update-AzWvdHostPool -ResourceGroupName az140pw -Name
 pwdeployment  -CustomRdpProperty redirectclipboard:i:1
```

Here's the output:

```
Windows PowerShell
Copyright (C) Microsoft Corporation. All rights reserved.

Try the new cross-platform PowerShell https://aka.ms/pscore6

PS C:\WINDOWS\system32> Connect-AzAccount

Account                      SubscriptionName   TenantId                                 Environment
-------                      ----------------   --------                                 -----------
ryan@ryanmangansitblog.com Azure subscription 1 6b358606-462c-40ce-96bc-5b2b81aa6230 AzureCloud


PS C:\WINDOWS\system32> Update-AzWvdHostPool -ResourceGroupName az140pw -Name pwdeployment  -CustomRdpProperty redirectc
lipboard:i:1

Location Name       Type
-------- ----       ----
uksouth  pwdeployment Microsoft.DesktopVirtualization/hostpools


PS C:\WINDOWS\system32>
```

Figure 7.9 – Cmdlets and output from running custom RDP property cmdlets

To check what RDP properties are applied to the host pool, you can use the following:

```
Get-AzWvdHostPool -ResourceGroupName <resourcegroupname> -Name
<hostpoolname> | format-list Name, CustomRdpProperty
```

The following provides an example of the usage:

```
get-AzWvdHostPool -ResourceGroupName az140pw -Name pwdeployment
| format-list name, customRdpProperty
```

The following screenshot shows the Get-AzWvdHostpool cmdlet output; as you can see, the redirect clipboard property we added is now set:

```
PS C:\WINDOWS\system32> get-AzWvdHostPool -ResourceGroupName az140pw -Name pwdeployment | format-li
st name, customRdpProperty


Name              : pwdeployment
CustomRdpProperty : redirectclipboard:i:1;


PS C:\WINDOWS\system32>
```

Figure 7.10 – Get-AzWvdHostpool cmdlets for checking the custom RDP properties

Adding or editing multiple custom RDP properties

To add multiple custom RDP properties, you can use the following PowerShell variables to add multiple properties with a semicolon, as follows:

```
$properties="<property1>;<property2>;<property3>"
```
```
Update-AzWvdHostPool -ResourceGroupName <resourcegroupname>
-Name <hostpoolname> -CustomRdpProperty $properties
```

The following provides an example of the usage:

```
$properties="redirectclipboard:i:1;use
multimon:i:1;drivestoredirect:s:*"
```
```
Update-AzWvdHostPool -ResourceGroupName az140pw -Name
pwdeployment -CustomRdpProperty $properties
```

The following screenshot shows the output from running the PowerShell cmdlet for adding multiple RDP properties:

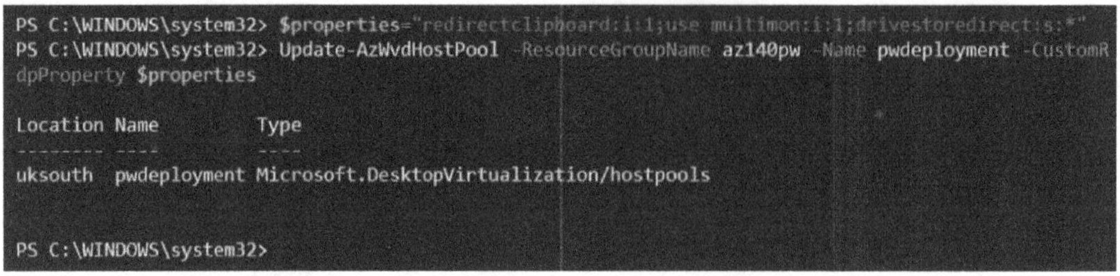

Figure 7.11 – Cmdlets for assigning multiple RDP properties using PowerShell

Using the same `get-AzWvdHostPool` powershell cmdlet, you can check to see if these properties have been applied.

The following screenshot shows the `get-azwvdhostpool` cmdlet being run to confirm that the RDP properties have been set:

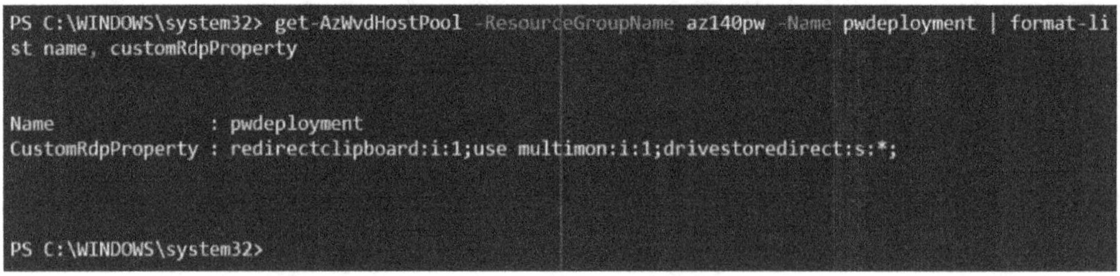

Figure 7.12 – get-azwvdhostpool cmdlets for checking the custom RDP properties have been set

Resetting all custom RDP properties using PowerShell

To reset the RDP properties to the default, you would use the following cmdlets:

```
Update-AzWvdHostPool -ResourceGroupName <resourcegroupname>
-Name <hostpoolname> -CustomRdpProperty ""
```

The following provides an example of the usage:

```
Update-AzWvdHostPool -ResourceGroupName az140pw -Name
pwdeployment -CustomRdpProperty ""
```

The following screenshot shows the reset PowerShell cmdlets being run:

```
PS C:\WINDOWS\system32> Update-AzWvdHostPool -ResourceGroupName az140pw -Name pwdeployment -CustomR
dpProperty ""

Location Name          Type
-------- ----          ----
uksouth  pwdeployment  Microsoft.DesktopVirtualization/hostpools


PS C:\WINDOWS\system32>
```

Figure 7.13 – Cmdlets for resetting the custom RDP properties with PowerShell

Again, you can use the same `get-AzWvdHostPool` cmdlet; you can check to see if these properties have been applied. The following screenshot shows the RDP properties being reset:

```
PS C:\WINDOWS\system32> get-AzWvdHostPool -ResourceGroupName az140pw -Name pwdeployment | format-li
st name, customRdpProperty


Name              : pwdeployment
CustomRdpProperty :


PS C:\WINDOWS\system32>
```

Figure 7.14 – get-azwvdhostpool cmdlets for checking the reset has been completed

In this section, we looked at configuring custom RDP properties for host pools. This covered both the configuration through the Azure portal and using PowerShell. In the next section, we take a look at configuring load balancing methods on host pools.

Methods for configuring Azure Virtual Desktop load balancing

In the previous chapter, we looked at the different types of session load balancing. We will now take a look at configuring load balancing within the Azure portal and PowerShell.

This section examines configuring the load balancing method for Azure Virtual Desktop using both the Azure portal UI and PowerShell.

Let's now take a look at how to configure load balancing.

Configuring load balancing

We'll now look at configuring host pool load balancing. The following steps walk you through configuring load balancing within the Azure portal:

1. Sign in to the Azure portal using the following URL: `https://portal.azure.com`.

2. Search for and select **Azure Virtual Desktop** under **Services**.

3. On the **Azure Virtual Desktop** page, select **Host pools**.

4. Select the name of the host pool you want to edit.

5. Select **Properties**.

6. Select the load balancing algorithm you want for this host pool in the drop-down menu.

7. Enter the required **Max session limit** into the field:

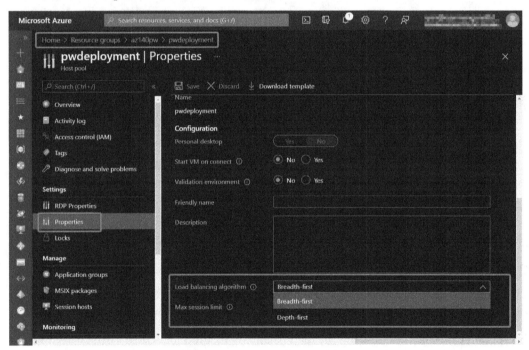

Figure 7.15 – Change the load balancing method of a host pool in the Azure portal

8. Select **Save**. This applies the new load balancing settings.

You have now configured your load balancing settings. Let's move on to the next section, where we will take a look at the option to configure load balancing settings using PowerShell.

Using PowerShell to configure load balancing methods

Before you can use PowerShell to customize your host pool load balancing methods, you will need to set up and load the PowerShell module for Azure Virtual Desktop as a prerequisite. I showed you how to do this in *Chapter 5, Implementing and Managing Storage for Azure Virtual Desktop*.

Breath-first load balancing

In this subsection, we take a look at the breadth-first load balancing method using PowerShell. Breadth-first is the default configuration when deploying pooled session hosts in a host pool. As a recap, this method distributes connections evenly to available session hosts within the host pool.

> **Important Note**
>
> MaxSessionLimit is used to control the maximum number of sessions allowed per session host in the Azure Virtual Desktop host pool. When using depth-first load balancing, the value is used to determine when to stop allocating users to one host and start sending user sessions to the next host.

The following cmdlets are used for configuring the load balancing methods:

```
Update-AzWvdHostPool -ResourceGroupName <resourcegroupname>
-Name <hostpoolname> -LoadBalancerType 'BreadthFirst'
-MaxSessionLimit ###
```

The following example demonstrates how to change/update the load balancing method:

```
Update-AzWvdHostPool -ResourceGroupName az140pw -Name
pwdeployment -LoadBalancerType 'BreadthFirst' -MaxSessionLimit
999999
```

Here's the output:

```
PS C:\WINDOWS\system32>
PS C:\WINDOWS\system32> Update-AzWvdHostPool -ResourceGroupName az140pw -Name pwdeployment -LoadBal
ancerType 'BreadthFirst' -MaxSessionLimit 999999

Location Name          Type
-------- ----          ----
uksouth  pwdeployment  Microsoft.DesktopVirtualization/hostpools


PS C:\WINDOWS\system32>
```

Figure 7.16 – Cmdlets for setting the load balancing method to breadth-first

To check that the setting has applied, you can run the following cmdlet:

```
Get-AzWvdHostPool -ResourceGroupName <resourcegroupname>
-Name <hostpoolname> | format-list Name, LoadBalancerType,
MaxSessionLimit
```

The following example demonstrates how to check that breadth-first has been set:

```
Get-AzWvdHostPool -ResourceGroupName az140pw -Name pwdeployment
| format-list Name, LoadBalancerType, MaxSessionLimit
```

Here's the output:

```
PS C:\WINDOWS\system32> Get-AzWvdHostPool -ResourceGroupName az140pw -Name pwdeployment | format-li
st Name, LoadBalancerType, MaxSessionLimit


Name             : pwdeployment
LoadBalancerType : BreadthFirst
MaxSessionLimit  : 999999


PS C:\WINDOWS\system32>
```

Figure 7.17 – Cmdlets for checking the load balancing method set on a host pool

Depth-first load balancing

Depth-first load balancing is used to populate session hosts with the highest number of connections that have not reached the maximum session limit threshold.

> **Important Note**
>
> You must enter a maximum session limit per session host within the host pool when configuring depth-first load balancing.

To set depth-first load balancing in your host pool, you need to use the following cmdlets:

```
Update-AzWvdHostPool -ResourceGroupName <resourcegroupname>
-Name <hostpoolname> -LoadBalancerType 'DepthFirst'
-MaxSessionLimit ###
```

The following provides an example of the usage:

```
Update-AzWvdHostPool -ResourceGroupName az140pw -Name
pwdeployment -LoadBalancerType 'DepthFirst' -MaxSessionLimit
999999
```

Here's the output:

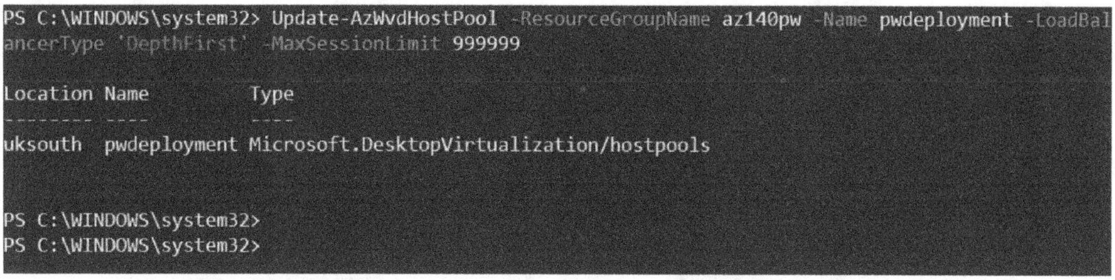

```
PS C:\WINDOWS\system32> Update-AzWvdHostPool -ResourceGroupName az140pw -Name pwdeployment -LoadBal
ancerType 'DepthFirst' -MaxSessionLimit 999999

Location Name           Type
-------- ----           ----
uksouth  pwdeployment Microsoft.DesktopVirtualization/hostpools


PS C:\WINDOWS\system32>
PS C:\WINDOWS\system32>
```

Figure 7.18 – Update cmdlet for changing the load balancing method of a host pool

To confirm settings have been applied, use the following cmdlets as shown in the breadth-first example:

```
Get-AzWvdHostPool -ResourceGroupName az140pw -Name pwdeployment
  | format-list Name, LoadBalancerType, MaxSessionLimit
```

Here's the output:

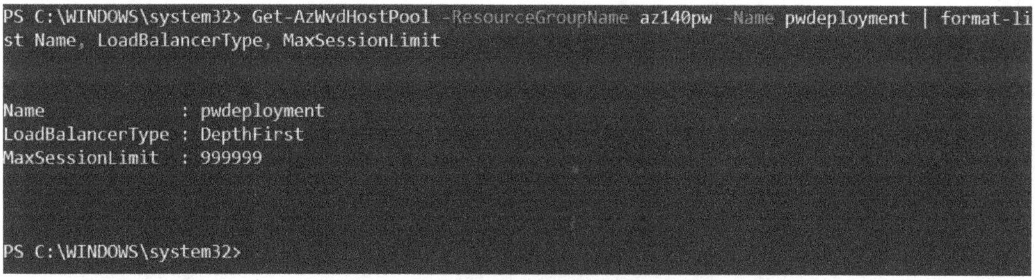

```
PS C:\WINDOWS\system32> Get-AzWvdHostPool -ResourceGroupName az140pw -Name pwdeployment | format-li
st Name, LoadBalancerType, MaxSessionLimit


Name             : pwdeployment
LoadBalancerType : DepthFirst
MaxSessionLimit  : 999999


PS C:\WINDOWS\system32>
```

Figure 7.19 – Cmdlets and output of checking the load balancing method of a host pool

This section looked at the configuration and updating of the load balancing method within a host pool. I covered both ways – the Azure portal UI and PowerShell. We'll now move on to assigning users to host pools.

Assigning users to host pools

Multi-session is great for when you want to provide a desktop experience to users where they all share the same compute resource of a session host. In this section, we take a look at assigning personal desktops to users. Personal host pools allow you to commit compute resource per user as you are allocating a session host per user. When you deploy a personal host pool, users are not assigned to specific session hosts. Instead, personal session hosts are used for specific use cases such as developers or users who need administrator access to the desktop. Other user cases include software license requirements that do not allow multiple users to connect to the device.

Assigning users to a session host in the Azure portal

In this subsection, we will look at assigning users to personal session hosts using the Azure portal.

> **Important Note**
>
> Please note this example is for assigning users and groups to personal desktops, however, the process is the same for both personal and multi-session based deployments.

The following steps show you how to assign a user to a personal desktop:

1. Sign in to the Azure portal at `https://portal.azure.com`.

2. Enter `Azure Virtual Desktop` into the search bar located at the top of the page.

3. Under **Services**, select **Azure Virtual Desktop**.

4. Within the **Azure Virtual Desktop** page, on the window's left-hand side, select **Host pools**.

5. Select the host pool you want to update.

6. Next, go to the menu on the left-hand side of the page and select **Application groups**:

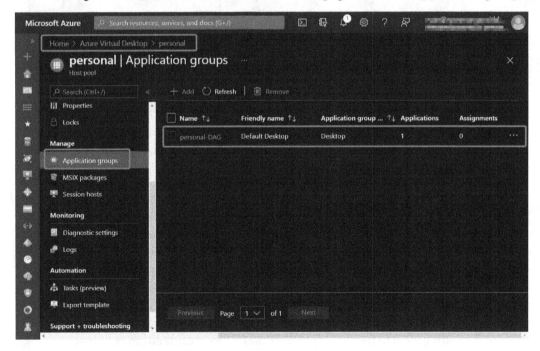

Figure 7.20 – The application groups within a host pool

7. Select the desktop app group name you want to edit, then select **Assignments** in the menu on the left-hand side of the window.

8. Select **+ Add**, then select the users or user groups you want to publish in the desktop app group:

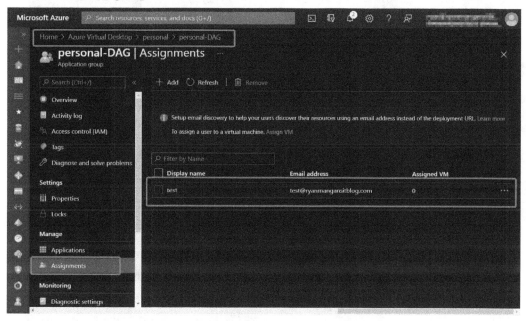

Figure 7.21 – User assignments within an app group

9. Select **Assign VM** in the information bar to assign a session host to a user.

10. Select the session host you want to assign to the user, then select **Assign**:

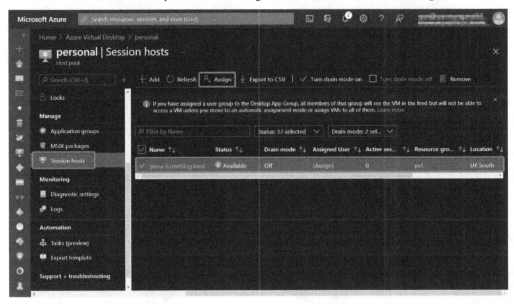

Figure 7.22 – The Assign button for assigning a user a personal session host within the host pool

11. Select the user you want to assign the session host to from the list of available users as shown in the following screenshot:

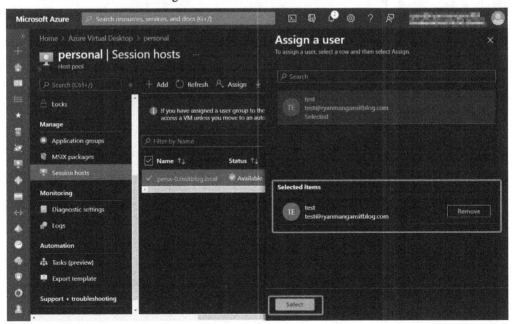

Figure 7.23 – Assign a user blade within the host pool

12. When you have finished, click **Select**.

There you have it – you have assigned a user to a session host:

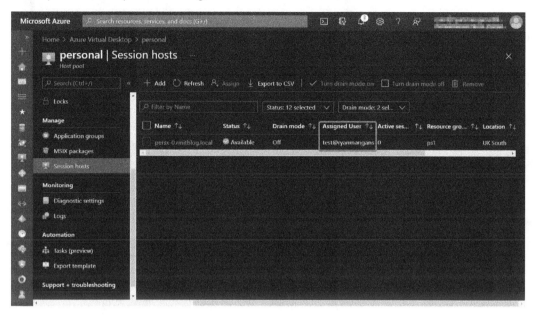

Figure 7.24 – User now assigned to a personal session host within the host pool

In this section, we looked at assigning users personal desktop hosts via the Azure portal UI. We will now take a look at how to do it via PowerShell.

Assigning users to host pools via PowerShell

Before you can use PowerShell to assign personal desktops, you will need to set up and load the PowerShell module for Azure Virtual Desktop as a prerequisite. I showed you how to do this in *Chapter 5*, *Implementing and Managing Storage for Azure Virtual Desktop*.

Configuring automatic assignment

In this subsection, we look at configuring automatic assignments, which is helpful for users who do not need or require a specific session host.

Automatic assignment works by first assigning users to the desktop in the personal host pool. Then, when the user opens the RD client and clicks on the advertised resources in their feed, they will be allocated an available session host, which completes the automatic assignment process.

To enable automatic assignment, you need to run the following PowerShell cmdlets:

```
Update-AzWvdHostPool -ResourceGroupName <resourcegroupname>
-Name <hostpoolname> -PersonalDesktopAssignmentType Automatic
```

The following example shows the assignment:

```
Update-AzWvdHostPool -ResourceGroupName ps1 -Name personal
-PersonalDesktopAssignmentType Automatic
```

Here's the output:

```
PS C:\WINDOWS\system32> Update-AzWvdHostPool -ResourceGroupName ps1 -Name personal -PersonalDesktop
AssignmentType Automatic

Location Name      Type
-------- ----      --
uksouth  personal Microsoft.DesktopVirtualization/hostpools


PS C:\WINDOWS\system32>
```

Figure 7.25 – Cmdlets for setting the personal assignment to automatic

To assign users to a personal desktop host pool, you use the following cmdlets:

```
New-AzRoleAssignment -SignInName <userupn> -RoleDefinitionName
"Desktop Virtualization User" -ResourceName <appgroupname>
-ResourceGroupName <resourcegroupname> -ResourceType
'Microsoft.DesktopVirtualization/applicationGroups'
```

The following provides an example of the usage:

```
New-AzRoleAssignment -SignInName testuser@ryanmangansitblog.com
-RoleDefinitionName "Desktop Virtualization User" -ResourceName
personal-DAG -ResourceGroupName ps1 -ResourceType 'Microsoft.
DesktopVirtualization/applicationGroups'
```

Here's the output:

```
PS C:\WINDOWS\system32> New-AzRoleAssignment -SignInName testuser@ryanmangansitblog.com -RoleDefini
tionName "Desktop Virtualization User" -ResourceName personal-DAG -ResourceGroupName ps1 -ResourceT
ype 'Microsoft.DesktopVirtualization/applicationGroups'


RoleAssignmentId    : /subscriptions/d96471f8-340c-42d6-92df-eba6fccca8e4/resourceGroups/ps1/provid
                      ers/Microsoft.DesktopVirtualization/applicationGroups/personal-DAG/providers/
                      Microsoft.Authorization/roleAssignments/e5750faa-0cb0-4b8a-964c-3ed6282052e8
Scope               : /subscriptions/d96471f8-340c-42d6-92df-eba6fccca8e4/resourceGroups/ps1/provid
                      ers/Microsoft.DesktopVirtualization/applicationGroups/personal-DAG
DisplayName         : test user
SignInName          : testuser@ryanmangansitblog.com
RoleDefinitionName  : Desktop Virtualization User
RoleDefinitionId    : 1d18fff3-a72a-46b5-b4a9-0b38a3cd7e63
ObjectId            : b4a25de1-014a-41a8-89de-10f82ba41ad3
ObjectType          : User
CanDelegate         : False
Description         :
ConditionVersion    :
Condition           :


PS C:\WINDOWS\system32>
```

Figure 7.26 – Assignment of a user to an app group

You can check in the following screenshot that the assignment worked:

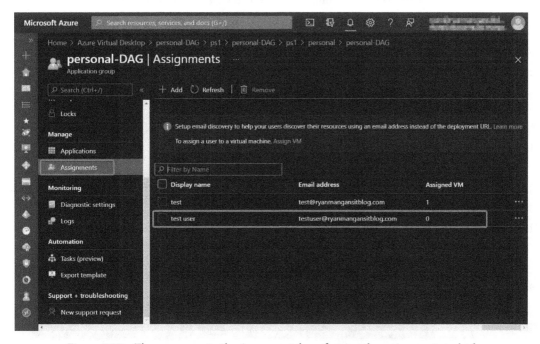

Figure 7.27 – The same user in the Azure portal confirming the assignment worked

As shown in the preceding screenshot, the user has been added to the app group.

> **Tip**
> You can also assign group object IDs to the app group rather than assigning individual users.

In this section, I showed you how to enable automatic assignment and assign users to an app group associated with a personal host pool. We will now look at direct assignments using PowerShell.

Configuring direct assignment using PowerShell

This section looks at assigning users to personal host pool session hosts using direct assignment. The key difference between direct assignment and automatic assignment is that with direct assignment, the user must be assigned to the personal session host before they can access the resources.

> **Remember**
> You need to follow the steps in *Chapter 5, Implementing and Managing Storage for Azure Virtual Desktop*, to configure PowerShell for Azure Virtual Desktop before proceeding.

Step 1: The first step is to configure the host pool for the direct assignment of users to session hosts. Use the following cmdlets to complete this:

```
Update-AzWvdHostPool -ResourceGroupName <resourcegroupname>
-Name <hostpoolname> -PersonalDesktopAssignmentType Direct
```

The following provides an example of the usage:

```
Update-AzWvdHostPool -ResourceGroupName <resourcegroupname>
-Name <hostpoolname> -PersonalDesktopAssignmentType Direct
```

The following screenshot shows the update of a host pool to direct assignment:

```
PS C:\WINDOWS\system32> Update-AzWvdHostPool -ResourceGroupName ps1 -Name personal -PersonalDesktop
AssignmentType Direct

Location Name      Type
-------- ----      ----
uksouth  personal  Microsoft.DesktopVirtualization/hostpools

PS C:\WINDOWS\system32>
```

Figure 7.28 – Cmdlets for setting the direct assignment type

> **Tip**
> You can change between direct and automatic personal session host assignments. All you need to do is run the cmdlets for your chosen configuration.

Step 2: Once we have set the host pool to `Direct`, as shown previously, we then need to assign a user to the personal desktop host pool:

```
New-AzRoleAssignment -SignInName <userupn> -RoleDefinitionName
"Desktop Virtualization User" -ResourceName <appgroupname>
-ResourceGroupName <resourcegroupname> -ResourceType
'Microsoft.DesktopVirtualization/applicationGroups'
```

As you will note from the previous section, the cmdlets are the same for assigning users to direct or automatic personal desktop host pools.

Step 3: The final step is to assign the user to a specific session host; you need to use the following cmdlets:

```
Update-AzWvdSessionHost -HostPoolName <hostpoolname> -Name
<sessionhostname> -ResourceGroupName <resourcegroupname>
-AssignedUser <userupn>
```

The following provides an example of the usage:

```
Update-AzWvdSessionHost -HostPoolName personal -Name persx-1.
rmitblog.local -ResourceGroupName ps1  -AssignedUser testuser@
ryanmangansitblog.com
```

The following screenshot shows the cmdlets for assigning a user to a specific session host:

Figure 7.29 – Assignment of a session host to a specific user

Once the cmdlets have been run successfully, you will then see the user assigned in the portal:

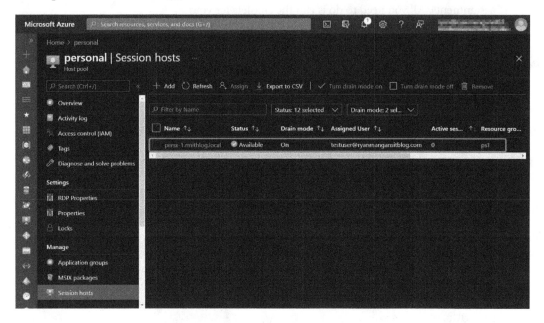

Figure 7.30 – Assignment in the Azure portal

There you have it – users assigned using direct assignment via PowerShell.

> **Important Note**
>
> Don't forget to link your application group to your workspace. Workspaces are a logical grouping of app groups. Each app group must be linked with a workspace for users to see the desktops and remote apps published to them. See the following screenshot, showing how to add an app group under the **Workspaces** tab.

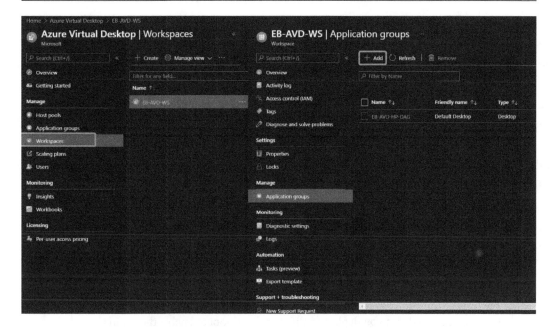

Figure 7.31 – Add an app group to a workspace in Azure Virtual Desktop

This section looked at the two options for personal session host assignment in Azure Virtual Desktop. We covered both automatic assignment and direct assignment.

We'll now move on to applying operating system and application updates on a running Azure Virtual Desktop host.

Applying OS and application updates on an Azure Virtual Desktop host

When it comes to updating Azure Virtual Desktop personal desktops or multi-session, it's recommended that you use Microsoft Endpoint Manager. However, you can carry out manual update tasks on the image and then update the version within the Azure Compute Gallery.

> **Important Note**
>
> The use of Azure Update Management is not supported for client Windows operating systems. You can read more here: `https://docs.microsoft.com/azure/automation/update-management/operating-system-requirements#supported-operating-systems.`

It is recommended that you use automatic enrollment to Microsoft Endpoint Manager using Group Policy. It is also advised that you use device credentials for enrollment rather than user credentials.

Configuring a validation pool

Validation pools are great for validating Azure Virtual Desktop service updates. Validation host pools are where services updates are applied in the first instance. This essentially allows you to monitor and test service updates before they are applied to your production or non-validation environment.

Validation host pools help you identify and discover issues from changes that are introduced from service updates. If you don't use a validation host pool, you may not discover any changes or errors introduced, which could impact your production environment.

> **Tip**
> It's recommended that you deploy a validation host pool to enable the testing of all future updates to the Azure Virtual Desktop service.

You can also change non-validation host pools to a validation environment; here is how:

1. Sign in to the Azure portal UI using the following URL: `https://portal.azure.com`.

2. Search for and select **Azure Virtual Desktop** within the search bar located at the top of the web page.

3. On the **Azure Virtual Desktop** page, from the left-hand side menu, select **Host pools**.

4. Select the name of the host pool you want to edit.

5. Select **Properties**:

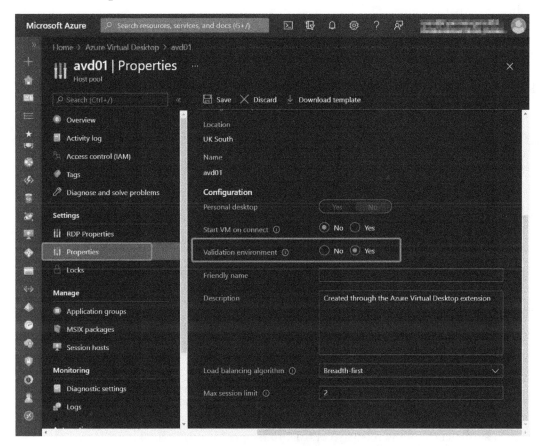

Figure 7.32 – Validation environment field within the properties of a host pool

6. Change **Validation environment** to **Yes** to enable the validation environment.

7. Select **Save**. Then the settings will be applied

To configure the validation environment using PowerShell, use the following cmdlets:

```
Update-AzWvdHostPool -ResourceGroupName <resourcegroupname>
-Name <hostpoolname> -ValidationEnvironment:$true
```

The following example shows you how to set an existing host pool to a validation environment:

```
Update-AzWvdHostPool -ResourceGroupName az140pw -Name
pwdeployment -ValidationEnvironment:$true
```

Here's the output:

```
PS C:\WINDOWS\system32> Update-AzWvdHostPool -ResourceGroupName az140pw -Name pwdeployment -Validat
ionEnvironment:$true

Location Name          Type
-------- ----          ----
uksouth  pwdeployment  Microsoft.DesktopVirtualization/hostpools


PS C:\WINDOWS\system32>
```

Figure 7.33 – Set a host pool to be a validation environment via PowerShell

There you have it – you've changed an existing host pool to a validation pool using the Azure portal and PowerShell. We'll now move on to looking at security and compliance settings that you can apply to session hosts.

Applying security and compliance settings to session hosts

Session hosts are virtual machines that run within your Azure subscription, which are connected to an Azure virtual network. The overall security of an Azure Virtual Desktop deployment depends on the security controls you apply to your session hosts.

Here are some tips for session host security: https://docs.microsoft.com/azure/virtual-desktop/security-guide.

Endpoint protection/detection and threat response and vulnerability management

It is advised that you should enable a supported endpoint production product on your Azure Virtual Desktop session hosts. There is the option of using Microsoft Defender antivirus or third-party vendors.

> **Tip**
> When configuring antivirus for Azure Virtual Desktop, make sure you exclude FSLogix VHD/VHDX and MSIX App Attach VHD/VHDX/CIMFS file extensions.

As security threats are becoming a daily occurrence and threats are becoming more complex, it is recommended that you deploy some form of **endpoint detection and response (EDR)** product to enable advanced detection and response capabilities. For example, you can use Microsoft Defender for Endpoint or others, including network virtual appliances that come with built-in threat detection capabilities that listen on the Azure virtual network.

You can use Azure Security Center to identify vulnerabilities in applications and operating systems. This helps you identify problems using vulnerability assessments. You can also use Microsoft Defender for Endpoint, which offers a level of vulnerability management for desktop operating systems and web content filtering. You can read more about web content filtering here: `https://docs.microsoft.com/microsoft-365/security/defender-endpoint/web-content-filtering`.

As shown in the previous section, Azure helps you address vulnerabilities within your environment by allowing you to schedule updates and apply patches to your session hosts. These can be both personal and pooled host pools.

Session screen locks

As the world has made a significant shift to working anywhere, especially from home, due to the global COVID-19 pandemic, you may want to consider configuring a machine's screen to lock during idle time, requiring the user to reauthenticate when they come back to unlock the screen. This is to prevent unauthorized access to company devices. This not only applies to Azure Virtual Desktop but should apply to all devices deployed in a business. It's also important to not get confused between screen locks and session timeouts. Screen locks are useful for thin client devices where the device is static and usually installed within the organization's offices. Session time outs are for remote connections where a user has not used the keyboard or mouse for a period of time and the session disconnects.

Configuring maximum inactive time and disconnection policies

A good security hardening technique for Virtual Desktop environments is configuring maximum inactive times and disconnection policies. The inactive time and disconnection policies can vary for each organization. However, it's suggested that 5 to 15 minutes is the time range you should consider when configuring these settings.

The following screenshot shows the user settings within a Group Policy Object for the **Set time limit for active but idle Remote Desktop Services sessions setting**. This setting is used for controlling idle settings.

You can configure the policy setting using the following group policy path **Computer Configuration\Administrative Templates\Windows Components\Remote Desktop Services\Remote Desktop Session Host\Session Time Limits**:

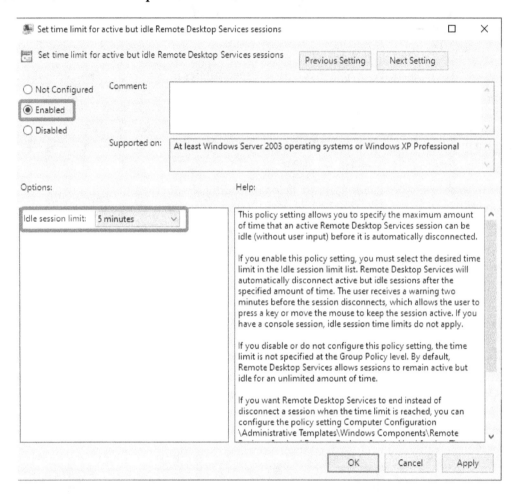

Figure 7.34 – Idle session limit set to 5 minutes

The following screenshot shows you the setting for **Set time limit for disconnected sessions**. This is used to remove any disconnected sessions from a Session Host after the specified time value set:

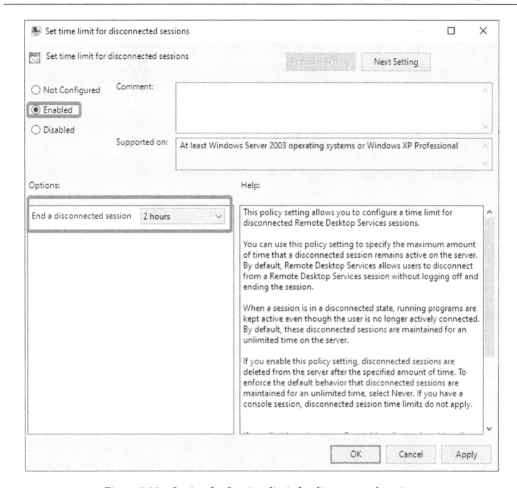

Figure 7.35 – Setting for Set time limit for disconnected sessions

The following screenshot shows all the policies you can configure within the `Session Time Limits` folder:

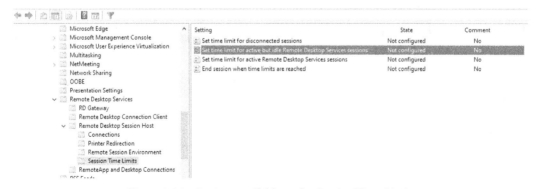

Figure 7.36 – Settings available under Session Time Limits

> **Important Note**
>
> Please note that disconnecting idle tasks such as rendering or simulations can interrupt users. It's advised that you check before enabling such policies.

Application security within session hosts

It is important to secure the applications running within the session host. It is recommended that you use tools such as Microsoft Security Policy Advisor (`https://docs.microsoft.com/en-us/DeployOffice/overview-of-security-policy-advisor`) to help identify possible issues with Microsoft 365 Apps for enterprise.

> **Tip**
>
> Remember to check other applications and apply the appropriate AppLocker and firewall rules to limit communication if not required for use within the organization.

Limiting operating system capabilities

It is advised that you go through a security hardening exercise to ensure you have limited security exposure and to reduce it if not. Some of the additional ways of achieving this are to use Group Policy and RDP custom policies.

You can control device redirection by redirecting drives, USB devices, and printers to a user's local device remotely.

The following link details the different device redirections and the restrictions you can set:

`https://docs.microsoft.com/azure/virtual-desktop/configure-device-redirections`

You can find the full list of RDP settings here:

`https://docs.microsoft.com/windows-server/remote/remote-desktop-services/clients/rdp-files`

> **Recommendation**
>
> Microsoft recommends you assess/evaluate your security requirements and check which features you need and should disable.

A common VDI practice is to restrict Windows Explorer access by hiding local and remote drive mappings. This still applies with Azure Virtual Desktop. This prevents users from discovering unwanted information about systems and other users.

You should avoid direct RDP access to session hosts in your environment. If you need direct RDP access for administration or troubleshooting, enable just-in-time access, use Azure Bastion as covered in *Chapter 6, Creating Host Pools and Session Hosts*, or use Quick Assist if you are supporting a user.

Consider limiting user permissions for accessing local and remote file systems. You can restrict user permissions by ensuring that your local and remote file systems use access control lists with the least privilege configured. This ensures that users can only access what they need and can't change or delete critical resources.

Prevent users from installing and running unwanted software on session hosts. As mentioned previously, you can enable AppLocker for additional security on session hosts, ensuring that only the apps you allow can run on the host. You can also use app masking for applications you don't want specific user groups to see.

In this section, we took a look at some high-level session host security tips. However, we look at security in more detail in *Chapter 11, Managing Security*.

Summary

In this chapter, we built on the previous chapter, where we deployed a session host.

In addition, this chapter looked at configuring session hosts within a host pool. We learned how to deploy and configure a Windows Server session host licensing server to support the use of the Windows Server operating system within Azure Virtual Desktop. We then looked at the configuration of host pool settings, RDP properties, load balancing methods, and assigning users to host pools. We then finished off the chapter by learning how to apply operating system and application updates to a session host as well as applying security compliance settings to session hosts.

In the next chapter, we will take a look at creating and managing session host images.

Questions

1. When using server-based operating systems for Azure Virtual Desktop, what resource do you require?

2. What is the purpose of MaxSessionLimit within a host pool?

3. What considerations are there to be taken into account when configuring antivirus for Azure Virtual Desktop?

4. Which group policy would you set for controlling idle time out session settings within Azure Virtual Desktop?

Answers

1. *When using server-based operating systems, you will need an additional server to host the RD client access licenses that the server license will require.*

2. *MaxSessionLimit is used to limit the number of user sessions on a single session host.*

3. *Ensure that you have set the exclusion rules for both FSLogix profiles and MSIX app attach on the appropriate file shares/storage.*

4. *Set time limit for active but idle Remote Desktop Services sessions.*

8

Azure AD Join for Azure Virtual Desktop

In this chapter, we will look at **Azure Active Directory (Azure AD)** join for Azure Virtual Desktop. Using Azure AD join for Azure Virtual Desktop has many benefits for organizations, including **Single Sign-On (SSO)**, virtual machines just using one identity provider, and being able to avoid some of the complexities associated with having an Active Directory domain controller.

It is important to note that other services may still require an Active Directory Domain Services environment for access to applications and **Server Message Block (SMB)**.

In this chapter, we will take a look at the following:

- Prerequisites for Azure AD join for Azure Virtual Desktop
- Deploying an Azure AD-joined host pool
- Enabling user access
- Configuring local admin access

Prerequisites

It is important to note that there are a few limitations when using Azure AD join for Azure Virtual Desktop at the time of writing. As you may know, many Microsoft services, third-party platforms, and others require access to an Active Directory environment for authentication and user/group permissions. Therefore, it is important to assess your organization's current requirements to ensure that Azure AD join is a suitable solution:

- Azure AD join is only supported when using Azure Virtual Desktop for Azure Resource Manager. The classic version of Azure Virtual Desktop is not supported.

- The session hosts must be Windows 10 Enterprise Version 2004 or later.

- Azure AD-joined VMs don't currently support external users.

> **Important Note**
>
> Azure AD join is different from an Active Directory Domain Services controller in that the session host **Virtual Machines** (**VMs**) are automatically joined with the Azure AD tenant of the subscription that deploys the VMs. There is no way to specify a different Azure AD tenant for the host VMs. This means you will need to ensure that the required Azure tenant is linked to the subscription you wish to deploy the Azure AD-joined VM to.

Let's now look at deploying an Azure AD-joined host pool.

Deploying an Azure AD-joined host pool

In this section, we will look at deploying a host pool using Azure AD join.

Before we get started, I want to cover the use of FSLogix profile containers with Azure AD join. When using Azure AD join, there are a few slight differences compared to the traditional way when using Active Directory Domain Services. The following link takes you to the Microsoft documentation detailing how to configure FSLogix profile containers with Azure Files and Azure AD. Please note this feature is in preview at the time of writing: `https://docs.microsoft.com/azure/virtual-desktop/create-profile-container-azure-ad`.

Let's now move on and look at the creation of an Azure AD-joined host pool:

1. We first need to navigate to the Azure Virtual Desktop service to get started.

2. Proceed to create a new host pool.

3. Within the host pool creation screen, under the **Virtual Machine** tab, in the **Domain to join** section, select **Azure Active Directory**:

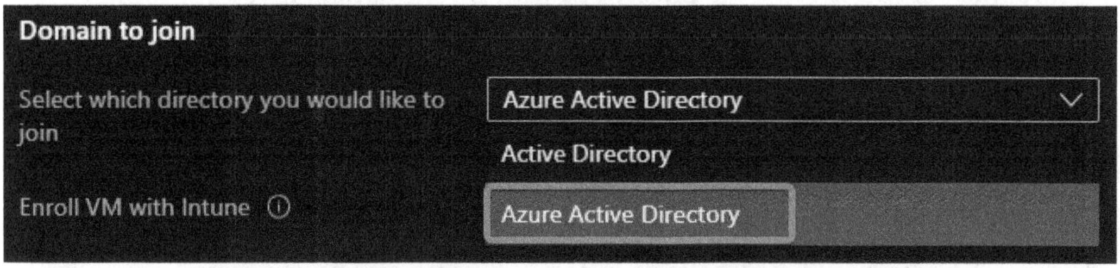

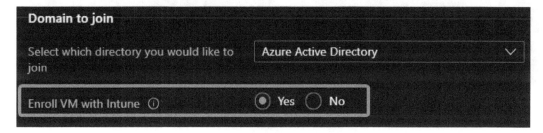

Figure 8.1 – Domain join options within the host pool creation wizard

4. When you select **Azure Active Directory**, you will see the **Enroll VM with Intune** option appear. You would use the **Enroll VM with Intune** option if you wanted to use Intune to manage policies, distribute software, and generally manage VMs:

Figure 8.2 – Screenshot showing the Enroll VM with Intune field

You can read more on Intune as a part of **Microsoft Endpoint Manager** (**MEM**) here: https://techcommunity.microsoft.com/t5/intune-customer-success/getting-started-with-microsoft-endpoint-manager/ba-p/2497614.

> **Important Note**
> You need to ensure that you have set up MEM before using the **Enroll VM with Intune** feature; otherwise, the host pool deployment will fail.

5. Once the deployment has finished, you should see an extension called **AADLoginForWindows**, which is used to create the Azure AD join and Intune enrollment if you selected the **Enroll VM with Intune** option. If you choose not to use Intune enrollment, you will need to configure customizations and policies locally using a master image:

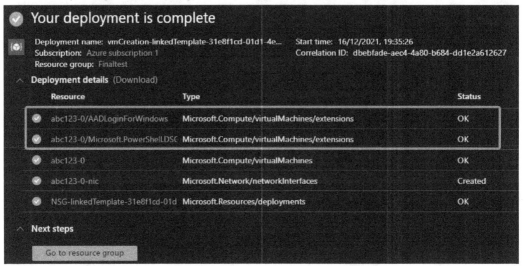

Figure 8.3 – Azure AD-joined host pool deployment successful

6. Once the deployment has been completed, you will see the device registered within Azure AD under **Devices | All Devices**, as shown in the following screenshot:

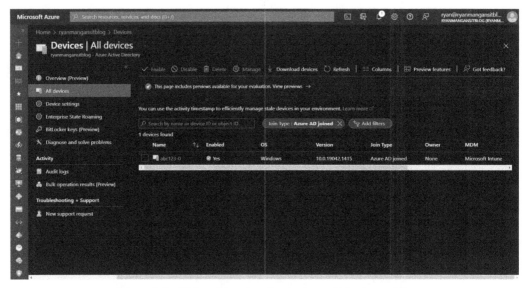

Figure 8.4 – VM registered under devices within Azure AD

7.   The device will also appear in MEM if enrolled with Intune:

Figure 8.5 – Endpoint Manager | All Devices

8.   You will also see the Azure AD registration within the **Audit logs** section when you navigate to **Azure Active Directory | Devices | Audit logs**, as shown in the following screenshot:

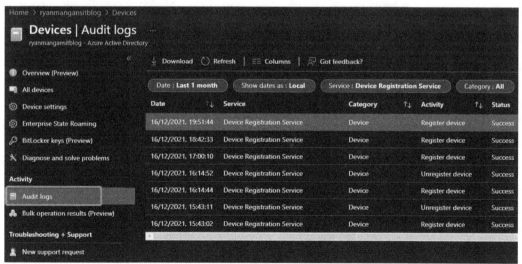

Figure 8.6 – Azure AD device registrations within the Audit logs section

9. If the VM does not appear to enroll or you would like to confirm enrollment, you can log in locally to the VM and use the following command using an elevated Command Prompt: `dsregcmd /status`:

Figure 8.7 – The dsregcmd /status command

10. Finally, you can also check the event logs using Event Viewer. The Azure AD registration logs are in the following section of Event Viewer: **Applications and Services Logs** | **Microsoft** | **Windows** | **User Device Registration** | **Admin**:

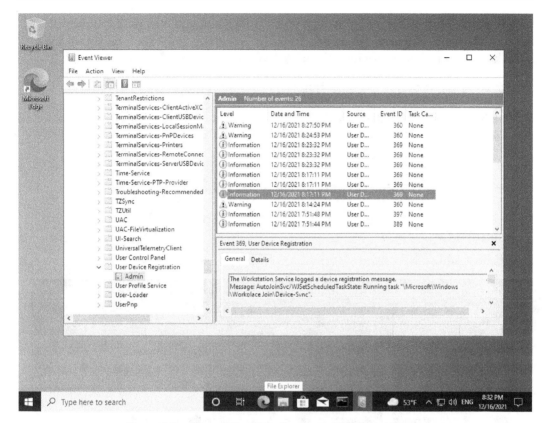

Figure 8.8 – Azure AD registration logs within Event Viewer

Now that we have deployed the Azure AD-joined host pool, we will now take a look at enabling access for users in the next section.

Enabling user access

Before users can sign in to the session hosts within the Azure AD-joined host pool, you must configure the required permission using **Role-Based Access Control** (**RBAC**). First, we need to add the required users and Azure AD groups to the host pool default desktop application group. We also need to add the **Virtual Machine User Login** RBAC role.

> **Important Note**
>
> The **Virtual Machine User Login** RBAC role is not an Azure Virtual Desktop role. This is required to enable access to sign in to a VM. The Azure role enables logon by applying the DataAction permission.

Depending on your requirements and host pool deployment, you may want to review the scope for this role. For example, assigning an Azure AD group at the resource group level may make more sense than assigning the RBAC role for each user per VM.

> **Important Note**
>
> It is not advised to set the **Virtual Machine User Login** RBAC role at the subscription level; you would essentially give all assigned users the ability to sign in to all VMs within the subscription.

To assign the **Virtual Machine User Login** role, do the following:

1. Go to your host pool resource group in the Azure portal and select **Access control (IAM)**.

2. Select **+ Add**:

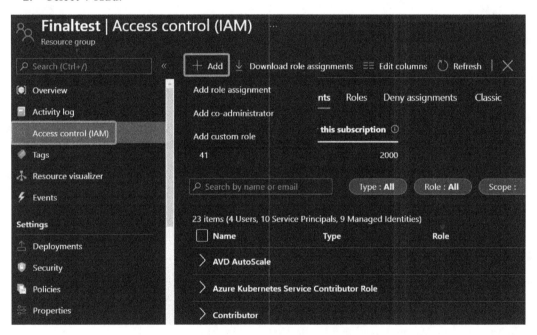

Figure 8.9 – The + Add button

3. On the **Add role assignment** page, select **Virtual Machine User Login**:

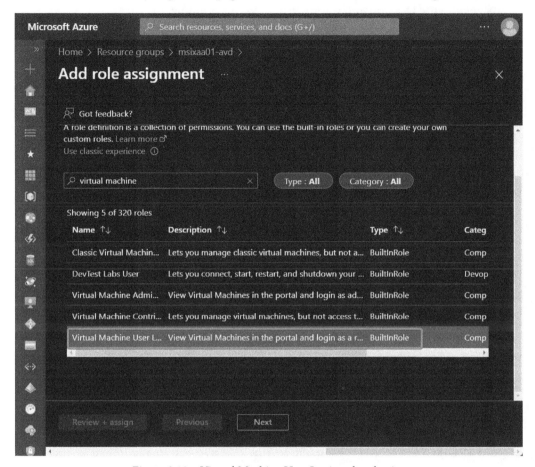

Figure 8.10 – Virtual Machine User Login role selection

4. Under **Members**, click **Select members** and select the required user group assigned to the Desktop application group; in this example, the user group is called `AZJoingroup`:

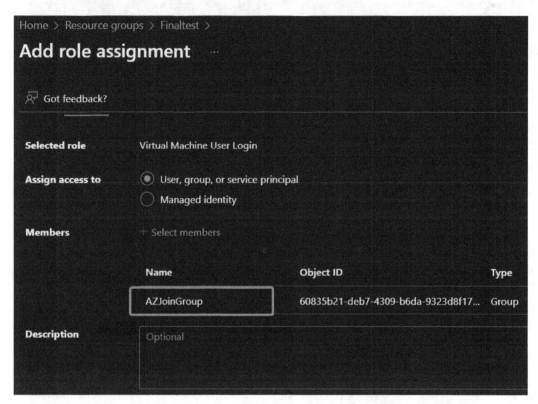

Figure 8.11 – The Add role assignment screen with the AZJoinGroup group added as a member

5. Click **Review + assign**.

6. You should now see **Virtual Machine User Login** appear on the **Access Control (IAM)** page, as shown in the following screenshot:

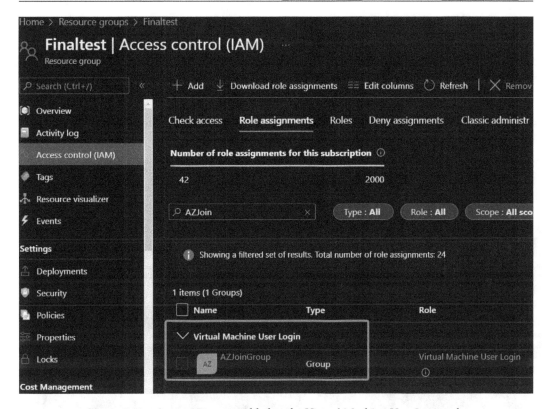

Figure 8.12 – Azure AD group added to the Virtual Machine User Login role

This section looked at assigning the **Virtual Machine User Login** role to give Azure user accounts access to VMs. In the next section, we will look at connecting to session hosts using the Windows Remote Desktop client.

Connect to Azure AD-joined session hosts using the Remote Desktop client

Before you can sign in to your Azure Virtual Desktop Azure AD-joined session host, you must ensure your local PC meets the following requirements:

- The local PC is Azure AD-joined to the same Azure AD tenant used for Azure Virtual Desktop.

- The local PC is hybrid AD-joined to the same Azure AD tenant used for Azure Virtual Desktop.

- You are using Windows 10 build 2004 or later and Azure AD registered with the same Azure AD tenant for Azure Virtual Desktop.

If you do not meet the preceding criteria, you can enable the RDSTLS protocol, an enhanced RDP security protocol. You can read more on RDSTLS here: `https://docs.microsoft.com/openspecs/windows_protocols/ms-rdpbcgr/83d1186d-cab6-4ad8-8c5f-203f95e192aa`.

You can add the RDSTLS protocol using a custom RDP property with the host pool: `targetisaddjoined:i:1`. You will also need to use the same custom RDP property when using web, Android, macOS, and iOS clients:

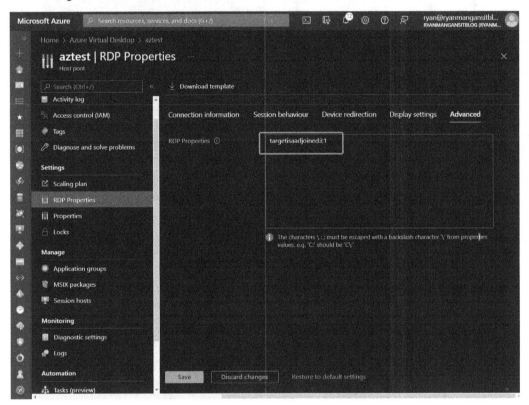

Figure 8.13 – Custom RDP property targetisaddjoined:i:1

Azure AD join host pool access uses the **Public Key User to User** (PKU2U) protocol for authentication. To sign in, both the session host and the local PC must have PKU2U set to **Enabled**. If you are using Windows 10 build 2004 or later, you can enable the protocol by following these steps:

1. Open Regedit and navigate to **HKLM | SYSTEM | CurrentControlSet | Control | Lsa | pku2u**.

2. Set **AllowOnlineID** to **1**.

You can also set this using Group Policy by completing the following steps:

1. Open either the local **Group Policy Object** (**GPO**) or create a GPO within Group Policy.

2. Navigate to **Computer Configuration | Policies | Windows Settings | Security Settings | Local Policies | Security Options**.

3. Under **Policy**, set **Network Security**: **Allow PKU2U authentication requests to this computer to use online identities** to **Enabled**.

In the next section, we will take a brief look at configuring local admin access when using Azure AD join.

Configuring local admin access

To give the user local admin access to a VM, you will need to assign the **Virtual Machine Administrator Login** role to the VM using the same process as shown in the *Enabling user access* section.

> **Important Note**
>
> It is recommended that you only assign users to the required VMs when assigning the **Virtual Machine User Login** role. For example, if you assign this role to a group at the subscription level, all users within the group would have local admin rights to all the VMs. This is not a recommended approach.

You can add the required user to the **Virtual Machine Administrator Login** role as shown in the following screenshot:

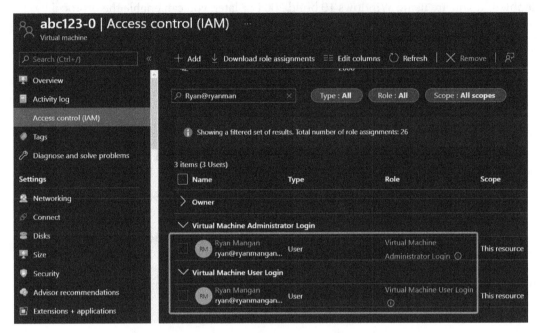

Figure 8.14 – Virtual Machine Administrator Login role assigned to the VM

Once you have added the required permissions, you should see the user account now logs in as an administrator:

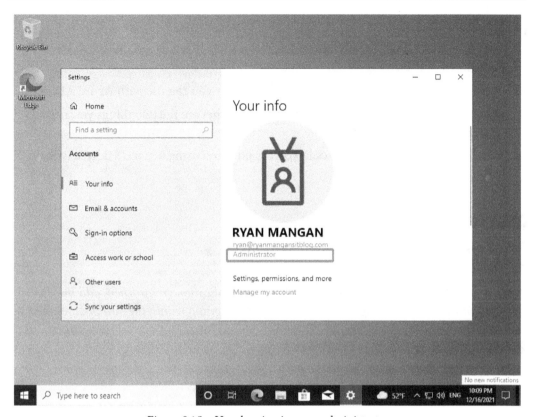

Figure 8.15 – User logging in as an administrator

This brief section looked at assigning local admin rights to an Azure AD-joined host pool.

Summary

This chapter looked at the Azure AD join feature for Azure Virtual Desktop. First, we looked at the prerequisites, then we studied deploying an Azure AD-joined host pool, and we finished off the chapter by looking at applying the required permissions and setting the custom RDP property for access on devices that are not Azure AD-joined or hybrid domain-joined. In the next chapter, we will take a look at creating and managing Session Host images.

Questions

1. Which command would you use to check to see whether a session host is Azure AD-joined?

2. What is the minimum version of Windows 10 that you can use with Azure AD join?

3. After deploying an Azure AD-joined host pool, what are the two things you need to do regarding permissions?

4. What custom RDP property should you assign when using a macOS device with an Azure AD-joined host pool?

Answers

1. `dsregcmd /status`

2. *Windows 10 Enterprise build 2004*

3. *Add the Azure AD group to the default desktop application group. Then, add the Virtual Machine User Login role for the Azure AD group within the host pool resource group.*

4. `targetisaddjoined:i:1`

9
Creating and Managing Session Host Images

In this chapter, we will look at creating a custom image that we can use with Azure Virtual Desktop and some of the customization, updates, and publishing capabilities that are available in the Azure Compute gallery. It is important to note that the images for Azure Virtual Desktop are one of its core components as this is what the user will access. It's important to ensure that you configure and optimize them correctly so that you provide a good user experience. We will also take a look at troubleshooting some of the **Operating System (OS)** issues related to Azure Virtual Desktop.

In this chapter, we will cover the following topics:

- Creating a gold image
- Modifying a Session Host image
- Creating and using an **Azure Compute Gallery (ACG)**
- Troubleshooting OS issues related to Azure Virtual Desktop

Creating a gold image

In this section, we will look at provisioning a **virtual machine (VM)** in Microsoft Azure and preparing it for Azure Virtual Desktop.

Creating a VM

To create a standardized template image for Azure Virtual Desktop, you will need to spin up a VM. In this section, we will look at doing just that.

To get started, you will need to navigate to the Azure portal at `https://portal.azure.com`. From there, follow these steps:

1. Type `virtual machines` in the search bar located at the top of the page.

2. Under **Services**, select **Virtual machines**.

3. On the **Virtual machines** page, select **Add** and then **Virtual machine**:

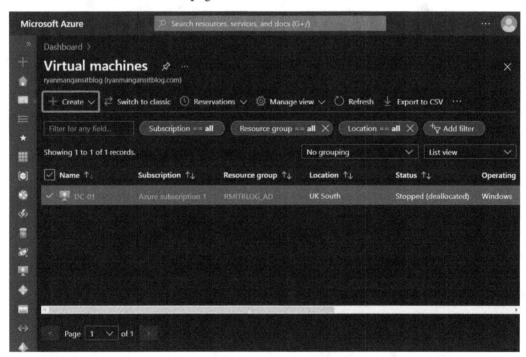

Figure 9.1 – The Virtual machines page

4. Under **Project details**, select the correct subscription and then choose to create a new resource group in the **Basics** tab. Type `myResourceGroup` for **Name**:

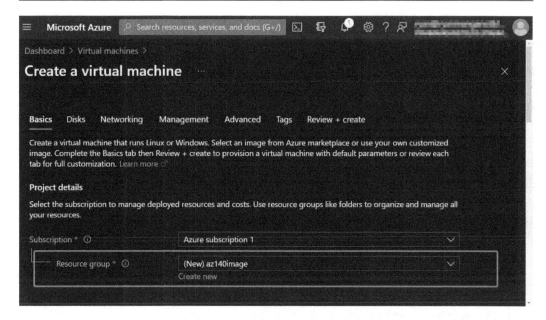

Figure 9.2 – The Create a virtual machine page

5. Under **Instance details**, enter a name under **Virtual machine name** and choose your required **Region**. Next, choose **Windows 10 Enterprise Multi-Session** for **Image** and select the required VM **Size**. Leave the other options as-is:

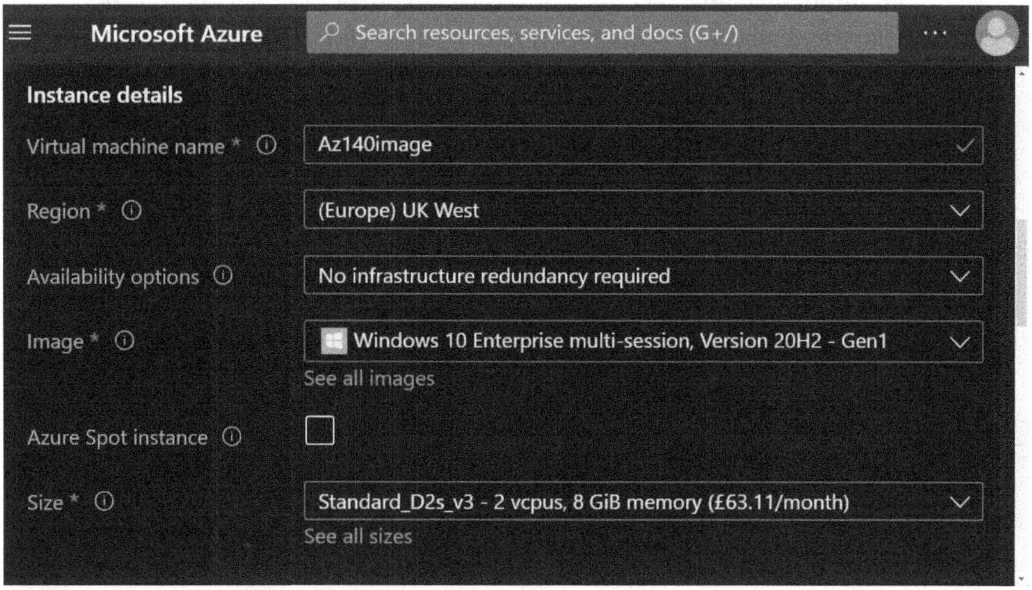

Figure 9.3 – Instance details when creating a virtual machine

6. Under **Administrator account**, enter a username and a password:

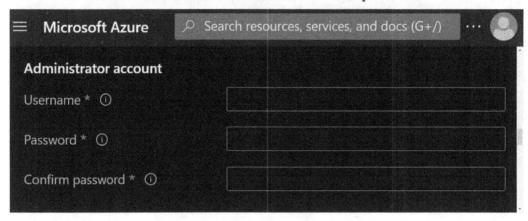

Figure 9.4 – The Administrator account section

> **Tip**
> Your password must be at least 12 characters long and meet the required
> complexity. For more information, go to `https://docs.microsoft.`
> `com/azure/virtual-machines/windows/faq#what-are-`
> `the-password-requirements-when-creating-a-vm-`.

7. Under **Inbound port rules**, choose **Allow selected ports** and then select **RDP
    (3389)** from the dropdown:

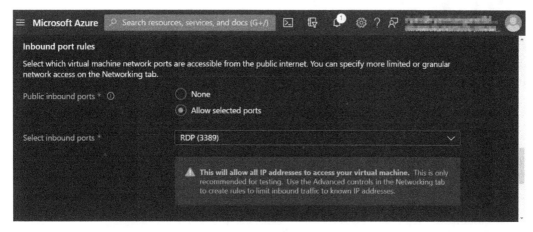

Figure 9.5 – Inbound port rules

8. Confirm the license eligibility for Windows 10 and click the **Review + create** button at the bottom of the page:

Figure 9.6 – Deployment is in progress

9. Once the deployment has finished, navigate to the VM by clicking **Go to the resource**.

Once you have created the VM, you are ready to connect to it.

Connecting to the VM

You can connect to an Azure VM using a remote desktop connection. You have two options – you can connect using a direct connection via a public IP address or connect using the local private IP address behind a VPN connection. Let's get started:

1. Navigate to the overview page of the VM you just deployed, select the **Connect** button, and then select **RDP**:

> **Important**
>
> Even though this section shows you how to connect using RDP via a public IP address, it is recommended that you connect over a VPN connection or Azure Bastion.
>
> In *Chapter 4, Implementing and Managing Networking for Azure Virtual Desktop*, we learned how to configure Azure Bastion. It is recommended that you use Azure Bastion as RDP is insecure.

Figure 9.7 – Using the Connect button to download an RDP file for the VM

2. On the **Connect with RDP** page, keep the default options to connect by IP address, over port 3389, as-is, and click **Download RDP file**:

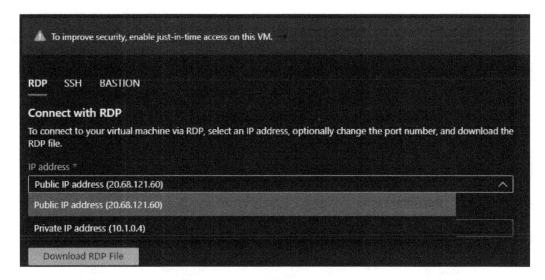

Figure 9.8 – The public and private IP address options for the RDP file

3.   Open the downloaded RDP file and click **Connect** when prompted:

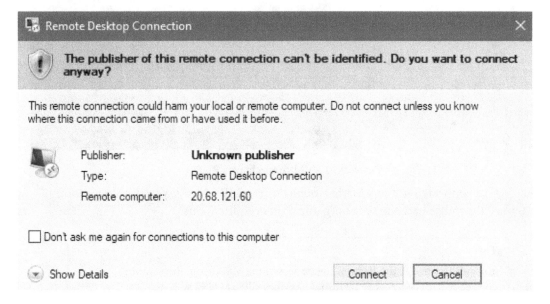

Figure 9.9 – RDP file connecting to the virtual machine

Once connected to the RDP session, you will see the session appear, as shown in the following screenshot:

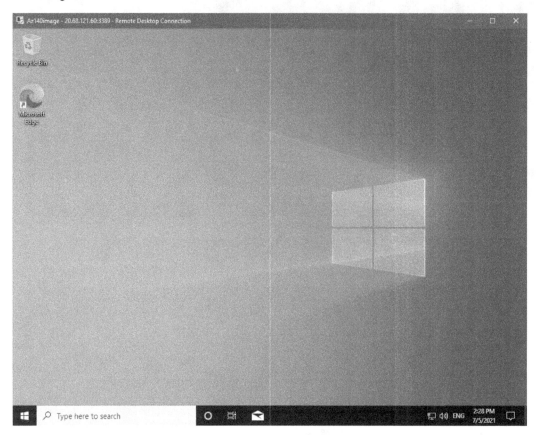

Figure 9.10 – VM connected via RDP

Once you've connected to the VM via a public or local IP address, you can then modify/customize the image based on your organization's requirements.

> **Tip**
>
> You can also use Azure Bastion to connect to the VM if you don't want to connect via the **Microsoft Terminal Services Client** (**MSTSC**).

In the next section, we are going to learn how to modify a Session Host image, including customizing and optimizing it.

Modifying a Session Host image

In this section, we will look at some of the *customizations/optimizations* you can apply to an image for Azure virtual Desktop.

> **Tip**
>
> When you're using Windows 10 Multi-Session images from Azure Gallery, FSLogix profile containers come pre-installed. It's recommended that you use an Azure Gallery template when possible.

Disabling automatic updates

When you're using pooled desktops, images are typically deployed centrally. First, updates are completed on the master image, and then VMs are redeployed to the host pool on the next scheduled maintenance window.

You should consider disabling Windows updates for Azure Virtual Desktop images as these should be carried out on the master image during a maintenance window. This enables control over patch updates and consistency through the deployed virtual desktop estate.

You may also want to consider configuring a validation environment, as discussed in *Chapter 7, Configuring Azure Virtual Desktop Host Pools*.

You can disable automatic updates directly on the Windows image using Regedit:

```
reg add "HKLM\SOFTWARE\Policies\Microsoft\Windows\
WindowsUpdate\AU" /v NoAutoUpdate /t REG_DWORD /d 1 /f
```

Alternatively, you can use a Group Policy to apply the same change, as detailed in the following steps:

1. Open **Local Group Policy Editor | Administrative Templates | Windows Components | Windows Update**.

2. Right-click **Configure Automatic Update** and set it to **Disabled**.

Now, let's install some language packs that we can use on the Azure Virtual Desktop image.

Installing language packs in Azure Virtual Desktop

To use multiple languages within Azure Virtual Desktop, you need to ensure that all the required languages are installed.

> **Tip**
>
> Windows 11 onwards will only allow language packs to be distributed as `.cab` files, which can be used for imaging. LIP languages that aren't distributed as `.cab` files will only be available as `.appx` packages, which can be acquired through the **Settings** app after logging in.

Before you start customizing your image with multiple languages, you will need to download the required files for the language configuration; these can be found at the following links:

- Language ISO files: `https://software-download.microsoft.com/download/pr/19041.1.191206-1406.vb_release_CLIENTLANGPACKDVD_OEM_MULTI.iso`

- Feature on-demand disk: `https://software-download.microsoft.com/download/pr/19041.1.191206-1406.vb_release_amd64fre_FOD-PACKAGES_OEM_PT1_amd64fre_MULTI.iso`

- Inbox Apps ISO for Windows 10, version 21H1: `https://software-download.microsoft.com/download/sg/19041.928.210407-2138.vb_release_svc_prod1_amd64fre_InboxApps.iso`

> **Important Note**
>
> Please note that the inbox apps that are included in the ISO are not the latest versions of the pre-installed Windows apps. You will need to update the apps using the Windows Store App and perform a manual search for updates after installing the additional languages.
>
> You can find all the language ISO files here: `https://docs.microsoft.com/azure/virtual-desktop/language-packs#prerequisites`.

When you're installing languages on Windows 10 version 2004, 20H2, and 21H1, it's recommended that you check the known issues to ensure you choose the correct ISO: `https://docs.microsoft.com/en-us/windows-hardware/manufacture/desktop/language-packs-known-issue`.

> **Tip**
>
> You can read more about language packs here: `https://docs.`
> `microsoft.com/en-gb/azure/virtual-desktop/`
> `language-packs`.

The following summary steps will show you how to create a custom Windows 10 Enterprise Multi-Session image and connect the repository as a drive letter:

1. Deploy an Azure VM, as shown previously. Then, go to Azure Gallery and select the current version of Windows 10 Enterprise Multi-Session that you plan on using.

2. Once you have deployed the VM, connect to the VM using RDP as a local administrator.

3. Make sure that your VM has all the latest Windows updates installed. Then, download the updates and restart the VM, if required.

4. Connect to the language package, features on-demand, and Inbox Apps file share repository and mount it to a letter drive (for example, drive Z). Note that you can use it on the root of C:\ if you have a large OS drive.

> **Important Note**
>
> Please note that the script should be customized to your needs and requirements. Running the entire script can take some time to complete.
>
> You can find the script for adding languages to run Windows images here: `https://github.com/PacktPublishing/Remote-`
> `Productivity-with-Windows-Virtual-Desktop/blob/`
> `main/B17392_07/Languages_winimage.ps1/`.

Once the script has finished running, you can check that the language packs have been installed correctly by navigating to **Start** | **Settings** | **Time & Language** | **Language**. If the language files have been installed, you will see them here.

Once you have confirmed that the licenses have been installed, you can install the inbox apps for each required language. Then, you can update the inbox apps by refreshing the pre-installed apps using the inbox app's ISO image. You can use the PowerShell script template to automate this process and update only the installed versions for the inbox apps with no internet access: `https://github.com/PacktPublishing/Remote-`
`Productivity-with-Windows-Virtual-Desktop/blob/main/B17392_07/`
`Update%20inbox%20Apps%20for%20Multi%20Language.ps1`.

Once you have finished, make sure that you disconnect the share you attached previously (for example, drive Z).

Tip

To ensure that modern apps can use the additional language packs, you should use the following PowerShell cmdlet, which is used to disable language pack cleanup:

```
Disable-ScheduledTask -TaskPath "\Microsoft\
Windows\AppxDeploymentClient\" -TaskName "Pre-
staged app cleanup"
```

You can also find this within the example script provided here: `https://
github.com/PacktPublishing/Remote-Productivity-
with-Windows-Virtual-Desktop/blob/main/B17392_07/
Languages_winimage.ps1/`.

Now, let's learn how to optimize an image.

Optimizing an image

In this section, we will look at two ways to optimize Azure Virtual Desktop images. Optimizing an image can improve the user experience for Azure Virtual Desktop users and can also improve user density per Session Host.

Important Note

Remember, turning off/disabling features and services can impact the functionality and behavior of the user desktop and applications that are running. Make sure that you fully understand what you are optimizing before applying it.

Using the VMware OS Optimization Tool

The VMware OS Optimization Tool allows you to analyze the current optimization state and available optimizations. You can even take a backup, which will allow you to roll back the changes you make.

To get started, download the VMware Optimization Tool by going to `https://flings.vmware.com/vmware-os-optimization-tool`:

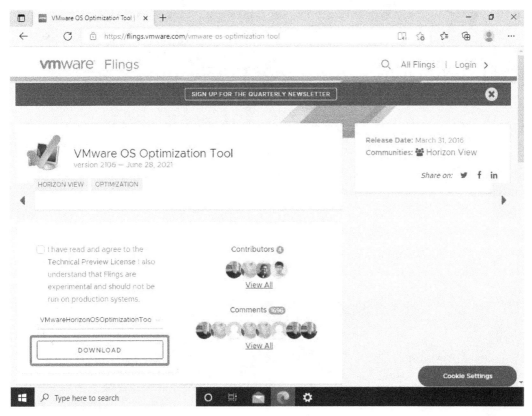

Figure 9.11 – VMware Flings download page for the Vmware OS Optimization Tool

Once it's been downloaded, run the application:

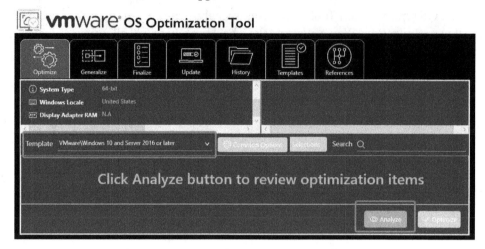

Figure 9.12 – Main page of VMware's OS Optimization Tool

You will be presented with the screen shown in the preceding screenshot. Next, select the required template and click **Analyze**.

Once the application has finished reviewing the configurations, you will see an analysis summary and several optimizations that you can apply. Once you have finished choosing the required optimizations for your image, you can go ahead and click on **Optimize**, which is located in the bottom right-hand corner, as shown in the following screenshot:

Figure 9.13 – The Analyze page of the VMware OS Optimization Tool

Once you have clicked **Optimize** and the process has finished, you will see a table of optimizations that have been applied to the image, as shown in the following screenshot:

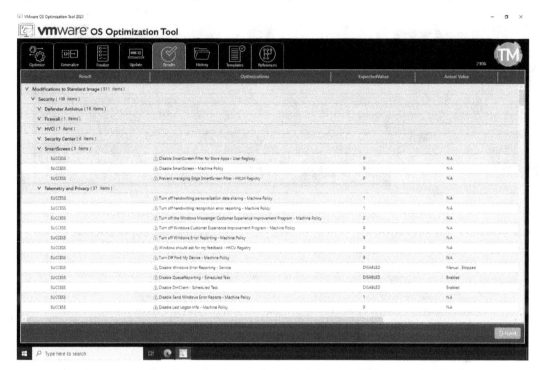

Figure 9.14 – Post-optimization results of the VMware OS Optimization Tool

If you need to roll back the configurations to the previous state, you can complete this by following these steps:

1. Click on **History**.

2. Select the template at the date and time you want to roll back to.

3. Click **rollback**.

The following screenshot shows these three steps, numbered as *1*, *2*, and *3*:

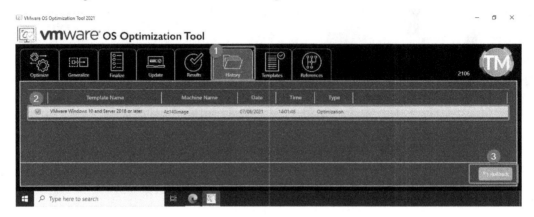

Figure 9.15 – History of the VMware OS Optimization Tool

There you have it. I have shown you how to analyze the current state, apply a set of optimizations, and roll them back if required.

> **Tip**
>
> You can export your selections using the **Export selections** button for future image creation. This means that you can import a different image into the VMware OS Optimization Tool and maintain optimizations from a previously tested configuration.

Virtual Desktop Optimization Tool

The second option would be to use the optimization tool and a set of PowerShell scripts that you can run on the template image to configure optimizations for the Virtual Desktop image.

You can access these scripts by going to the following GitHub repository `https://github.com/The-Virtual-Desktop-Team/Virtual-Desktop-Optimization-Tool`.

First, you will need to download the scripts from the aforementioned GitHub repository. Once you've downloaded them, you must find the build version of your OS – for example, `C:\temp\optfiles\ConfigurationFiles` – and change the required settings to **Enabled** (default) or **Disabled**. The following screenshot provides an example of the JSON configuration file for `AppxPackages.json`:

```
 1   □ [
 2   □   {
 3          "AppxPackage": "Microsoft.OneConnect",
 4          "VDIState": "Disabled",
 5          "URL": "https://www.microsoft.com/en-us/p/mobile-plans/9nblggh5pnb1",
 6          "Description": "Microsoft Mobile Plans app"
 7      },
 8   □   {
 9          "AppxPackage": "Microsoft.MSPaint",
10          "VDIState": "Enabled",
11          "URL": "https://www.microsoft.com/en-us/p/paint-3d/9nblggh5fv99",
12          "Description": "Paint 3D"
13      },
14   □   {
15          "AppxPackage": "Microsoft.BingWeather",
16          "VDIState": "Disabled",
17          "URL": "https://www.microsoft.com/en-us/p/msn-weather/9wzdncrfj3q2",
18          "Description": "MSN Weather app"
19      },
```

Figure 9.16 – Snippet of the AppxPackages.json file

Once you have finished customizing the configuration files, you need to run the optimization script using PowerShell.

First, open PowerShell as an administrator, then set the execution policy to Bypass:

```
Set-ExecutionPolicy -ExecutionPolicy Bypass
```

The following screenshot shows the set execution policy's bypass cmdlets that have been run:

```
Copyright (C) Microsoft Corporation. All rights reserved.

Try the new cross-platform PowerShell https://aka.ms/pscore6

PS C:\Users\sysadmin> Set-ExecutionPolicy -ExecutionPolicy Bypass

Execution Policy Change
The execution policy helps protect you from scripts that you do not trust. Changing the execution policy might
expose
you to the security risks described in the about_Execution_Policies help topic at
https:/go.microsoft.com/fwlink/?LinkID=135170. Do you want to change the execution policy?
[Y] Yes  [A] Yes to All  [N] No  [L] No to All  [S] Suspend  [?] Help (default is "N"): Y
PS C:\Users\sysadmin>
PS C:\Users\sysadmin>
PS C:\Users\sysadmin> _
```

Figure 9.17 – The set-execution policy cmdlet being run

Once set, you need to run the script. Remember to use the required Windows version you are using. In this example, you will note that -WindowsVersion is 2004:

```
.\Win10_VirtualDesktop_Optimize.ps1 -WindowsVersion 2004
-Verbose
```

The following screenshot shows the script being run and that the optimization process is in progress, as denoted by the progress bar:

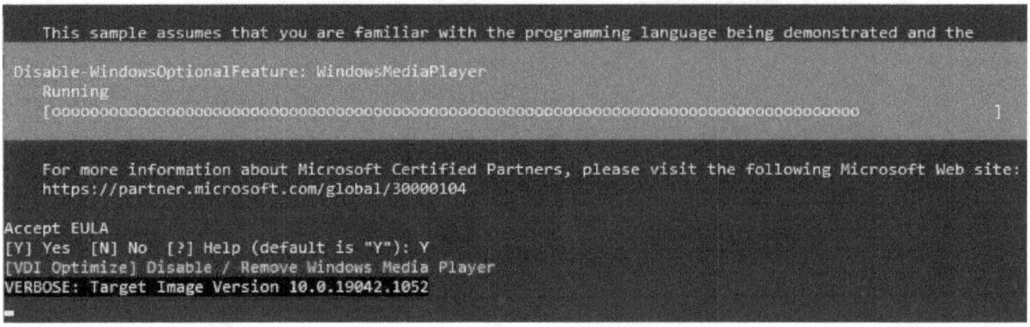

```
This sample assumes that you are familiar with the programming language being demonstrated and the

Disable-WindowsOptionalFeature: WindowsMediaPlayer
    Running
    [ooooooooooooooooooooooooooooooooooooooooooooooooooooooooooooooooooooooooooooooooooooooooo                    ]


    For more information about Microsoft Certified Partners, please visit the following Microsoft Web site:
    https://partner.microsoft.com/global/30000104

Accept EULA
[Y] Yes  [N] No  [?] Help (default is "Y"): Y
[VDI Optimize] Disable / Remove Windows Media Player
VERBOSE: Target Image Version 10.0.19042.1052
```

Figure 9.18 – Optimization script running

Once complete, the script will finish and prompt you to reboot:

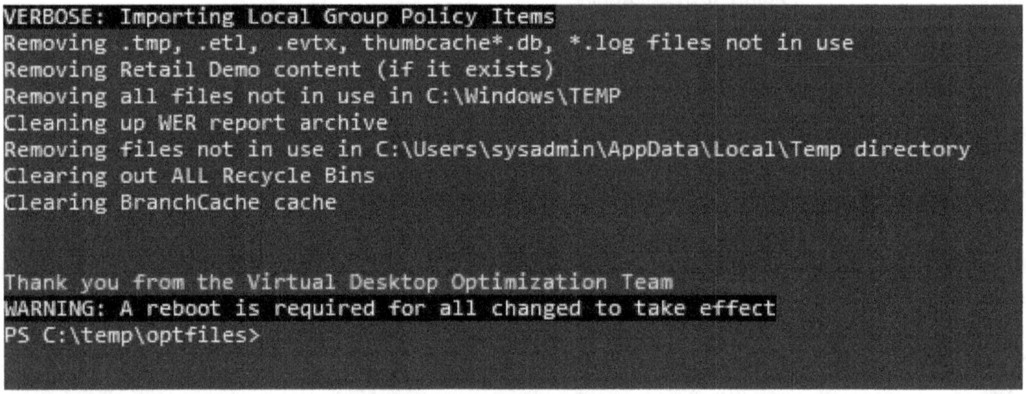

```
VERBOSE: Importing Local Group Policy Items
Removing .tmp, .etl, .evtx, thumbcache*.db, *.log files not in use
Removing Retail Demo content (if it exists)
Removing all files not in use in C:\Windows\TEMP
Cleaning up WER report archive
Removing files not in use in C:\Users\sysadmin\AppData\Local\Temp directory
Clearing out ALL Recycle Bins
Clearing BranchCache cache


Thank you from the Virtual Desktop Optimization Team
WARNING: A reboot is required for all changed to take effect
PS C:\temp\optfiles>
```

Figure 9.19 – Optimization script finished

Once you have rebooted, you may notice that the processes and threads may have reduced within the **TaskManager** | **Performance** tab.

The following screenshot shows the number of processes and threads before optimization:

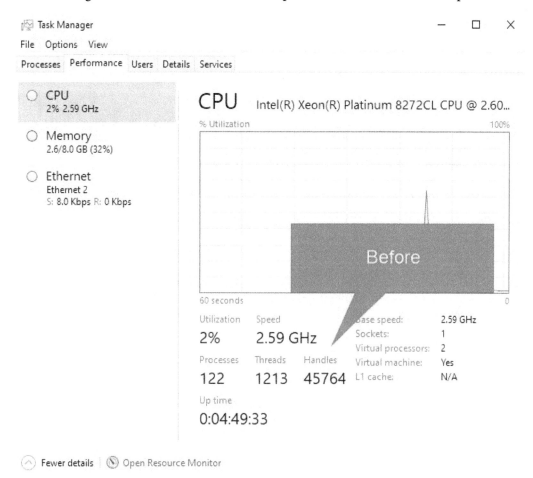

Figure 9.20 – The number of processes, threads, and handles before optimization

The following optimization screenshot shows a reduction in processes, threads, and handles:

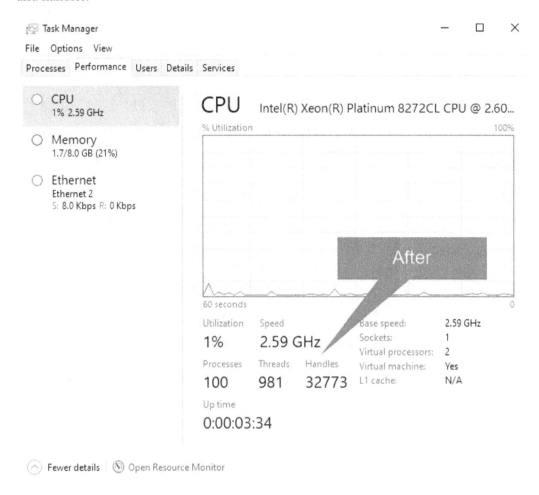

Figure 9.21 – The number of processes, threads, and handles after optimization

> **Important Note**
> The Azure Virtual Desktop optimization script is community-driven and not supported by Microsoft.

Remember, optimizations have an impact on the user experience and some can be difficult to restore. So, ensure you create a snapshot before applying such changes to your image as it is not as easy to roll back using the Virtual Desktop optimization script.

In the next section, we will look at capturing an image template.

Capturing an image template

In this section, we will look at capturing an image template so that you can distribute the same image across multiple hosts within a host pool or even multiple host pools.

Important Note

Before you capture a VM in an image, make sure that you run the following command first:

```
C:\Windows\System32\Sysprep\Sysprep.exe /oobe /
generalise/shutdown
```

Once you've run this, make sure that the VM has been stopped in Azure. Then, you can proceed with the capture process.

It is also important to note that installing Microsoft Store apps or updating existing Store apps before generalizing a Windows image can cause Sysprep to fail. Sysprep also requires all apps to be provisioned for all users. When you update an app from the Microsoft Store, that application will become associated with the user account. You will then see the following error message:

```
<package name> was installed for a user, but not
provisioned for all users. This package will not
function properly in the Sysprep image.
```

This will be located within the Sysprep log file, here: `%WINDIR%\System32\Sysprep\Panther`.

You can read more about Sysprep here: `https://docs.microsoft.com/windows-hardware/manufacture/desktop/Sysprep--generalize--a-windows-installation?view=windows-11`.

To capture a template, follow these steps:

1. First, you need to navigate to the Azure portal (`https://portal.azure.com/`) to manage the VM image. Then, search for and select **Virtual machines**.
2. Select your VM from the **Virtual Machine** list.

3. On the **Virtual machines** page for the VM, go to the top menu and click the **Capture** button:

Figure 9.22 – The Capture button located within the VMs page

The **Create image** page will then appear.

4. For **Name**, use the pre-populated name or enter a new name that you would like to use for the image:

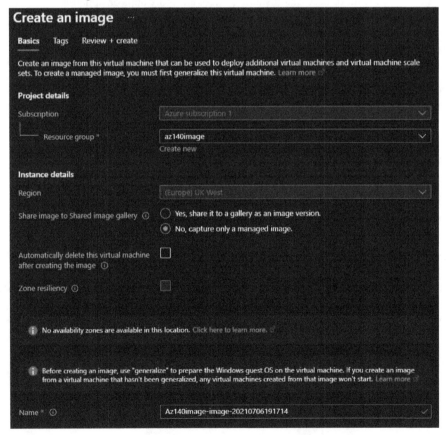

Figure 9.23 – The Create an image page within the Azure portal

For **Resource group**, use the existing one, select one from the dropdown, or create a new one.

5. For **Instance details**, ensure you select the **No, capture only a managed image within the share image** option to create a managed image only.

6. To delete the source VM once the image has been created, select **Automatically delete this virtual machine after creating the Image**.

7. If you want to use the image in any availability zone, select **On** for **Zone resiliency**.

8. Select **Create** to create the image; this will start the image creation process.

9. Once the image has been created, you can find it as an image resource in the list of resources in the resource group:

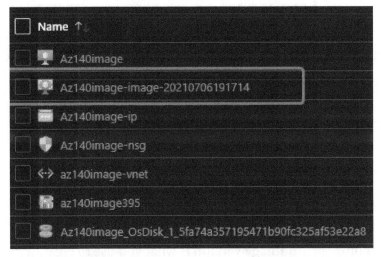

Figure 9.24 – Image created – post-creation process

In this section, we created an image from a VM and customized it. I will now show you how to create and use an Azure Compute Gallery.

Creating and using an Azure Compute Gallery (ACG)

A **Shared Image Gallery** (**SIG**) is a service that distributes images that can be shared across multiple regions and subscriptions within an **Azure Active Directory** (**AAD**) tenant. This is extremely useful for Azure Virtual Desktop as SIGs enable easy deployment of standard company desktop/server image templates across multiple Azure Regions. One of the other benefits of SIGs is that you can have different image versions and the newest can be referenced easily.

The following table details the different resource types within a SIG:

> **Tip**
> It is recommended that you become familiar with the terms within the following table before continuing.

Resource	Description
Image source	This is a resource that can be used to create an **image version** in an image gallery. An image source can be an existing Azure VM that is either generalized or specialized, a managed image, a snapshot, or an image version in another image gallery.
Image gallery	Like the Azure Marketplace, an **image gallery** is a repository for managing and sharing images, but you control who has access to it.
Image definition	Image definitions are created within a gallery and carry information about the image and the requirements for using it internally. This includes whether the image is for Windows or Linux, release notes, and the minimum and maximum memory requirements. It is a definition of a type of image.
Image version	An **image version** is what you use to create a VM when you're using a gallery. You can have multiple versions of an image as needed for your environment. Like a managed image, when you use an **image version** to create a VM; the image version creates new disks for the VM. Image versions can be used multiple times.

The preceding table was taken from Microsoft's documentation: `https://docs.microsoft.com/en-us/azure/virtual-machines/windows/shared-images-portal`.

This section provided an overview of ACG and some of the specific terms that are used. In the next section, we will look at creating an ACG.

Creating your first Azure Compute Gallery

In this section, you will learn how to create an ACG, ready for you to capture an image inside it:

> **Important Note**
>
> SIG has been renamed **Azure Compute Gallery (ACG)**. Note that some of the new names have not been fully updated on the Microsoft documentation site. You can read more here: `https://docs.microsoft.com/azure/virtual-machines/create-gallery`.

1. Sign into the Azure portal by going to `https://portal.azure.com`.

2. Type **Azure Compute Gallery** in the search box and select **Azure Compute Gallery** from the results.

3. On the **Azure compute galleries** page, click the **Add** button:

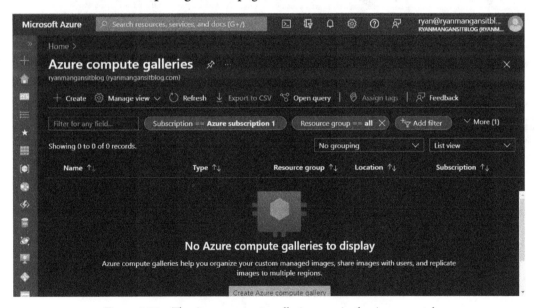

Figure 9.25 – The Azure compute galleries page in the Azure portal

4. On the **Create Azure compute gallery** page, ensure you select the correct subscription.

5. For **Resource group**, select **Create new** and enter the required resource group name.

6. For **Name**, provide a name for the name of the gallery.

7. Choose the required **Region**.

8. You can enter a short description of the gallery, such as it being a desktop VM gallery, for testing purposes:

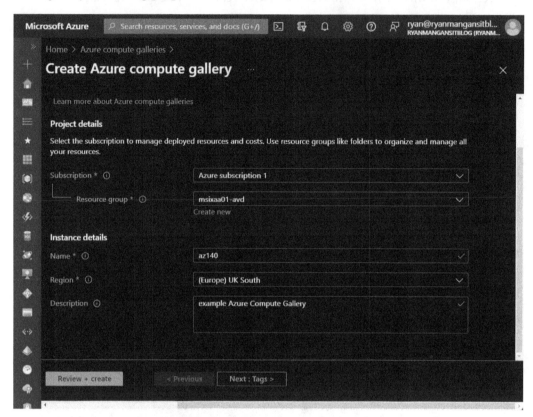

Figure 9.26 – The Create Azure compute gallery page

9. Then, click **Review + create**.

10. Once the validation process has been completed, select **Create**.

11. Once the deployment has finished, select **Go** to be taken to the resource. This will open ACG:

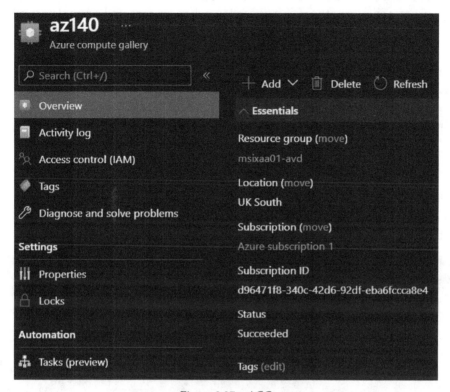

Figure 9.27 – ACG

There you have it; we have now created an ACG and are ready to add image definitions. In the next section, we will capture an image in an ACG and create an image definition and our first version.

Capturing an image in an Azure Compute Gallery

In this section, we will capture an image in the ACG we created previously. Similar to the capture process shown in the previous section, when we captured a template, we can capture the image from a generalized VM within the **Virtual machines** page:

> **Important Note**
>
> What does a generalized VM mean? Before you can deploy a Windows image to your Azure Virtual Desktop environment, you need to run a process called Generalize. This essentially removes computer-specific information such as the computer's **security identifier (SID)** and other items, such as drivers. This process enables you to turn the OS into a deployable template.

1. Select your VM from the **Virtual Machine** list.

2. On the **Virtual machines** page for the VM, from the top menu, click the **Capture** button:

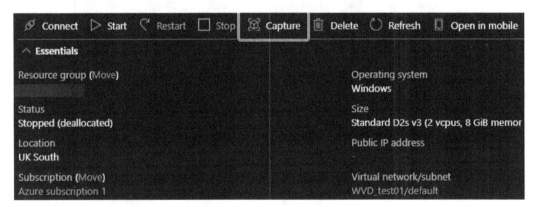

Figure 9.28 – The Capture button on the VMs page in the Azure portal

3. The **Create image** page will appear.

4. Select the required resource group and ensure you select **Yes** to share the image to your ACG:

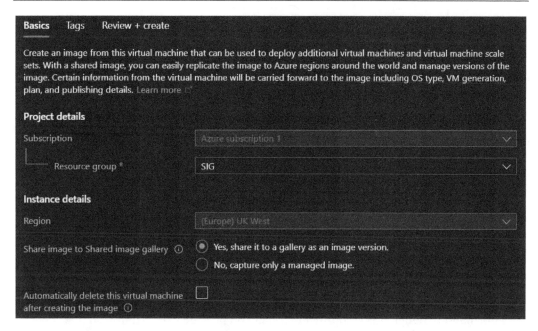

Figure 9.29 – The Capture page for capturing an image in an ACG

5. Select the **Automatically delete this virtual machine after creating the virtual machine** check box if required.

6. Choose an availability zone if required (if your chosen region supports this).

7. Select the target image gallery we created previously and state if the image was generalized or specialized:

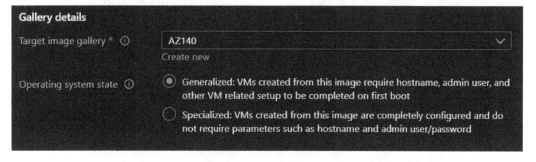

Figure 9.30 – The Target image gallery and OS state options

8. Create a new target image definition or use an existing one if you created one previously.

> **Important Note**
>
> An image definition's purpose is to carry information about the image and its requirements. This information is for IT use, and you can include release notes, as well as the minimum/maximum memory. You can also enter a publisher, offer, and SKU code, which is typically used for Azure Marketplace deployments.
>
> **The Azure Marketplace uses the following terminology**:
>
> **Publisher**: The organization that created the image; for example, `MicrosoftWindowsServer`.
>
> **Offer**: The name of a group of related images that have been created by a publisher; for example, `WindowsServer`.
>
> **SKU**: An instance of an offer, such as the major release of a distribution; for example, 2019-Datacenter Version, which is the version number of the image's SKU.

If you are not using the Azure Marketplace, you don't have to enter descriptive information, though it is recommended that you provide a description so that other IT admins can identify the specific image definition.

As shown in the following screenshot, I have provided the **Publisher**, **Offer**, and **SKU** fields with non-descriptive information. However, it is recommended that **Publisher** is set to your organization's name, **Offer** is set to the OS type (Windows 11), and **SKU** is set to the version (MultiSession):

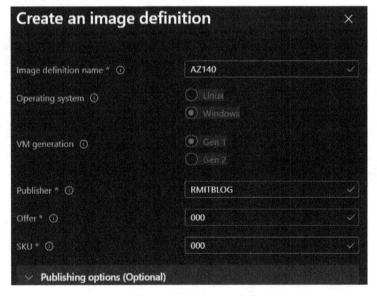

Figure 9.31 – The Create an image definition page

9. In this example, we created a new image definition:

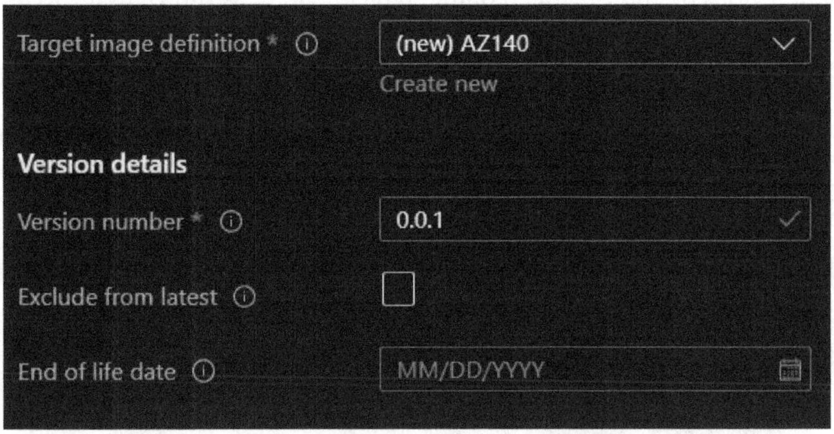

Figure 9.32 – Version details for an image definition

The following are the four fields within the **Version details** section:

- **Version number**: The version number is used as the name of the image version. The format for this is MajorVersion.MinorVersion.Patch. When you specify to use **latest** while creating a VM page or via PowerShell, the latest image is chosen based on the highest major version, then minor version, then patch.

- **source** can be a VM, managed disk, snapshot, managed image, or another image version.

- The **Exclude from latest** setting allows you to keep a version from being used as the latest image version.

- The **End of life date** field is used to indicate the end-of-life date for the image version. End-of-life dates are for informational purposes only, and users can still create VMs from versions past the set end-of-life date.

10. You can use the **Replication** to configure the replication of the template across different regions by entering the required target regions, as shown in the following screenshot:

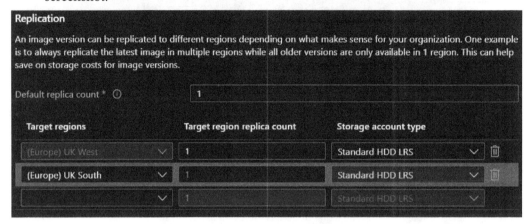

Figure 9.33 – The Replication section for specifying target regions that you would like to replicate the image to

11. Then, click on **Review + Create**.

Once you've finished, click **Go to resource**. You will see the new image version:

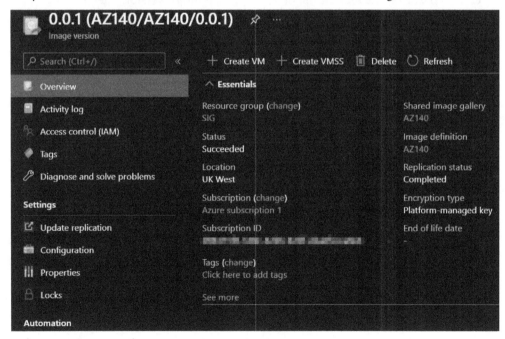

Figure 9.34 – Image version

With that, we have captured an image in the ACG; this has created both an image definition and an image version. Next, we will look at creating an image definition without using the capture feature shown previously.

Creating an image definition from the Shared Image Gallery

This section will show you how to create a new image definition from the ACG:

1. On the page for your recently created image gallery, select **Add a new image definition** at the top.

2. Under **Add new image definition to the Azure Compute Gallery**, for **Region**, select the required **Region**:

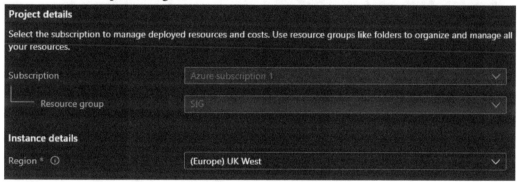

Figure 9.35 – The Image definition page

3. For **Image definition name**, enter a name.

4. For **Operating system**, select your source VM.

5. For **VM generation**, select the option based on your source VM type. These are typically Gen 1, though you can build Gen 2 images.

6. For **Operating system state**, select an option based on your source VM.

7. For **Publisher**, enter an appropriate name.

8. For **Offer**, enter an appropriate name.

9.   For **SKU**, enter an appropriate name:

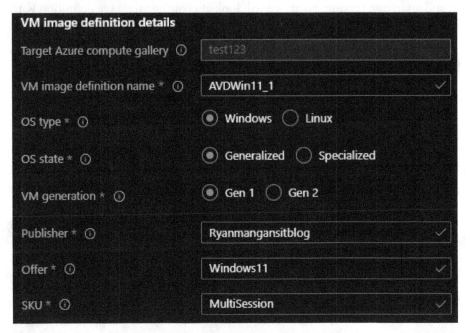

Figure 9.36 – Required image definition details

10. When you're finished, click **Review + create**.

11. Once the image definition has been validated, click **Create**.

12. When the deployment has finished, click **Go to the resource**.

In this short section, we looked at creating an image definition from a SIG. Now, let's learn how to create an image version.

Creating an image version

In this section, we will learn how to create an image version within the image definition:

> **Tip**
> Image versions are useful for updating images and their general management.

1.   Within the page of your created image definition, select **Add version** from the top of the page:

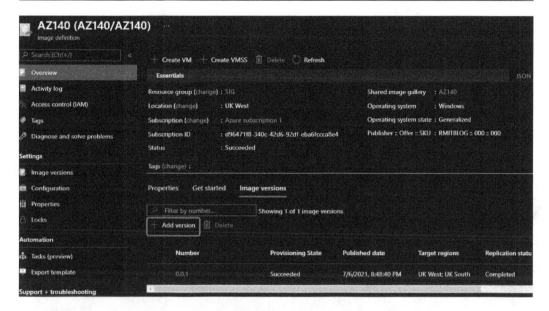

Figure 9.37 – The Add version button on the image definition

2. For **Region**, select the region where you want to create the image.

3. For **Version number**, enter a number, such as 1.0.0. The image version name must follow the major.minor.patch format and use integers.

4. For **Source image**, select your source-managed image from the dropdown.

    The following table shows the specific details for each source type:

Source	Other Fields
Disks or snapshots	- For the OS disk, select the required disk or snapshot from the dropdown.
	- To add a data disk, type the LUN number and then select the data disk from the dropdown.
Image version	- Select the source gallery from the dropdown.
	- Select the correct image definition from the dropdown.
	- Select the existing image version that you want to use from the dropdown.
Managed image	Select the source image from the dropdown.
	The managed image must be in the same region that you chose under Instance details.
VHD in a storage account	Select **Browse** to choose the storage account for the VHD.

The preceding table was taken from Microsoft's documentation: `https://docs.microsoft.com/azure/virtual-machines/linux/shared-images-portal`.

5. For **Exclude from latest**, leave it set to **No**.

6. For **End-of-life date**, choose a date from the calendar. This can be a few weeks, months, or even years.

7. In the **Replication** tab, select the required storage type from the dropdown:

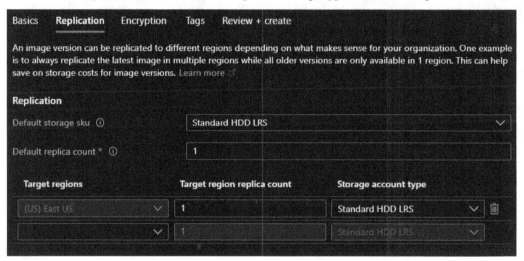

Figure 9.38 – The replication options for the image version

8. Enter a number for **Default replica count**. You can also override this for each Azure Region you add.

9. You need to replicate to the source region. This means that the first replica in the list will be in the region where you created the image. You can add more replicas by selecting the required region from the dropdown and adjusting the replica count as necessary.

10. When you are done, click **Review + create**. Azure will validate your configuration.

11. When the image version passes validation, click **Create**.

12. When the deployment is finished, click **Go to the resource**.

13. It may take a while to replicate the image to all of the target regions.

In this section, we looked at creating an image version. Now, let's learn how to troubleshoot OS image issues related to Azure Virtual Desktop.

Troubleshooting OS issues related to Azure Virtual Desktop

In this section, we will learn how to troubleshoot Session Host configuration issues. We will focus on the most common issues, including domain joins and communication between the Azure Virtual Desktop service and session host agent.

VMs are not joined to the domain

VMs not joining a domain typically occurs because the username and password that were entered during the host pool's setup/adding VMs were incorrect. Make sure that you check your password and use the full UPN of your Active Directory domain; for example, `domJoin.company.local`.

> **Important Note**
>
> When you're using AAD joined hosts, you would expect to see the hosts joined without the domain extension shown previously.

The other issue that may be preventing your VMs from joining the domain is a networking-related one, specifically **DNS**. Ensure that you have configured DNS correctly so that it points to your Active Directory Domain Service's infrastructure before trying to deploy session hosts.

> **Tip**
>
> Ensure that the account that you used for the domain join does not have **multi-factor authentication** (**MFA**) configured. You should use a service account with its password expiry set to disabled. You should also make sure that the account has delegated permissions to make sure the account can join multiple devices to the domain.

You should also check that you have configured the correct permissions for the domain join account; otherwise, the domain join process will fail. As shown in the following screenshot, there is no check password feature in the form. It is advised that you write the password out in text form and copy and paste it into the form to ensure it's correct:

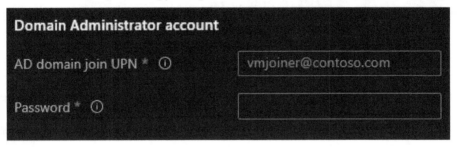

Figure 9.39 – Active Directory details for a domain join when adding VMs to a host pool

In this section, we looked at how to troubleshoot domain joins issues when deploying session hosts to a host pool within Azure Virtual Desktop. We will now look at some of the Azure Desktop Agent and Bootloader issues that may occur.

Azure Desktop Agent and Virtual Desktop Bootloader are not installed

For Azure Virtual Desktop to see the Session Hosts, you need to ensure that the Session Hosts have Azure Virtual Desktop Agent and Azure Virtual Desktop Bootloader installed. You can check this by reviewing the installed programs via **Control Panel | Programs | Programs and Features**. Alternatively, you can review the `scriptlog.log` file by navigating to the `c:\windows\temp\ScriptLog.log` file path. The log file will show error messages to help you diagnose the root cause.

> **Important Note**
> Azure Desktop Agent and Virtual Desktop Bootloader should not be installed on the master image. This is installed automatically through a VM deployment for a host pool or a manual process.

If the `ScriptLog.log` file is missing, this would indicate that the Azure Resource Manager template had the incorrect permissions entered into it or that these credentials do not have the required permissions. Likewise, if PowerShell DSC was unable to start and run, this would indicate a permissions issue, that the hostname is incorrect, or that MFA is enabled, causing the sign-in process to fail.

The next section will look at Azure Virtual Desktop Agent not registering issues.

Azure Virtual Desktop Agent is not registering with the Azure Virtual Desktop service

If you encounter an issue where the Session Host is unavailable within the Azure Virtual Desktop portal, this is typically due to the agent not communicating correctly with the Azure Virtual Desktop service. It is advised that you check connectivity from the Session Host to the Azure Virtual Desktop service using Sysinternals tools such as PSPing.

You can download PSPing from `https://docs.microsoft.com/en-us/ Sysinternals/downloads/psping/`.

To test your connectivity, run the following as an administrator within the command line:

> **Important Note**
>
> For those who have already deployed an AVD environment, you can use the `WVDAgentUrlTool.exe` tool, which can be found in the `C:\Program Files\Microsoft RDInfra\RDAgent_*` folder.

```
psping rdbroker.wvdselfhost.microsoft.com:443
```

The following screenshot shows using PSPing to confirm that the host can communicate with the Rdbroker for Azure Virtual Desktop:

```
Microsoft Windows [Version 10.0.19042.1052]
(c) Microsoft Corporation. All rights reserved.

C:\Users\sysadmin>cd Desktop

C:\Users\sysadmin\Desktop>psping.exe rdbroker.wvdselfhost.microsoft.com:443

PsPing v2.10 - PsPing - ping, latency, bandwidth measurement utility
Copyright (C) 2012-2016 Mark Russinovich
Sysinternals - www.sysinternals.com

TCP connect to 104.40.191.174:443:
5 iterations (warmup 1) ping test:
Connecting to 104.40.191.174:443 (warmup): from 10.0.0.6:61634: 6.73ms
Connecting to 104.40.191.174:443: from 10.0.0.6:61635: 8.22ms
Connecting to 104.40.191.174:443: from 10.0.0.6:61636: 9.71ms
Connecting to 104.40.191.174:443: from 10.0.0.6:61637: 8.91ms
Connecting to 104.40.191.174:443: from 10.0.0.6:61638: 6.88ms

TCP connect statistics for 104.40.191.174:443:
  Sent = 4, Received = 4, Lost = 0 (0% loss),
  Minimum = 6.88ms, Maximum = 9.71ms, Average = 8.43ms

C:\Users\sysadmin\Desktop>_
```

Figure 9.40 – The output of PSPing when testing communication with the broker

> **Tip**
> This test is also useful if the Azure Virtual Desktop agent is not reporting a heartbeat when you run the `Get-AzWvdSessionHost` PowerShell cmdlet.

Once you have checked your network connectivity and confirmed that this is not the issue, you should follow these steps to update the agent manually:

1. Download a new version of the Azure Virtual Desktop agent on the problematic Session Host VM.

2. Open Task Manager and, within the **Service** tab, stop the `RDAgentBootLoader` service from running.

3. Run the installer for the downloaded copy of Azure Virtual Desktop Agent.

4. When you're prompted for the registration token, remove the `INVALID_TOKEN` entry and click **Next** (no token is required).

5. Complete the installation wizard and close it.

6. Open Task Manager and start the `RDAgentBootLoader` service.

If the Azure Virtual Desktop Agent registry entry called `IsRegistered` shows a value of `0`, then the registration token has expired. You will need to generate a new registration token to fix this:

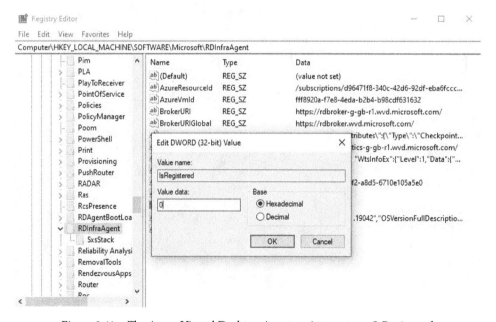

Figure 9.41 – The Azure Virtual Desktop Agent registry entry – IsRegistered

You can check this using a Powershell cmdlet.

7. If there's already a registration token, remove the token using the following command:

```
Remove-AzWvdRegistrationInfo
```

8. Run the `New-AzWvdRegistrationInfo` cmdlet to generate a new token.

9. Confirm that the `-ExpriationTime` parameter has been set to 3 days.

> **Further Information**
>
> For more information on common Virtual Desktop Agent issues, you can find a complete list of errors and troubleshooting guidance at `https://docs.microsoft.com/azure/virtual-desktop/troubleshoot-agent`.

This section looked at some of the troubleshooting issues that may affect how the image communicates with Azure Virtual Desktop. We will now look at basic performance troubleshooting in Azure Virtual Desktop.

Basic performance troubleshooting in Azure Virtual Desktop

In this section, we will look at ways to identify and resolve common performance issues that may occur on Session Hosts within an Azure Virtual Desktop environment.

Four key resources can impact performance on a Session Host, as follows:

- **Central Processing Unit (CPU)**
- **Random Access Memory (RAM)**
- **Storage (Disk)**
- **Network**

The typical performance issues you may experience include capacity, constraints, and overall performance degradation or lag.

First, we will look at troubleshooting CPU performance issues.

CPU troubleshooting

CPU constraints are a common issue with session-based desktops. Performance and high CPU utilization issues can occur for several reasons and not be due to a single app or service. The web browser can be one such suspect, especially if hardware rendering has been left set to *on* once the master image has been optimized. You can view your CPU usage by going to Task Manager, and then go to **Azure monitoring features** within the Azure portal for specific VM and using Sysinternals Process Explorer:

> **Tip**
>
> You can download process explorer here: `https://docs.microsoft.com/Sysinternals/downloads/process-explorer`.

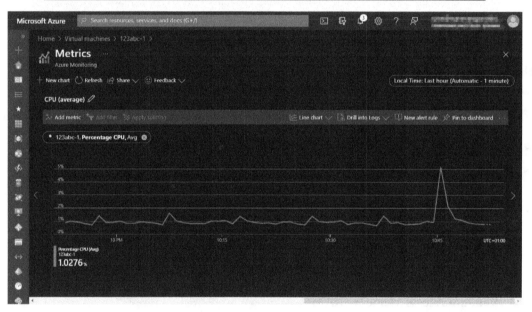

Figure 9.42 – The CPU utilization of a session host within Azure monitoring features

The following screenshot shows using the Sysinternals process explorer to gauge the CPU usage when monitoring the performance of an OS:

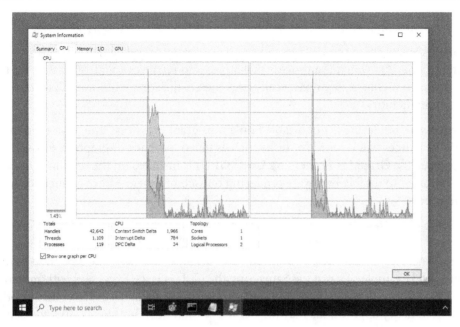

Figure 9.43 – CPU utilization of a session host using the Sysinternals process explorer

The following screenshot shows using the Sysinternals process explorer to monitor running processes to see which are consuming the most CPU and memory. This is a great tool for identifying processes that are consuming excessive resources:

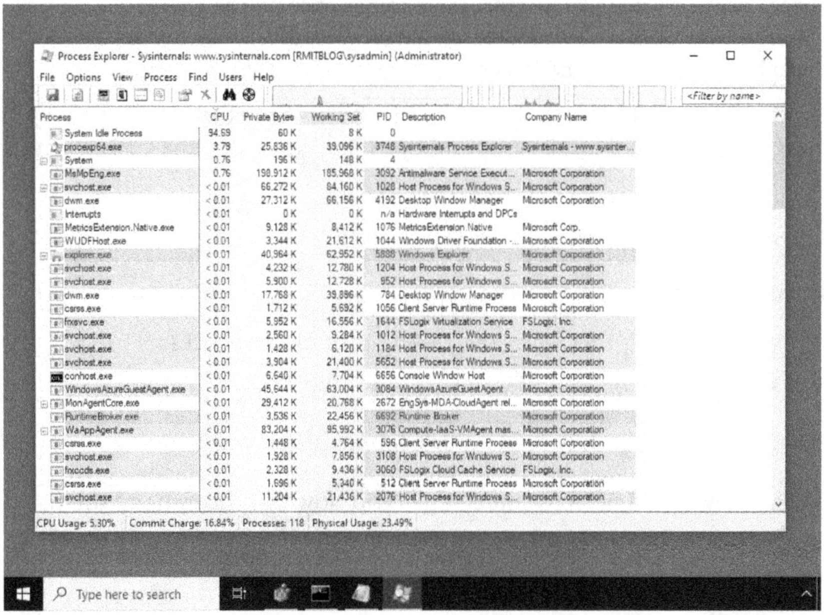

Figure 9.44 – Sysinternals process explorer (running processes) on a Session Host

The following are some useful tips for when you're troubleshooting CPU resource issues:

- Low RAM can cause the CPU to spike and also increase disk activity due to memory paging, which is a process that stores and retrieves data from a disk for use in the main memory. Paging typically uses the OS disk or a temporary disk to use in the main memory.

- If hardware rendering is not disabled on a non-graphic process unit VM, then more CPU resources will be used for tasks such as video playback or graphics software. However, if a **Graphics Processing Unit (GPU)** is installed on the session host, you do not need to disable hardware rendering on web browsers, Office applications, and others.

- Specific processes may be causing performance issues on the Session Host. You can use Sysinternals Process Explorer to view CPU time, allowing you to review your processes, the time they've run for, and if they are causing the system to hang. One good example of a process impacting the CPU is large Excel files with macros. Additionally, multiple users on the same Session Host using large Excel files or other resource-heavy applications may impact the session host. In this case, it's advised that you move these power users to higher spec Session Hosts or personal pools.

> Tip
> It is recommended that you build more session hosts with fewer CPUs. This is advised because when you increase the number of cores, the system's synchronization overhead also increases. Smaller resourced VMs would perform better than fewer and larger specification VMs.

Here are a few examples of potential symptoms you may see when the CPU is under contention:

- Slow/lagging switching between windows.
- The loading cursor appears for long periods.
- The log on and log off process is slow, taking minutes to process.
- Applications are consistently going into a not responding state or locking/crashing.
- Web pages are jumping, slow to load, or become unresponsive.

Now, let's look at a few RAM performance issues and how to spot some of them.

RAM challenges

Modern applications consume more RAM. For example, when you combine Microsoft Office Suite, Microsoft Teams, and have multiple other applications open simultaneously, this can impact RAM consumption. When RAM reaches high consumption or becomes full, it will revert to the page file as secondary storage for the main memory.

The challenge with page file is speed. For example, a **Solid State Drive** (**SSD**) could have a typical write speed of 456 MB per second, whereas RAM writes at estimated speeds of 12,800 MB per second. When all the RAM has been consumed, the performance drops as secondary storage is being used. This performance drop will be seen by users and will most likely cause performance degradation for multiple users on a session host.

You can view your session host RAM utilization in Azure monitoring, as shown in the following screenshot:

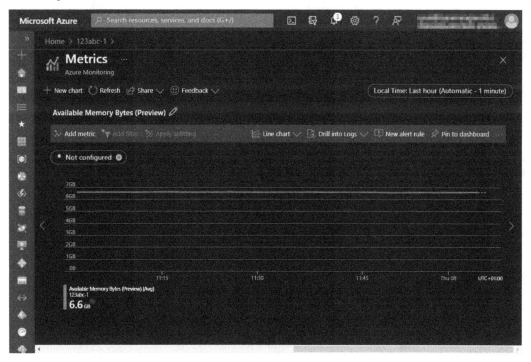

Figure 9.45 – Available RAM on a session host in Azure monitoring

The following are some tips for troubleshooting RAM issues:

- Try to spread your users across multiple Session Hosts. You can manage this using the **Depth** and **Breadth** load balancing modes.

- One of the ways to address issues with a session that has become saturated would be to enable stop drain and ask a subset of users to log off and then back on. This will clear resources, free up RAM, and restore the expected user experience for the remaining users on that session host.

- Leaving users in an idle state and not rebooting Session Hosts can cause longer-term resource consumption issues. Therefore, it is advised that users log off and that the session hosts are restarted regularly.

Some of the symptoms you may see with RAM issues are as follows:

- Applications crashing

- Windows errors stating that there's low memory

- A slow log on and log off experience, which will be visible

- Applications locked in a **Not responding** state

- Application launch times are slow

- Running applications causes performance degradation and they are slow to use

We now move on to the next section where we look at disk performance and troubleshooting.

Disk performance troubleshooting

This is a common problem as it's easy to forget about the OS disk when it comes to multi-session deployments. Within Microsoft Azure, different sized disks have different performance outputs, which are measured in **input/output operations per second (IOPS)**. To avoid any disk performance degradation, you should size the disk based on IOPS and factor in the expected total number of users per session host. P15 Azure Managed Disks or higher is recommended to ensure there's enough IOPS to serve all users and applications in use. Every environment can be different; it is advised to baseline your requirements for IOPS by using one or two users on a Session Host to generate IOPS consumption. You can then see the total usage of the disk over a set period from the test users carrying out their typical day-to-day tasks.

You can then use the data that's been collected to calculate the requirements and estimate the required IOPS based on a set number of users per Session Host.

See the following link for a list of the premium SSD disk sizes and their allocated IOPS: https://docs.microsoft.com/en-us/azure/virtual-machines/disks-types#premium-ssd-size.

> **Tip**
> It is also important to note that choosing a VM that's the wrong size may limit the throughput that's allowed by the disk. So, you must check the VM specs as well as the disk IOPS output. The following link provides a table detailing the max IOPS per VM size: https://docs.microsoft.com/en-us/azure/virtual-machines/dav4-dasv4-series#dav4-series.

The following command can help you identify disk performance issues by spotting high disk queues:

```
typeperf -si 2 "\PhysicalDisk(*)\Avg. Disk Queue Length"
```

The following screenshot shows the output of the current disk queue length of the OS. This is a great tool for identifying any issues with the disk performance on the OS:

```
Microsoft Windows [Version 10.0.19042.1052]
(c) Microsoft Corporation. All rights reserved.

C:\Users\sysadmin>typeperf -si 2 "\PhysicalDisk(*)\Avg. Disk Queue Length"

"(PDH-CSV 4.0)","\\123abc-1\PhysicalDisk(0 C:)\Avg. Disk Queue Length","\\123abc-1\PhysicalDisk(1 D:)\Avg. Disk Queue
ngth","\\123abc-1\PhysicalDisk(_Total)\Avg. Disk Queue Length"
"07/07/2021 22:46:32.066","0.000178","0.000000","0.000178"
"07/07/2021 22:46:34.066","0.000517","0.000000","0.000517"
"07/07/2021 22:46:36.082","0.000870","0.000000","0.000870"
"07/07/2021 22:46:38.097","0.000071","0.000000","0.000071"
"07/07/2021 22:46:40.113","0.000286","0.000000","0.000286"
"07/07/2021 22:46:42.113","0.000000","0.000000","0.000000"
"07/07/2021 22:46:44.128","0.000441","0.000000","0.000441"
"07/07/2021 22:46:46.129","0.000238","0.000000","0.000238"
"07/07/2021 22:46:48.144","0.001872","0.000000","0.001872"
"07/07/2021 22:46:50.144","0.000497","0.000000","0.000497"
"07/07/2021 22:46:52.160","0.000000","0.000000","0.000000"
"07/07/2021 22:46:54.175","0.000210","0.000000","0.000210"
"07/07/2021 22:46:56.191","0.000974","0.000000","0.000974"
"07/07/2021 22:46:58.207","0.001537","0.000000","0.001537"
"07/07/2021 22:47:00.222","0.001956","0.000000","0.001956"
"07/07/2021 22:47:02.238","0.000101","0.000000","0.000101"
"07/07/2021 22:47:04.238","0.002081","0.000000","0.002081"
"07/07/2021 22:47:06.254","0.000314","0.000000","0.000314"
"07/07/2021 22:47:08.269","0.000090","0.000000","0.000090"
"07/07/2021 22:47:10.269","0.001163","0.000000","0.001163"
"07/07/2021 22:47:12.285","0.001131","0.000000","0.001131"
"07/07/2021 22:47:14.285","0.010351","0.000000","0.010351"
```

Figure 9.46 – Disk queue output from running typeperf

For a centralized view of potential disk performance issues, you can use Azure Monitor or Log Analytics. Azure Monitor and Log Analytics will be covered in *Chapter 18, Monitoring and Managing Performance and Health*.

The following are some key points regarding disk troubleshooting:

- You should not use standard disks for multi-session environments.

- When you're deploying multi-session host pools, it is advised to use p-type SSD disks.

- Prevent users from using streaming services such as radios and music as this can impact the disk.

Now, let's take a look at the symptoms. The following are some disk performance symptoms:

- Files take a long time to open and save

- Slow switching between screens

- Logon and logoff times are long

- Applications stop responding or repeatedly show **Not responding** before becoming active again

- Applications are slow to launch

This section looked at disk performance issues, as well as some troubleshooting hints and tips that you can use to resolve some of the issues you may face.

Networking troubleshooting

Networking issues can occur in three areas: the user endpoint device, Azure Virtual Desktop's management service, and the session host itself. When you're reviewing network issues, it is recommended that you start with the client device and then look at the Azure Virtual Desktop management service and session host connectivity.

There are four typical network contention issues that you can experience:

- A jittery mouse or delayed typing

- Audio degradation or distortion

- The connection to Azure Virtual Desktop keeps dropping

- The screen goes blank and reappears frequently

These issues are usually found on the user side, all of which can be due to many different reasons. However, it is important to follow the necessary processes and check all three areas. There can be issues with the broker service, gateway communication, and even the Session Host agent service.

You can also review the connection information by right-clicking on the **Session** title bar, as shown in the following screenshot:

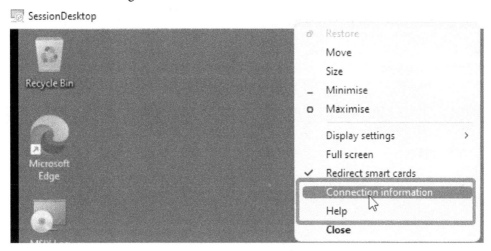

Figure 9.47 – The menu that appears after right-clicking the Session desktop title bar

Click the **Connection information** button to see the **Connection information** window appear. Click **show details** to view the connection details for the client connection. Note that the round trip time, available bandwidth, and frame rate are shown here:

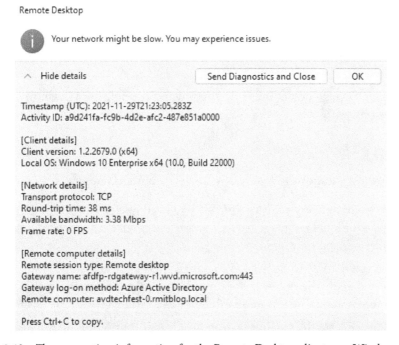

Figure 9.48 – The connection information for the Remote Desktop client on a Windows device

The following are some tips for identifying network issues:

- Conduct a broadband/ISP speed test to understand if the user has network connectivity issues to the public network.

- Use tools such as PSPing to test connectivity to `www.microsoft.com` and `rdweb.microsoft.com:443`, as well as the broker service shown in the previous section.

- Force session hosts to **redeploy**, which moves the VM within a specific region to another physical host.

- Check the status of the session host using PowerShell.

Using Azure Virtual Desktop's **Insights** dashboard to view end user latency and poor user bandwidth. Azure Monitor and Azure Virtual Desktop Insights will be covered in *Chapter 18, Monitoring and Managing Performance and Health*.

This section looked at some hints and tips for spotting possible issues and resource contentions that may impact or affect your Session Hosts and connecting users.

Summary

In this chapter, we looked at creating a gold image for Azure Virtual Desktop, as well as modifying the session image, including customizing it, optimizing it, and capturing it in an image template. Then, we created an ACG, including creating image definitions and image versions. Finally, we looked at troubleshooting the OS and diagnosing possible performance and resource contention issues.

In the next chapter, we will look at managing access and configuring IT admin and user security permissions.

Questions

Answer the following questions to test your knowledge of this chapter:

1. When you're configuring a custom image, you need to ensure that modern apps can use the additional language packs. What Powershell cmdlet would you use to disable pre-stage app cleanup?

2. You have created a VM to be used as the image master. You install applications on the image and apply the necessary optimizations and configurations. What should you do before making the image distributable as a template?

3. You need to replicate the custom session host image to multiple Azure Regions. Which Azure service would you use to complete this task?

Answers

1. *Disable-ScheduledTask -TaskPath "\Microsoft\Windows\AppxDeploymentClient\"*
   -TaskName "Pre-staged app cleanup"

2. *At the command prompt, run the Sysprep command*

3. *Azure Compute Gallery*

Section 4: Managing Access and Security

This section covers two key topics of managing user access and security for Azure Virtual Desktop.

This part of the book comprises the following chapters:

- *Chapter 10, Managing Access*
- *Chapter 11, Managing Security*

10
Managing Access

In this chapter, we will journey through the process of managing access within **Azure Virtual Desktop** (**AVD**). First, we look at planning, managing, and restricting access to AVD resources. This consists of exploring how **Role-Based Access Control** (**RBAC**) works in combination with the permissions that must be synchronized with the Active Directory domain. Also, we will briefly look at group policy and the value it brings to a virtual desktop environment.

In this chapter, we will cover the following topics:

- Introduction to Azure RBAC
- Planning and implementing Azure role-based controls
- The delegated access model
- Assigning RBAC roles to IT admins
- Creating a custom role using rights assignments
- Configuring user restrictions by using Azure AD groups

Introduction to Azure RBAC

Azure RBAC stands for **Azure Role-Based Access Control**. Essentially, this feature allows you to apply access management to your Azure management groups/subscriptions. In addition, Azure RBAC enables you to configure granular control with access to Azure resources and specify which user/admin actions can be taken with the resources you have granted access to.

Here are some examples of the access control conditions you can set:

- Allow one user to manage virtual machines in a specific subscription and another user to only manage networks. This is an example of separating the network controls from the virtual machine controls.

- Provide access to a specific user to only manage all of the resources within a specific resource group.

- Grant access to an application to access specific resources or a resource group.

Lets now take a look at the components of the Desktop Virtualization Contributor:

- Security principle
- Role definition
- Scope

Let's discuss these elements in more detail:

- **Security principle**: A security principle is an object that represents a user, group, service principles, or managed identity. You can assign a role to any of these security principles:

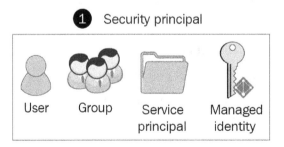

Figure 10.1 – The different security principles

- **Role definition**: A role definition is a collection of permissions that you can assign for different operations. These can then be assigned to the security principle. Azure does include several built-in roles, so you don't have to configure custom roles, but you can if you want to. A good example is the virtual machine contributor role that allows a user to create and manage virtual machines.

- **Scope**: The scope refers to the resources you apply to grant access to. There are four levels within the scope that you can specify, including the management group, subscription, resource group, and the specific resources themselves:

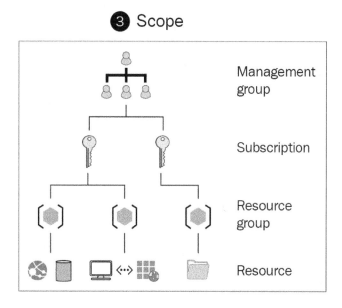

Figure 10.2 – The different scope levels

Now that we have reviewed the three core elements of RBAC in more detail, let's move on to role assignments.

Essentially, a role assignment is a process of assigning a role definition to a security principle and at the required scope level (that is, applying RBAC permissions to users and groups).

> **Tip**
>
> You can find the complete list of Azure's built-in roles at `https://docs.`
> `microsoft.com/azure/role-based-access-control/`
> `built-in-roles`.

In this section, we learned about the basics of Azure RBAC; next, let's look at the built-in roles of AVD and learn how to use RBAC with AVD.

Planning and implementing Azure roles and RBAC for AVD

As with all Azure resources, AVD uses Azure RBAC to assign roles and permissions to both users and IT admins, as mentioned earlier. In this section, we will take a look at the RBAC roles that can be used within AVD, and I will show you how to apply these role assignments and create custom roles.

> **Tip**
> RBAC roles that are specific to AVD do appear in the AZ140 exam. It is advised that you pay attention to these different roles, as you might see a question in the exam.

AVD has many built-in management roles that you can use for host pools, app groups, and workspaces. This provides you with more granular control over administrative tasks, which can be extremely useful in larger organizations. It is recommended that all organizations leverage RBAC roles to use the least-privilege model ensuring access to systems is carefully controlled.

Additionally, it is important to note that the roles are named in compliance with Azure's least-privilege methodology and standard role naming conventions.

> **Tip**
> AVD does not have a specific owner role. However, you can use the Azure standard owner role for service objects. It is recommended that you follow the least-privilege methodology when assigning admin permissions to AVD administrators.

The following screenshot shows the specific desktop virtualization roles that are available in RBAC:

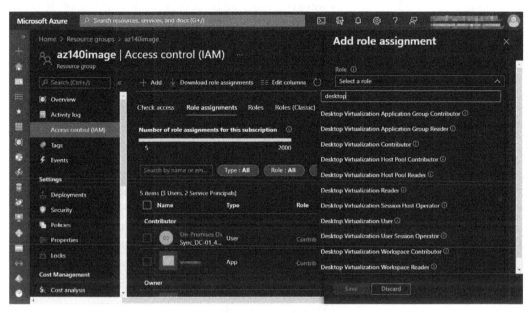

Figure 10.3 – The Access control menu within an Azure resource

The following table details the built-in roles for AVD that you can use to separate management roles from host pools, app groups, and workspaces. You will note that these roles are for the management of AVD, not user access:

Role	Description
Desktop Virtualization Contributor	The Desktop Virtualization Contributor role enables you to manage all aspects of the deployment. However, it doesn't grant you access to compute resources. Note that you will also need the User Access Administrator role to publish app groups to users or user groups.
Desktop Virtualization Reader	The Desktop Virtualization Reader role allows you to view everything in the deployment but doesn't let you make any changes.
Desktop Virtualization Host Pool Contributor	The Host Pool Contributor role enables the management of all aspects of host pools, including access to resources. You do need an extra contributor role, Virtual Machine Contributor, to create virtual machines. Additionally, you will need the AppGroup and Workspace contributor roles to create a host pool using the portal or use the Desktop Virtualization Contributor role.

Role	Description
Desktop Virtualization Host Pool Reader	The Host Pool Reader role enables you to view everything within the host pool but does not allow you to make any changes.
Desktop Virtualization Application Group Contributor	The Application Group Contributor role enables the management of all aspects of app groups. If you want to publish app groups to users or user groups, you will also need to add the User Access Administrator role.
Desktop Virtualization Application Group Reader	The Application Group Reader role enables you to view everything in the app group and will not allow you to make any changes.
Desktop Virtualization Workspace Contributor	The Workspace Contributor role enables the management of all aspects of the workspaces. To get information on applications added to the app groups, you will also need to assign the Application Group Reader role.
Desktop Virtualization Workspace Reader	The Workspace Reader role enables you to view everything in the workspace but won't allow you to make any changes.
Desktop Virtualization User Session Operator	The User Session Operator role enables you to send messages, disconnect sessions, and use the `logoff` function to sign sessions out of the session host. However, this role doesn't enable you to perform session host management such as removing the session host, changing the drain mode setting, and more. This role can view assignments, but you cannot modify admins. It is recommended that you assign this role to specific host pools. If you give this permission at a resource group level, the admin will have read permissions on all host pools under a resource group.
Desktop Virtualization Session Host Operator	The Session Host Operator role enables you to view and remove session hosts and change the drain mode. The session host operator can't add session hosts using the Azure portal because they don't have write permissions for host pool objects. If the registration token is valid (generated and not expired), you can also use this role to add session hosts to the host pool outside of the Azure portal. This is subject to ensuring the admin has compute permissions through the Virtual Machine Contributor role.

The `https://docs.microsoft.com/azure/virtual-desktop/rbac` link details the up-to-date list of RBAC roles for AVD.

Now we will take a look at the delegated access model for AVD.

The delegated access model

Delegated access in AVD lets you specify the level and total amount of access that a particular user is allowed. This can be done by assigning a role that can be built-in or custom.

> **Important Note**
>
> The delegated access model is based on the Azure RBAC model. Essentially, you can customize roles with granular controls ensuring the least-privilege methodology is followed as per security best practices. You should also note that the `Desktop Virtualization User` role is the lowest role and is required for user access to the AVD environment.

You can read more about AVD delegated access at `https://docs.microsoft.com/azure/virtual-desktop/delegated-access-virtual-desktop`.

This section looked at different built-in RBAC roles for AVD and briefly covered the delegated access model. Now we will move on to look at how to configure RBAC through the Azure portal.

Assigning RBAC roles to IT admins

This section looks at assigning RBAC roles to specific resources and resource groups for AVD.

Within a subscription, resource group, or a specific resource, you will see **Access control (IAM)** in the menu options:

Figure 10.4 – The Access control (IAM) menu button is shown in each Azure resource

This is where you can assign roles to users, groups, and service principals. As mentioned earlier, these are called security principles.

To assign a security principle to a role that is within scope, you can click on the **Access control** button; as shown in this example, this is at the subscription level. Click on **Add | Add role assignment (Preview)**:

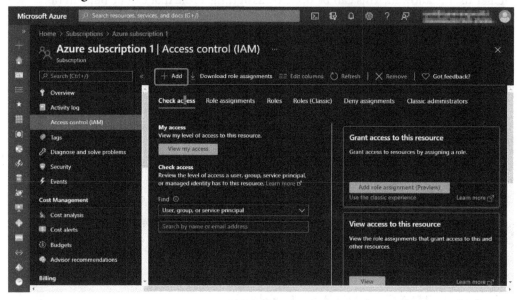

Figure 10.5 – The buttons for adding role assignments

Then, you should see the **Add role assignment** tab appear. Select the role you require, select the security principle, and then click on **Save**:

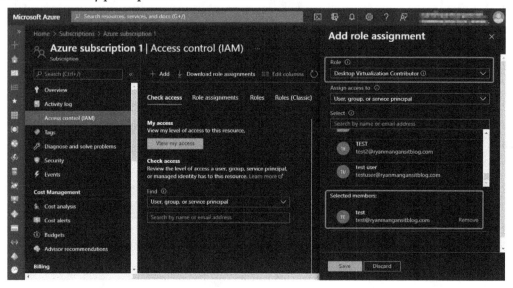

Figure 10.6 – The selection of a role and user when adding a role assignment

Now you will see the **Desktop Virtualization Contributor** role with the user account assigned in the bottom section of the screenshot (*Figure 10.7*):

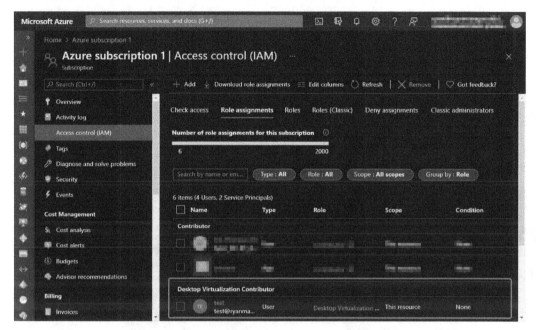

Figure 10.7 – The new role assignment added to the resource

There you have it; you have just assigned a user account to the desktop virtualization contributor RBAC role at the subscription level. Additionally, as a best practice, it is recommended that you assign roles to Azure Active Directory groups that offer more flexibility and security rather than specific users.

Important Note

Deny assignments are created and managed by Azure. You cannot directly create your own deny assignments.

Now, let's look at how to do the same using PowerShell.

The PowerShell way to assign role assignments

Before you can start assigning roles via PowerShell, first, you need to ensure that the AVD PowerShell model is set up. Please refer to the *Setting up PowerShell for Azure Virtual Desktop* section in *Chapter 6, Creating Host Pools and Session Hosts*.

To assign a user to an app group using PowerShell, you could use the following cmdlets:

```
New-AzRoleAssignment -SignInName <userupn> -RoleDefinitionName
"Desktop Virtualization User" -ResourceName <appgroupname>
-ResourceGroupName <resourcegroupname> -ResourceType
'Microsoft.DesktopVirtualization/applicationGroups'
```

Here's the result of using the preceding command:

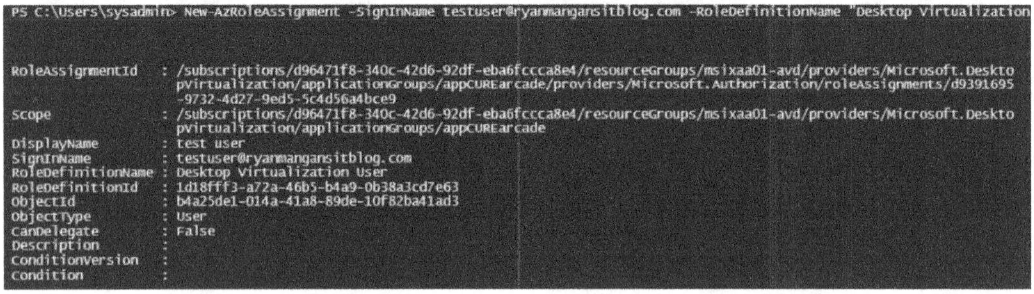

Figure 10.8 – Using New-AzRoleAssignement

To assign a group, you can use the following:

```
New-AzRoleAssignment -ObjectId <usergroupobjectid>
-RoleDefinitionName "Desktop Virtualization User" -ResourceName
<appgroupname> -ResourceGroupName <resourcegroupname>
-ResourceType 'Microsoft.DesktopVirtualization/
applicationGroups'
```

When using a group, you need to use the object ID, which can be found within the Azure Active Directory page within the Azure portal. Within groups, select the required group. You will then see the object ID that is required:

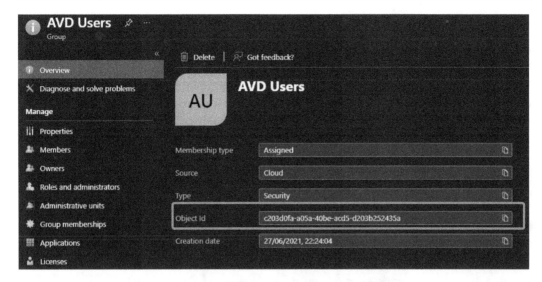

Figure 10.9 – An example group and its associated object ID

Once you have the required object ID for the associated group, you are ready to assign the desktop virtualization user role definition:

Figure 10.10 – An example of assigning a role assignment to a group using PowerShell

You can read more about assigning roles using PowerShell at https://docs. microsoft.com/azure/role-based-access-control/role-assignments-powershell.

In the next section, we will look at how to create a custom role using the Azure portal.

Creating a custom role using the Azure portal

The following section provides high-level steps regarding how to create a custom role assignment. Custom role assignments are useful when you want to grant very specific actions to admins and users. In larger organizations, you might wish to create more granular roles to suit your IT department's support structures or other use cases:

1. The following screenshot shows the **Access control (IAM)** menu within a resource. You can see the **Add custom role** option within the drop-down menu:

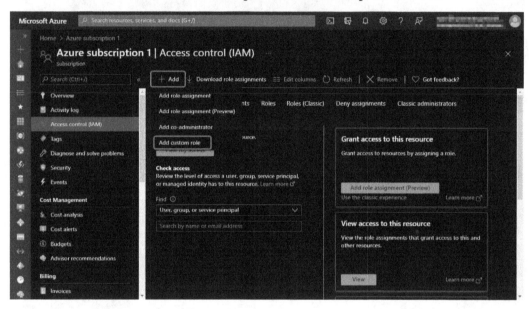

Figure 10.11 – The add function of a custom role

2. When clicking on the **Add custom role** option, you will see the **Create a custom role** page appear. Enter a role name, description, and choose the base permissions. It is recommended that you clone a role rather than start from scratch. You can also start from JSON if you wish.

3. As shown in the following screenshot, we are cloning a role. In this case, we will use the **Desktop Virtualization User** role. Once you have filled out the form, click on **Next**:

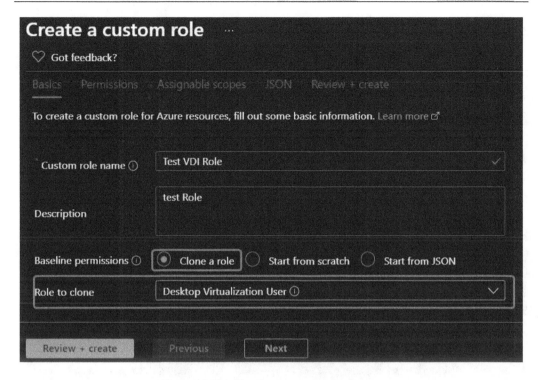

Figure 10.12 – The Create a custom role page

4. On the **Permissions** tab, you will see two buttons: **Add permissions** and **Exclude permissions**. To add permissions, click on the **Add permissions** button:

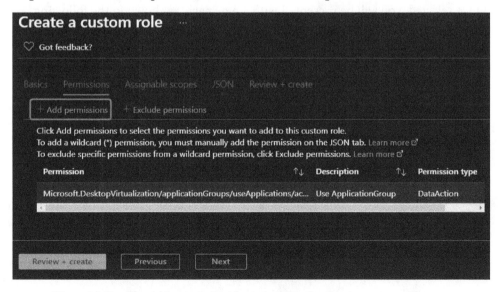

Figure 10.13 – The Add permissions button within the Create a custom role page

5. You will then see the **Add permissions** page appear. You can use the search bar to search for specific permissions, as shown in the following screenshot:

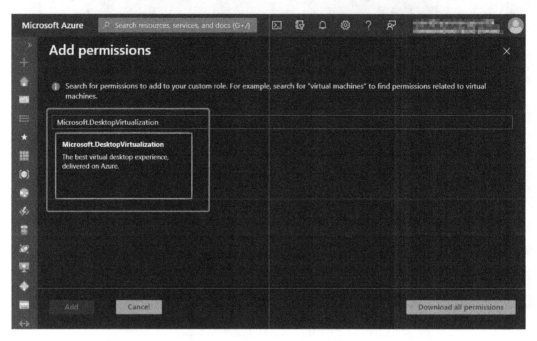

Figure 10.14 –Searching for Microsoft.DesktopVirtualization permissions

6. In this example, I will select the **Microsoft.DesktopVirtualisation** permissions. Once selected, you will be presented with a new page, as shown in the following screenshot. Select the permissions you want; these can be either **Actions** or **Data Actions**:

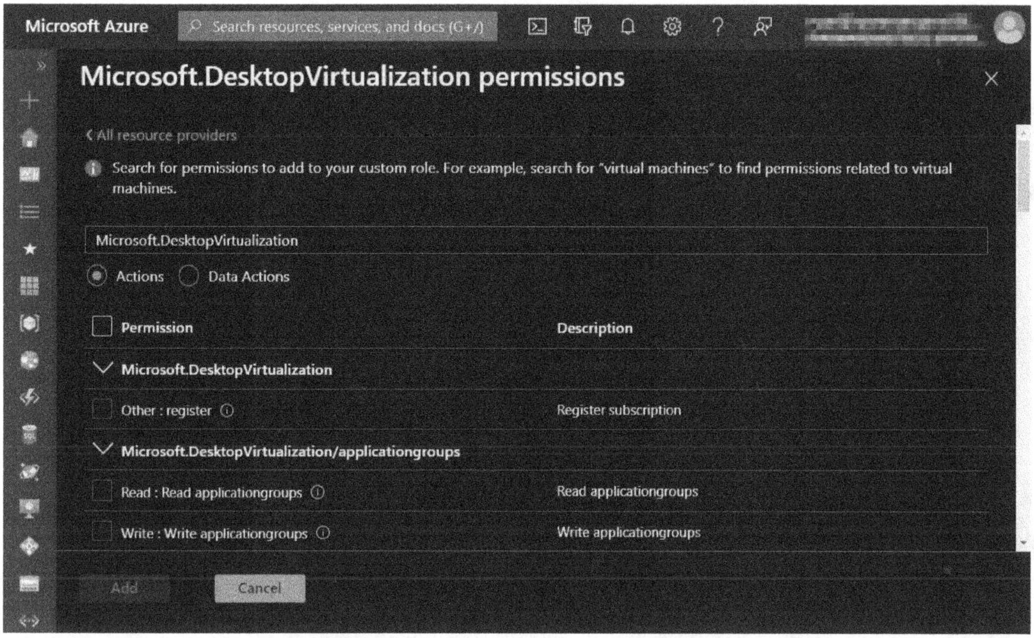

Figure 10.15 – The Microsoft.Desktopvirtualization permissions page with the add custom role

> **Tip**
> **Actions** are an array of strings that specify the management operation that the role allows. **DataActions** refers to an array of strings that specifies the data operations the role allows to be performed on the data within that object. You can read more at `https://docs.microsoft.com/azure/role-based-access-control/custom-roles#how-to-determine-the-permissions-you-need`.

7. Once you have selected the required permissions, click on **Add**.

8. You will then see the added permission appear with the **Create a custom role** page:

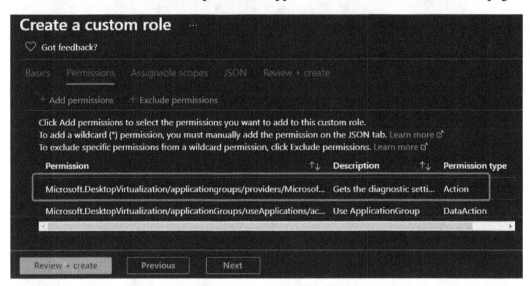

Figure 10.16 – The added role of getting diagnostic settings

9. Once you have finished adding permissions, click on the **Review + create** button, as shown in the preceding screenshot.

10. Check what you have configured and, once complete, proceed by clicking on the **Create** button:

Figure 10.17 – The custom role configured before creating

11. Once created, you can search for the customer role underneath the **Roles** tab within the access control page:

Figure 10.18 – The newly created custom role

This concludes the creation of a custom role. In the next section, we will look at how to manage local roles, groups, and right assignments on session hosts.

Managing local roles, groups, and rights assignments on AVD session hosts

In this section, we will take a look at managing local roles, groups, and rights assignments. When working in a pooled desktop environment, it's important to ensure that each session host is configured to ensure the user experience is identical for each host within the pool. When configuring local roles, groups, and rights assignments, you can configure these on the gold master image (image template) or configure group policy to apply to single or multiple host pools centrally.

> **Tip**
> Using group policy is great when working with multiple host pools, as you don't need to worry about customizing the image with roles, groups, and rights assignments.

The use of local roles and groups might be required for specific requirements such as applications or allowing additional access permissions to the local operating system.

For example, if you are using FSLogix profile containers, you might wish to have a specific group of users assigned to the FSLogix profile containers.

Let's suppose you need to apply local groups to all session hosts within a pool. In that case, you can use the restricted groups setting via group policy. This allows you to configure local groups and apply them to your session hosts within an organizational unit.

The following example shows you a screenshot of **Group Policy Management Editor | Computer Configuration | Policies | Security Settings | Restricted Groups**.

The **Restricted Groups** setting is a great way to automatically configure local groups to session hosts.

The following screenshot shows the restricted groups setting within the **Computer Configuration** tab, underneath **Windows Settings**:

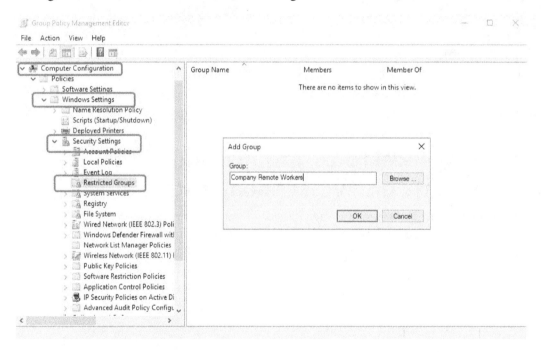

Figure 10.19 – The creation of a group within the Restricted Groups setting

The example in the following screenshot shows how you can add members to a group that can be either users or groups. Additionally, you can link this group to a member of another group. For example, the screenshot shows the **Company Remote Workers** group has been added and configured with a domain security group:

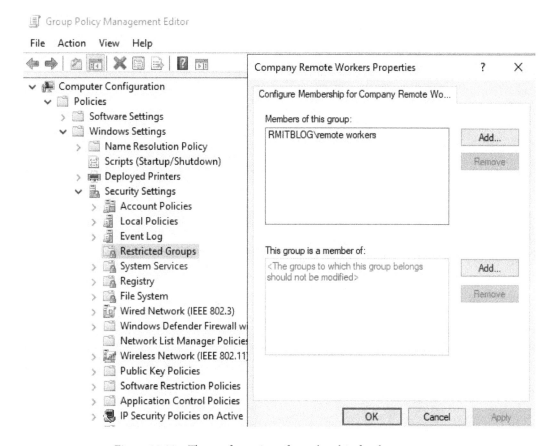

Figure 10.20 – The configuration of membership for the new group

Now that we have covered the **Restricted group** settings, let's take a look at **User Rights Assignments**.

User Rights Assignments are used for customizing specific items such as preventing the change of a time zone or making changes to a specific application; you can even configure who can shut down the session host. Again, as stated earlier, the configuration and customization of user rights assignments are unique to the organization, and it is recommended that rights assignments are carefully considered and tested.

The following screenshot shows the group policy setting for rights assignments under **Computer Configuration | Policies | Windows Settings | Security Settings | User Rights Assignment**:

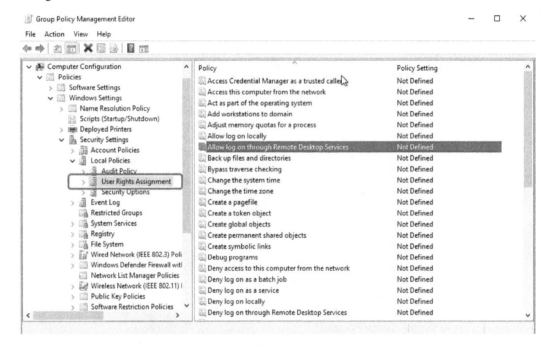

Figure 10.21 – The User Rights Assignment settings you can configure within group policy

You can use group policy to customize a wide range of optimizations/customizations and controls for AVD. Where possible, you should use group policy; however, it's important to note that some group policy settings could impact login performance compared to configuring directly on the image template.

> **Group Policy Tip**
>
> **LSDOU**: A really good acronym to remember when it comes to group policy is LSDOU. This means Local Group Policy objects are applied first, **LS**, then, **Domain (D)**, and, finally, Organizational Unit **OU** policies.
>
> **Block Inheritance**: This can be used if you want to ignore group policies above the OU your session hosts reside in. It is important to note that any enforced GPOs still apply when block inheritance is set.
>
> **Loopback**: This is useful for desktop virtualization environments, as you can take the user settings and apply them to a group of session hosts (user settings linked to the computer OU will be applied). Remember to ensure that both user and computer objects are added to the scope tab of the group policy object for this to work, and ensure the GPO status is set to enabled.
>
> Please note Loopback is known to slow down group policy processing.

The next section looks at configuring user restrictions by using Azure AD group policies and AD policies.

Configuring user restrictions by using Azure Active Directory Domain Service group policies

Using group policy to restrict visibility and access to items such as the operating system disk and removing the restart button from the start menu are typically done via group policy. It is recommended, where possible, to use group policy rather than direct configurations on the image template.

If you are using Azure Active Directory group policies, you will need to build a Windows Server management virtual machine that is joined to the Azure Active Directory Domain Services. Additionally, you will need a user account that is a member of the Azure AD DC administrators group in your Azure AD tenant. You can read more about the requirements and setup process at `https://docs.microsoft.com/azure/active-directory-domain-services/manage-group-policy`.

> **Tip**
>
> You can now use AVD with Intune for configuring policies and controls; for more information, please refer to `https://docs.microsoft.com/en-us/mem/intune/fundamentals/azure-virtual-desktop`.

Summary

This chapter looked at the Azure roles and the specific RBAC for AVD resources. I, hopefully, refreshed your memories of Active Directory and discussed some useful tips for managing local roles, groups, and rights assignments. Then, we finished by looking at the requirements for Azure Active Directory Domain Service to be able to use group policies.

In the next chapter, we will look at the application of security and compliance.

Questions

1. You have a group policy object named `user_personalization` that only contains user settings. The policy is linked to the AVD Session host OU. What should you configure for the settings within the policy to apply to users when they sign in to the session hosts?

2. Which Desktop Virtualization role allows you to manage all aspects of the AVD service?

3. What are the three key elements of RBAC?

Answers

1. *Loopback processing*

2. *Desktop Virtualization Contributor*

3. *Security principle, role definition, and scope*

11
Managing Security

In this chapter, we'll take a look at security and compliance settings for **Azure Virtual Desktop** (**AVD**). First, we'll look at planning and implementing **multi-factor authentication** (**MFA**) and Conditional Access policies for AVD. Next, we'll look at Microsoft Defender for Cloud and the benefits of turning this feature on and enabling Azure Defender. To finish the chapter, we'll look at Microsoft Defender Antivirus and additional configurations you can apply to streamline the security signature updates to session hosts.

This chapter covers the following topics:

- Planning and implementing MFA
- Managing security by using Microsoft Defender for Cloud
- Using Microsoft Defender for Cloud for AVD
- Enabling Azure Defender for AVD
- Configuring Microsoft Defender Antivirus for AVD

Introduction to MFA

MFA is an authentication layer you can add to the sign-in process as a way of improving sign-in security. When accessing corporate accounts, apps, or other services, the user is required to provide additional identity verification. This additional verification can be scanning a fingerprint or entering a code received by a phone or token-generating device.

> **Important Note**
>
> The security threat landscape is consistently changing, with new threats appearing daily. It is advised as a best practice that organizations use MFA as a standard practice to harden the sign-in process to protect users and corporate data.

How does Azure MFA work?

Azure **Active Directory** (**AD**) MFA works by the user requiring two or more authentication methods to complete a sign-in process. The first method is typically a password. Trusted devices such as a phone or hardware key or biometrics such as a fingerprint or face scan can be used as a second method.

> **Important Note**
>
> Azure AD MFA also offers a feature known as secure password reset. This can be enabled when users register for Azure AD MFA, which appears as an additional step.

You can use the following forms of authentication when using Azure MFA:

- Microsoft Authenticator app
- OATH hardware token (preview)
- OATH software token
- SMS
- Voice call

The verification when using Azure MFA looks similar to the following screenshot:

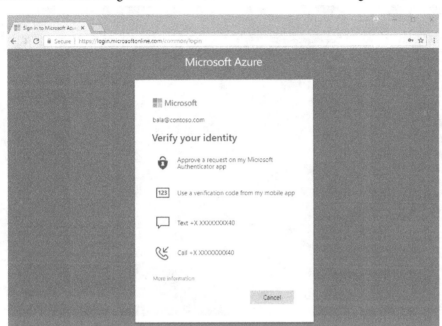

Figure 11.1 – Azure MFA prompt during a user sign-in process

You have the option of configuring the security defaults to enable Authenticator for all users or choosing conditional access policies that can be used to control specific events and applications. You can configure conditional policies to allow regular sign-in or to include a prompt for additional verification when a user is remote or on a personal device.

Let's now take a look at the security defaults available to you on Azure.

Security defaults

Security defaults are a feature that helps simplify security hardening when applying MFA to your organization's Azure tenant. When applying preconfigured security settings, you essentially set the following:

- Requiring all users to register for Azure AD MFA
- Requiring administrators to do MFA
- Blocking legacy authentication protocols
- Requiring users to do MFA when necessary

- Protecting privileged activities such as access to the Azure portal

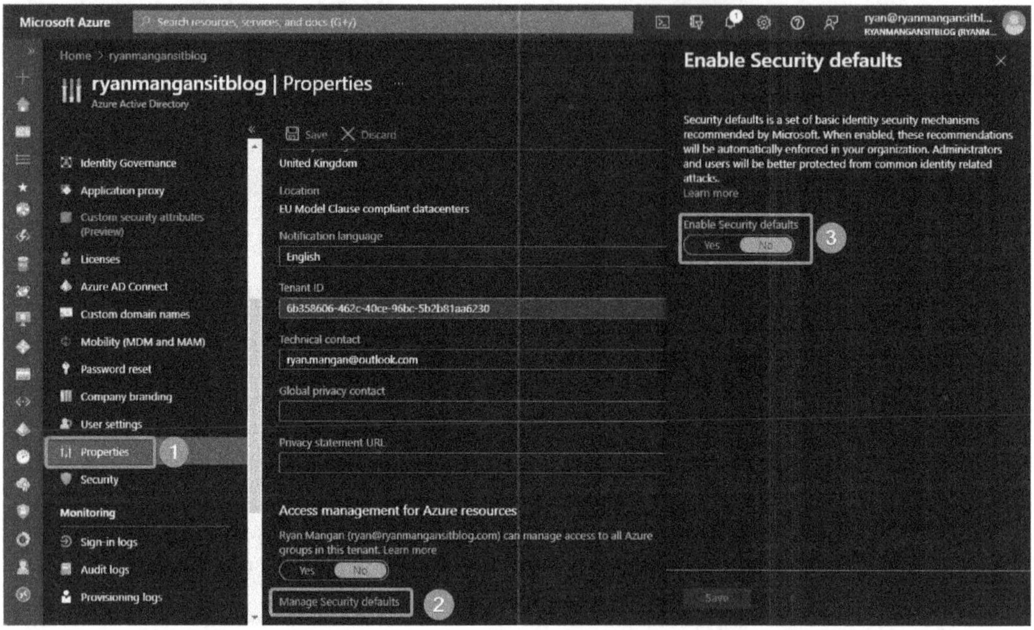

Figure 11.2 – Manage Security defaults section

You can read more on security defaults here: `https://docs.microsoft.com/azure/active-directory/fundamentals/concept-fundamentals-security-defaults`.

Conditional Access

As the technology ecosystem continues to evolve and change day by day, the way people work and access corporate resources changes. This can also be described as the *modern security perimeter*, which essentially refers to users and device identities that access corporate data and network resources from outside the corporate network.

When looking at conditional access, we need to first understand the three core principles: signals, decisions, and enforcements.

> **Important Note**
>
> To use conditional access policies, you need the Azure AD Premium P1 license. You can read more here: `https://www.microsoft.com/security/business/identity-access-management/azure-ad-pricing?rtc=1`.

Let's now take a look at these three components that are required for conditional access organizational policies:

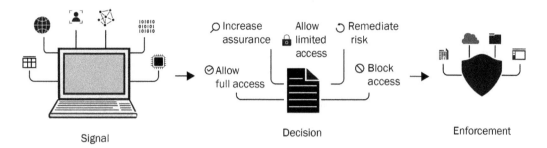

Figure 11.3 – The three components of Conditional Access policies

Signals

The following are taken into consideration when making policy decisions using conditional access:

Signal	Description
User and group membership	Policies can be targeted to specific users or group membership, enabling granular control over access to the organizational resource.
IP location information	Trusted locations are common as if a user needs to pass through an organization's physical security controls, such as security cards or biometrics, they may not need to use MFA at their desk.
Device	You can control access to specific devices or types of devices.
Application	You can control the required access controls based on the application the user is trying to connect to.
Real-time calculated risk detection	You can use advanced signals such as real-time or calculated risk detection based on identity risk sign-in behavior. This means if the behavior of an identity is deemed unusual, then access can be blocked until the admin takes manual intervention.
Microsoft Defender for Cloud apps	Application access and sessions can be monitored and controlled in real time, providing improved security controls as well as improved visibility of activities within your cloud environment.

Decisions

The following table details the two decisions and the options available when you select **Grant Access**:

Decision	Description
Block Access	This is the most restrictive decision.
Grant Access	You can configure one or many of the following controls with the Grant Access decision: • Require MFA • Require device to be marked as compliant • Require Hybrid Azure AD joined device • Require approved client app • Require app protection policy (preview)

Enforcement

The following is a list of examples of some of the applied policies you can set:

- Blocking risky sign-in behaviors
- Requiring MFA for Azure management tasks
- Blocking sign-ins for users attempting to use legacy authentication protocols
- Requiring trusted locations for Azure AD MFA registration
- Requiring MFA for users with administrative roles
- Blocking or granting access from specific locations
- Requiring organization-managed devices for specific applications

You can read more on the three components of Conditional Access here: `https://docs.microsoft.com/azure/active-directory/conditional-access/overview`.

The following diagram shows the use of the three components in actions to enforce conditional access on the required apps and data for your organizations:

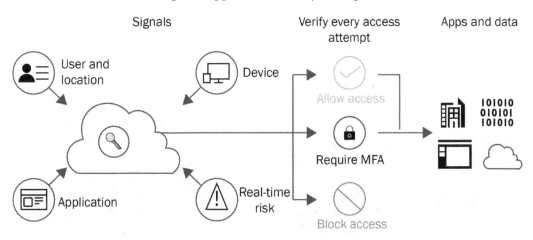

Figure 11.4 – Logical diagram of how Conditional Access works

We'll now move on to take a look at the planning and implementation of MFA.

Planning and implementing MFA

This section goes into detail on how to implement MFA for AVD. We will navigate through the process step by step. The benefit of MFA is that it provides an extra layer of security for users, and only the user with access to the token can log in, reducing the risk of unauthorized access to the network and IT resources.

The prerequisites for getting started are as follows:

- You first need to assign a license to users that includes Azure AD Premium P1 or P2.

- You also need to create a new Azure AD group for MFA and ensure that you have included the users you want to assign MFA to.

- Ensure you enable Azure MFA for all required users.

For more information on the prerequisites, please see the following link: https://docs.microsoft.com/en-us/azure/active-directory/authentication/howto-mfa-getstarted#prerequisites-for-deploying-azure-ad-mfa.

You also need to ensure that your users are configured to use MFA. This is done by following the steps I have summarized here:

1. First, sign in to the Azure portal using an administrator account.

2. Select **Azure Active Directory** from the left-hand menu, then select **Users** | **All users**.

3. Select **Per-user MFA**. The following screenshot shows the **All users** section within Azure AD:

Figure 11.5 – The All users page within Azure AD

4.   The following screenshot shows the **Enable** button for enabling a user to use MFA:

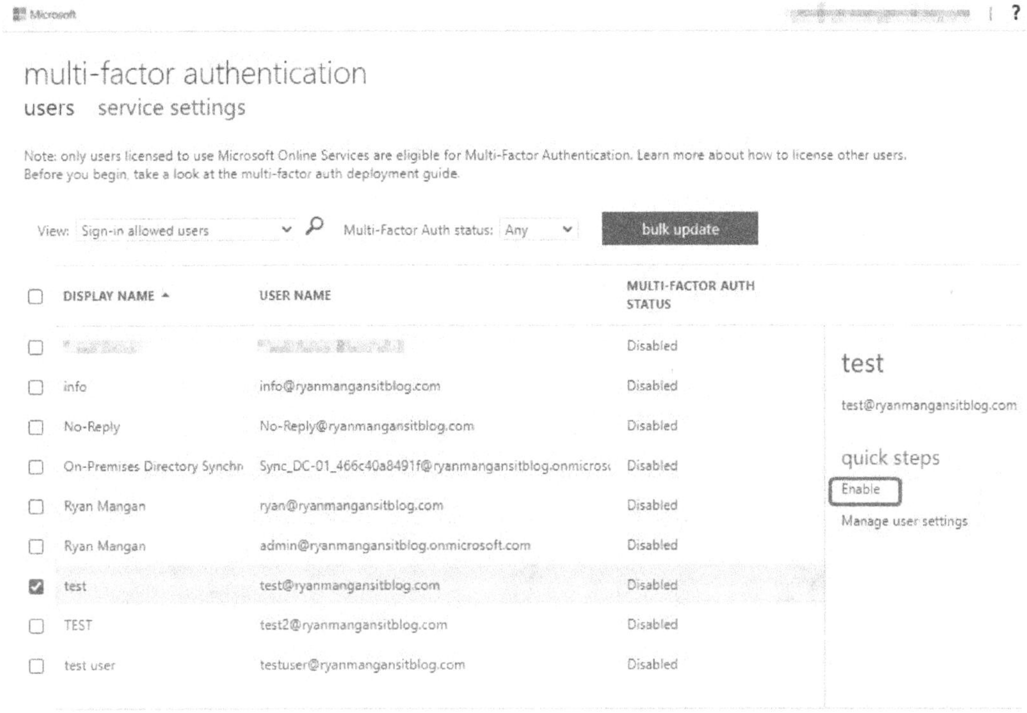

Figure 11.6 – The multi-factor authentication page for enabling MFA for users found in the
Office.com portal

To configure multi-factor user states, see the following link: `https://docs.`
`microsoft.com/azure/active-directory/authentication/howto-mfa-`
`userstates`.

> **Tip**
> It is recommended that you do not manually change the user state to
> **Enforced** unless the user is already registered or understands there will be an
> interruption in connections to legacy authentication protocols.

In the following subsection, we take a look at configuring the required conditional access
policy for AVD to enforce MFA.

Creating a conditional access policy for MFA

In the previous section, we discussed conditional access policies and the three components: signals, decisions, and enforcements. We'll now take a look at creating a conditional access policy.

The following steps guide you through creating a conditional Access policy that requires MFA when connecting to AVD:

1. Log in to the Azure portal as an administrator.

2. Navigate to **Azure Active Directory | Security | Conditional Access**. This screenshot shows the **Security** menu within the **Azure Active Directory** menu in the Azure portal:

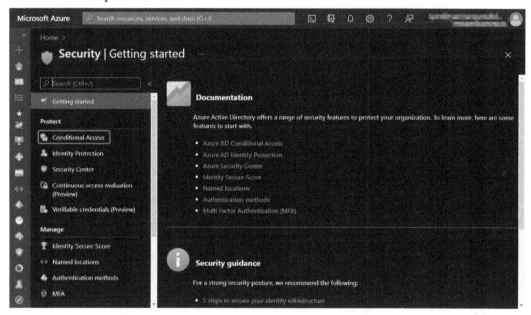

Figure 11.7 – Conditional Access option on the Azure AD page

3. Select **+ New policy**. This screenshot shows the button to add a new conditional access policy:

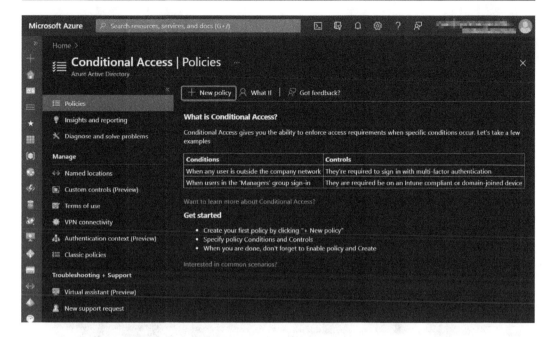

Figure 11.8 – Add new policy button

4. Enter a name for your policy.

5. Under the **Assignments** section, select **users and groups**. Under **Include,** click on **select users and groups | users and groups** and choose the group you created in the prerequisites stage. Click on **Done**.

6. Under **Cloud apps or actions | Include**, click on **Select apps**. Select one of the following apps based on which version of AVD you're using.

> **Tip**
> Please note you may find that the name has not changed from Windows Virtual Desktop, and it is advised you check for both.

If using AVD, choose this app: **Azure Virtual Desktop** (app ID 9cdead84-a844-4324-93f2-b2e6bb768d07).

The following screenshot shows the details filled in for creating a new conditional access policy, which we will apply to AVD as specified in the **Cloud apps | Include** section:

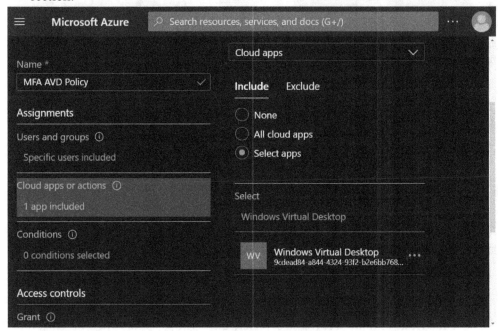

Figure 11.9 – Cloud apps AVD

Tip

To find the app ID of the app you want to select, navigate to **Enterprise Applications** and select **Microsoft Applications** from the **Application type** drop-down menu. You can read more here: `https://docs.microsoft.com/azure/active-directory/manage-apps/view-applications-portal?tabs=azure-portal#search-for-an-application`.

7. Next, navigate to **Conditions | Client apps**. In **Configure**, select **Yes**, and then select where to apply the policy:

- If you want the policy to apply to the web client, then select **Browser**.

- If you want to apply the policy to other clients, then select **Mobile apps and desktop clients**.

- If you want to apply the policy to all clients, then select both the checkboxes.

The following screenshot shows the conditions set for this conditional access policy; you will note that both **Browser** and **Mobile apps and desktop clients** have been set for this policy:

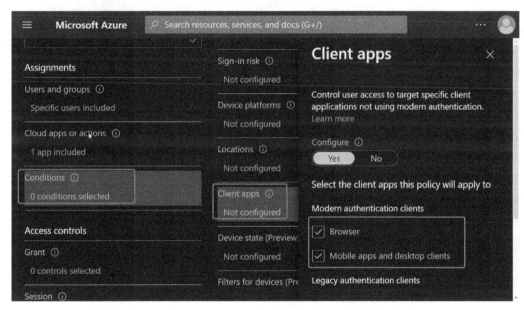

Figure 11.10 – Conditions being set for browser and mobile apps and desktop clients

8. Once you've selected the required client apps as shown in *Figure 9.10*, click **Select**, and then click on **Done**.

9. Under **Access controls | Grant**, select **Grant access | Require multi-factor authentication**, and then **Select**.

The following screenshot shows the configuration of access controls, specifically the **Grant access** control. By setting **Require multi-factor authentication**, you force the user to complete two-factor verification to access the resources configured within the conditional access policy:

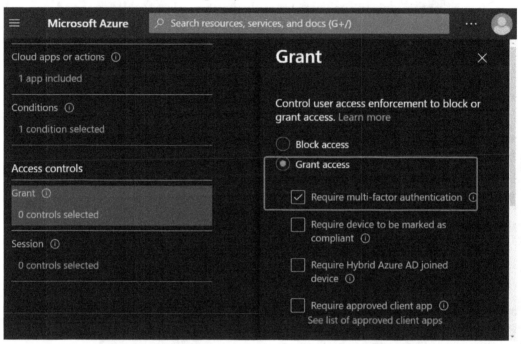

Figure 11.11 – Control for enforcing MFA for granting access to the cloud app

10. Under **Access controls | Session**, select **Sign-in frequency**, set the value to the time you want between MFA prompts, and then click on **Select**. For example, setting the value to **4** and the unit to **Hours** will require MFA if a connection is launched 4 hours after the last.

The following screenshot shows the customization of the sign-in frequency setting. You can set a specific time before a user needs to reauthenticate:

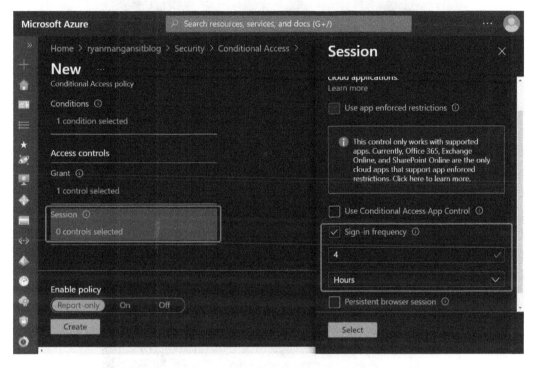

Figure 11.12 – Sign-in frequency setting for enforcing re-authentication

11. Confirm the settings and set **Enable policy** to **On**. The following screenshot shows that **Enable policy** has been turned on for the conditional access policy:

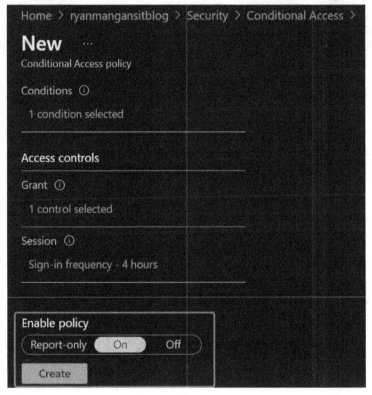

Figure 11.13 – Setting the policy to On

12. Select **Create** to enable your policy.

There you have it; you have enabled MFA and configured the required conditional access policy for AVD.

> **Tip**
>
> It is advised that you use **Report-only** before introducing this to a production environment. **Report-only** allows you to identify any issues and ensure the configured conditional access policy is functioning correctly.

This section looked at enabling MFA for users and then configuring an AVD conditional access policy. The next section looks at managing security by using Microsoft Defender for Cloud.

Managing security by using Microsoft Defender for Cloud

Microsoft Defender for Cloud was previously known as Azure Security Center and Azure Defender. I want to set some context around the reasoning and detail of the responsibilities split between Microsoft and the customer.

We previously spoke about some advanced security features, such as reverse connect, which reduces the risk of exposing virtual desktop resources directly to the public network. We'll now look at the security responsibilities and some of the Azure security best practices available to you.

Here are the security areas you're responsible for in your AVD deployment. Note that the value under the **Customer responsibility** column is **Yes** if the customer is responsible and **No** if Microsoft is responsible:

Security areas	Customer Responsibility
Identity	Yes
User devices (mobile and PC)	Yes
App security	Yes
Session host OS	Yes
Deployment configuration	Yes
Network controls	Yes
Virtualization control plane	No
Physical hosts	No
Physical network	No
Physical datacenter	No

This table was taken from the following Microsoft link:

```
https://docs.microsoft.com/en-us/azure/virtual-desktop/
security-guide#security-responsibilities
```

As detailed in the table, Microsoft takes care of the physical aspects of the cloud infrastructure and the virtualization control plane. The customer is responsible for everything else. This is why it makes sense to use Microsoft Defender for Cloud to assist with security hardening all the required components for your AVD environment.

> **Important Note**
>
> Microsoft Defender for Cloud is an essentially security posture manager that has two offerings, the first being a free version and the second option known as enhanced security, which offers a number of security features and tools to help you harden your environment.
>
> Microsoft Defender for Cloud represents a number of security services that are specific to different workloads, such as databases, storage accounts, containers, and key vaults.

Microsoft Defender for Cloud helps you harden your resources, as well as mapping your current security posture and tracking future changes to help protect against cyber attacks and streamline your IT security. As Microsoft Defender for Cloud is natively integrated, it provides a simple and easy way to deploy Defender to secure your resources by default.

Take a look at the three core needs when managing security with Microsoft Defender for Cloud:

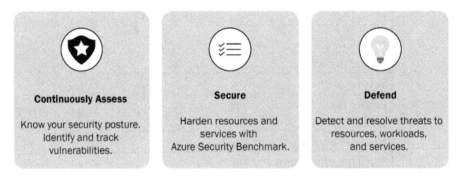

Figure 11.14 – The three core needs when managing the security of your resources in the cloud or on-premises

For a detailed breakdown of Microsoft Defender for Cloud, take a look at the following link: `https://docs.microsoft.com/azure/defender-for-cloud/defender-for-cloud-introduction`.

The following table describes the three core security requirements used within Defender for Cloud:

Security requirement	Defender for Cloud solution
Continuous assessment – Understand your current security posture.	Secure score – A single score so that you can tell, at a glance, your current security situation: the higher the score, the lower the identified risk level.
Secure – Harden all connected resources and services.	Security recommendations – Customized and prioritized hardening tasks to improve your posture. You implement a recommendation by following the detailed remediation steps provided in the recommendation. For many recommendations, Defender for Cloud offers a Fix button for automated implementation!
Defend – Detect and resolve threats to those resources and services.	Security alerts – With the enhanced security features enabled, Defender for Cloud detects threats to your resources and workloads. These alerts appear in the Azure portal and Defender for Cloud can also send them by email to the relevant personnel in your organization. Alerts can also be streamed to SIEM, SOAR, or IT Service Management solutions as required.

The table is taken from the Microsoft documentation site: `https://docs.microsoft.com/azure/defender-for-cloud/defender-for-cloud-introduction`.

Important Note

Please note that when using custom/third-party technologies such as **network virtual appliances** (**NVAs**), you may get false positive alerts from Microsoft Defender for Cloud regarding best practices. These alerts or recommendations become a false positive because you are effectively bypassing the default Azure configurations with a third-party security feature/technology. One good example is the use of port forwarding that is typically enabled for an NVA. This would flag an alert in Microsoft Defender for Cloud. However, port forwarding must pass traffic through the NVA and thus must be enabled on the NVA.

Microsoft Defender for Cloud provides a security score, which is essentially a set of recommendations and best practices for improving your AVD environment:

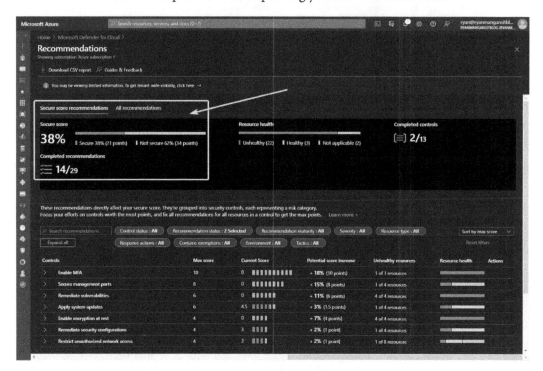

Figure 11.15 – Security score and list of recommendations below

The good news is that recommendations are prioritized to help you select the most important. There is also the **Fix** option to help you quickly identify and address any vulnerabilities. This is important to note. The **Fix** button helps with some issues but does not provide full coverage. It's advised that you conduct internal security reviews to ensure that you meet the requirements for your organization's security posture:

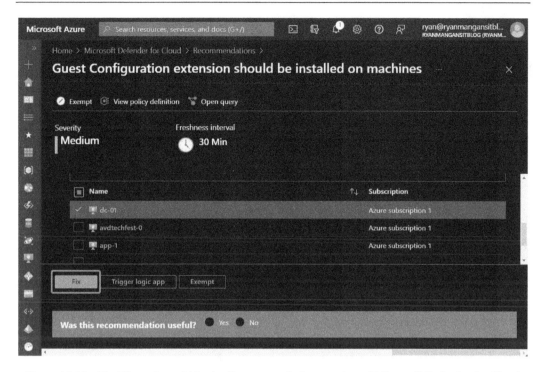

Figure 11.16 – The Fix option within the Recommendations section of Microsoft Defender for Cloud

---

Important Note

The recommendations will update when changes in the IT ecosystem occur, meaning that new recommendations will be provided when the security landscape changes, such as new vulnerabilities arising or new/better ways to maintain your AVD environment's security develop.

The next section takes a look at securing your AVD security environment and enabling enhanced security within Microsoft Defender for Cloud.

Securing AVD using Microsoft Defender for Cloud

As summarized in the introduction to this section, the customer is responsible for the following areas under the shared responsibility model:

- Network
- Deployment configuration
- Session host operating system
- Application security
- Identity

Security posture is a term used to reference the overall cybersecurity strength of an organization. It can also be used to predict, prevent, and respond to ever-changing threats. Therefore, it is advised that you examine both the required level of threat protection and the security posture for your AVD environment.

The misconfiguration of the network and/or virtual machines can increase the attack surface or possibly compromise an endpoint.

> **Important Note**
>
> You need to ensure that all management ports are closed on your AVD virtual machines. No direct access to session hosts from the public network is required. If you want direct access to virtual machines, it is advised to use Azure Bastion or connect over a VPN.

We cover endpoint protection in the next section; however, it is necessary to call out the following security controls to protect users from browsing to malicious sites or connecting to malicious devices.

Here is a list of benefits Microsoft Defender for Cloud offers for improving security posture and threat protection for AVD when enabling Azure Defender:

- Secure configuration assessment and Secure Score
- Industry-tested vulnerability assessment
- Host-level detections
- Agentless cloud network micro-segmentation and detection
- File integrity monitoring
- Just-in-time virtual machine access
- Adaptive application controls

The following table shows different security areas and what Microsoft Defender for Cloud offers in terms of capabilities:

Azure Virtual Desktop security area	Azure Security Center security posture enhancement capabilities	Microsoft Defender for Cloud threat protection capabilities
Network security	Secure configuration assessment and security score Just-in-time virtual machine access	Agentless cloud network micro-segmentation and detections
Deployment configuration	Secure configuration assessment and security score Session host operating system	Not available
Session host operating system	Industry-tested vulnerability assessment	Host-level detections
Application security	Industry-tested vulnerability assessment File integrity monitoring Adaptive application controls	Host-level detections
Identity	Secure configuration assessment and security score	Agentless cloud network micro-segmentation and detections

This section provided a high-level overview of Microsoft's and the customer's security responsibilities. In addition, it provided an introduction to Microsoft Defender for Cloud to set the scene for the following sections of this chapter. We'll now move on to take a look at using Microsoft Defender for Cloud and Azure Defender for AVD.

Using Microsoft Defender for Cloud and AVD

Out of the box, you can use Microsoft Defender for Cloud to provide continuous assessments and security recommendations, fixes, and Azure security scores, which can be used to gauge your security posture.

Enabling Azure Defender opens up additional features, including just-in-time virtual machine access, adaptive application controls/network hardening, compliance dashboards/reports, threat protection for Azure virtual machines, and non-Azure servers.

> **Important Note**
> It is important to note that Microsoft Defender for Cloud is a **security posture manager** (SPM).

The following screenshot shows the differences between Microsoft Defender for Cloud being switched on and off:

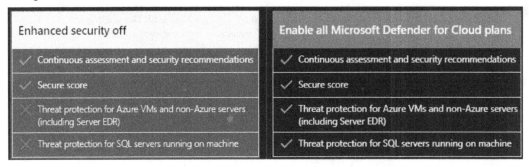

Enhanced security off	Enable all Microsoft Defender for Cloud plans
✓ Continuous assessment and security recommendations	✓ Continuous assessment and security recommendations
✓ Secure score	✓ Secure score
✓ Threat protection for Azure VMs and non-Azure servers (including Server EDR)	✓ Threat protection for Azure VMs and non-Azure servers (including Server EDR)
✗ Threat protection for SQL servers running on machine	✓ Threat protection for SQL servers running on machine

Figure 11.17 – The different features available when Microsoft Defender for Cloud is on and off

To access Microsoft Defender for Cloud, you will see an icon in the main window of the Azure portal with the Security Center icon. When you click this, you will be taken to the **Overview** window of Microsoft Defender for Cloud, as shown in the following screenshot:

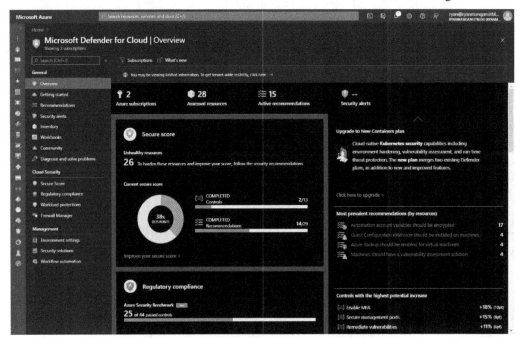

Figure 11.18 – Microsoft Defender for Cloud Overview page

Within Microsoft Defender for Cloud, you can review and configure various security controls/policies and review best practices. A lot of the content within Microsoft Defender for Cloud is out of scope for this book; however, we will take a brief look at what you can use for AVD to improve your desktop virtualization security posture.

You can take a look at your resources via the inventory, as highlighted in the following screenshot. This lets you see which resources are configured with monitoring agents, turn Azure Defender on/off, and see recommendations.

The following screenshot shows the **Inventory** page of Microsoft Defender for Cloud. This page is used for reviewing all resources, including total, unhealthy, unmonitored, and unregistered subscriptions:

Figure 11.19 – Microsoft Defender for Cloud Inventory page

One final part I wanted to cover before we move on to enabling Microsoft Defender for Cloud is the **Recommendations** page. This provides a centralized list of recommendations to improve your Azure security score, as well as gauging your current state and future security score.

> **Tip**
> Did you know that the regulatory compliance feature within Microsoft Defender for Cloud is part of the free module?

The following screenshot shows the list of recommendations for Azure Security Center based on the current score and configuration of the Azure subscription:

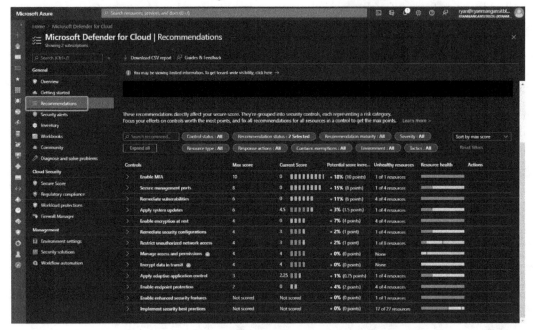

Figure 11.20 – Recommendations page within Azure Security Center

In this section, we looked at Microsoft Defender for Cloud and how it can help improve your AVD's security posture. The next section takes a look at enabling Azure Defender for AVD.

Enabling enhanced security for AVD

This section summarizes the basic steps for enabling enhanced security for Microsoft Defender for Cloud on your Azure subscription. This will allow you to use the more advanced features of Security Center at a cost.

The link to pricing can be found here: `https://azure.microsoft.com/pricing/details/azure-defender/`.

> **Important Note**
>
> You will need to enable enhanced security for Microsoft Defender for Cloud
> for each subscription you use.

The basic steps for enabling Azure Defender on your Azure subscription are as follows:

1. Navigate to Security Center located on the left-hand menu. Within the **Microsoft Defender for Cloud** menu, select **Environment settings**. The following screenshot shows the **Environment settings** menu option, which lists the subscriptions:

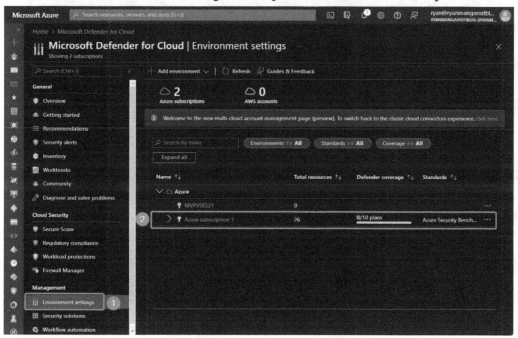

Figure 11.21 – Pricing and settings page in Microsoft Defender for Cloud

2. Click on the required Azure subscription.

3. Select **Enable all Microsoft Defender for Cloud plans**.

> **Important Note**
>
> It is important to note that if you select the option for **Enable all Microsoft Defender for Cloud plans**, this will onboard all resources within the subscription. If you want to onboard only a subset, you will need to manually onboard the specific required resources.

The following screenshot shows the option to turn Microsoft Defender for Cloud on and off:

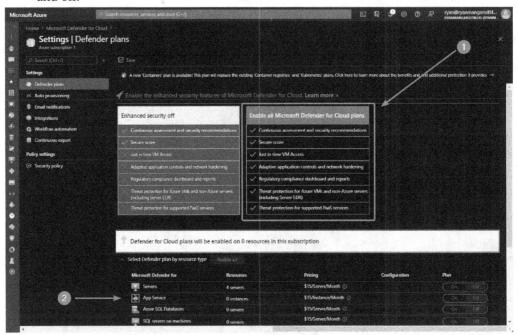

Figure 11.22 – Selecting Enable Microsoft Defender for Cloud plans on the Defender plans page

4. Select the resource types that you would like to enable on the **Defender plans** page. The following screenshot shows the different plans you can configure when you want to enable enhanced security:

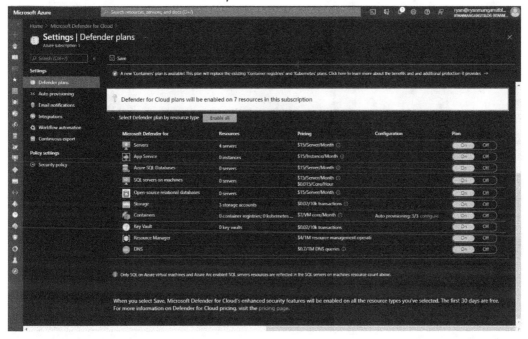

Figure 11.23 – Selected plans and saving the chosen plans

Once you have chosen the resource types (plans) you require, click **Save**.

5. Then, navigate back to the main Microsoft Defender for Cloud page and click **Workload protections** from the left-hand menu. The following screenshot shows the **Workload protections** page within Microsoft Defender for Cloud:

Figure 11.24 – Workload protections page detailing the coverage graphically

As shown in the preceding screenshot, you can see that you can now review Azure Defender's coverage. This concludes the enablement of enhanced security within Microsoft Defender for Cloud for AVD.

For more information on Microsoft Defender for Cloud, check out this link for the planning and operations guide: `https://docs.microsoft.com/azure/defender-for-cloud/security-center-planning-and-operations-guide`.

In the next section, we'll look at configuring Microsoft Defender Antivirus for session hosts and useful configurations for ensuring antimalware signatures are constantly updated.

Configuring Microsoft Defender Antivirus for session hosts

This section takes a look at Microsoft Defender Antivirus for session hosts. Before we look at scans and prevent notifications, I want to first take a look at offloading security intelligence updates onto a host machine.

The benefit of doing this is to reduce the impact on the CPU, disk, and memory resources of the session hosts when security intelligence updates are processed. You can manage Microsoft Defender Antivirus using Group Policy; however, you can also use System Center Configuration Manager, Intune, and other third-party **mobile device management** (**MDM**) platforms.

See the following link from Microsoft on deploying Microsoft Defender Antivirus: `https://docs.microsoft.com/microsoft-365/security/defender-endpoint/deployment-vdi-microsoft-defender-antivirus`.

What is the difference between Microsoft Defender Antivirus and Microsoft Defender for Endpoint?

Microsoft Defender for Endpoint is an additional license you can purchase that essentially offers an extra layer of security to your endpoints. It is an enterprise endpoint security platform that offers additional features to antivirus offerings, including advanced threat detection.

The following table details why you should consider both Microsoft Defender Antivirus and Microsoft Defender for Endpoint together:

#	Advantage	Why it matters
1	Antivirus signal sharing	Microsoft applications and services share signals across your enterprise organization, providing a stronger single platform. See `https://www.microsoft.com/security/blog/2018/12/03/insights-from-the-mitre-attack-based-evaluation-of-windows-defender-atp/`.
2	Threat analytics and your score for devices	Microsoft Defender Antivirus collects underlying system data used by threat analytics and Microsoft Secure Score for Devices. This provides your organization's security team with more meaningful information, such as recommendations and opportunities to improve your organization's security posture.
3	Performance	Microsoft Defender for Endpoint is designed to work with Microsoft Defender Antivirus, so you get better performance when you use these offerings together.
4	Details about blocked malware	More details and actions for blocked malware are available with Microsoft Defender Antivirus and Microsoft Defender for Endpoint.
5	Network protection	Your organization's security team can protect your network by blocking specific URLs and IP addresses.
6	File blocking	Your organization's security team can block specific files.
7	Attack Surface Reduction	Your organization's security team can reduce your vulnerabilities (attack surfaces), giving attackers fewer ways to perform attacks. Attack surface reduction uses cloud protection for a number of rules.
8	Auditing events	Auditing event signals are available in endpoint detection and response capabilities. (These signals are not available with non-Microsoft antivirus solutions.)
9	Geographic data	Compliant with ISO 270001 and data retention, geographic data is provided according to your organization's selected geographic sovereignty.
10	File recovery via OneDrive	If you are using Microsoft Defender Antivirus together with Office 365, and your device is attacked by ransomware, your files are protected and recoverable.
11	Technical support	By using Microsoft Defender for Endpoint together with Microsoft Defender Antivirus, you have one company to call for technical support.

The preceding table was taken from the following Microsoft link: `https://docs. microsoft.com/microsoft-365/security/defender-endpoint/ why-use-microsoft-defender-antivirus`.

> **Important Note**
>
> The Microsoft Defender Antivirus feature was introduced in Windows 10 version 1903; however, it has been backported to Windows 10 version 1703 and above.

Let's now take a look at configuring some of the Microsoft Defender Antivirus features.

In this example, you will use Group Policy to enable the Microsoft shared security intelligence feature:

> **Important Note**
>
> The shared security intelligence feature is used to offload the processing required by an endpoint in terms of unpackaging and installing security intelligence updates. Using a network or local path reduces the resource utilization of a client when security intelligence updates are applied.

1. On the management machine with Group Policy installed, open the Group Policy management console, right-click the Group Policy object you want to configure, and then click **Edit**.

2. In **Group Policy Management Editor**, navigate to **Computer configuration**.

3. Click the **Administrative** templates.

4. Expand the tree to **Windows components | Microsoft Defender Antivirus | Security Intelligence Updates**.

5. The following screenshot shows the **Security Intelligence Updates | Define security intelligence location for VDI clients** policy location:

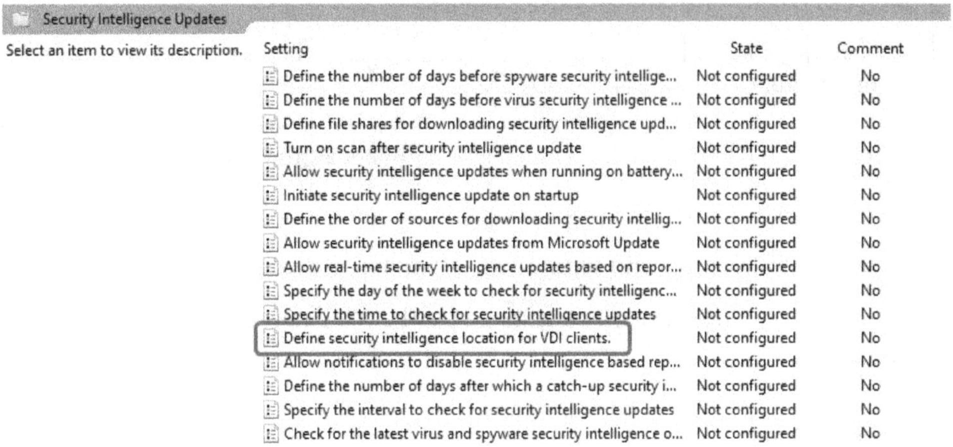

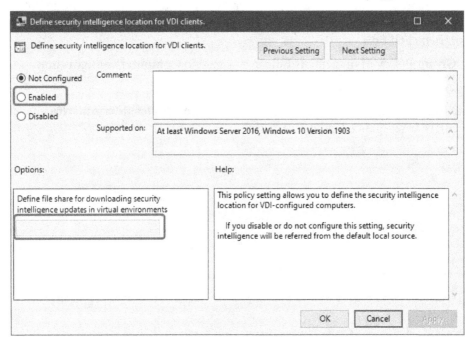

Figure 11.25 – The Define security intelligence location for VDI clients policy within the Security Intelligence Updates policy folder

Double-click **Define security intelligence location for VDI clients**, and then set the option to **Enabled** within the form. A field should then automatically appear:

Figure 11.26 – Configuration form for Define security intelligence location for VDI clients

6. Enter `\\<fileshare\>\av-update` (for help with this value, we will look at how to download these updates shortly).

7. Click **OK** to close the form with the new configuration.

8. Deploy the Group Policy object to the virtual machines you want to test.

> **Tip**
>
> You can also use PowerShell to enable the feature using the following cmdlet: `Set-MpPreference -SharedSignaturesPath \\<fileshare>\av-update`. You can deliver these on each machine or use the Custom Script Extension.

Getting the latest updates

To download and unpack the latest security updates, it's advised that you configure a PowerShell script as a scheduled task to automatically update the file share with new security update definitions when they are released:

```
$vdmspathbase = "$env:systemdrive\av-update\{00000000-0000-
0000-0000-"

$vdmspathtime = Get-Date -format "yMMddHHmmss"

$vdmspath = $vdmspathbase + $vdmspathtime + '}'

$vdmspackage = $vdmspath + '\mpam-fe.exe'


New-Item -ItemType Directory -Force -Path $vdmspath | Out-Null


Invoke-WebRequest -Uri 'https://go.microsoft.com/
fwlink/?LinkID=121721&arch=x64' -OutFile $vdmspackage


cmd /c "cd $vdmpath & c: & mpam-fe.exe /x"
```

Setting the scheduled task to run the PowerShell script

The following steps guide you in setting a scheduled task to run the PowerShell script:

1. On your chosen management machine, open the *Start* menu and type `Task Scheduler`. Open and select **Create task...** on the side panel.

2. Enter the name as `Security intelligence unpacker` or another name of your choosing. Go to the **Trigger** tab. Select **New...** | **Daily** and select **OK**.

3. Go to the **Actions** tab. Select **New....** Enter `PowerShell` in the **Program/Script** field. Enter `-ExecutionPolicy Bypass c:\av-update\vdmdlunpack.ps1` in the **Add arguments** field. Select **OK**.

4. You can also choose to configure additional settings if you require.

5. Select **OK** to save the configured scheduled task.

You can start the update manually by right-clicking on the task and clicking **Run**.

Manually downloading and unpacking

If you would prefer to configure manually, this is what to do to replicate the script's behavior:

1. Create a new folder on the machine root called `av_update` to store intelligence updates; for example, create the `c:\av_update` folder.

2. Create a subfolder under `av_update` with a GUID name, such as `{00000000-0000-0000-0000-000000000000}`.

    Here's an example: `c:\av_update\{00000000-0000-0000-0000-000000000000}`.

    > **Important Note**
    >
    > In the *Getting the latest updates* section, you will note that the script includes the date, month, and year within the GUID so that a new folder is created for each update. This can be changed so that files are downloaded to the same folder each time.

3. Download a security intelligence package from `https://www.microsoft.com/wdsi/definitions` into the GUID folder. The file should be named `mpam-fe.exe`.

4. Open a Command Prompt window and navigate to the GUID folder you previously created. Use the `/X` extraction command to extract the files, for example, `mpam-fe.exe /X`.

> **Tip**
> The session host virtual machines will pick up the updated package when a new GUID folder is created with an update package or whenever the existing folder is updated with new packages.

The next section looks at configuring quick scans for AVD session hosts.

Configuring quick scans

This section takes a quick look at configuring the group policy for specifying the scan type. In the example, we will be configuring a quick scan:

1. In Group Policy Editor, go to **Administrative templates | Windows components | Microsoft Defender Antivirus | Scan**:

Scan			

Specify the scan type to use for a scheduled scan
 	
Edit policy setting
 	
Requirements:
At least Windows Server 2012, Windows 8 or Windows RT
 	
Description:
This policy setting allows you to specify the scan type to use during a scheduled scan. Scan type options are:
  1 = Quick Scan (default)
  2 = Full Scan
 	
If you enable this setting, the scan type will be set to the specified value.
 	
If you disable or do not configure this setting, the default scan type will used.
	Setting	**State**	**Comment**

	Turn on reparse point scanning	Not configured	No
	Create a system restore point	Not configured	No
	Run full scan on mapped network drives	Not configured	No
	Scan network files	Not configured	No
	Configure local setting override for maximum percentage o...	Not configured	No
	Configure local setting override for the scan type to use for ...	Not configured	No
	Configure local setting override for schedule scan day	Not configured	No
	Configure local setting override for scheduled quick scan ti...	Not configured	No
	Configure local setting override for scheduled scan time	Not configured	No
	Configure low CPU priority for scheduled scans	Not configured	No
	Define the number of days after which a catch-up scan is fo...	Not configured	No
	Turn on removal of items from scan history folder	Not configured	No
	Specify the interval to run quick scans per day	Not configured	No
	Start the scheduled scan only when computer is on but not i...	Not configured	No
	Specify the scan type to use for a scheduled scan	Not configured	No
	Specify the day of the week to run a scheduled scan	Not configured	No
	Specify the time for a daily quick scan	Not configured	No
	Specify the time of day to run a scheduled scan	Not configured	No

Figure 11.27 – The Specify the scan type to use for a scheduled scan policy in the Scan policy folder

2. Select **Specify the scan type to use for a scheduled scan** and then edit the policy setting. The following screenshot shows the **Specify the scan type to use for a scheduled scan** form set to **Enabled** and the scan type set to **Quick scan**:

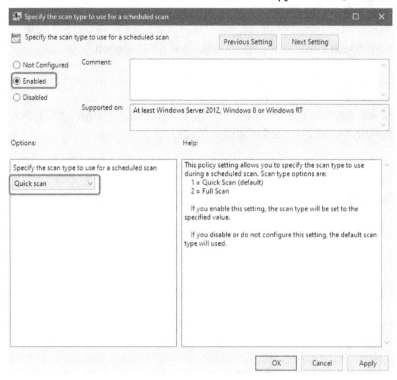

Figure 11.28 – Policy form for configuring the scan type

3. Set the policy to **Enabled**, and then under **Options**, select **Quick scan**.

4. Select **OK**.

5. Deploy your Group Policy object.

This section showed you how to configure a quick scan for AVD session hosts. We will now take a look at how to suppress notifications for Microsoft Defender Antivirus.

Suppressing notifications

This section looks at how you can suppress Microsoft Defender Antivirus notifications. Follow these steps detailed to configure it:

1. In Group Policy Editor, go to **Windows components | Microsoft Defender Antivirus | Client Interface**. The following screenshot shows the **Microsoft Defender Antivirus | Client Interface | Suppress all notifications** policy:

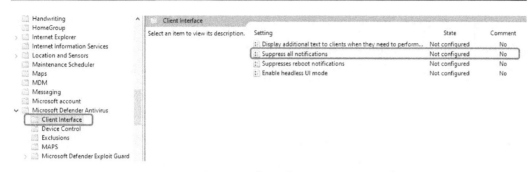

Figure 11.29 – Suppress all notifications in Group Policy

2. Select **Suppress all notifications** and then edit the policy settings. The following screenshot shows the **Suppress all notifications** policy set to **Enabled**:

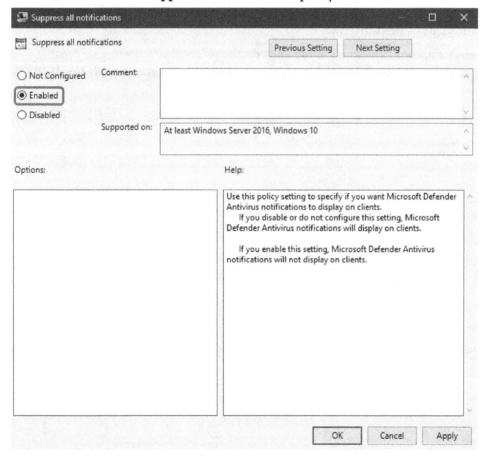

Figure 11.30 – Suppress all notifications policy form

3. Set the policy to **Enabled**, and then select **OK**.

4. Deploy your Group Policy object.

This section looked at suppressing all notifications for Microsoft Defender Antivirus. Next, we'll look at enabling headless UI mode, which essentially hides the UI from the user.

Enabling headless UI mode

Headless UI mode is a great feature for AVD as it hides the UI from the end user. This means that the IT admin is in full control and schedules scans when required.

The following steps detail how to configure headless UI mode:

1. In Group Policy Editor, navigate to **Windows components | Microsoft Defender Antivirus | Client Interface**.

2. Select **Enable headless UI mode** and edit the policy. The following screenshot shows the **Microsoft Defender Antivirus | Client Interface | Enable headless UI mode** policy:

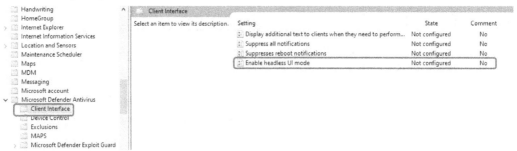

Figure 11.31 – The Enable headless UI mode policy within the Client Interface folder for Microsoft Defender Antivirus

3. Set the policy to **Enabled**. The following screenshot shows the enabled headless UI mode:

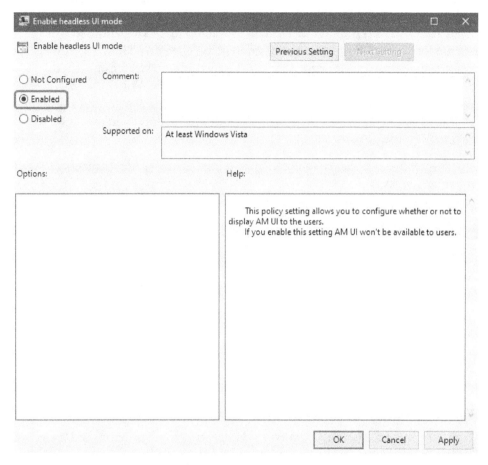

Figure 11.32 – The Enable headless UI mode policy form

4. Click **OK**.

5. Deploy the Group Policy object.

In this section, we looked at enabling headless UI mode to hide Microsoft Defender Antivirus from the users' view.

Summary

This chapter provided an insight into Microsoft Defender for Cloud with a focus on AVD. We started the chapter off by looking at enabling MFA and then configuring a conditional access policy to enforce MFA on AVD. We then moved on to looking at the security responsibilities of both Microsoft and the customers. We then dived into Microsoft Defender for Cloud, the value it offers Azure customers, and how you can use it to improve your AVD security posture as well as the security of the Azure resources running more widely within your subscription(s). To finish off the chapter, we looked at Microsoft Defender Antivirus at a high level, focusing on some of the features you may want to configure for AVD.

In the next chapter, we will change topics to look at implementing and managing FSLogix profile containers in AVD.

Questions

1. What is the difference between Microsoft Defender Antivirus and Microsoft Defender for Endpoint?

2. What are the three core principles required for setting up a Conditional Access policy?

3. What does the security defaults policy do in regards to Azure MFA?

4. What are the two options when configuring Azure Defender for Cloud?

Answers

1. *Microsoft Defender Antivirus is native to the operating system. Microsoft Defender for Endpoint is an additional service for which you require a license.*

2. *Signals, decisions, and enforcements.*

3. *Applies a default set of preconfigured security settings.*

4. *Enhanced security off and enhanced security on.*

Section 5:
Managing User
Environments and Apps

The section of the book looks at the management and configuration of user environments and apps for Azure Virtual Desktop.

This part of the book comprises the following chapters:

- *Chapter 12, Implementing and Managing FSLogix*
- *Chapter 13, Configuring User Experience Settings*
- *Chapter 14, MSIX App Attach*
- *Chapter 15, Installing and Configuring Apps on a Session Host*

12
Implementing and Managing FSLogix

In this chapter, we take more of an in-depth look at FSLogix and the benefits associated with it. First, in *Chapter 5*, *Implementing and Managing Storage for Azure Virtual Desktop*, we covered some of the planning requirements for FSLogix and storage, and now we move on to the implementation and management of FSLogix.

FSLogix profile containers enable you to roam user data between computing session hosts. This allows you to remove the user's dependency on a specific device. The benefits of this include the fact that the user's sign-in times are minimized as they don't have to create a new profile with each logo, along with providing the flexibility of connecting to different business desktops/remote apps with the same user profile experience.

To summarize how FSLogix works, it uses both a filesystem driver and a registry filter driver, which handles any filesystem or registry requests that allow the user profiles to be redirected.

Here are the topics that will be covered in this chapter:

- Installing and configuring FSLogix

- Configuring antivirus exclusions

- Configuring profile containers

- Configuring Cloud Cache

- Microsoft Teams exclusions

- FSLogix profile container best practices

Installing and configuring FSLogix

The following conceptional architecture diagram shows how FSLogix works within the Windows operating system:

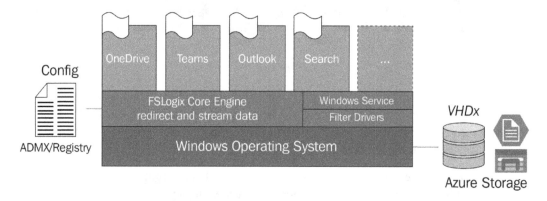

Figure 12.1 – Architecture diagram of FSLogix

The preceding architecture diagram shows how the FSLogix filter driver sits within an operating system and some of the services it redirects. The diagram depicts the redirection of user data using filter drivers to a remote storage solution.

Now, let's take a brief look at the license requirements for FSLogix profile containers.

License requirements for FSLogix profile containers

To use FSLogix profile containers, you must have one of the following licenses:

- Microsoft 365 E3/E5

- Microsoft 365 A3/A5/Student Use Benefits

- Microsoft 365 F1/F3

- Microsoft 365 Business

- Windows 10 Enterprise E3/E5

- Windows 10 Education A3/A5

- Windows 10 VDA per user

- **Remote Desktop Services (RDS) Client Access License (CAL)**

- RDS **Subscriber Access License (SAL)**

- Azure Virtual Desktop per-user access license

You will note that these license requirements are the same as those for accessing the Azure Virtual Desktop service.

Let's now take a quick look at the key capabilities of FSLogix profile containers.

FSLogix key capabilities

We now take a look at the key capabilities/benefits of using FSLogix profile containers:

- Redirect user profiles to a network storage location. Mounting the profile as a VHD(X) and using the profile over the network eliminates delays often associated with other solutions that copy profiles to and from the network location. In addition, this provides a seamless experience for the end user. When using FSLogix, the experience is similar to native local profiles where the operating system looks for the data in C:\users, which has been redirected using FSLogix.

- FSLogix also offers the ability to redirect only the required portion of the profile that contains Office data by using FSLogix Office Container. Office Container allows your organization, which is already using an alternate profile solution, to enable Office in a pooled virtual desktop environment.

- FSLogix Profile Container is used with Cloud Cache to create resilient and highly available user profile environments. Cloud Cache places a portion of the profile VHD(X) on the local hard drive. Cloud Cache also provides the administrator with the ability to specify multiple remote profile locations. Local Cache, with multiple remote profile containers, insulates users from network and storage failures, making this an excellent solution for enterprise and disaster recovery scenarios.

Now that we have covered the basics of what FSLogix is, let's take a look at installing the FSLogix components for profile containers.

FSLogix installation and configuration

In this section, I will provide instructions on how to download and install FSLogix.

Before we get started, I want to set out the steps for deploying FSLogix profile containers at a high level. The following diagram shows the steps for configuring FSLogix profile containers:

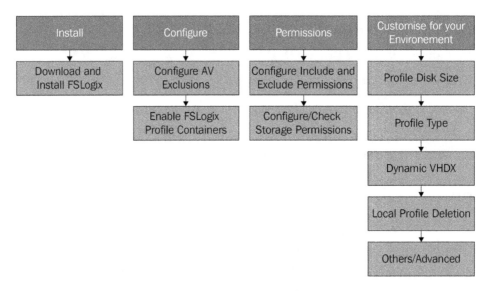

Figure 12.2 – Process diagram detailing the high-level steps for deploying FSLogix

As you can see, in the following two sections, *FSLogix installation and configuration* and *Configuring profile containers*, we will look at the four areas of deployment set out in the preceding diagram. You may want to refer back to this to ensure that you have configured all the required steps.

Getting started

> **Important Note**
>
> To obtain the latest copy of FSLogix, you can download it from the following link: `https://aka.ms/fslogix/download`.

To configure both profile containers and office containers, you must download and install FSLogix Apps on the session host. FSLogix Apps install all the required core drivers and components for FSLogix to work.

> **Tip**
>
> When using the Azure Marketplace templates, FSLogix will come preinstalled on the Windows 10 Multi-Session + Microsoft 365 app image template.

Once you have downloaded and unzipped the files, follow these steps:

1. Navigate to the `FSLogix_Apps_2.9.7838.44263\x64\Release` directory and run the installer named `FSLogixAppsSetup.exe`.

2. Click **Install**, as shown in the following screenshot of the installer.

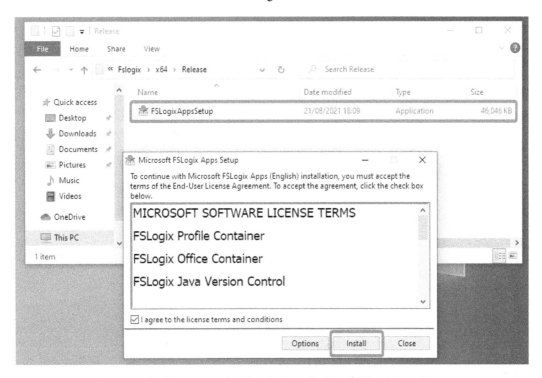

Figure 12.3 – Screenshot showing the installation of FSLogixAppsSetup

3. Once installed, you should see the **Setup Successful** message from the installer.

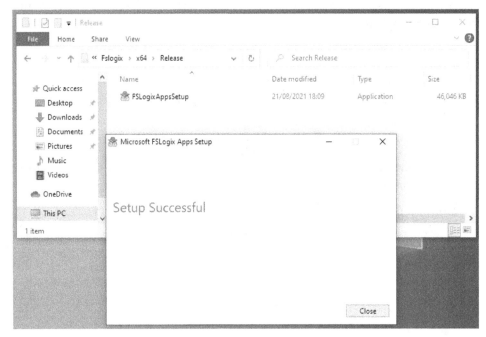

Figure 12.4 – Screenshot showing the FSLogix Apps Setup complete

4. You can also check to ensure that the files are present as FSLogix is installed on the following path: `C:\Program Files\FSLogix\Apps`.

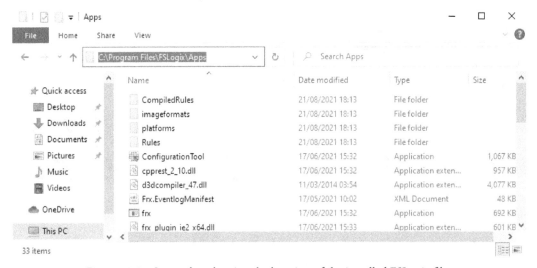

Figure 12.5 – Screenshot showing the location of the installed FSLogix files

You should now see the FSLogix files within the `Program Files` directory.

> **Tip**
> To install silently, use the following switches: `"C:\temp\Fslogix\Win32\Release\FSLogixAppsSetup.exe" /install / quite /norestart`.

We now move on to configuring the required antivirus exclusions for FSLogix profile containers.

Configuring antivirus exclusions

This section looks at the required antivirus file and process exclusions as are necessary for FSLogix. Even if you are using Microsoft Defender Antivirus, it is recommended that you configure the recommended exclusions.

The following table shows the files, processes, and Cloud Cache file exclusions you should configure in your Azure Virtual Desktop environment:

Excluded Files	Excluded Processes	Exclude when using Cloud Cache (files)
`%ProgramFiles%\FSLogix\Apps\frxdrv.sys`	`%ProgramFiles%\FSLogix\Apps\frxccd.exe`	`%ProgramData%\FSLogix\Cache\*.VHD`
`%ProgramFiles%\FSLogix\Apps\frxdrvvt.sys`	`%ProgramFiles%\FSLogix\Apps\frxccds.exe`	`%ProgramData%\FSLogix\Cache\*.VHDX`
`%ProgramFiles%\FSLogix\Apps\frxccd.sys`	`%ProgramFiles%\FSLogix\Apps\frxsvc.exe`	`%ProgramData%\FSLogix\Proxy\*.VHD`
`%TEMP%\*.VHD`		`%ProgramData%\FSLogix\Proxy\*.VHDX`
`%TEMP%\*.VHDX`		
`%Windir%\TEMP\*.VHD`		
`%Windir%\TEMP\*.VHDX`		
`\\storageaccount.file.core.windows.net\share\*.VHD`		
`\\storageaccount.file.core.windows.net\share\*.VHDX`		

Configuring exclusions using PowerShell

The following script can be used to configure your template image with the required exclusions for FSLogix profile containers. You will note that this particular script is for Microsoft Defender. The script essentially adds exclusions for the profile container virtual disks, both VHD and VHDX:

```
# A140 FSLOGIX AV Exc
#Defender Exclusions for FSLogix
   $Cloudcache = $false                    # Ensure you Set for true if
using cloud cache
   $StorageAcct = "
storageacct"  # Enter a Storage Account Name

   $filelist = ' # Files to be excluded
   "%ProgramFiles%\FSLogix\Apps\frxdrv.sys", '
   "%ProgramFiles%\FSLogix\Apps\frxdrvvt.sys", '
   "%ProgramFiles%\FSLogix\Apps\frxccd.sys", '
   "%TEMP%\*.VHD", '
   "%TEMP%\*.VHDX", '
   "%Windir%\TEMP\*.VHD", '
   "%Windir%\TEMP\*.VHDX", '
   "\\$Storageacct.file.core.windows.net\share\*.VHD", '
   "\\$Storageacct.file.core.windows.net\share\*.VHDX"

   $processlist = ' # processes to be excluded
   "%ProgramFiles%\FSLogix\Apps\frxccd.exe", '
   "%ProgramFiles%\FSLogix\Apps\frxccds.exe", '
   "%ProgramFiles%\FSLogix\Apps\frxsvc.exe"

Foreach($item in $filelist){
     Add-MpPreference -ExclusionPath $item}
Foreach($item in $processlist){
     Add-MpPreference -ExclusionProcess $item}

   If ($Cloudcache){
     Add-MpPreference -ExclusionPath "%ProgramData%\FSLogix\
Cache\*.VHD"
```

```
        Add-MpPreference  -ExclusionPath  "%ProgramData%\FSLogix\
Cache\*.VHDX"
```
```
        Add-MpPreference  -ExclusionPath  "%ProgramData%\FSLogix\
Proxy\*.VHD"
```
```
        Add-MpPreference  -ExclusionPath  "%ProgramData%\FSLogix\
Proxy\*.VHDX"}
```

Now that we have installed FSLogix on the session host/session host template, we can proceed with configuring profile containers.

Configuring profile containers

In this section, we run through the configuration of FSLogix profile containers. The configuration of profile containers to redirect user profiles is relatively straightforward as this consists of several registry settings you can add to the master image template or roll out using group policy.

The two areas we will look at are the configuration of the storage location and the setup of the Include and Exclude user groups.

> **Important Note**
> Ensure that you exclude your VHD(X) files from any antivirus software.

Before you can configure group policy, you need to ensure that the FSLogix adm/admx files are copied into the correct policy definition folder or central store. These files can be found in the downloaded ZIP archive I showed in the previous section.

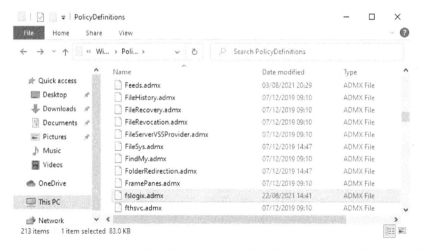

Figure 12.6 – Screenshot showing the FSLogix ADMX file added to the PolicyDefinitions folder

Once FSLogix is added to the `PolicyDefinitions` folder/**Group Policy Central Store**,
you will see the folder appear within **Computer Configuration | Administrative Templates | FSLogix**.

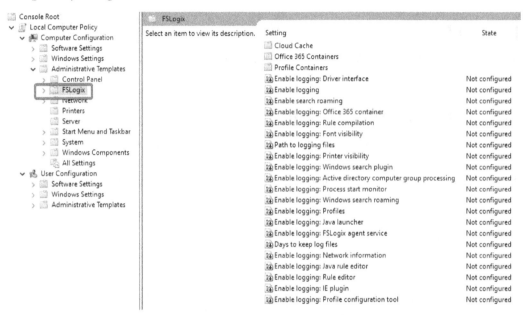

Figure 12.7 – Screenshot showing the FSLogix folder within group policy

Two required settings must be applied for FSLogix profile containers to work. These are (1) the setting to enable profile containers, and (2) specifying the **VHDLocations** storage location.

To configure these, perform the following steps:

1. Create a group policy object within Active Directory.

2. Navigate to the FSLogix policies within **Computer Configuration | Administrative Templates | FSlogix**.

3. Select the **Profile Containers** folder:

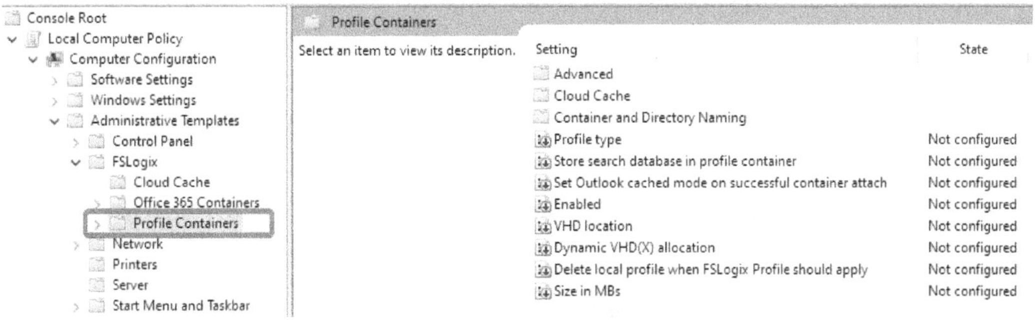

Figure 12.8 – Screenshot showing the Profile Containers folder in group policy

4. Open the **Enabled** policy, set it to **Enabled**, and then click **OK**.

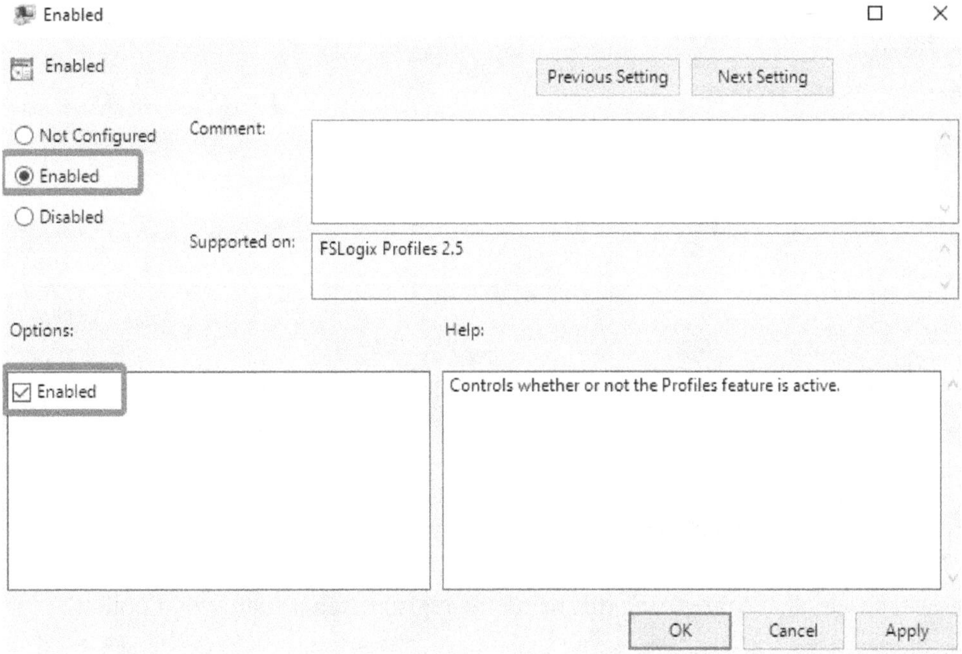

Figure 12.9 – Screenshot showing the FSLogix profile containers Enabled policy

5. Then, open the VHD location policy and enter a file path to store your user's roaming profile containers. Then, click **OK**.

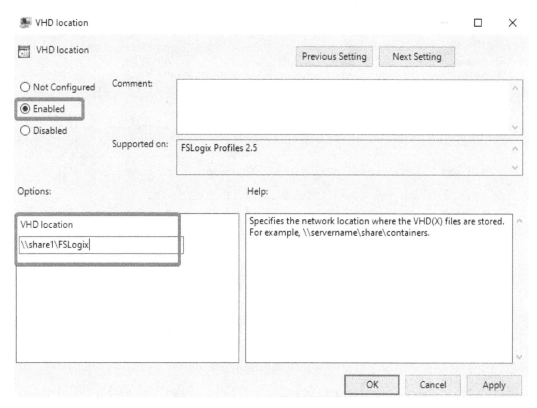

Figure 12.10 – Screenshot showing the VHD location path for storing FSLogix profiles

> **Tip**
> It is recommended that you use Azure Files for smaller deployments and Azure NetApp Files for enterprise FSLogix deployments.

Let's now take a look at configuring this using the registry rather than group policy.

Configuring using the registry

You can also configure FSLogix profile containers within the registry. You do this by enabling FSLogix profile containers and setting the path configuration settings with the following registry path: HKLM\SOFTWARE\FSLogix\Profiles.

The following table lists the two mandatory settings that must be configured for FSLogix Profile Containers to work:

Value	Type	Configured Value	Description
Enabled (Mandatory setting)	DWORD	1	0: Profile containers disabled. 1: Profile containers enabled
VHDLocations (Mandatory setting)	MULTI_SZ or REG_SZ		A list of filesystem locations to search for the user's profile VHD(X) file. If one isn't found, one will be created in the first listed location. If the VHD path doesn't exist, it will be created before it checks whether a VHD(X) exists in the path. These values can contain variables that will be resolved. Supported variables are %username%, %userdomain%, %sid%, %osmajor%, %osminor%, %osbuild%, %osservicepack%, %profileversion%, and any environment variable available at the time of use. When specified as an REG_SZ value, multiple locations can be separated by a semi-colon.

The table is taken from the Microsoft documentation: `https://docs.microsoft.com/en-us/fslogix/configure-profile-container-tutorial#configure-profile-container-registry-settings`.

The following screenshot shows you what the configuration looks like within the registry:

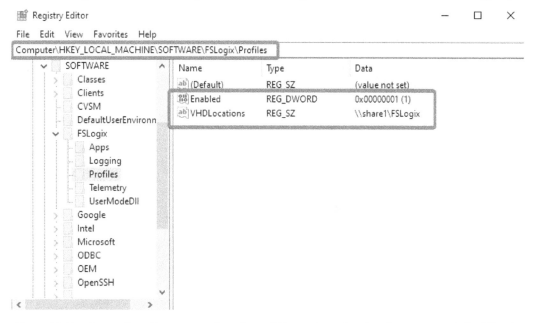

Figure 12.11 – Screenshot of registry settings for enabling and configuring the storage path for FSLogix

This configures the basics for getting started with FSLogix profile containers.

FSLogix Include/Exclude Lists

We will now take a look at FSLogix Profile Exclude and Include Lists.

> **Important Note**
> By default, the Everyone group is added to the *FSLogix Profile Include List* group.

When configuring profile containers, you need to consider the local administrators and other user accounts that should remain as local profiles. The way to do this is to enter users or groups into the FSLogix Profile Exclude List.

You can do this by navigating to **Local Users and Groups** > **Select Groups**, and you will see the **FSLogix Profile Exclude List** group. Within this group, add the users and groups you would like to exclude.

Figure 12.12 – Screenshot showing the Exclude List for FSLogix profile containers

There may be cases where you want to remove everyone's configuration from the Include List; however, this does not need to be changed in most deployments.

The following table details the permissions you should configure on the storage for FSLogix profile containers.

User Account	Folder	Permissions
Users	This Folder Only	Modify
Creator/Owner	Subfolders and Files Only	Modify
Administrator (optional)	This Folder, Subfolders, and Files	Full Control

In the next section, we take a look at Cloud Cache and its benefits.

Configuring Cloud Cache

Cloud Cache is a technology (a part of FSLogix) that enables you to use multiple remote locations continually updated during the user session. One of the use cases for Cloud Cache is disaster recovery and business continuity as it provides real-time, active-active redundancy for a profile container.

If the main or a storage provider becomes unavailable, Cloud Cache will continue to function/operate with the other storage providers. If an unavailable storage provider becomes available within the user session, it will be updated with the local cache. If the provider does not become available until after the user has signed out of their session, then the storage provider will be updated during the next session.

> **Important Note**
> When using Cloud Cache, all profile data writes go through the local cache first, and then the remote storage locations.

It is important to note that configuring Cloud Cache differs from configuring the typical FSLogix profile containers. The settings are configured in the same way as in the group policy or registry; however, you need to ensure that you remove any settings in the **VHDLocations** policy as Cloud Cache uses **CCDLocations**.

You should also note that the value when configuring Cloud Cache is also different to profile containers. Instead of entering the UNC path, you will need to use the value described below. Finally, you will note that I have detailed both SMB shares and the use of Azure Page Blob storage.

> **Important Note**
>
> To use Azure Blob storage, you must generate an access key within the chosen Azure storage account.

Cloud Cache storage configuration types	
Type	**Value example**
SMB Share	`type=smb,connectionString=\\Location1\Folder1;` `type=smb,connectionString=\\Location2\folder2`
Azure Page Blobs	`type=azure,connectionString="DefaultEndpointsProtocol=https;` `AccountName=;AccountKey=;EndpointSuffix="`

We now take a closer look at configuring Cloud Cache and the associated steps.

Configuring Cloud Cache

The following diagram shows the steps for configuring Cloud Cache; you will note that the diagram covers all the bases for existing FSLogix profile container implementations and greenfield deployments.

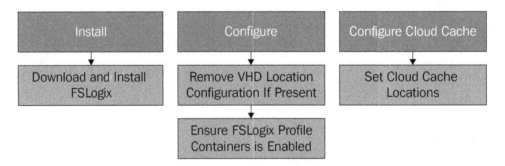

Figure 12.13 – Screenshot showing the process diagram for FSLogix Cloud Cache

We will skip the installation step as this was shown in the previous, *Installing and configuring FSLogix* section.

To configure Cloud Cache, we need to enable and configure the group policy object `Cloud Cache Locations`:

1. Within **Group Policy**, navigate to **Computer Configuration** > **FSLogix** > **Profile Containers** > **Cloud Cache** > **Cloud Cache Locations**.

2. Set the policy to **Enabled** and enter the storage paths described in the policy description and the **Cloud Cache Storage Configuration types** table, as shown in the following screenshot:

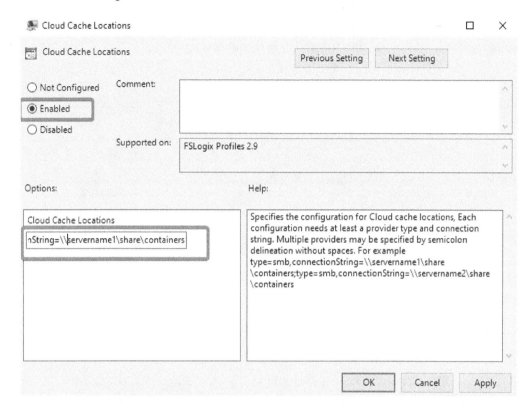

Figure 12.14 – Screenshot showing the Cloud Cache locations policy within group policy

3. Once you have set the policy to **Enabled** and entered the required Cloud Cache locations, click **OK**.

You can also configure this using the registry on the Image template by using the following:

Registry Value	Type	Value
CCDLocations	REG_SZ / MULTI_SZ	`type=smb,connectionString=<\Location1\` `Folder1>;type=smb,connectionString=<\Location2\folder2>`
Enabled	DWORD	`1`

The preceding table was taken from the following Microsoft page:

`https://docs.microsoft.com/en-us/fslogix/configure-cloud-cache-tutorial#configuring-cloud-cache-for-office-container`

As shown in the following screenshot, you can see that **CCDLocations** has been set with the storage provider locations, and that FSLogix is enabled:

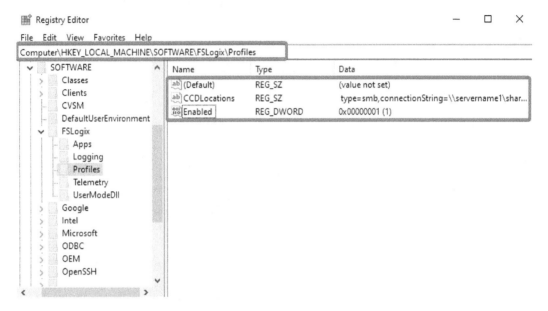

Figure 12.15 – Screenshot showing the registry method for configuring Cloud Cache

> **Note**
> There are several additional configurations for FSLogix Cloud Cache; however, they are not covered within this book.

In this section, we looked at how to configure Cloud Cache for user profile roaming. In the next section, we will take a look at Microsoft Teams exclusions for FSLogix.

Microsoft Teams exclusions

Microsoft Teams has a caching folder that can cause bloat on your user profile disk. The following details show how you can set an exclusion using an XML file to prevent both the media stack folder and `meeting-addin\Cache` from being stored in the profile container.

You first need to create an XML file with the required exclusions; you can do this using `notepad.exe` or another text editing tool. You then enter the required exclusions:

- media-stack folder
- meeting-addin\Cache (`%appdata%\Microsoft\Teams\meeting-addin\Cache`)

The XML file should look something like the following example:

```
?xml version="1.0" encoding="UTF-8"?>
<FrxProfileFolderRedirection ExcludeCommonFolders="0">
<Excludes>
<Exclude Copy="0">AppData\Roaming\Microsoft\Teams\media-stack</Exclude>
<Exclude Copy="0">AppData\Roaming\Microsoft\Teams\meeting-addin\Cache</Exclude>
</Excludes>
</FrxProfileFolderRedirection>
```

You may have noticed from the preceding example that the exclude is configured with `Copy="0"`. This means that no files are copied in or out.

You can configure other redirection values:

- `1` = Copy files to base. Any existing file in an excluded folder will be copied to base.
- `2` = Copy files back to the virtual profile. Any modified file in the base will be copied back to the profile on user sign-out.
- `3` = Files are copied from/to base. This is a combination of options 1 and 2.

Once you have configured your XML file, you need to save and store this. The session host needs to access the redirection file from a folder share. In this example, I have configured the local `C:\RedirectFiles` directory; however, you may wish to use the Active Directory NETLOGIN share.

To configure FSLogix to use the redirection file, you will need to follow the steps listed here:

1. Within **Group Policy**, navigate to **Computer Configuration** > **Administrative Templates** > **FSLogix** > **Profile Containers** > **Advanced** > **Provide RedirXML file to customize redirections**.

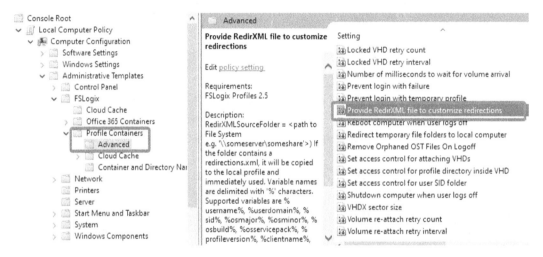

Figure 12.16 – Screenshot showing the redirection policy in group policy for configuring custom redirections

2. Enter the path for the folder directory. This can be a local path on the Template image or a network share, as described above. You only specify the folder, not the file itself.

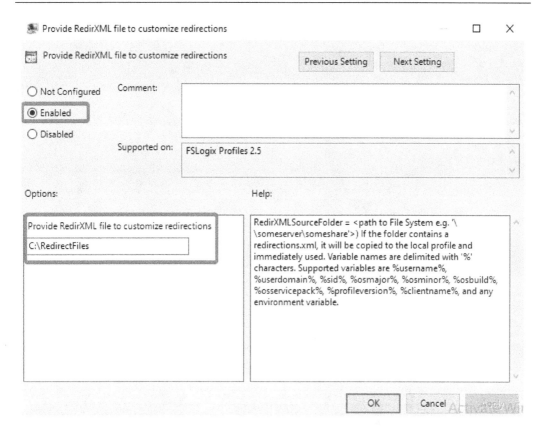

Figure 12.17 – Screenshot showing the policy for pointing to the RedirXML folder

3. Once you have added and enabled the policy and entered the path, click **OK**.

There you have it. We have configured redirection exclusions for Microsoft Teams.

To configure via the registry, enter the following values:

Value	Type	Configured Value	Description
RedirXMLSourceFolder	REG_SZ	Folder path or share path	If the folder contains a redirections.xml file, it will be copied to the local profile and used immediately.

You need to create a registry string value as detailed in the preceding table under the following registry path: `Computer\HKLM\SOFTWARE\FSLogix\Profiles`.

The following screenshot shows how this should look once you have added the registry value:

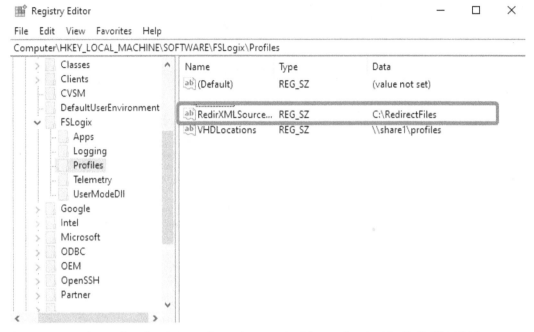

Figure 12.18 – Screenshot showing you the registry method for configuring the RedirXLM folder source

You can now test to see whether redirection is working for your FSLogix roaming profile users.

For more information on setting up Azure Files, please refer to *Chapter 5, Implementing and Managing Storage for Windows Virtual Desktop.*

You can also read more from Microsoft's site here: https://docs.microsoft.com/en-us/azure/virtual-desktop/fslogix-containers-azure-files.

FSLogix profile container best practices

This short section details the best practices for enterprises. There are a few settings you can apply to your FSLogix deployment to improve management and the cleanup of profiles.

The following table shows some of the best practice settings when configuring FSLogix profile containers within an enterprise:

Setting	Value	Reason
DeleteLocalProfileWhenVHDShouldApply	1	The benefits of this are to prevent errors when logging in and also clean up any local profiles that may appear following a storage issue.
SizeInMBs	30000	Set the size of the profile disk.
VolumeType	VHDx	VHD disks offer limited management capability however VHDX do. It is recommended that you use VHDX when configuring FSLogix profile containers.
FlipFlopProfileDirectoryName	1	This setting is recommended for making it easier to search for the specific profile container user folder on the network share. When enabled, the SID folder is created as %username%%sid% instead of the default %sid%%username%.

In this section, we briefly took a look at some of the best practices/recommended configurations you should apply when configuring FSLogix profile containers.

Summary

In this chapter, we ran through the implementation of FSLogix profile containers and Cloud Cache. First, we started with the basics of installing the software on a session host and the configuration of antivirus exclusions, and then we moved on to what is required to set up profile containers. We then discussed the need to remove the profile containers' VHDLocation path when configuring Cloud Cache and some of your other options. We then took a look at creating profile exclusions for Microsoft Teams and finished off the chapter by looking at a few enterprise best practices you can configure for FSLogix.

In the next chapter, we will take a look at configuring user experience settings. We will talk about Universal Print, group policy configurations, and troubleshooting both user profile issues and Azure Virtual Desktop clients.

Questions

1.   What are the maximum concurrent handles you can have in Azure Files?

2.   When configuring the storage path for FSLogix Cloud Cache, what is the correct value for the storage location?

3.   What is the reason for configuring Microsoft Teams exclusions for FSLogix profile containers?

4.   What do you need to do before you can start configuring and using FSLogix profile containers?

Answers

1.   *2,000 handles.*

2.   *CCDLocations.*

3.   *Microsoft Teams has a caching folder that can cause bloat on your user profile disk.*

4.   *Ensure that you download and install FSLogix Apps. Remember that if you are using a Microsoft gallery image, this is usually installed as part of the image. Always check beforehand.*

13
Configuring User Experience Settings

In this chapter, we will look at user experience. We will start by looking at the powerful capabilities of Universal Print before looking at Microsoft Endpoint Manager. Then, we will look at Start Virtual Machine (VM) on Connect, which is very useful for those who want to reduce the cost and control the startup of VMs. After that, we will cover Screen Capture protection for protecting corporate data, FSLogix profile troubleshooting, and provide some useful information on remote desktop client connection issues.

The following topics will be covered in this chapter:

- Configuring Universal Print
- Configuring user settings using Microsoft Endpoint Manager
- Start VM on Connect
- Screen capture
- Troubleshooting FSLogix profile issues
- Troubleshooting client connection issues

> **Important Note**
>
> For more information on configuring persistent and non-persistent desktops and configuring **Remote Desktop** properties for a host pool, please refer back to *Chapter 7, Configure Azure Virtual Desktop Host Pools*.

We will kick off this chapter by looking at Universal Print and the fundamentals of how the product works.

Configuring Universal Print

What is Universal Print? This is a cloud-managed print service that's provided by Microsoft through Microsoft Azure. Universal Print runs solely on Microsoft Azure. So, when it's deployed with Universal Print-compatible printers, you do not require any on-premises infrastructure to use the service.

The service is essentially a Microsoft 365 subscription-based service that you can use to centralize print management through the Universal Print portal. It's important to note that this service is fully integrated into Azure Active Directory and supports single sign-on scenarios.

This section will look at Universal Print and how you can use this Azure service with Azure Virtual Desktop.

Let's take a quick look at its architecture:

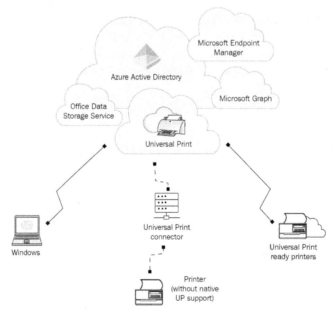

Figure 13.1 – The component architecture of universal print

The universal print service leverages the following components:

Component	Description
Universal Print	Cloud print service.
Azure Active Directory	User and device identity and authorization service.
Office Data Storage Service	Print queue data storage service.
Microsoft Endpoint Manager	Client device printer provisioning policy service.
Microsoft Graph	Printer management API.
Universal Print connector	A component that handles communication between printers and the Universal Print service.
Universal Print ready printer	A printer that has built-in support for communicating with Universal Print.
Printer (without native UP support)	A printer that needs to be registered using the Universal Print connector to communicate with Universal Print.

The preceding table was taken from the following Microsoft site: `https://docs.` `microsoft.com/universal-print/fundamentals/universal-print-` `whatis#architecture`.

Now, let's look at the required licensing and Universal Print's prerequisites.

Before we look at Universal Print, we must look at the required licensing for using the service. The following subscriptions include Universal Print:

- Microsoft 365 Enterprise F3, E3, E5, A3, and A5
- Windows 10 Enterprise E3, E5, A3, and A5
- Microsoft 365 Business Premium

If you have issues accessing the Universal Print service with any of the correct licenses, you need to ensure that you have checked the **Universal Print Service Plan**. To check this, follow these steps:

1. Within the Azure portal, go to **Azure Active Directory | Licenses | All products**.
2. Select the product from the list shown.
3. Navigate to the **Service plan details** section in the left-hand menu.

4.   Check if Universal Print is in the service plan list:

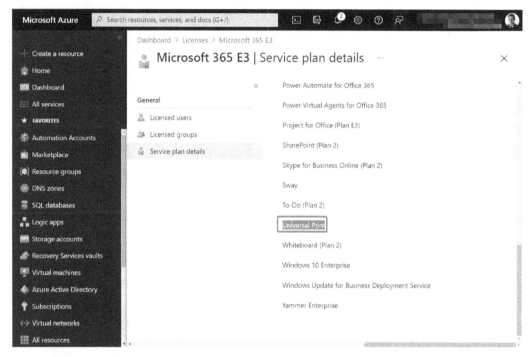

Figure 13.2 – Universal Print listed in the service plan for Microsoft 365 E3

5.   If this is included in one or more product licenses, you need to ensure that the required licenses are assigned to those users who require the Universal Print service.

Next, let's look at the requirements we need to have in place for configuring Universal Print.

Important Note

Where is print data stored? Universal Print stores all print queues in its office data storage. This is the same storage that's used to store Office 365 mailboxes and OneDrive files. A job can be queued for a few days. If the job is not claimed by a printer within 3 days, the job gets marked as aborted. You may see jobs stay within Universal Print for up to 10 days. Please note that when print jobs are sent using Universal Print, they are cloud encrypted.

Prerequisites for Universal Print

In this section, we will look at the prerequisites for Universal Print:

- You will need a Universal Print (eligible) license that has been assigned to the user by a Global Administrator.

- To configure and manage Universal Print, the IT administrator must have a Universal Print-eligible license assigned.

- To configure and manage Universal Print, an administrator must be assigned either of the following two **Azure Active Directory** (**Azure AD**) roles: Printer Administrator or Global Administrator.

- To install and print from Universal Print, you need a client device running a Windows client OS that's at version 1903 or beyond. Where possible, use the latest operating system for the best user experience. For a list of partner integrations that you can use for Universal Print, please go to `https://docs.microsoft.com/universal-print/fundamentals/universal-print-partner-integrations`.

- An internet connection.

Ensure that the following firewall rules have been applied to the device that's been chosen to host the connector. If you are using a Windows client device, remember that you will need to disable the hibernation/sleep controls and that you also need to ensure that the following firewall rules are set at the perimeter and on the client device:

- `*.print.Microsoft.com`
- `*.microsoftonline.com`
- `*.azure.com`
- `*.msftauth.net`
- `go.microsoft.com`
- `aka.ms`

> **Important Note**
> Make sure that both TCP 443 and 445 are open on the firewall to ensure you don't experience any issues when using Universal Print.

Universal Print administrator roles

There are two designated limited Azure administrator roles that you can use to manage Universal Print. The following table details these two roles:

Name	Description
Printer Administrator	Users with this role have full access to manage all the aspects of printers in Universal Print.
Printer Technician	Users in this role can register and un-register printers and set the printer's status.

The preceding table was taken from the following Microsoft resource: `https://docs.microsoft.com/universal-print/fundamentals/universal-print-administrator-roles`.

Now, let's learn how to set up Universal Print.

Setting up Universal Print

When it comes to setting up Universal Print, first, we need to deploy a Universal Print connector that enables printers to communicate with the Universal Print service.

> **Important Note**
> Some in-market printers do not support the required Universal Print protocols. It is most likely that printer manufacturers will offer printer firmware upgrades that add Universal Print support directly to the printer; however, you need to use the Universal Print connector for those that do not.

The connector's purpose, as per its name, is to make sure that a wide range of printers can connect to and communicate with the Universal Print service. All those printers with the Universal Print protocol within their firmware don't require the Universal Print connector.

The key functions of the connector are as follows:

- The connector enables IT admins to register printers with the Universal Print service.
- It reports a print job's status and the printer's status to the Universal Print service.
- The connector collects print jobs from the Universal Print service and delivers them to their target printer.

> **Important Note**
> The print connector passes jobs to the print spooler without locally storing the files the user intends to print. However, depending on their size, the connector may need to store the file to ensure it is submitted successfully to the spooler. In some cases, the deletion may not be successful and IT admin intervention will be required to clear these no longer needed files.

Connector prerequisites

Ensure that the following firewall rules are applied to the device chosen to host the connector. If you are using a Windows client device, remember that you will need to disable hibernation/sleep controls and that you also need to ensure the required firewall rules are set as detailed in the *Prerequisites for Universal Print* section.

The recommended operating system is Windows 10 64-bit Pro or Enterprise on build 1809 onwards. If you are using a server, you will need a minimum of Windows Server 2016 64-bit. Both Windows Server 2019 and 2022 are supported.

> **Important Note**
> When you create a print connector, a device object is created in Azure AD with an object ID.

Installing the connector

Follow these steps to install the connector:

1. First, you will need to download the connector file from the following link: `https://aka.ms/UPConnector`.

> **Important Note**
> For those using proxy services, you can use bitsadmin to set the proxy. You can find more information on this here: `https://docs.microsoft.com/windows-server/administration/windows-commands/bitsadmin-util-and-setieproxy`.

2. Once you have downloaded the installation files, run the .exe file and follow the steps to install it, as guided by the wizard:

Figure 13.3 – The Universal Print connector installer wizard

3. Once installed, you will be prompted to launch the connector. Click the **Launch** button, as shown in the following screenshot:

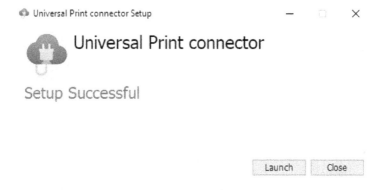

Figure 13.4 – The Universal Print connector has been installed successfully

Once the Universal Print connector has been launched, you will see the option to sign in. Go ahead and sign in using the administrator account that's been assigned to the Universal Print license:

Important Note

Make sure that the user account that's used to configure the Universal Print connector's configuration has either the role of **Printer Administrator** or **Global Administrator**.

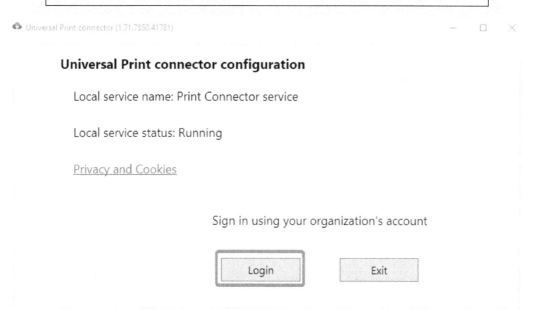

Figure 13.5 – Universal Print connector configuration form

4. Once you've signed in, you will see a box appear within the Universal Print connector form showing the connector name label and text box for registration. Enter a name and register:

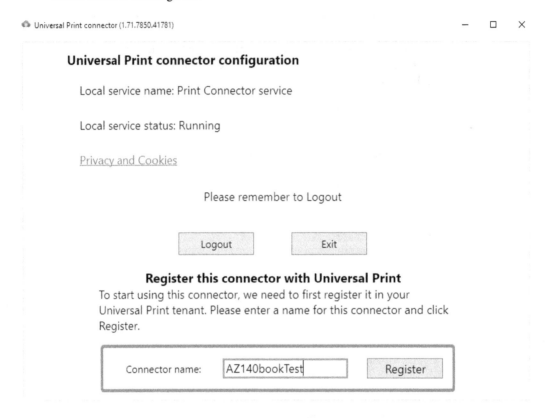

Figure 13.6 – Successfully signing in for the Universal Print connector with the registration field shown

5. At this point, you will see the registration loading screen:

Figure 13.7 – Registration progress message/progress bar

6. Once you've registered successfully, you will see the configuration page:

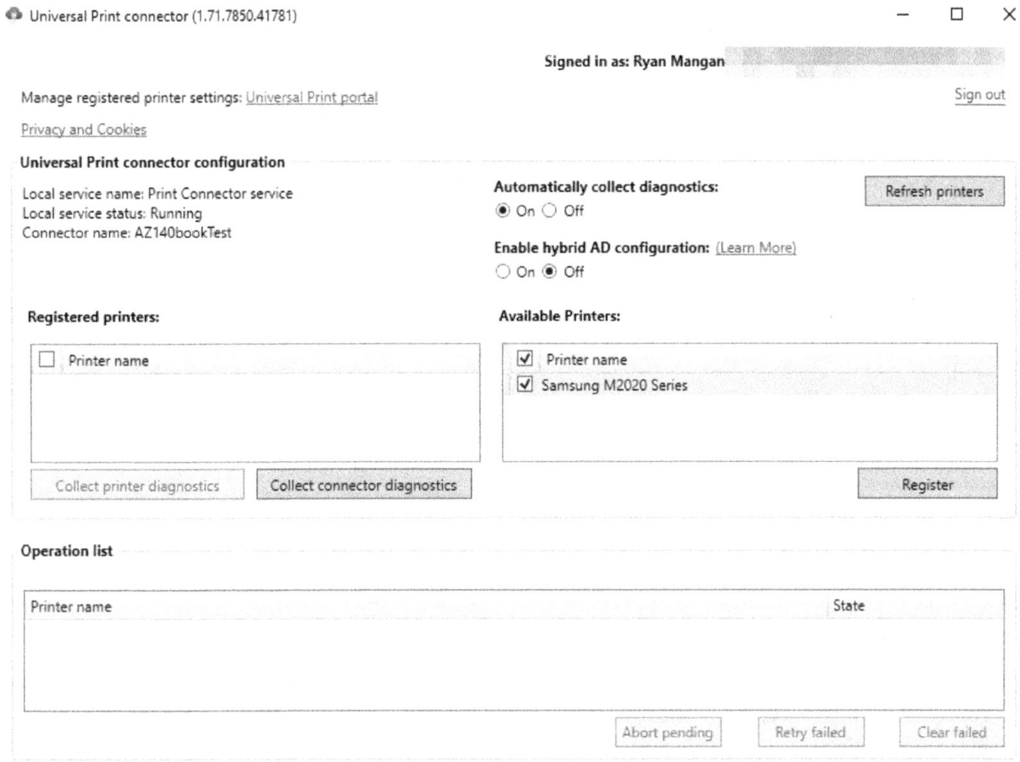

Figure 13.8 – Registered Universal Print connector listing the available printers to register

Within the Universal Print portal, you will see the connector under **Universal Print | Connectors**:

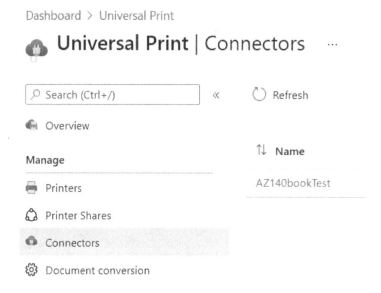

Figure 13.9 – Registered Universal Print connectors

In this subsection, we looked at the Universal Print connector's prerequisites and installed the connector on a device. Now that we have installed the Universal Print connector, we can register the printer.

Registering printers using the Universal Print connector

In this section, we'll learn how to register printers with Universal Print using the Universal Print connector we installed in the previous section.

Important Note

Ensure that you have configured the correct external URLs through the perimeter security and localhost firewall.

There are essentially three steps to registering a printer with Universal Print:

1. Select the printers you want to register from the available list and click the **Register** button. The printers will appear in the **Available Printers** list if the registration process is successful:

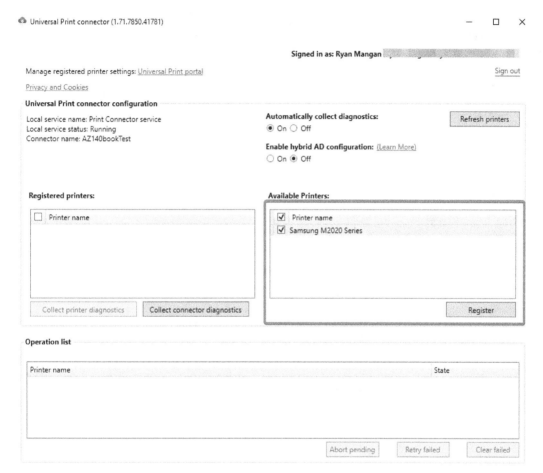

Figure 13.10 – Available printers that can be registered

The registration process can take between 10 to 30 seconds on a typical internet connection. It may take longer, so please be patient.

> **Important Note**
>
> The option to set **Enable Hybrid AD Configuration** to **Enable** is used for those organizations that use both Active Directory as well as Azure AD. In this type of setup, the user account exists in both Directory services.

You can read more about Hybrid AD Configuration here: `https://docs.microsoft.com/en-us/universal-print/fundamentals/universal-print-hybrid-ad-aad-environment-setup#what-is-a-hybrid-adconfiguration.`

2. Once the registration process is complete, you will see the printer(s) appear in the **Registered printers** section, as shown in the following screenshot:

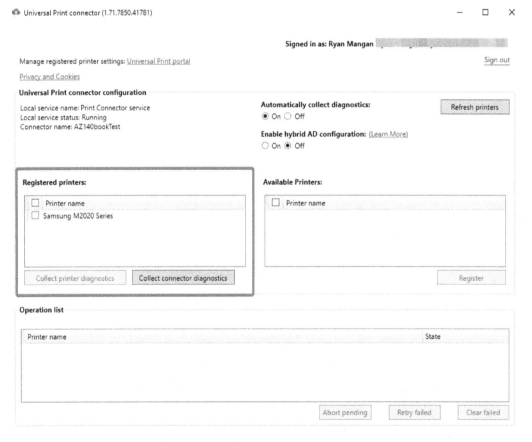

Figure 13.11 – The printer is now registered

Now that we have registered the printer, you should see the newly registered printer within **Azure portal | Universal Print | Printers**:

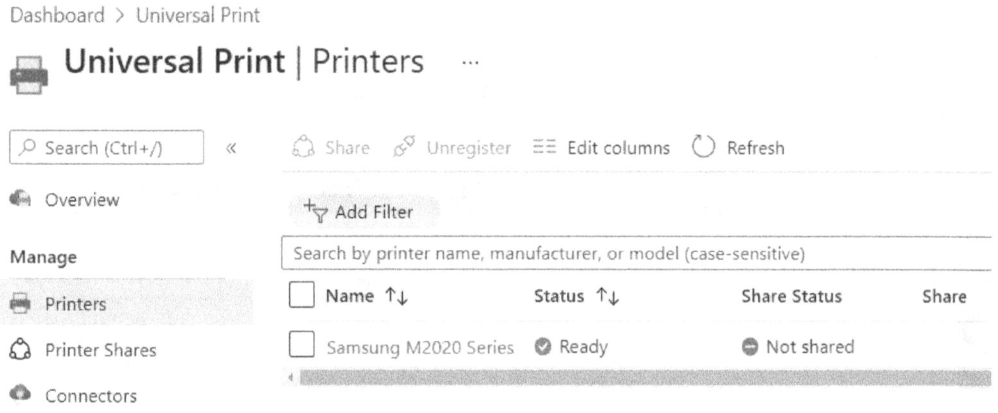

Figure 13.12 – Printers registered within the Azure Universal Print page

If the printer registration process fails, you will note that it will remain in the operations list and show a failure in the status section. You can retry the failed registration process and clear it using the buttons at the bottom left of the form, as shown in the preceding screenshot.

Now that we have registered a printer with Universal Print, we can assign permissions to the registered printers and share them.

Assigning permissions and sharing printers

Now that we have installed the print connector and registered the printers, the next stage is to share the printer. This means making the printer accessible to users. Before a user can print to a printer, the printer must be shared, thus granting access.

The quickest way to share a printer is to navigate to **Printer Shares** and click the **Add** button (https://portal.azure.com/#blade/Universal_Print/MainMenuBlade/PrinterShares):

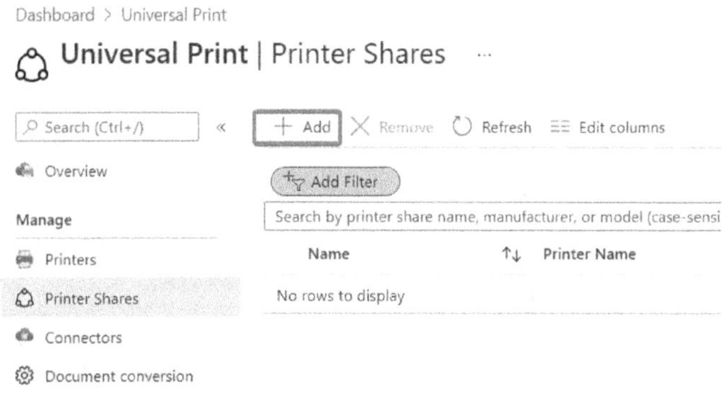

Figure 13.13 – The Printer Shares page with the Printer Shares function highlighted

Once you have clicked the **Add** button, the **Create printer share** blade will appear. Enter the share name, the printer/printers, and the selected Azure users/Azure groups or allow access to everyone in your organization. Once you have entered the correct information for the share, click **Share Printer**:

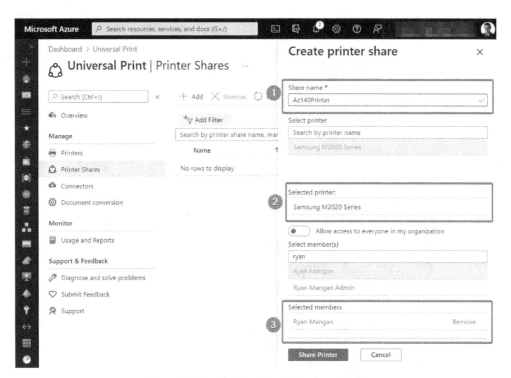

Figure 13.14 – The Create printer share blade

Once created, you will see the printer share appear on the **Printer Shares** page within Universal Print, as per the following screenshot:

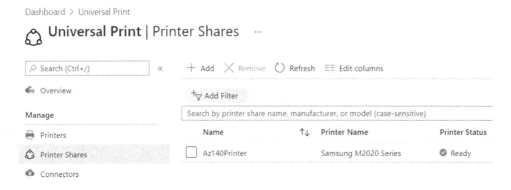

Figure 13.15 – Universal Print – the Printer Shares page

When you click on **Printer Shares**, you will see options for managing access control, which is where you can add more users to the printer share, have the opportunity to delete the printer share, and swap the printer, as shown in the following screenshot:

Figure 13.16 – Printer Share details

> **Tip**
>
> When a printer needs to be replaced, you can use the **Swap Printer** button to choose another printer that has been registered with Universal Print.

In this section, we learned how to assign printers to a printer share and how to assign user (member) permissions to use the Universal Print service. Now that we have configured printer sharing, we must add the Universal Print printer to a Windows device.

Adding a Universal Print printer to a Windows device

In this final section on configuring Universal Print, we will assign a printer to a Windows device. The following are the prerequisites we must have before we can add the printer to the user's device:

- The user's device needs to be Azure AD joined, Azure AD registered, or hybrid domain joined.
- The Universal Print printer must have been shared, and the user must have been assigned the appropriate permissions to use the printer.
- The user must have the appropriate license for Universal Print.

There are typically three steps to adding a Universal Print printer to a device:

1. Navigate to **Settings** on the Windows client and search for **Printers & scanners**:

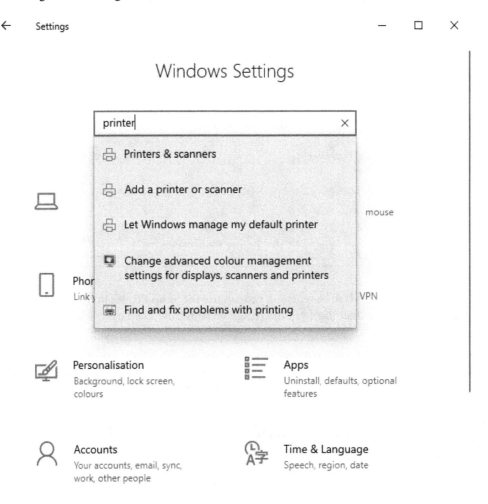

Figure 13.17 – The Windows Settings page

2. Click **Add a printer or scanner** to start scanning for printers. You should then see the Universal Print printer appear, as shown in the following screenshot, as **Az140Printer**:

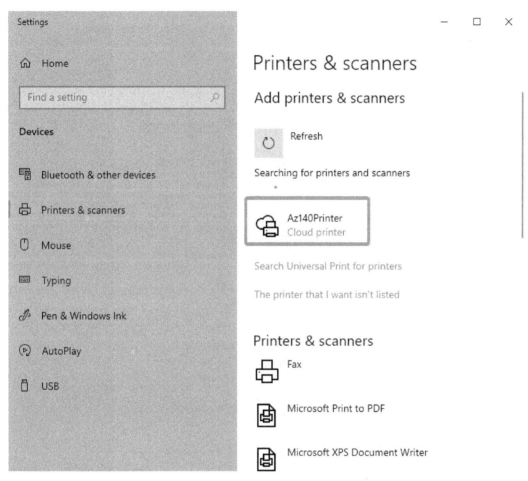

Figure 13.18 – The Printers & scanners page

3. Once the printer has been installed, you will see it appear as ready and that it's in the **Printers & scanners** list:

> **Important Note**
>
> It is advised that you don't change the driver for Universal Print printers as this could cause the printer to stop printing.

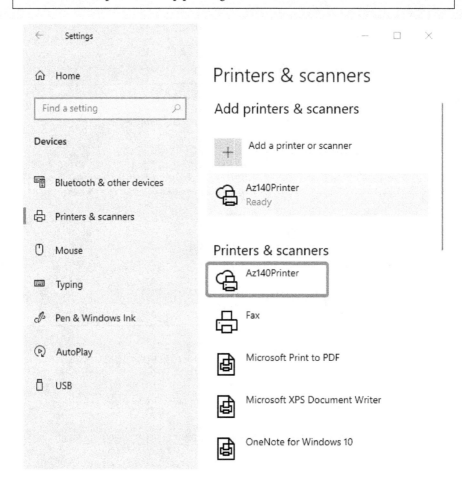

Figure 13.19 – Universal Printer added to the client device

There you have it – with that, we have deployed Universal Print for Azure Virtual Desktop. The key takeaway from this section is that you need to install a connector on a device on-premises to register the printers within the Azure Universal Print portal page. Then, unless you have a printer that supports the Universal Print protocols out of the box, you need to share the printer and assign the necessary permissions. Once they have been shared, you can add the printer to user devices that have the required license to use Universal Print.

In the next section, we will look at user settings in Group Policy and Microsoft Endpoint Manager.

Configuring user settings using Microsoft Endpoint Manager

This section will briefly look at ways you can configure and manage user settings on Azure Virtual Desktop. You can manage user settings using local policies and registry entries, group policy settings, and Microsoft Endpoint Manager.

Endpoint Manager is a cloud-based platform that focuses on both mobile and device management. This type of service offering is referred to as **Mobile Device Management (MDM)** or **Mobile Application Management (MAM)**.

Microsoft Endpoint Manager enables you to control and manage your organization's devices and how they are used. This is the same for Azure Virtual Desktop and Microsoft's latest offering, which is known as Windows 365 or, as some call it, Cloud PC.

In the **Devices | Windows** section, there are several Windows policies you can configure. This includes compliance, configuration, the use of PowerShell scripts, and Windows updates/feature updates.

Let's take a brief look at creating a Configuration Profile for Azure Virtual Desktop users:

> **Important Note**
> Intune/Endpoint Manager supports both Windows 10 Enterprise machines and Windows 10 Enterprise Multi-Session for Azure Virtual Desktop.

1. To create a profile, navigate to **Devices | Windows | Configuration profiles**. Then, click **Create profile**:

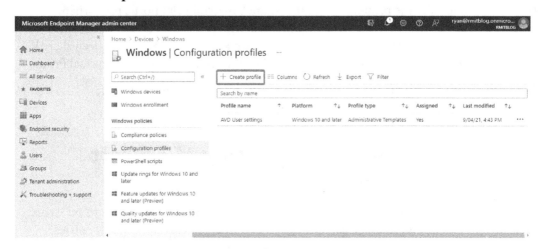

Figure 13.20 – The Windows Configuration profiles page within Microsoft Endpoint Manager

2. Once you click **Create profile**, a blade will appear on the left-hand side, where you can choose your platform and the profile type. In this example, we chose **Windows 10 and later** as the platform and **Templates** as the profile type. We have also selected the administrative templates that you would find in a group policy:

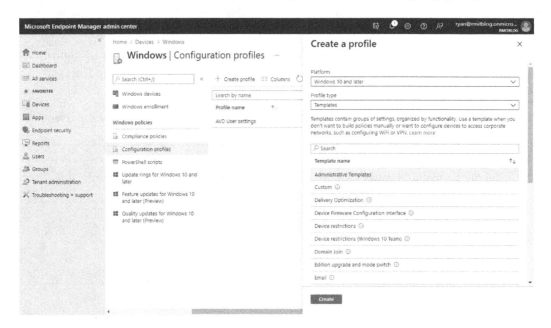

Figure 13.21 – The Create a profile blade within the Configuration profiles page

3. Once you have finished selecting your requirements, click the **Create** button. A wizard form will appear with four sections called **Basics**, **Configuration settings**, **Scope tags**, and **Assignments**. You can click **Review + create** to check the configurations you have specified.

    Enter a name and description for the configuration policy:

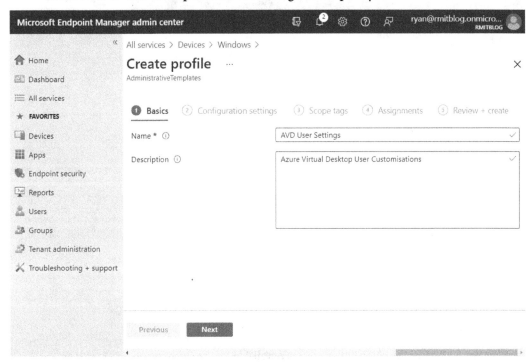

Figure 13.22 – The Create profile page when creating a new configuration profile

4. Click **Next** to move on to the **Configuration settings** section of the **Create profile** wizard form. Within the **Configuration settings** page, you can select both user and computer settings. In this example, I am going to choose a few user settings to lock down the desktop:

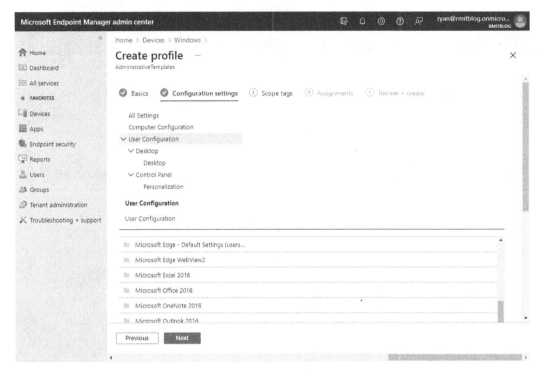

Figure 13.23 – Configuration options that are available for the computer and user settings

As you can see, there are several different policies you can enable to lock down a desktop. These are the same ones that you would find in a group policy or the local policy on the session host itself.

5. Choose the policies you require and, once complete, click **Next**:

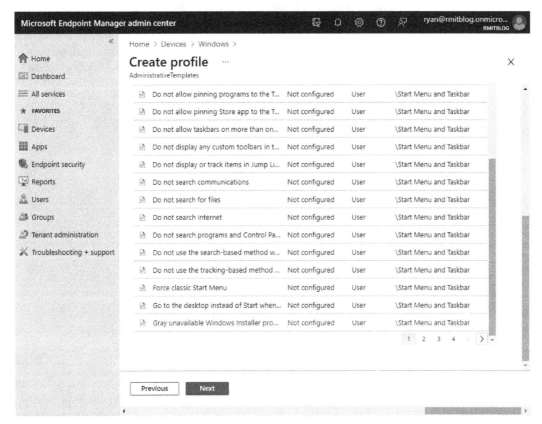

Figure 13.24 – Some of the policies you can add to the configuration profile

6. You should now see the **Scope tags** section. A scope tag is like a virtual version of an Active Directory **Organizational Unit (OU)** that can be used to assign/group devices to configuration profiles and compliance policies:

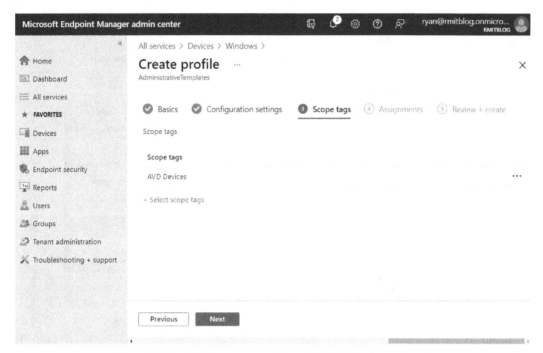

Figure 13.25 – The Scope tags setting with AVD Devices selected

7. Once you have finished adding your scope tags, you can start assigning users. In this example, we will assign all users. You can add users or groups; however, you cannot mix user and device groups across the included and excluded groups:

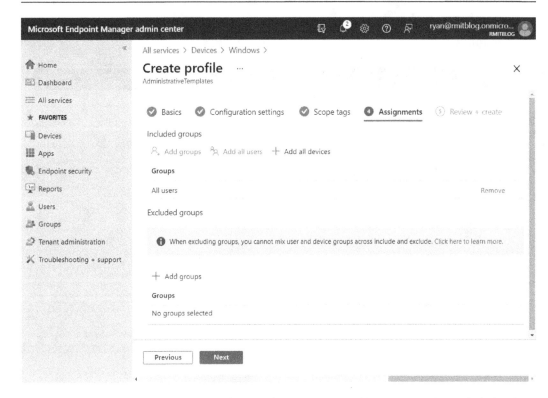

Figure 13.26 – The Assignments tab of the configuration policy allows you to select included and excluded groups

8. Once you have finished configuring the assignment, click **Review + create**.

    As shown in the following screenshot, I have selected three user configuration items in this policy that will be rolled out to the Azure Virtual Desktop session hosts.

9. Once you are happy with the settings/configuration, click **Create** to create the policy:

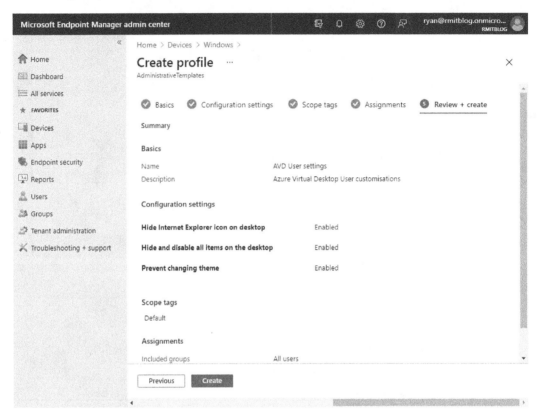

Figure 13.27 – The Review + create page of the Create profile page

Once created, you will see the new policy within the **Configuration policies** page:

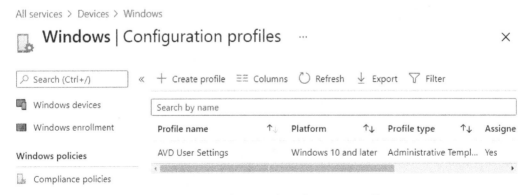

Figure 13.28 – The created configuration profile

There you have it – we have created our first configuration policy for Azure Virtual Desktop using Microsoft Endpoint Manager! You can learn more about Microsoft Endpoint Manager by reading *Mastering Microsoft Endpoint Manager*, by *Christiaan Brinkhoff, Per Larsen, Packt Publishing*.

This section looked at how we can assign configuration policies to Azure Virtual Desktop session hosts using Microsoft Endpoint Manager. In the next section, we will look at configuring Start Virtual Machine on Connect.

Start Virtual Machine on Connect

In this section, we will look at the Start **VM** on Connect feature. This offers a cost-saving mechanism for organizations as Start Virtual Machine on Connect essentially allows you to turn VMs on when required; when they are not needed, the user can turn them off. Start Virtual Machine on Connect is a great way for you to boot VMs on demand. This can be useful for personal desktops or resources that shut down every evening, as scheduled by the IT department.

The following screenshot shows Start Virtual Machine on Connect in action:

Figure 13.29 – Start Virtual Machine on Connect

Important Note

Start Virtual Machine on Connect is available for personal and pooled host pools and uses the Azure portal and PowerShell.

We now take a look at using the Azure portal to configure Start Virtual Machine on Connect.

Configuring with the Azure portal

Now, let's look at the configuration within the Azure portal:

1. Within the Azure portal, navigate to **Subscriptions**.

2. Within the required subscription, go to **Access Control (IAM)**.

3. Select the **Add custom role** button.

4. You will then see the **Create custom Role** page.

5. Select **Start from JSON** and upload the Start_VM_On_Connect. json file, which you can download from here: https://github.com/ PacktPublishing/Remote-Productivity-with-Windows-Virtual- Desktop/blob/main/B17392_07/Start_VM_on_connect.json.

   The JSON template should look something like this:

   ```
   { "properties": { "roleName": "Start VM on connect
   (Custom)", "description": "Start VM on connect
   with AVD (Custom)", "assignableScopes": [ "/
   subscriptions/<EnterSubscriptionHere>" ], "permissions":
   [ { "actions": [ "Microsoft.Compute/virtualMachines/
   start/action", "Microsoft.Compute/virtualMachines/read"
   ], "notActions": [], "dataActions": [], "notDataActions":
   [] } ] }}
   ```

   The following screenshot shows where you would import the JSON configuration file for the custom role:

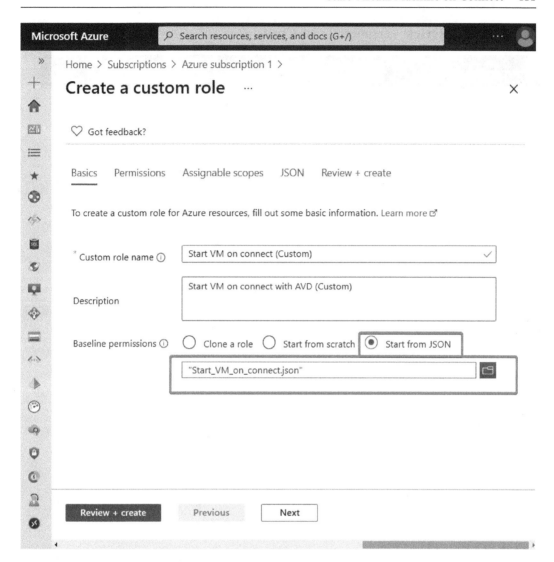

Figure 13.30 – The Create a custom role page within the Azure portal

6. Once imported, you will see that the form fields have been populated and that, as you navigate through the tabs, the required permissions have been assigned.

7. Navigate to **Review + create** and click **Create**:

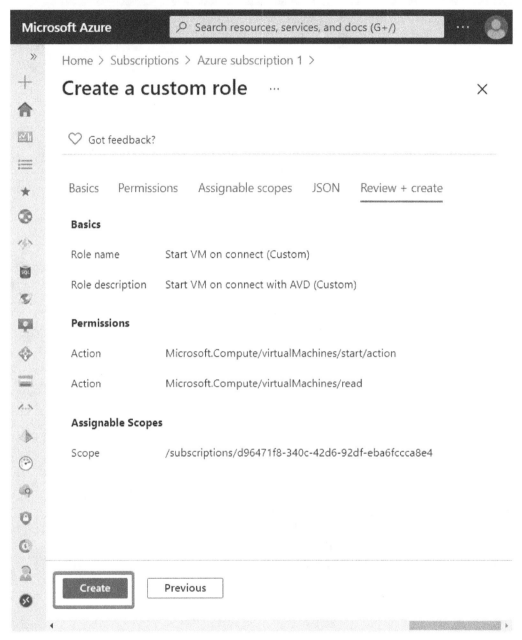

Figure 13.31 – The Review + create tab of the Create a custom role page

8. The final step is to assign the custom role you just created to Windows Virtual Desktop (soon to be renamed Azure Virtual Desktop):

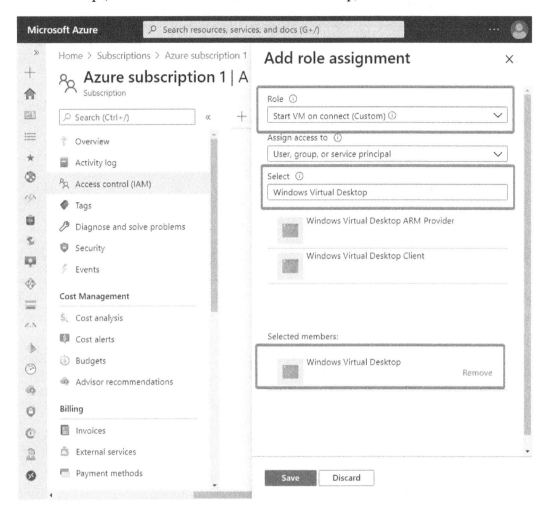

Figure 13.32 – Assigning the Windows Virtual Desktop service to the Start Virtual Machine on Connect custom role

Once you have completed this step, you will be ready to enable Start Virtual Machine on Connect within the required host pool.

This section looked at setting up Start Virtual Machine on Connect by creating a custom role and assigning the Windows Virtual Desktop (soon to be renamed Azure Virtual Desktop) service to the role.

In the next section, we will look at screen capture protection for Azure Virtual Desktop.

Enabling screen capture protection for Azure Virtual Desktop

The screen capture protection feature can be used as a data leak prevention tool to prevent sensitive information from being captured on endpoint clients. When this feature is enabled, remote content will be automatically blocked or hidden in screenshots and screen shares.

> **Important Note**
>
> The Remote Desktop Client hides content from any malicious software that may be capturing the screen.

Prerequisites

Screen capture protection is an Azure Virtual Desktop feature that is configured at a session host level and is enforced on the client. You can only use screen capture protection with Windows Desktop Clients for full desktops only. However, macOS clients using version 10.7.0 or later support screen capture protection for both RemoteApp and full desktops.

Configuring screen capture protection

In this subsection, we will configure screen capture protection:

> **Tip**
>
> This example shows you how to configure the Session Host itself. However, you can use the Group Policy Central store within Active Directory to do this.

1. To configure screen capture protection, you will need to download a set of administrative templates and add them to the session host/session host template.

2. You can download the template files from here (`AVDGPTemplate.cab`) and extract the `.cab` file and ZIP archive's contents: `https://github.com/PacktPublishing/Remote-Productivity-with-Windows-Virtual-Desktop/blob/main/B17392_07/AVDGPTemplate.cab`.

3. Then, you need to copy the `terminalserver-avd.admx` file to the `%windir%\policyDefninitions` folder.

4. A similar process must be followed for the `adml` file – copy it to the `%windir%\policyDefninitions\en-us` folder.

5. Once both files have been copied to their required locations, you can check that the policies have been added correctly by opening the local group policy editor and navigating to **Computer Configuration | Administrative Templates | Windows Components | Remote Desktop Services | Remote Desktop Session Host | Azure Virtual Desktop**.

6. You should then see the **Enable screen capture protection** policy:

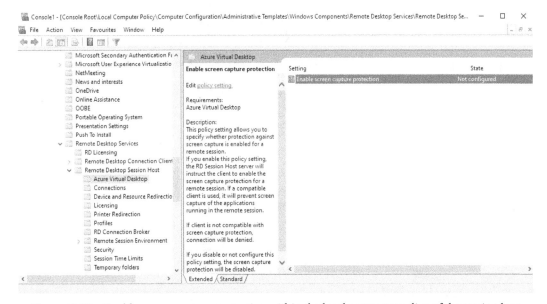

Figure 13.33 – Enable screen capture protection within the local computer policy of the session host

7. Set the policy to **Enabled**:

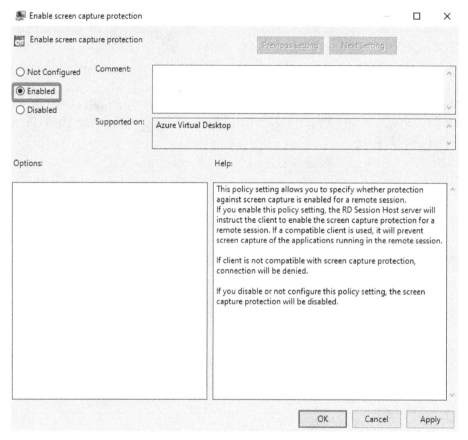

Figure 13.34 – The Enable screen capture protection page

8. Once enabled, you will need to reboot the host if you want to test it.

> **Important Note**
>
> There is no guarantee that the feature will fully restrict protected content, and it is recommended that you test it before rolling it out to a production environment. It is also recommended that you consider restricting access to items such as the clipboard, drive, and printer redirection as well as using screen capture protection. It is also important to understand that users cannot use local collaboration software such as Microsoft Teams when the screen capture protection feature is enabled.

In this section, we looked at how to configure and enable screen capture protection for Azure Virtual Desktop. Now, let's learn how to troubleshoot FSLogix profile containers.

Troubleshooting FSLogix profiles

This section will provide an overview of troubleshooting FSLogix profile containers. We will provide a few pointers to help you when you're diagnosing profile-related issues.

The quickest way to get insight into FSLogix profile issues is to review the logs using the FSLogix profile status utility. This enables you to view both administrative and operational profile-related events. You can find the profile status utility here: `C:\Program Files\FSLogix\Apps\frxtray.exe`.

> **Tip**
>
> You can review the logs for FSLogix remotely via `%ProgramData%\`
> **FSLogix**`\Logs`.

Using the FSLogix profile status utility and cross-referencing the status codes will help you quickly diagnose an issue. You can find the list of status codes on the Microsoft Docs site at `https://docs.microsoft.com/fslogix/fslogix-error-codes-reference`:

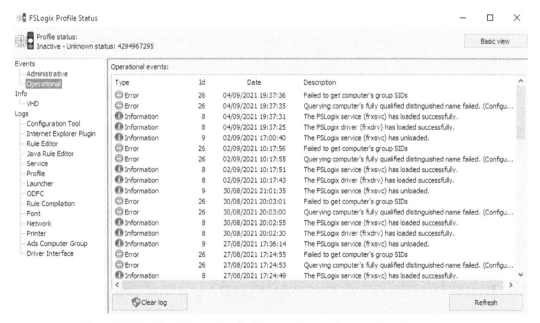

Figure 13.35 – The FSLogix Profile Status utility tool's operational events page

You can also review VHD/VHDX disk usage and size using the FSLogix profile status utility tool and view logs that are specific to a particular area, such as the profile or service.

> **Important Note**
>
> You can review the FSLogix logs via the Event Viewer by going to **EventViewer - Applications and Services Logs | Microsoft | Fslogix**.

You can read more about FSLogix profile logs by going to the Microsoft Docs site: `https://docs.microsoft.com/fslogix/logging-diagnostics-reference`.

One of the more typical issues related to FSLogix profile containers is ensuring that you have enabled the service on the session host or via Group Policy central management. Also, ensure that you have specified a valid VHD location (`VHDLocations`) and that the permissions have been set correctly for the profile to be mounted for the user trying to log on.

> **Important Note**
>
> When you're using the FSLogix cloud cache, `VHDLocations` is replaced with `CCDLocations`.

A couple of final closing issues to watch out for when troubleshooting FSLogix profile containers are that the user or group in question is not in the FSLogix profile's excluded group, that a local profile doesn't already exist for the user or group of users, and that there is space available on the selected profile storage.

> **Important Note**
>
> For more information on configuring FSLogix profile containers, please refer back to *Chapter 12, Implementing and Managing FSLogix*.

In this section, we looked at troubleshooting FSLogix profile container issues within Azure Virtual Desktop. We provided a high-level summary and discussed the FSLogix profile status utility, as well as some common problems to watch out for. In the next section, we will look at troubleshooting Azure Virtual Desktop clients.

Troubleshooting Azure Virtual Desktop clients

In this section, we will look at troubleshooting Azure Virtual Desktop client issues and some hints and tips to help you on your way with diagnosing problems.

You need to ensure that your user can communicate with the Azure Virtual Desktop service and on corporate devices; you should add the correct firewall rules to do so.

The following table details the required URLs that the client should be able to access:

Address	Outbound TCP port	Purpose	Client(s)	Azure Gov
`*.wvd.microsoft.com`	443	Service traffic	All	`*.wvd.microsoft.us`
`*.servicebus.windows.net`	443	Troubleshooting data	All	`*.servicebus.usgovcloudapi.net`
`go.microsoft.com`	443	Microsoft FWLinks	All	None
`aka.ms`	443	Microsoft URL shortener	All	None
`docs.microsoft.com`	443	Documentation	All	None
`privacy.microsoft.com`	443	Privacy statement	All	None
`query.prod.cms.rt.microsoft.com`	443	Client updates	Windows Desktop	None

The preceding table was taken from `https://docs.microsoft.com/azure/virtual-desktop/safe-url-list#remote-desktop-clients`.

In the next section, we will look at testing connectivity to help you troubleshoot any issues.

Testing connectivity

This subsection will look at how to test that the client can communicate correctly with Azure Virtual Desktop. We will look at two tests – one that uses PsPing and another that uses nslookup.

You can also complete client tests using Sysinternals PsPing, which allows you to test connectivity from the client to the Azure Virtual Desktop service.

You can download PsPing from `https://docs.microsoft.com/sysinternals/downloads/psping`.

The test that was run in the following screenshot essentially pings the RDweb service using port 443; that is, `"psping64.exe" -t rdweb.wvd.microsoft.com:443`.

As you can see, the device can communicate with the service:

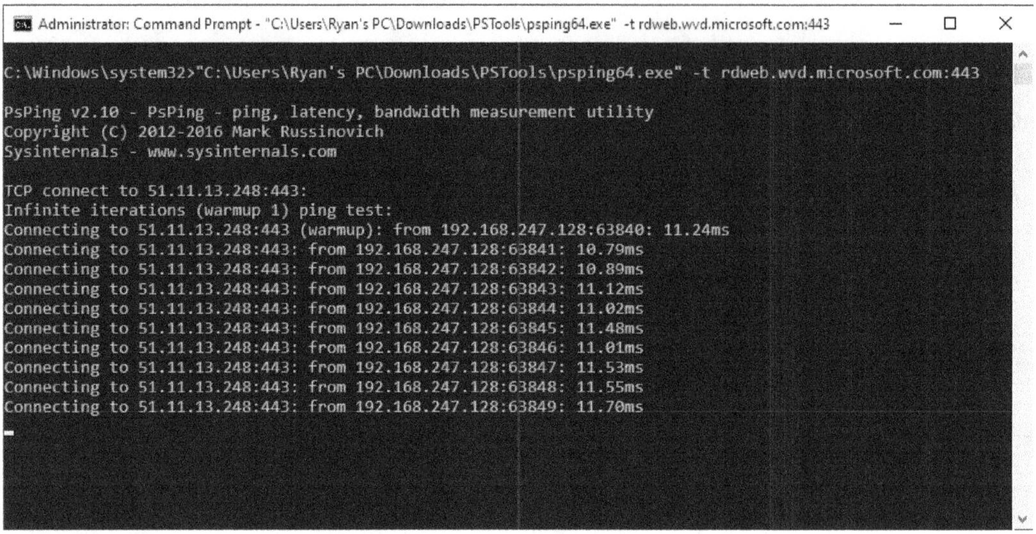

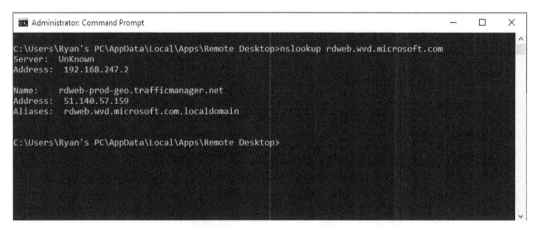

Figure 13.36 – PsPing testing port 443's connectivity to the Azure Virtual Desktop Rdweb service

You can also use `nslookup` to ensure that DNS is working as expected:

```
nslookup rdweb.wvd.microsoft.com
```

You should see the following output. If DNS is working, it should resolve with IP addresses and other information, such as aliases:

Figure 13.37 – PsPing testing DNS connectivity to the Azure Virtual Desktop Rdweb service

Now that we have looked at how to test client connectivity to the Azure Virtual Desktop service, let's learn how to reset the client.

Resetting the Remote Desktop Client

If you find that a user's Remote Desktop Client stops responding, cannot be opened, or you receive messages such as certificate errors, you may want to try resetting the client as a way to resolve the issue:

```
"%userprofile%\appdata\local\apps\Remote Desktop\msrdcw.exe" /
reset
```

The result of the preceding query is shown in the following screenshot:

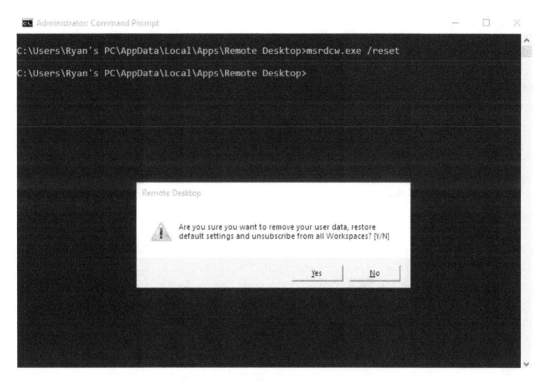

Figure 13.38 – Command line for resetting the Remote Desktop client

You can also add the [/f] switch to force the reset without receiving a popup message. This is useful if you want to automate the process of resetting multiple devices using an endpoint manager or other tool.

To reset with the force switch, you can use the following command:

```
"%userprofile%\appdata\local\apps\Remote Desktop\msrdcw.exe" /
reset /f
```

Now that we have covered resetting the remote desktop client, let's move on to the next section, where we will learn what to do if the remote desktop client is showing no resources.

Remote Desktop Client is showing no resources

If your client is showing no resources, this is usually because the user has been taken out of the app group. If there has been a resource move between resource groups, this can impact the configuration of Azure Virtual Desktop. If no resources exist, check the app groups first. It is also advised that the user logs out of the client and re-authenticates to see if the issue persists.

In this section, we looked at troubleshooting Azure Virtual Desktop clients. We looked at troubleshooting and confirming connectivity, including testing connectivity to the Azure Virtual Desktop service using PsPing from Sysinternals and nslookup to ensure that DNS is working correctly.

Summary

In this chapter, we started by learning about Universal Print, which offers a modern, flexible print solution for organizations and compliments Azure Virtual Desktop as both services are built inside Microsoft Azure. We then looked at Microsoft Endpoint Manager and the benefits it offers Azure Virtual Desktop in the sense that you can centralize and configure configuration policies for users using scope tags. Next, we looked at a relativity new feature to the Azure Virtual Desktop portfolio known as screen capture protection, which offers better protection for sensitive workspaces. We looked at how to add the required policies and configure them. Finally, we looked at troubleshooting FSLogix profile containers and troubleshooting the Remote Desktop client.

The next chapter is very exciting as we look at installing and configuring apps on a session host.

Further reading

Step-by-Step: Configure and manage Microsoft Universal Print: `https://techcommunity.microsoft.com/t5/itops-talk-blog/step-by-step-configure-and-manage-microsoft-universal-print/ba-p/2227224`

Questions

Answer the following questions to test your knowledge of this chapter:

1. Does Screen Capture Protection support both remote apps and full desktops when you're using a Windows client?

2. Name the two Universal Print roles within Azure Virtual Desktop.

3. Where can you retrieve the FSLogix logs from a session host?

4. When you're troubleshooting a Remote Desktop client on a Windows operating system, what command you would use to remove your user data, restore the default settings, and unsubscribe from all workspaces?

Answers

1. *Windows clients only support full desktop screen capture protection at the time of writing.*

2. *Printer Administrator and Printer Technician.*

3. *%ProgramData%\FSLogix\Log.*

4. *"%userprofile%\appdata\local\apps\Remote Desktop\msrdcw.exe" /reset*

14

MSIX App Attach

In this chapter, we take a deep dive into MSIX app attach and the various terms and features associated with it. We then look at how to create an MSIX package and MSIX image. Then we progress on to configuring MSIX app attach and publishing a remote app using MSIX app attach. To finish off the chapter, we cover high-level troubleshooting for common issues.

In this chapter, we look at the following:

- Configuring dynamic application delivery by using MSIX app attach
- What is MSIX?
- What does it look like inside MSIX?
- What is MSIX app attach?
- MSIX app attach terminology
- An overview of how MSIX app attach works
- Prerequisites
- Creating an MSIX package
- Creating an MSIX image
- Configuring Azure files for MSIX app attach
- Importing the code-signed certificate

- Uploading MSIX images to Azure Files
- Configuring MSIX app attach
- Publishing an MSIX app to a RemoteApp
- Troubleshooting MSIX app attach

Configuring dynamic application delivery by using MSIX app attach

In this section, we'll look at MSIX app attach – a dynamic application delivery capability for Azure Virtual Desktop. This is a relatively new technology to the application delivery market that offers the ability to deliver applications to users by logging on or in-session. Let's learn more about it in detail.

What is MSIX?

MSIX is a modern application packaging format and development framework positioned as the future application packaging format. When combined with MSIX app attach, it provides a modern and dynamic application delivery mechanism.

MSIX offers a container-based packaging solution for Windows applications, simplifying the application installation process for IT admins and users. Applications packaged using MSIX run in a lightweight application container. The MSIX app and child processes run inside this container and are isolated using the filesystem and registry virtualization rather than natively on the operating system.

MSIX applications can read the global registry. Additionally, an MSIX app writes to its own virtual registry and application data folder. This app data is then deleted when the app is uninstalled or reset using the apps and features settings page. Other applications do not have access to the virtual registry or virtual filesystem of an MSIX application.

> **Tip**
> Services work slightly differently from typical applications where the service runs outside of the container. If an application has a service, the service component does not run within the container.

Existing applications can be repackaged or converted to MSIX using the Microsoft MSIX packaging tool or via third-party packaging products such as appCURE.

Here are some of the benefits of using MSIX as a packaging format:

- Clean removal: When you remove MSIX apps, you can delete all associated application data. As a result, no data remains in the registry or filesystem. However, there is the caveat that you must ensure the MSIX package has not written any configurations outside the container.

- Container-type technology that isolates the application from the rest of the operating system for security reasons.

- Predictable and secure deployment.

- The MSIX packaging format removes the deduplication of files across applications, and Windows manages the shared files across different applications. The applications are independent of each other, so updates will not impact other applications that share the file. A clean uninstall is guaranteed even if the platform manages shared files across applications.

Let's now explore the inner workings of MSIX and how the container architecture works.

What does it look like inside MSIX?

To recap on the previous section, we looked at applications that are packaged in an MSIX lightweight container. The MSIX package writes to its own virtual registry and application data folder. It is important to note that the application processes run inside that container.

Applications installed in the MSIX packaging format are located in the `C:\program files\WindowsApps` folder. Each package folder contains a set of standard files required for the MSIX application to communicate with the Windows operating system API.

The following figure shows the structure of a typical MSIX package:

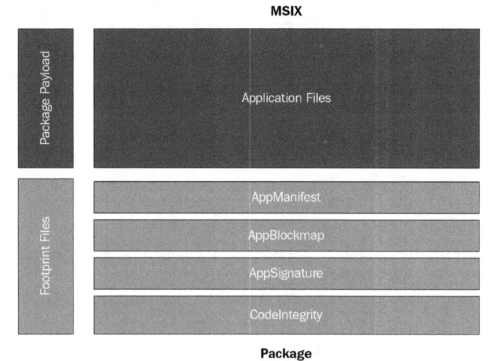

Figure 14.1 – Structure of an MSIX package

The following table details the core contents of an MSIX package:

File	Description
App payload	Contains the app code files and assets
AppxBlockMapp.xml	Contains a verified and secure list of all the files within the package
AppxManifest.xml	Essentially the configuration file for the MSIX package and contains the identity of the package and its dependencies
AppxSignature.p7x	Contains the signature of the package that the operating system must trust before the application can be installed

Now that we have finished looking at the fundamentals of MSIX, we will progress with looking at MSIX app attach.

What is MSIX app attach?

MSIX app attach a relatively recent technology advancement and addition to the Azure Virtual Desktop feature portfolio. This technology facilitates the delivery of applications to a user session within Azure Virtual Desktop by dynamically attaching the applications in an MSIX image. This new capability delivers applications on logon and/or in-session hence the term dynamic.

One of the critical benefits of MSIX app attach over other application delivery technologies is that it has been designed to deliver applications that do not impact or delay user login times. It also offers reduced management that IT needs to perform as applications are not installed natively on the Azure Virtual Desktop image. This allows organizations to modernize/enhance their virtual desktop estate and move from dedicated/specific virtual machines for applications. When using MSIX app attach, applications are delivered dynamically to any VM that a user may log in to. This saves on complexity, time, and costs.

The following figure depicts some of the benefits of MSIX app attach:

Single-instance storage	Resistance to tampering
• MSIX app attach uses one instance of the MSIX application to deliver to all hosts without consuming extra space	• After an MSIX package has been expanded into an MSIX image, the latter is read-only and locked down for modification by the Operation system
Improvied user experience	**Simplified gold image management**
• Providing the ability to attach applications in session or at logon	• As departmental/group applications

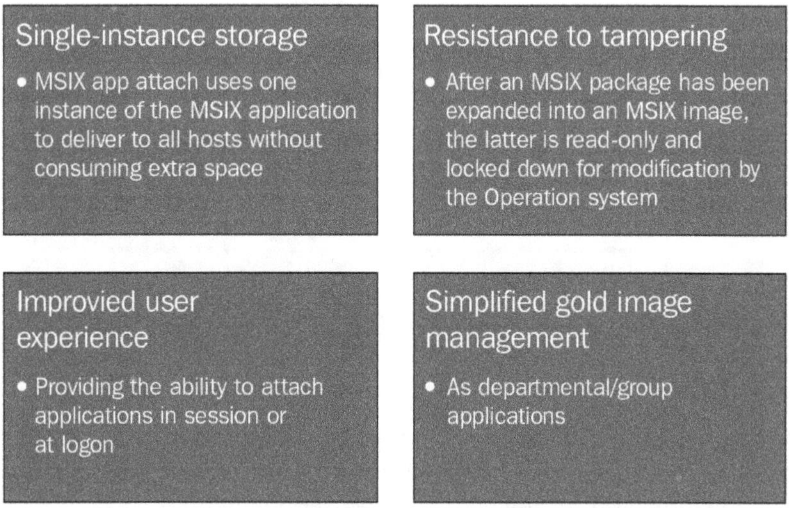

Figure 14.2 – The four key benefits of MSIX app attach

> **Important Note**
> It is important to note that MSIX app attach requires that an MSIX package is in an expanded state, also known as an MSIX image (a virtual disk or **Composite File System (CimFS)** image). Expanding is the process term for taking the MSIX package, unzipping it, and applying the appropriate system permissions to the file structure inside the chosen virtual disk or **CimFS** image.

The following figure illustrates both FSLogix profile containers and MSIX app attach in Azure Virtual Desktop:

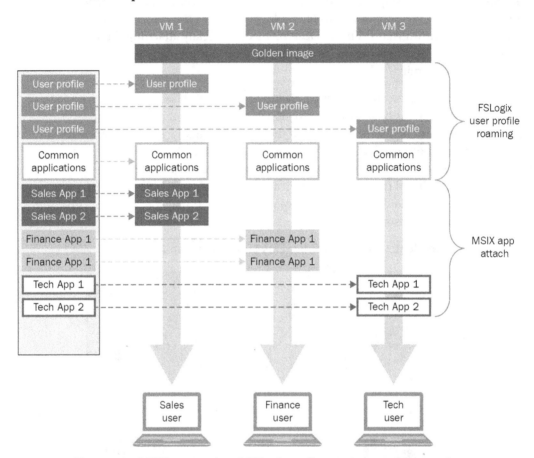

Figure 14.3 – MSIX app attach and FSLogix profile containers working together

From the preceding diagram, you will note that typical applications are installed within the operating system image. The user profiles are attached on logon, and departmental/group applications are dynamically delivered to the user on logon.

> **Important Note**
> The term *dynamically* refers to the process of attaching a virtual disk or CimFS image to the operating system rather than the traditional method of installing an application natively.

MSIX app attach terminology

There are five different process stages to call out for MSIX app attach in terms of terminology:

Term	Definition
Stage	Azure Virtual Desktop notifies the operating system that an application is available. This means the virtual disk containing the MSIX package (also known as the MSIX image) is mounted.
Register	MSIX app attach users a per-user process to make the application available to the user.
Delayed or deferred registration	Complete registration of the application is delayed until the user decides to run the application.
Deregistration	The application is no longer available to you after you sign out.
Destage	The application is no longer available from the VM following the shutting down or restarting of the VM.

We'll now move on to looking at how MSIX app attach works within Azure Virtual Desktop.

An overview on how MSIX app attach works

There are typically five steps to delivering applications using Azure Virtual Desktop and MSIX app attach:

1. You would sign in and select the host pool you should have access to from the Azure Virtual Desktop client. The process is similar to opening published desktops or RemoteApp applications from the Azure Virtual Desktop environment.

2. You're assigned a virtual machine within the host pool from which a RemoteApp or Remote Desktop session is created. Then, the Azure Virtual Desktop client interacts with the session.

3. If the user profile is configured, the FSLogix agent on the session host provides the user profile from the file share. The file share can be Azure Files, Azure NetApp Files, or an **infrastructure as a service (IaaS)** file server.

4. Applications that are assigned to you are read from the Azure Virtual Desktop service.

5. MSIX app attach applications are registered to the operating system for you from the attached MSIX virtual disk. For example, the virtual disk might be on an IaaS file share or Azure NetApp Files.

The following diagram highlights the preceding five key steps:

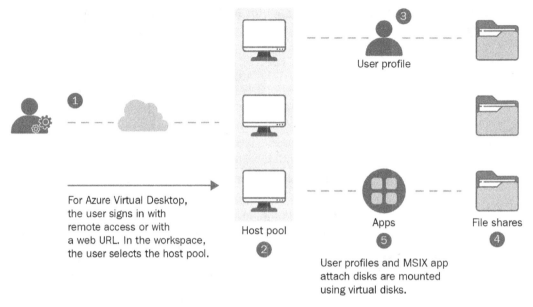

For Azure Virtual Desktop, the user signs in with remote access or with a web URL. In the workspace, the user selects the host pool.

Host pool

User profile

Apps

File shares

User profiles and MSIX app attach disks are mounted using virtual disks.

Figure 14.4 – Five steps for delivering MSIX app attach to Azure Virtual Desktop users

Now that we have covered the basics of MSIX app attach, we'll move on to the prerequisites and getting started with MSIX app attach.

Prerequisites

Before we can start provisioning MSIX images and applications to users, we first need to package some applications into the MSIX app attach format.

> **Important Note**
>
> You will need a code-signing certificate to create MSIX packages, and MSIX app attach. The certificate can either be a public, domain, or self-signed certificate.

The five steps to prepare your package for MSIX applications are as follows:

Step	Description
Create an MSIX package	The first step is to create an MSIX package containing the application you want to deliver dynamically.
Create an MSIX image	Create an MSIX image using the MSIX package you created in the previous step.
Configure Azure Files for MSIX app attach (it's recommended that Azure NetApp Files is used for enterprise deployments)	Configure Azure Files, including the required permissions for the file share.
Upload the MSIX images	Upload your prepared MSIX image.
Code-signed certificate	Install the required certificate (self-assigned or otherwise) on all the required session hosts for use with MSIX app attach.

It is important to note that you cannot use Azure Active Directory Domain Services with MSIX app attach.

> **Tip**
> Azure Files has a maximum concurrent handle limit of 2,000. It is advised that enterprises use Azure NetApp Files when planning to use MSIX app attach. Read more on this limitation here: `https://docs.microsoft.com/en-us/azure/storage/files/storage-files-scale-targets#file-scale-targets`.

In the next section, we look at creating an MSIX package.

Creating an MSIX package

Before we can create an MSIX image, we need the application in the correct format, which is an MSIX package. You will first need to package your application with the MSIX packaging tool or a third-party tool such as **appCURE Studio**.

> **Important Note**
> MSIX app attach does not support automatic application updates. Therefore, you must disable automatic updates on the operating system. Otherwise, you could end up with unusable applications for the end user(s) if updates occur. It is also important to note that you may need to turn off auto-updating within the application if it supports such a feature.

To turn off automatic updates on the operating system image, you need to run the following script within Command Prompt:

```
rem Disable Store auto-update:
reg add HKLM\Software\Policies\Microsoft\WindowsStore /v
AutoDownload /t REG_DWORD /d 0 /f
Schtasks /Change /Tn "\Microsoft\Windows\WindowsUpdate\
Automatic app update" /Disable
Schtasks /Change /Tn "\Microsoft\Windows\WindowsUpdate\
Scheduled Start" /Disable
rem Disable Content Delivery auto download apps that they want
to promote to users:
reg add HKCU\Software\Microsoft\Windows\CurrentVersion\
ContentDeliveryManager /v PreInstalledAppsEnabled /t REG_DWORD
/d 0 /f
reg add HKLM\SOFTWARE\Microsoft\Windows\CurrentVersion\
ContentDeliveryManager\Debug /v ContentDeliveryAllowedOverride
/t REG_DWORD /d 0x2 /f
```

> **Important Note**
>
> You can create your own MSIX packages or you can download them from the **Integrated Software Vendor** (**ISV**). More and more ISVs are turning to MSIX as the packaging format of choice. A good example is Mozilla Firefox. You can read more here: http://gecko-docs.mozilla.org-11.s3.us-west-2.amazonaws.com/browser/installer/windows/installer/MSIX.html.

To get started with creating your first MSIX package, you will need to download the MSIX package tool from the following URL:

https://www.microsoft.com/p/msix-packaging-tool/9n5lw3jbcxkf

The following screenshot shows the main UI page of the MSIX packaging tool:

Figure 14.5 – The main page of the MSIX packaging tool

We'll now move on to look at packaging a simple application in the MSIX packaging format.

Packaging a simple application in an MSIX container

Before we take a look at creating a package, I want to briefly cover some of the options available to you when you create an MSIX package. Firstly, even though it's common, you don't have to package one app per MSIX package. What this means is you can package multiple packages in the same MSIX package if required.

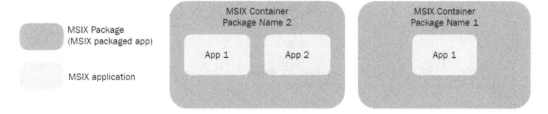

Figure 14.6 – Two different options when creating an MSIX package

Before we create an MSIX package, we need a certificate. As an example, I will create a self-signed certificate.

To create a self-signed certificate, you can use the following PowerShell script:

```
New-SelfSignedCertificate -Type Custom -Subject "CN=RMSITBLOG,
O=Ryanmangansitblog, C=GB" -KeyUsage DigitalSignature
-FriendlyName "Your friendly name goes here" -CertStoreLocation
"cert:\CurrentUser\ my" -TextExtension @("2.5.29.37={text}1.3.6
.1.5.5.7.3.3", "2.5.29.19={text}")
```

Once you have the CER certificate, you can use the following PowerShell cmdlets to convert it into a PFX certificate:

```
$password = ConvertTo-SecureString -String -Force -AsPlainText
Export-PfxCertificate -cert "Cert:\CurrentUser\My\" -FilePath
.pfx -Password $password
```

We'll now move on to looking at creating an MSIX package:

1. First, download and install the MSIX Packaging Tool.
2. Launch the application and you should see the following screen:

Figure 14.7 – The home page of the MSIX Packaging Tool

3. Click the cog located in the top-right and corner of the home page.

4. Scroll down to the certificate section:

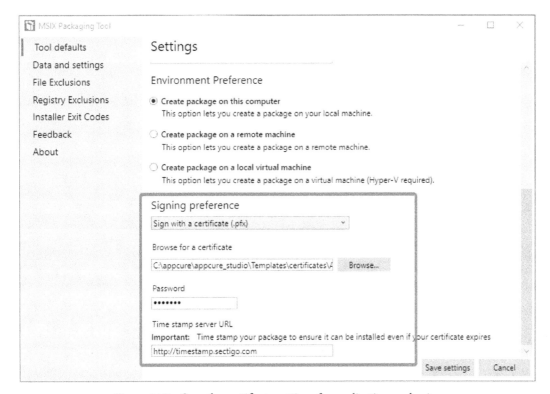

Figure 14.8 – Save the certificate settings for application packaging

5. Select **Sign with a Certificate (.pfx)** and enter the path of the certificate and password.

6. Optional, however somewhat important, enter a time stamp URL so that your packages do not stop working when the certificate expires.

7. Click **Save settings**.

We'll now move on to creating the MSIX package:

1. On the home page of the MSIX Packaging Tool, click **Application package**:

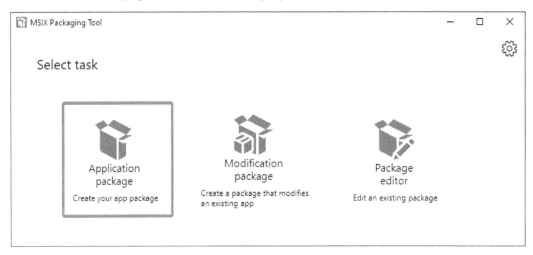

Figure 14.9 – Application package icon highlighted

2. Select **Create package on this computer**:

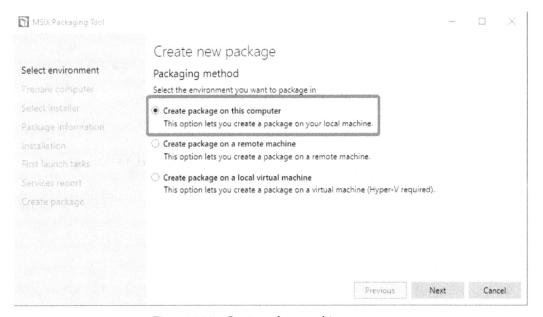

Figure 14.10 – Create package on this computer

3. Click **Next**.

4. Within the **Create new package** screen, you will see two sections, **Additional preparations** and **Recommended action items**:

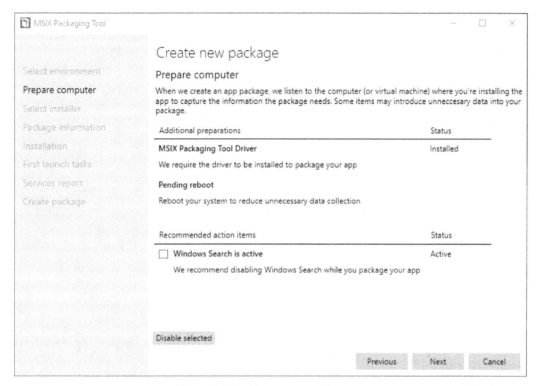

Figure 14.11 – Prepare computer page

5. Check the box **Windows Search is active** and click **Disable selected**.

6. Then click **Next**:

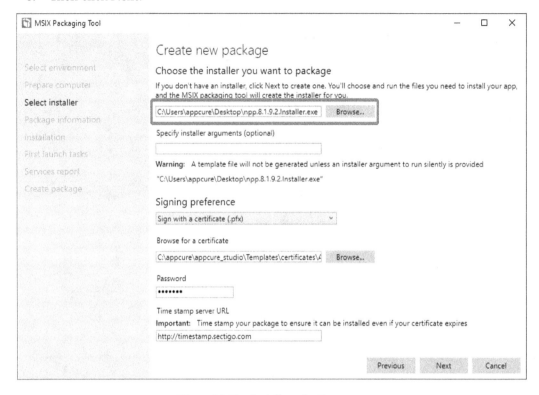

Figure 14.12 – Installer selection page

Important Note

Please note that if you have not set a time stamp server URL, then when the certificate expires, you will no longer be able to use the app. This will require the application to be signed again with an in-date certificate.

---

7. Select the application installer you want to use. In this example, we are using Notepad++.

8. You will also note that the certificate settings we previously configured are now shown within the **Signing preference** section.

9. Click **Next** to continue.

10. You will now be presented with the **Package information** page.

11. All fields marked with an asterisk are mandatory:

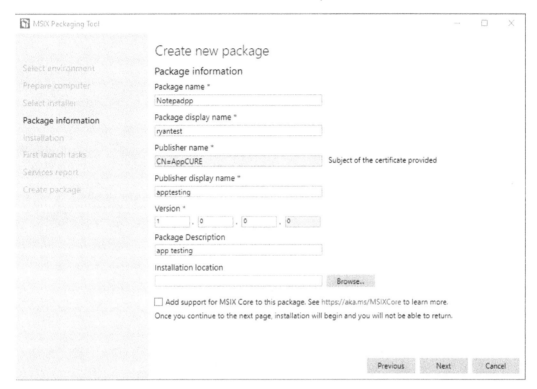

Figure 14.13 – Package information page

Type

It's important that the private key and CN (organization's name) matches the package for the code-signing process to work when the package is created. You should see the notification alongside the publisher name field stating **Subject of the certificate provided**. If you do not see this, then you may want to check your certificate.

---

12. Once you have filled out all the application information, you can proceed with the next page, **Installation**. Click **Next**.

13. You will then see the **Installation** page and the application installer will launch:

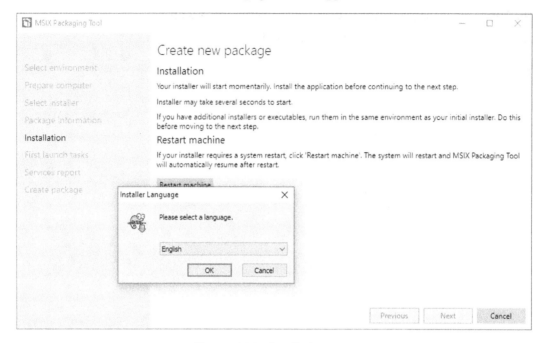

Figure 14.14 – Installation page

14. Follow the steps to install the package and launch it on install completion.

15. Once installed and launched, make the required setting changes within the app and, when complete, close the application.

16. Click **Next** within the MSIX Packaging Tool:

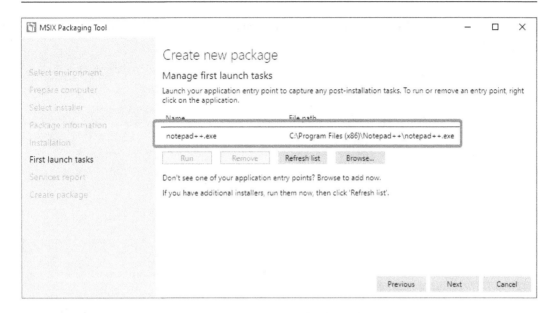

Figure 14.15 – Entry points for the application

17. Ensure you have set the required entry points on the **Manage first launch tasks** page, then click **Next**. You will then be prompted with the following:

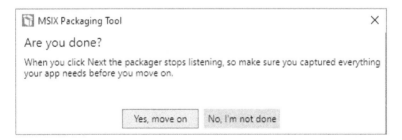

Figure 14.16 – Prompt

18. Click **Yes, move on** if you have finished installing apps.

19. On the **Services report** page, exclude any services if required. In this example, there are none. Click **Next** to continue.

20. On the final page, **Create package**, select the save location and click **Create package**:

Figure 14.17 – Package successfully created

21. The final step is to launch the app to make sure it's working:

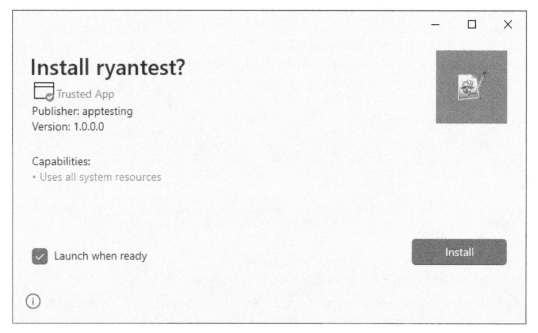

Figure 14.18 – MSIX package ready to install on the operating system

There you have it – we just walked through the steps of creating an MSIX package.

The final point to cover in this section is the Package Editor feature within the MSIX Packaging Tool.

Using the Package Editor feature offers the ability to set app capability declarations for the MSIX package, which are essentially used for specifying specific access to areas of the Windows APIs and resources such as pictures, music, and devices such as a microphone or camera:

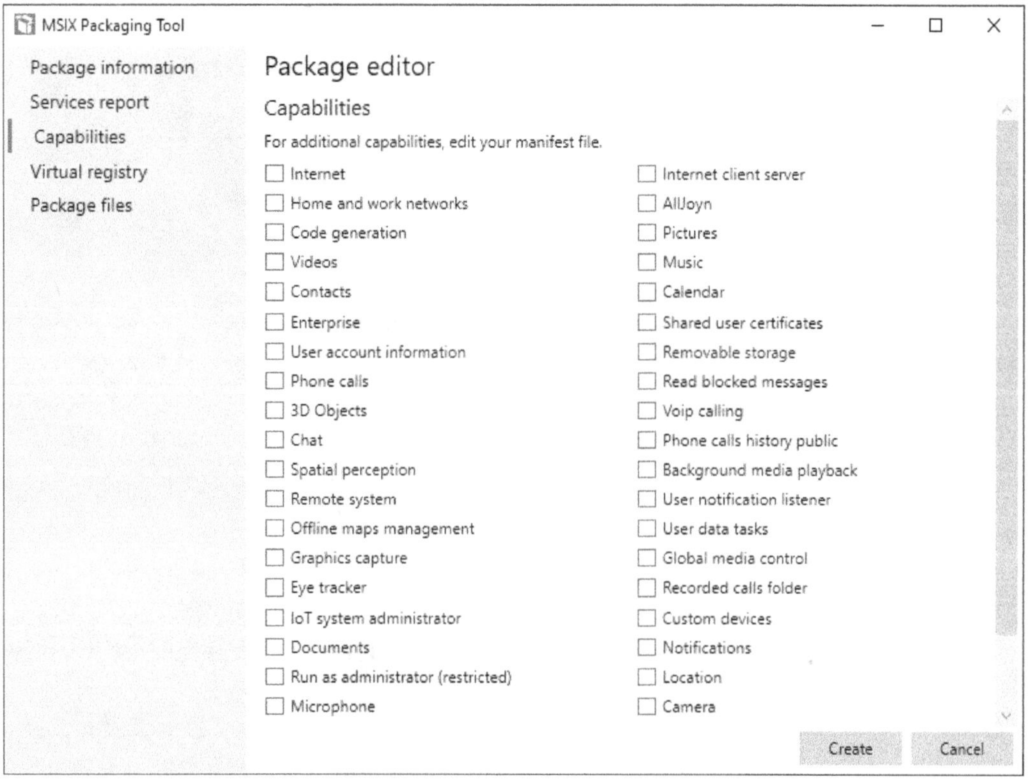

Figure 14.19 – Package editor

The Package Editor also enables the ability to add and remove files and modify the virtual registry, which includes the importing and exporting of registry settings.

Let's now move on to taking a look at creating an MSIX image.

Creating an MSIX image

An MSIX image is essentially one of three different disk types: VHD, VHDX, or a CIM image. These virtual disks/images are mounted or attached to the session host, and the content is then registered using the native operating system APIs.

The following figure shows the typical structure of an MSIX image. As you can see from the key elements, three layers make up the structure of the MSIX image:

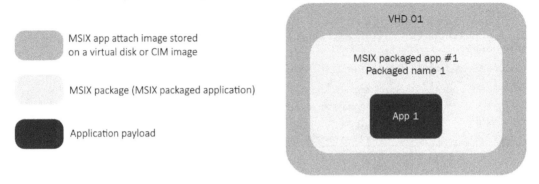

Figure 14.20 – An illustration of the structure of an MSIX image

What is the Composite File System (CimFS)?

The CIM image is essentially a file-backed image format that is a similar concept to WIM. Read more on WIM here: `https://docs.microsoft.com/en-us/windows-hardware/manufacture/desktop/wim-vs-ffu-image-file-formats`.

The term composite is used as it can contain multiple file system volumes that can be mounted individually but still share the same data files.

The following figure shows you the three types of files that you should expect to see when creating a CIM image:

Name	Date modified	Type	Size
objectid_fc0b3d45-5988-4edc-8a38-361...	24/02/2021 16:38	File	33 KB
objectid_fc0b3d45-5988-4edc-8a38-361...	24/02/2021 16:38	File	227 KB
objectid_fc0b3d45-5988-4edc-8a38-361...	24/02/2021 16:38	File	12 KB
region_fc0b3d45-5988-4edc-8a38-3611...	24/02/2021 16:38	File	1,056 KB
region_fc0b3d45-5988-4edc-8a38-3611...	24/02/2021 16:38	File	1,251,348 ...
region_fc0b3d45-5988-4edc-8a38-3611...	24/02/2021 16:38	File	170 KB
testapp.cim	24/02/2021 16:38	CIM File	1 KB

Figure 14.21 – The structure of a composite image (CIM)

When you create a CIM image, you will see three file types in the folder: ObjectID, region files containing the data, and the composite image file, `.cim`, that contains the metadata.

> **Tip**
>
> When creating a CIM image, it's advised that you create one per folder. If you create multiple CIM images in the same folder it will be very difficult for you to separate the package files. This is something I call CIM sprawl.
>
> The following link will help you address this issue: `https://ryanmangansitblog.com/2021/02/11/msix-app-attach-how-to-manage-cimfs-file-sprawl-tips-and-tricks/`.

CimFS does offer performance benefits compared to traditional virtual disk types (VHD and VHDX). You can read more on the performance benefits here: `https://docs.microsoft.com/en-us/azure/virtual-desktop/app-attach-glossary#cim`.

Creating an MSIX image

To create an MSIX image, you will need to download the MSIXMGR tool used for creating MSIX images. You can download the MSIXMGR tool from here: `https://aka.ms/msixmgr`.

The following steps detail the process to expand an MSIX file:

1. Download the MSIXMGR tool if you haven't already.

2. Unzip `MSIXMGR.zip` into a local folder.

3. Open Command Prompt in elevated mode.

4. Find the local folder from *step 2*.

5. Run the following command in Command Prompt to create an MSIX image:

   ```
   msixmgr.exe -Unpack -packagePath -destination
   [-applyacls] [-create] [-vhdSize ] [-filetype ]
   [-rootDirectory ]
   ```

Here's an example of the use of the MSIXMGR tool:

```
msixmgr.exe -Unpack -packagePath "C:\apps\notepadpp_1.0.0.0_
x64__ekey3h7rct2nj.msix" -destination "C:\apps\testapp.vhdx"
-applyacls -create -vhdSize 2048 -filetype VHDX -rootDirectory
MSIX
```

The output should look similar to the following screenshot:

```
Administrator: Command Prompt                                    —    □    ×

C:\appcure\appcure_studio\Core\msixmgr>msixmgr.exe -Unpack -packagePath "C:\Users\Ryan'
s PC\Desktop\232323\pt1.MSIX" -destination "C:\Users\Ryan's PC\Desktop\apples.vhdx" -ap
plyacls -create -vhdSize 1024 -filetype VHDX -rootDirectory MSIX
Successfully created virtual disk
Stopping the Shell Hardware Detection service
Stopping dependent services if necessary.
Successfully initialized and partitioned the disk.
Formatting the disk.
Successfully formatted disk
Starting the Shell Hardware Detection service
Successfully started the Shell Hardware Detection Service
Finished unpacking packages to: C:\Users\Ryan's PC\Desktop\apples.vhdx


C:\appcure\appcure_studio\Core\msixmgr>
```

Figure 14.22 – The output of running the msixmgr.exe cmdlet

Once you have created your MSIX image, we need to progress to configuring Azure Files for MSIX app attach:

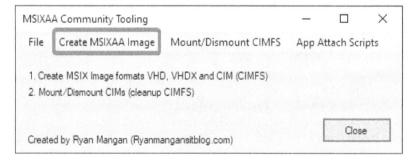

Figure 14.23 – MSIXAA community application main page

Select the **Create MSIXAA Image** button on the main form. This will then load the MSIXAA image creation form.

Within the form shown in the following screenshot, you have the option to create an MSIX image of one of the three types of MSIX images. Once you have selected the MSIX package you want to convert into an MSIX image and completed the required fields of the form, you can proceed to create an MSIX image by clicking **Create MSIX Image**:

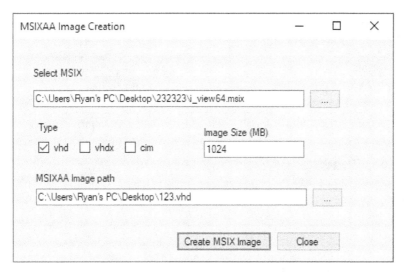

Figure 14.24 – MSIXAA community tooling app that can be used to create MSIX images

You can also use the MSIXAA Community Tooling application found on GitHub: `https://github.com/RMITBLOG/MSIX_APP_ATTACH/releases/download/2.1/MSIXAA_27052021.msi`.

For more information on using the Microsoft MSIXMGR tool, you can visit this link: `https://docs.microsoft.com/azure/virtual-desktop/app-attach-msixmgr`.

For more information on creating MSIX packages and images with appCURE, see the following link: `https://www.appcure.io`.

Configuring Azure Files for MSIX app attach

In this section, we take a look at configuring Azure Files for MSIX app attach. This is an important step as incorrectly configuring the storage and permissions will impact users when applications are trying to attach and register within user sessions. The file share is a process similar to FSLogix in terms of setting up. However, a significant difference is you need to ensure that the specific permissions are assigned correctly.

> **Important Note**
>
> Make sure the storage used has a latency of less than 400 ms as per Microsoft's recommendations.

There are nine steps required for configuring Azure Files for MSIX app attach. The following table summarizes these steps:

Step	Description
One	Create an **Active Directory Domain Services (AD DS)** security group for the session hosts you wish to use with MSIX app attach.
Two	Add the computer accounts for all session host VMs as members of the created group. Ensure you reboot the VMs after adding the computer accounts to the group.
Three	You then need to sync the AD DS group to Azure Active Directory.
Four	Create a storage account.
Five	You will then need to create a file share under the storage account by following the instructions for creating an Azure file share.
Six	Join the storage account to AD DS.
Seven	Add the storage file data SMB share contributor role to the synced AD DS group that contains the computer object of the session hosts.
Eight	To be able to manage the file share, you need to grant NTFS permissions on the file share to the computer object's AD DS group.
Nine	Grant NTFS permission for the user or user group containing the user accounts, sourced from AD DS.

Let's now take a look at these steps in more detail:

1. We first need to create the security group within Active Directory Domain Services. To do this, we would create a security group in Active Directory, as shown in the following screenshot:

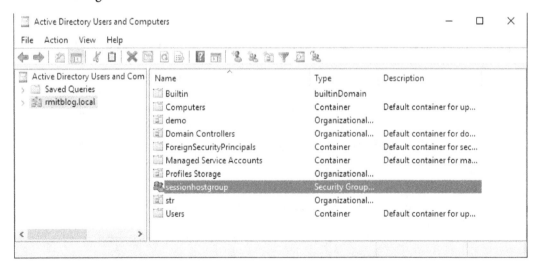

Figure 14.25 – The session host group being created

2. Once the group has been created, we then add the computer accounts to the group, as shown in the following screenshot:

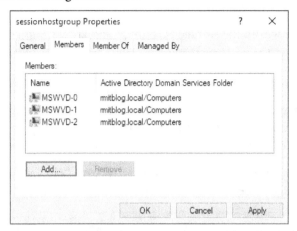

Figure 14.26 – Session host computer accounts added to the synchronized AD group

3. Once complete, you then need to ensure the security group has been synchronized with Azure Active Directory to ensure that the computer accounts are synced:

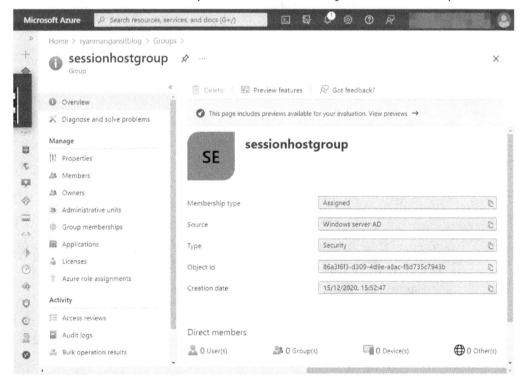

Figure 14.27 – Active Directory Domain Services group synchronized with Azure Active Directory

4. Create an Azure storage account as shown in *Chapter 5, Implement and Manage Storage for a Windows Virtual Desktop Environment*, in the *Configure storage accounts* section.

5. Create a file share within the storage account as shown in *Chapter 5, Implement and Manage Storage for a Windows Virtual Desktop Environment*, in the *Configure file shares* section.

6. Join the storage account to Active Directory Domain Services. To complete these steps, you will need to follow the guidance in the Microsoft documentation detailed here: `https://docs.microsoft.com/azure/storage/files/storage-files-identity-auth-active-directory-enable`.

    Once configured, you should see the **Active Directory** field shows **Configured** on the **File shares** page | **File share settings** as shown in the following screenshot:

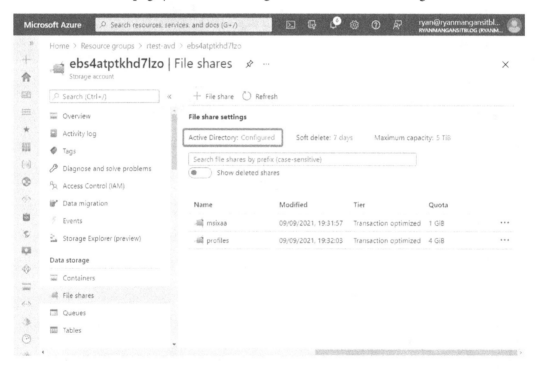

Figure 14.28 – Active Directory is configured for Azure Files

7. Add the storage file data SMB share contributor role to the synced AD DS group that contains the computer object of the session hosts:

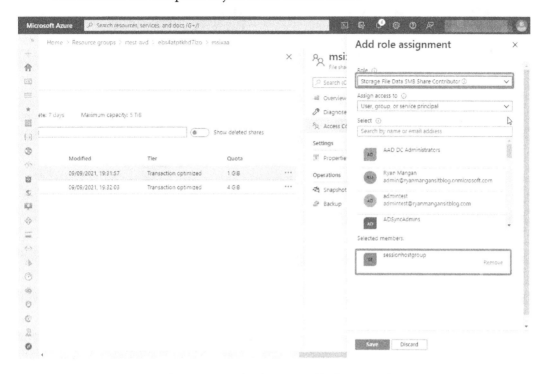

Figure 14.29 – Role assignment for the storage file data SMB share contributor role assigned to the session host group

8. Grant NTFS permissions on the file share to the computer object's AD DS group:

Figure 14.30 – Adding the sessionhostgroup group to grant NTFS permissions
for the session hosts on the file share

9. Grant NTFS permission for the user or user group containing the user accounts, sourced from AD DS:

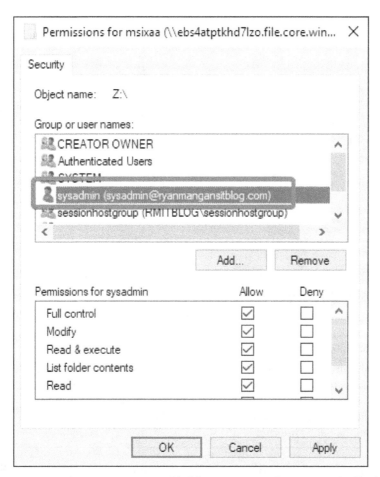

Figure 14.31 – Admin user account added for accessing and managing the file share

Important Note

It is recommended that you reboot the session hosts once the configurations are complete, as access may fail until reboots have been completed.

Once all steps are complete and you have rebooted the session hosts, you should be able to navigate to the share path using the Active Directory user account you set in *step 9* to test connectivity to the file share:

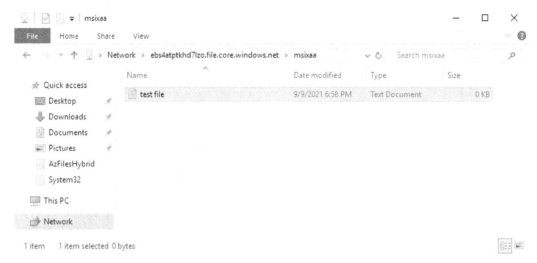

Figure 14.32 – Active Directory access to the Azure Files file share and a test file created to prove permissions are configured correctly

> **Important Note**
>
> You can also use private endpoints when using Azure Storage to improve security. This enables you to configure network traffic between clients on the VNet and storage account to traverse over the VNet via a private link rather than publicly. This essentially means using the Microsoft backbone network rather than the public internet.

This section provided a high-level overview of configuring the Azure Files File share for MSIX app attach, including the nine steps required for Active Directory authentication. In the next section, we look at how to install the certificate to all the required session hosts using MSIX app attach.

Importing the code-signed certificate

Before we upload MSIX images into the file share, we'll take a look at installing the code-signed certificate on all required session hosts.

You can essentially use three types of code-signed certificate with MSIX app attach:

- Self-signed certificates
- Public code signed certificates
- Internal certificate authority certificates

> **Tip**
>
> Enterprises should use public code-signed certificates or an internal certificate authority. It's not recommended that you use a self-signed certificate for production use. It is also important to note that you should time stamp your application packages as if the certificate expires and you have not signed the MSIX package, then the app will stop working.

To install the certificate on a session host, you would open a new MMC snap-in for the local computer. You would then add the **Certificates (Local Computer)** snap-in and click **OK**:

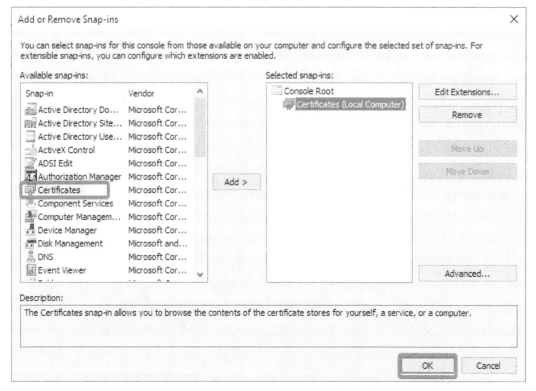

Figure 14.33 – MMC snap-in and adding the Certificates snap-in for the local computer

Once you are in the **Certificates (Local Computer)** snap-in, right-click within the Certificates window, typically the middle panel within the MMC console. Right-click and select **All Tasks | Import**:

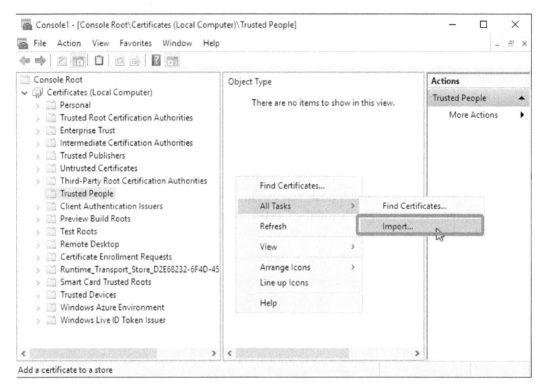

Figure 14.34 – Import button within the MMC snap-in

You now need to follow the wizard by selecting the certificate you want to import and ensure that you import it to the **Trusted People** certificate store:

> Tip
> You have the choice of importing the certificate as **Current User** or **Local Computer**. There is no right or wrong answer as it's dependent on your chosen design. Some may argue that controlling the installation of a certificate per user has security benefits, whereas other organizations may prefer the local machine certificate installation option.

Figure 14.35 – Trusted People

Once imported, you will see the certificate inside the Trusted People folder as can be seen in the following screenshot:

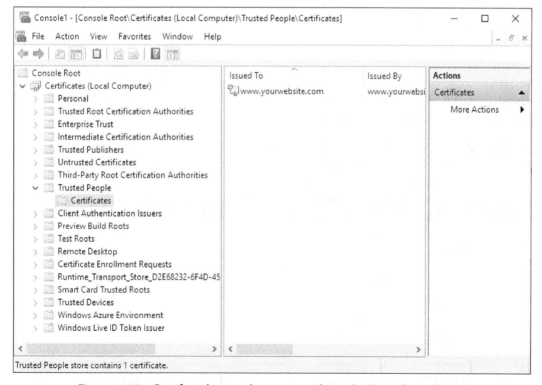

Figure 14.36 – Certificate has now been imported into the Trusted People store

You have now completed the steps for installing a code signing certificate on a session host.

> **Important Note**
> It is recommended that you deploy the certificate to a template image or use custom script extensions to automate the deployment of certificates to your session hosts.

Now that we have covered creating and installing certificates, we'll move on to looking at uploading MSIX images to Azure Files.

Uploading MSIX images to Azure Files

In this section, we will briefly look at how to upload the required MSIX images to Azure Files.

> **Tip**
> In larger environments, it is recommended that you package your applications on an isolated session host to keep file transfer times down. You will appreciate this as it's much faster to copy files from a packaging virtual machine within Azure than it would be from on-premises to Microsoft Azure.

The most common method for transferring MSIX image files to Azure Files is by connecting to the SMB share directly on your network. However, there are a few other tools and methods you can use, such as the following:

- The Azure portal: You can upload files within the Azure portal using your web browser. You simply click the upload icon within the share as shown in the following screenshot:

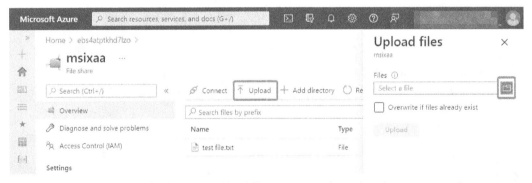

Figure 14.37 – The feature to upload files to Azure Files within the Azure portal

- You can also use AzCopy, which is a command-line transfer tool. You can download this from the following URL: `https://docs.microsoft.com/azure/storage/common/storage-use-azcopy-v10`.

  AzCopy also offers the capability to preserve file permissions during copying, similar to how Robocopy works if you have ever used it.

- The final tool I wanted to cover is **Storage Explorer**. This is a standalone application that you can run on the packaging machine. It simplifies the transfer of files to Azure Files and other storage offerings within Microsoft Azure.

  You can download Storage Explorer here: `https://www.storageexplorer.com/`.

The following screenshot shows the Microsoft Azure Storage Explorer application:

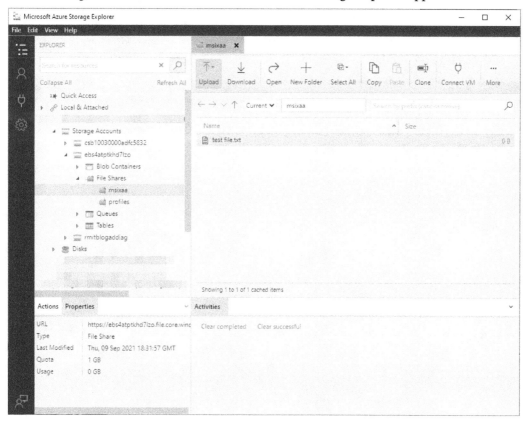

Figure 14.38 – Storage Explorer

This section looked at some of the options available to you for uploading files to Azure Files. Now that we have covered all the pre-MSIX app attach configuration tasks, we'll move on to look at configuring MSIX app attach.

Configuring MSIX app attach

In this section, we'll look at adding MSIX packages to a host pool within the Azure portal:

> **Important Note**
>
> Ensure you have installed the required code-signed certificates before proceeding with the steps detailed in this section. The configuration will fail on certificate validation if not installed on each session host within the host pool.

1. To add MSIX packages, you will need to navigate to the **MSIX packages** blade located within the host pool. You will see the icon and the name **MSIX packages** in the **Manage** section in the menu on the left side:

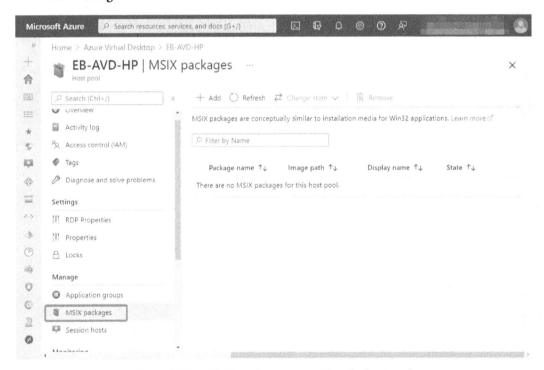

Figure 14.39 – MSIX packages page within the host pool

2. To add a package, you would simply have to click the **Add** button located within the menu bar.

The following steps detail how to add MSIX packages to your host pool. In the **Add MSIX package** tab, enter the following values:

1. For **MSIX image path**, enter a valid UNC path pointing to the MSIX image on the file share (for example, `\\storageaccount.file.core.windows.net\msixshare\appfolder\MSIXimage.vhd`). Select **Add** to query the MSIX container to check whether the path is valid when you're done:

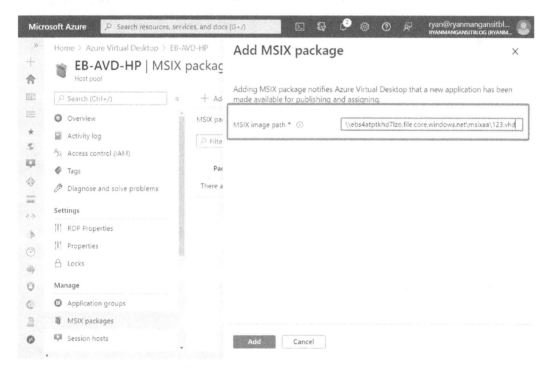

Figure 14.40 – Add MSIX package blade

2. To configure the MSIX package, select the required MSIX package name from the drop-down menu in the **MSIX package** field. This menu will only be populated if you've entered a valid image path in the **MSIX image path** textbox. If there is an error, you will see an error message appear onscreen in message format.

3. For package applications, make sure the list contains all the MSIX applications you want to be available to users.

4. Alternatively, enter a display name if you want your package to be more user-friendly in your user deployments:

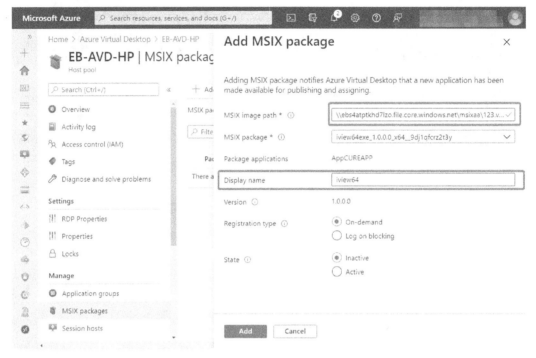

Figure 14.41 – Add MSIX package blade and the package we are adding in this example

5. Ensure the version number is correct.

6. Select the **Registration type** you want to use. This will depend on your needs:

   - **On-demand** registration essentially postpones the complete registration of the MSIX application until the user has launched the application. This is the registration type Microsoft recommends.

   - **Log on blocking** is used to only register apps while the user is signing in. This is not recommended for most deployments as it can increase sign-in times for users.

7. For the **State** field, select your preferred state:

    - The **Active** status is used to enable users to interact with the package.

    - The **Inactive** status instructs Azure Virtual Desktop to ignore the package and not deliver the package to users.

8. When you're done, select **Add**.

9. Once complete, you will see the package appear on the **MSIX packages** page, as shown in the following screenshot:

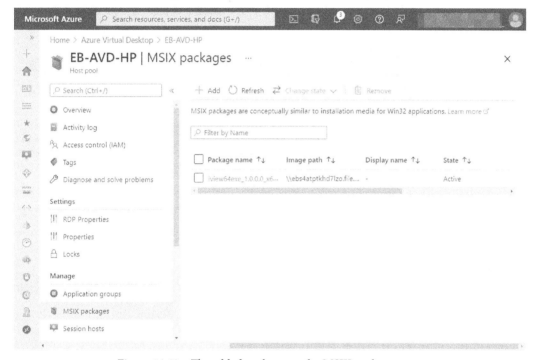

Figure 14.42 – The added package on the MSIX packages page

Now that we have added an MSIX package to the host pool, we'll now move on to assigning packages to an application group, also known as publishing an MSIX app to an application group.

Publishing an MSIX app to a RemoteApp

This section looks at assigning MSIX apps to a RemoteApp application group.

The following steps will guide you through publishing MSIX apps to application groups as remote apps:

> **Important Note**
> You can deliver MSIX applications to both remote app and desktop app groups. In this example, we are creating a remote app group for MSIX packages. To add applications to a desktop app group, navigate to the desktop app group and add the applications you require.

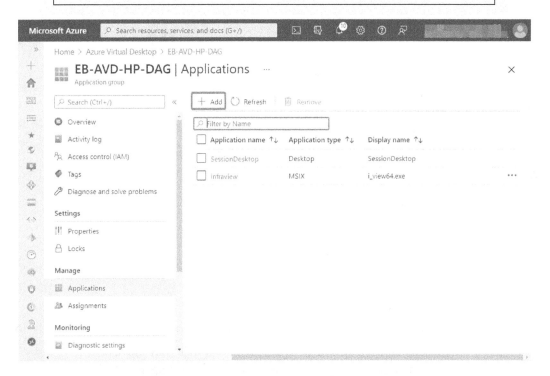

Figure 14.43 – The Add button to add applications to a desktop application group

1. Navigate to the **Azure Virtual Desktop** page within the Azure portal, then select the **Applications group** button.
2. Click **Create**.

3. You will then be presented with the page **Create an application group**:

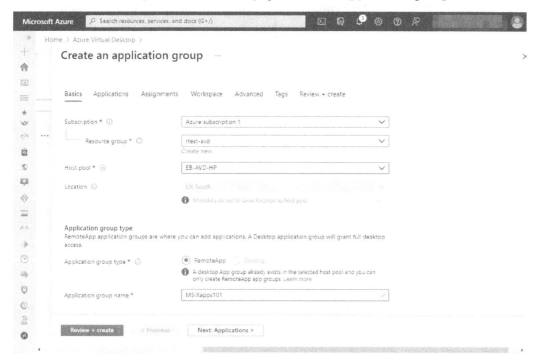

Figure 14.44 – Create an application group page

4. Within the **Basics** tab, select the **Host pool** and provide an application group name, then click **Next**.

5.   You will then be presented with the **Applications** tab, where you can add applications by clicking **Add applications**. This will open the **Add application** blade, as shown in the following screenshot:

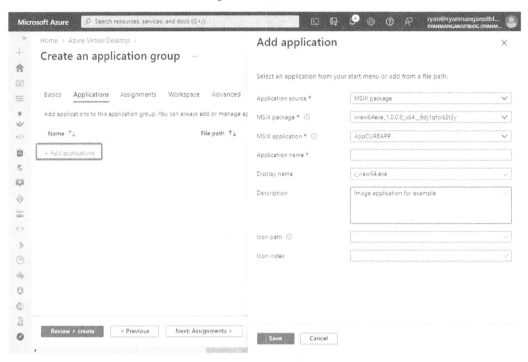

Figure 14.45 – Add application

6.   Once you have added the application(s), you can proceed to the next tab, **Assignments**. This is where you select the users and/or groups you would like to access the published applications. Once complete, click **Next**, which will show the **Workspace** tab.

7. Within the **Workspace** tab, set the **Register Application Group** to **Yes**, then click **Next**.

8. You can enable diagnostic settings and add **Tags**. If you don't need these two features, skip to **Review + create** and check your configuration:

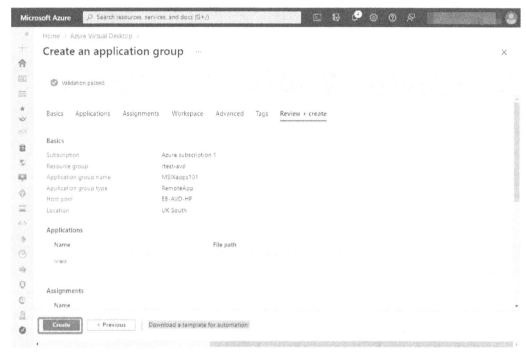

Figure 14.46 – The Review + create section of Create an application group

9. Once the application group is created, you can add more apps and remove them as
    you see fit:

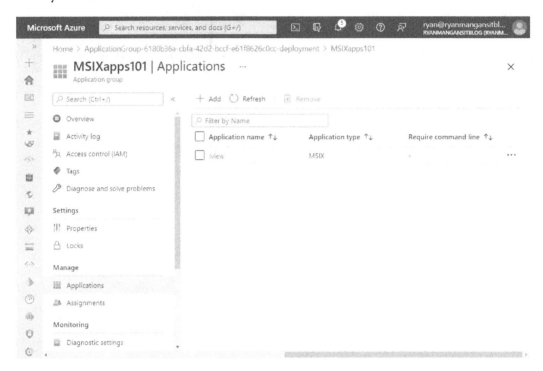

Figure 14.47 – The created application group

There you have it – we have created an application group and assigned an MSIX package.

> **Important Note**
>
> When publishing applications, the default time for the update will be 5
> minutes. The IT admin can adjust this. To change the default check interval,
> you can use the following registry key that checks it in the order of minutes:
>
> ```
> [HKEY_LOCAL_MACHINE\SOFTWARE\
> Microsoft\RDInfraAgent\MSIXAppAttach]
> "PackageListCheckIntervalMinutes"=dword:00000001
> ```

You should now see the application within the Remote Desktop client, and when
launching the app, you should see the app appear as shown in the following three
screenshots:

Figure 14.48 – Remote app published to the user's Remote Desktop client

The following screenshot shows the ICON for Iviewer:

Figure 14.49 – Remote app on the taskbar

The following screenshot shows the Iviewer application launched as an MSIX app attach package:

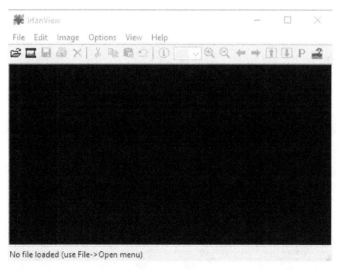

Figure 14.50 – MSIX app attach application launched as a remote app

When establishing a desktop session, you should see a mounted virtual disk, and the application should appear in the Start menu:

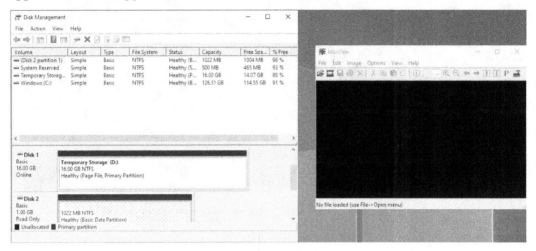

Figure 14.51 – Application delivered using MSIX app attach

This concludes the section on configuring MSIX app attach. In this section, we looked at creating an application group and assigning MSIX packages. In the next section, we move on to looking at some troubleshooting hints and tips.

Troubleshooting

In this section, we'll look at some of the common issues when working with MSIX app attach.

> **Important Note**
>
> To use MSIX app attach, you need to use one of the following supported versions: Windows 10 Build 2004 onwards, Windows 11, and Windows Server 2022.
>
> You will not be able to use MSIX app attach on any other version of Windows or Server operating systems.
>
> It is also important to note that MSIX app attach using Azure Virtual Desktop is not supported when using Azure Active Directory joined virtual machines.

One of the most common issues is the certificate not being installed on the target session hosts or having expired. You need to ensure that the certificate is installed on all the required session hosts and the MSIX image certificate is in date or time-stamped.

When expanding the MSIX image, you need to make sure that the required ACL permissions are applied or the applications within the MSIX image will be unusable.

Another issue that we covered in this chapter is NTFS and role-based access control permissions before adding MSIX images to the Azure portal. If these are incorrect, when configuring the MSIX package, you will be prompted with an error message as shown in the following screenshot:

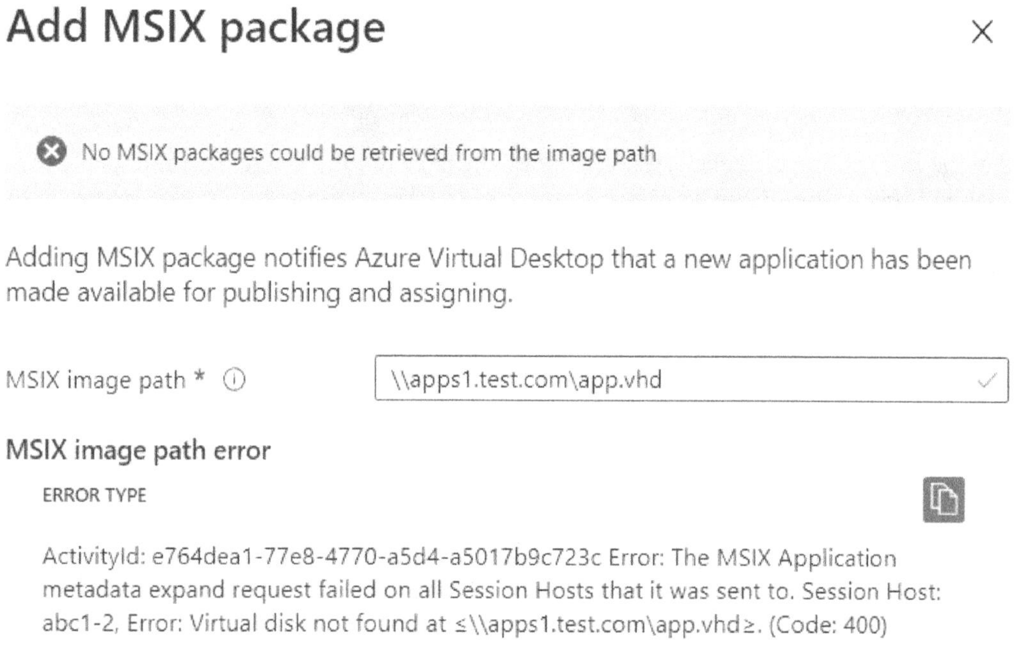

Add MSIX package   ✕

 No MSIX packages could be retrieved from the image path

Adding MSIX package notifies Azure Virtual Desktop that a new application has been made available for publishing and assigning.

MSIX image path * ⓘ   \\apps1.test.com\app.vhd   ✓

MSIX image path error

ERROR TYPE

Activityld: e764dea1-77e8-4770-a5d4-a5017b9c723c Error: The MSIX Application metadata expand request failed on all Session Hosts that it was sent to. Session Host: abc1-2, Error: Virtual disk not found at ≤\\apps1.test.com\app.vhd≥. (Code: 400)

Figure 14.52 – An error relating to the session hosts not seeing the virtual disk

You can also view the MSIX event logs, and MSIX app attach event logs using the tool MSIX Log Explorer, which is a free tool you can download from here: `https://github.com/RMITBLOG/MSIX_APP_ATTACH/releases/tag/1`.

The following screenshot shows MSIX Log Explorer, which can be used to view the events of both MSIX and MSIX app attach on Azure Virtual Desktop session hosts:

Figure 14.53 – The MSIX Log Explorer community tool

One of the final points to check is to make sure you exclude the storage path and MSIX image extensions using third-party antivirus to prevent any performance issues or bottlenecks.

> **Tip**
> The two most common issues with MSIX app attach are certificate and storage permissions. Always check that permissions are configured correctly and each session host in the host pools has the correct certificates installed.

You can read more on MSIX troubleshooting here: `https://docs.microsoft.com/windows/msix/msix-core/msixcore-troubleshoot`.

In this section, we looked at some of the common issues or problems relating to MSIX app attach. Remember to check those certificates!

Published MSIX app attach applications not showing in the Start menu

In this short section, I cover an issue that can occur relating to newly published MSIX app attach apps not showing in the Start menu. This issue is related to applications that have been removed still showing in the Start menu and new applications not showing. This issue itself is related to the redirection of the Start menu to the profile container.

To fix this issue if it occurs, you would create an FSLogix profile container redirection exclusion using the `redirections.xml`. This is a topic we covered in *Chapter 12, Implement and Manage FSLogix*, in the *Microsoft Teams exclusions* section.

You would essentially need to exclude the following from the FSLogix profile container: the `%localappdata%\packages\Microsoft.Windows.StartMenuExperienceHost_cw5n1h2txyewy\TempState` folder and the `%localappdata%\packages` folder.

This would be added to the `redirections.xml` file and it should look similar to the following:

```xml
<?xml version="1.0" encoding="UTF-8"?>
<FrxProfileFolderRedirection ExcludeCommonFolders="0">
<Excludes>
<Exclude Copy="0">AppData\Local\Packages\Microsoft.Windows.
StartMenuExperienceHost_cw5n1h2txyewy\TempState</Exclude>
<Exclude Copy="0">AppData\Local\Packages</Exclude>
</Excludes>
</FrxProfileFolderRedirection>
```

Ensure you follow the same configuration process as stipulated in *Chapter 12, Implement and Manage FSLogix*, in the *Microsoft Teams exclusions section*.

In this short section, we looked at how to solve the challenge of newly published MSIX app attach applications not showing in the Start menu.

Summary

In this chapter, we took a detailed look at MSIX app attach and learned how to configure it for Azure Virtual Desktop. We discussed the creation of MSIX packages and MSIX images, the configuration of Azure Files, and the configuration and publication of MSIX packages using MSIX app attach in Azure Virtual Desktop. In the next chapter, we will take a look at some of the other capabilities Azure Virtual Desktop has to offer including FSLogix Application Masking, deploying applications as remote apps and Microsoft Teams AV redirection.

Further reading

You'll find a list of approved Microsoft third-party packing partners here: `https://docs.microsoft.com/windows/msix/desktop/desktop-to-uwp-third-party-installer`.

Questions

1. Which certificate store would you use for MSIX and MSIX app attach?

2. Can you use Azure Active Directory Domain Services with MSIX app attach?

3. Which are three different code-signed certificate types you can use with MSIX and MSIX app attach?

4. What is the registry key for setting the MSIX app attach package check interval for Azure Virtual Desktop?

Answers

1. *The Trusted People store*

2. *AADDS is not supported*

3. *Self-signed, domain, and public certificates.*

4. *[HKEY_LOCAL_MACHINE\SOFTWARE\Microsoft\RDInfraAgent\MSIXAppAttach] "PackageListCheckIntervalMinutes"=dword:00000001*

15
Configuring Apps on a Session Host

In this chapter, we take a look at configuration applications for Azure Virtual Desktop. We start by looking at Application Masking, used to hide applications from users who do not require those specific applications. We then cast our eyes over deploying an application as a RemoteApp. As we progress through the chapter, we will also implement OneDrive for Business on a multi-session environment, implementing Microsoft Teams AV redirection. Then, we will finish off the chapter with some troubleshooting advice and guidance on application issues relating to Azure Virtual Desktop.

In this chapter, we look at the following:

- Configuring Application Masking
- Deploying RemoteApp applications
- Configuring and managing OneDrive for Business for a multi-session environment
- Configuring and managing Microsoft Teams AV redirection
- Implementing and managing multimedia redirection
- Managing internet access for Azure Virtual Desktop sessions

Application Masking

Application Masking is a part of the FSLogix portfolio that can manage access to applications, fonts, and other items based on criteria. The Apps RuleEditor is used to create app masking rules, edit rules, manage user and group assignments, and test created rule sets. This is incredibly useful for controlling application access via user groups.

To get started with Application Masking, you need to install the application FSLogixAppRuleEditorSetup.exe, which can be downloaded with the other FSLogix products here: https://aka.ms/fslogix/download.

Rule types available

Application Masking supports the following four rule types:

- **Specify Value rule**: Used to assign a value for the specified item
- **App Container rule**: Used to redirect applications or app data to a specified VHD
- **Redirection rule**: Used to redirect applications or app data to a specified item
- **Hiding rule**: Used to redirect applications or app data to a specified criteria

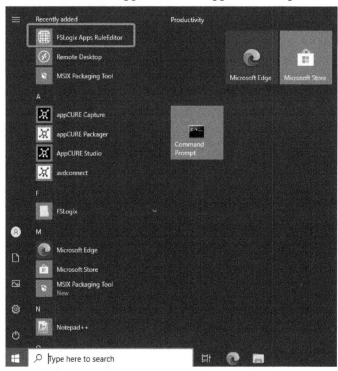

Figure 15.1 – FSLogix Apps RuleEditor icon in the Start menu

1. Now let's create our first rule:

2. Once the FSlogix Apps **RuleEditor** has been launched, click **File** and then **New** to create a new rule:

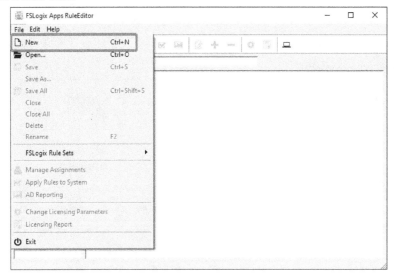

Figure 15.2 – Creating a new rule in the FSLogix Apps RuleEditor

3. You will now need to enter a file name for the rule we are about to create:

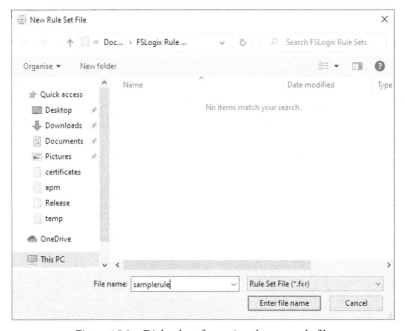

Figure 15.3 – Dialog box for saving the new rule file

4. Once you have added a name and clicked **Enter file name**, you will see the following **Rule Set** form appear:

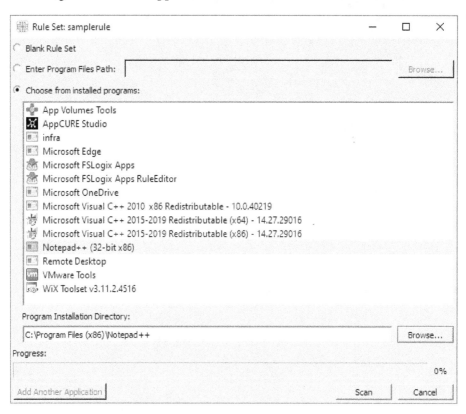

Figure 15.4 – The Rule Set form where we select an application from the installed programs list

5. We will choose a program from the installed programs for this example. Select **Notepad++** and click **Scan**. Once the scan has been completed, you can click the **Ok** button, which has changed from **Scan** to **Ok**:

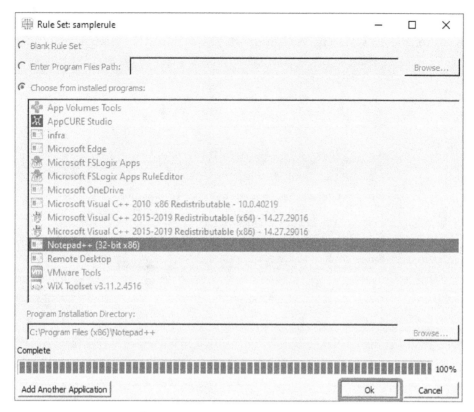

Figure 15.5 – The scan has been completed and you can now click Ok

6. You should now see the hiding rule for **Notepad++**:

Figure 15.6 – A hiding rule has been created

7. To manage assignments, right-click on **samplerule** as shown in the following screenshot and click **Manage Assignments**. This will load the **Assignments** page:

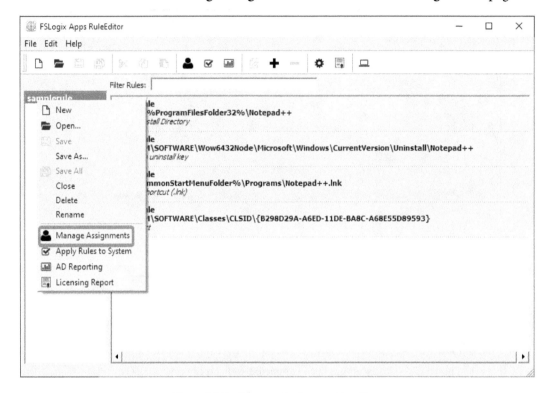

Figure 15.7 – Manage Assignments option

8. Within the **Assignments** page, you can add the required user/group permissions for this rule:

Important Note

There are several options available to you when it comes to assignments. You have a choice of not only user and group but also additional options including process, network location, computer, directory container, and environment variable.

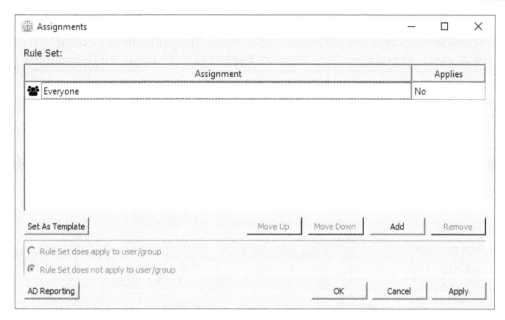

Figure 15.8 – Assignments form where you can set different assignments such as users and groups

Important Note

Good practice would be to use Active Directory groups to break down applications into department groups or groups relating to specific requirements. This then essentially enables granular access and better IT administrator control for user access to applications using FSLogix Application Masking.

9. Now that we have finished configuring the rule, you may want to test it before we deploy to a production environment. To do that, we would click the checkbox in the main form taskbar as shown in the following screenshot:

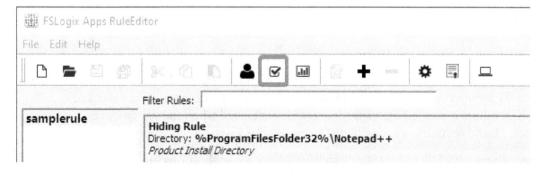

Figure 15.9 – The test check button on the taskbar

10. Once you have finished testing using the built-in test capability, the next step is to publish these rules to the session hosts. To do this, you would simply need to copy the created rule to the `c:\Program Files\FSLogix\Apps\Rules` path.

11. Once you have completed the task in *step 9*, you should see the rule name you created earlier with a different extension, `fxac`, in `C:\Program Files\FSLogix\Apps\Rules\CompiledRules`:

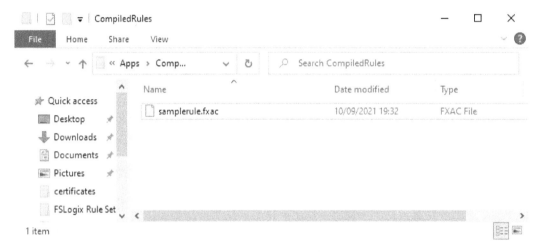

Figure 15.10 – The compiled rule once you've added the rule to C:\Program Files\FSLogix\Apps\Rules

> **Important Note**
> You can use traditional file transfer technologies or apply the rules within a master image by copying the rule file to the required location. You can also use custom script extensions to distribute the rules.

To summarize, we have created a simple hiding rule from the installed programs. After that, you can apply many custom/granular configurations and controls to your rule sets, including redirection rules, specify value rules, and app container (VHD) rules.

Application file containers

In this section, we take a look at creating application file containers. App containers allow IT admins to move applications and application data directories to VHD and VHDX volumes. The FSLogix app virtual disk is attached when the directory contents are accessed, and redirection is completed to the attached volume.

The auto-attach VHD feature is an excellent feature for applications that cannot use MSIX app attach and for those native apps that are large in size, which can impact the overall size of gold images. In addition, redirected applications are immediately available when needed.

VHD creation

The first thing we need to do to configure application file containers is to create a virtual disk. You can do this using the FSLogix toolset, specifically the `frx.exe` CLI tool.

You first need to navigate to the program folders where the tool is located as detailed here: Cd `"C:\Program Files\FSLogix\Apps"`.

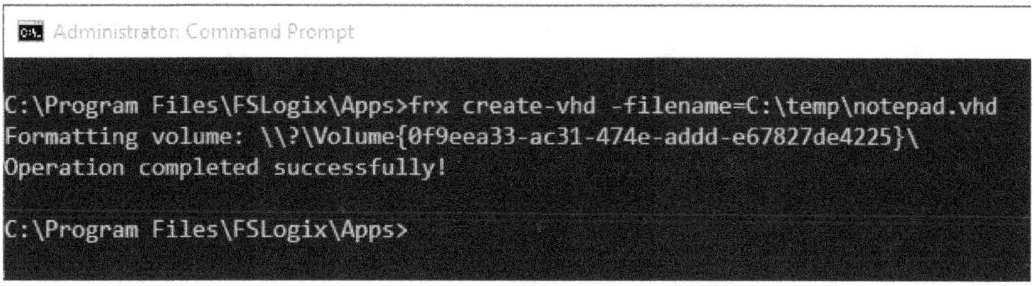

```
Administrator: Command Prompt

C:\Program Files\FSLogix\Apps>frx create-vhd -filename=C:\temp\notepad.vhd
Formatting volume: \\?\Volume{0f9eea33-ac31-474e-addd-e67827de4225}\
Operation completed successfully!

C:\Program Files\FSLogix\Apps>
```

Figure 15.11 – Run the frx tool to create a new VHD file

Once the VHD file has been created, you need to copy the application directories to the VHD. This can be done by using the frx tool.

> **Tip**
>
> You can create both VHD and VHDX virtual disks. It is recommended that you use VHDX virtual disks as you have more flexibility in terms of management using PowerShell.

As per the steps to create a VHD, you first need to navigate to the `FSLogix\apps` path, which is Cd `"C:\Program Files\FSLogix\Apps"`.

You then need to run the following commands to copy the application directory to the previously created virtual disk:

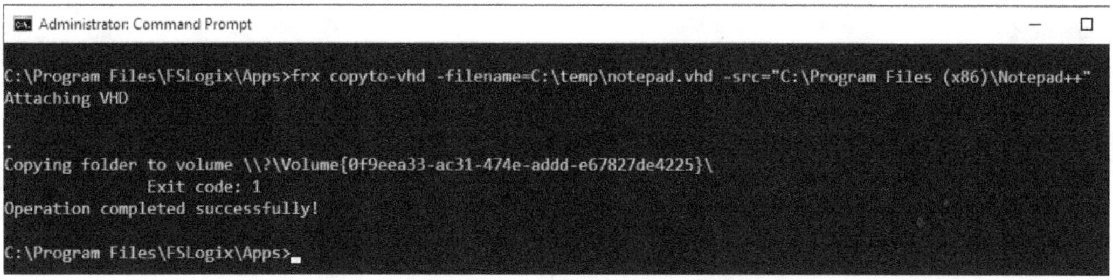

```
Administrator: Command Prompt                                          —    □

C:\Program Files\FSLogix\Apps>frx copyto-vhd -filename=C:\temp\notepad.vhd -src="C:\Program Files (x86)\Notepad++"
Attaching VHD
.
Copying folder to volume \\?\Volume{0f9eea33-ac31-474e-addd-e67827de4225}\
          Exit code: 1
Operation completed successfully!

C:\Program Files\FSLogix\Apps>
```

Figure 15.12 – Application files copied to the VHD

Now that we have completed the steps to create the VHD and copied the files from the application directory to the VHD, we can move on to the VHD deployment section.

VHD deployment

You can store your application disks on a local path or network path as long as the latency does not impact performance. If you decide to store your application file containers on a network store, you will need to ensure the session host has read permissions to the network drive – the same requirements MSIX app attach has. For details on configuring storage permissions for application file containers, please refer to *Chapter 14, MSIX App Attach in the Configuring Azure Files for MSIX App Attach section*.

Rule creation

Now we have the VHD file stored in the required location, the next step is to create an app container (VHD) rule using the FSLogix App RuleEditor tool.

To do this, we will create an app container VHD rule specifying the folder path we wish to redirect and the location of the VHD/VHD disk:

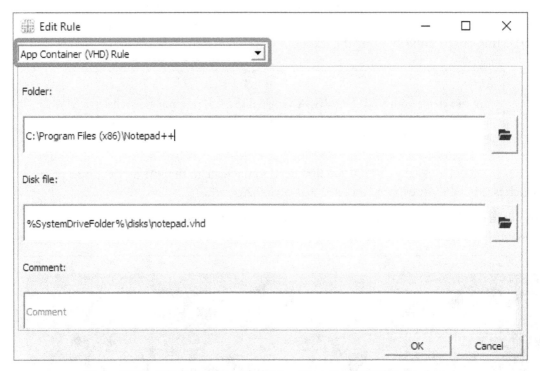

Figure 15.13 – Edit Rule form with the App Container (VHD) Rule selected

Once you have finished configuring the rule, save and make a copy of the rule ready for the next step.

Rule deployment

To deploy the redirection shown in the first section of this chapter, you will need to copy the created rules into the `C:\Program File\FSlogix\Apps\Rules` folder on all the required session hosts.

> **Important Note**
> The application folder path must be present on the session host for redirection to work. Therefore, you will need to delete the folder contents once the disk copy has been completed. However, the empty folder must remain.

Once deployed, you will see a VHD disk mounted, and the application directory populated with the application files from the mounted disk:

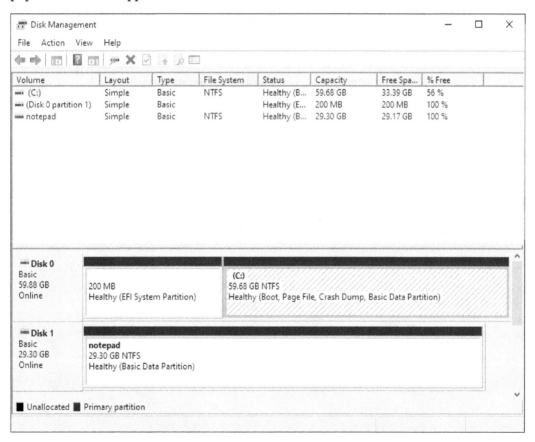

Figure 15.14 – Attached application file container for Notepad

In this section, we looked at implementing application masking. We started off by creating a hiding rule via assignments. We then took a look at application file containers where we copied the contents of an application to a VHD and then created the redirection rule so that the VHD became the app file source. We'll now move on to deploying applications as a RemoteApp.

Deploying an application as a RemoteApp

Please note that before proceeding with this section you will need to ensure applications have been installed on the session host first.

In this section, we take a look at deploying a RemoteApp within Azure Virtual Desktop. RemoteApps are essentially configured within the application groups. As mentioned in previous chapters, there are two types of application groups – one being a desktop app group and the second, a RemoteApp group.

> **Reminder**
>
> You can use MSIX app attach to deliver applications to RemoteApp user sessions.

Work through the following steps to create a RemoteApp group:

1. Sign in to the Azure portal and search for `Azure Virtual Desktop`.
2. On the **Azure Virtual Desktop** page, select **Host pools** and then select **Application groups**.
3. Click **Create** to create a new application group:

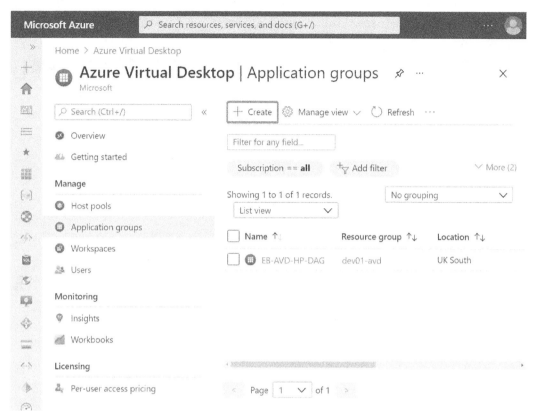

Figure 15.15 – Application groups page within Azure Virtual Desktop

4. Within the **Basics** tab, select the required **Subscription**, **Resource group**, and **Host pool**:

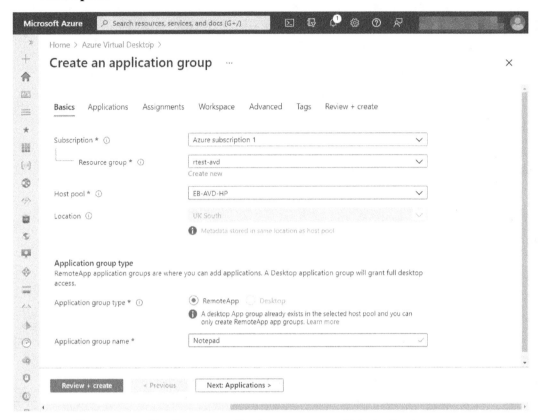

Figure 15.16 – The Create an application group page within Application groups

5. Ensure **Application group type** is set to **RemoteApp** and enter a name:

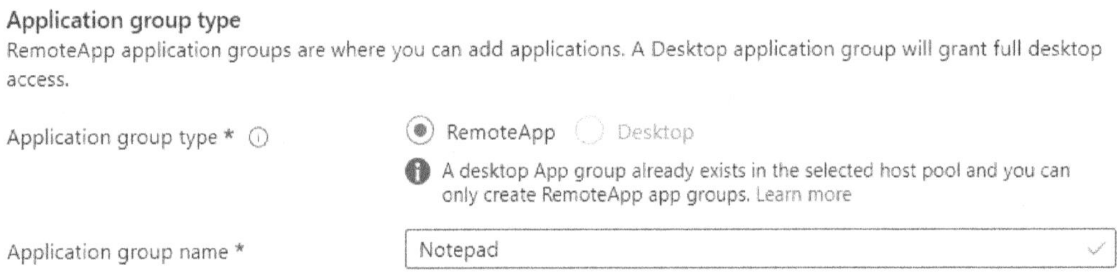

Application group type

RemoteApp application groups are where you can add applications. A Desktop application group will grant full desktop access.

Application group type * ⓘ   ◉ RemoteApp ◯ Desktop

ⓘ A desktop App group already exists in the selected host pool and you can only create RemoteApp app groups. Learn more

Application group name *   Notepad   ✓

Figure 15.17 – The Application group type section

6. Once you have filled out the required fields, click **Next: Applications** to move on to the **Applications** tab.

7. Select **Start menu** as the application source and the application in this example is **Notepad**:

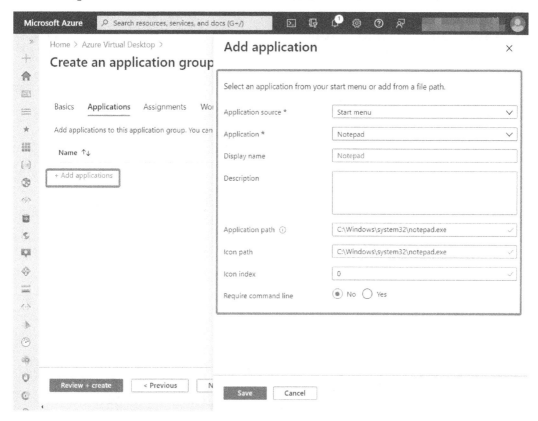

Figure 15.18 – The Add application blade within an application group

8. Enter a **Display name** for the application and leave the other options as is, then click **Save**.

9. Once you have finished adding applications, click **Next: Assignments** to move on to the **Assignments** tab:

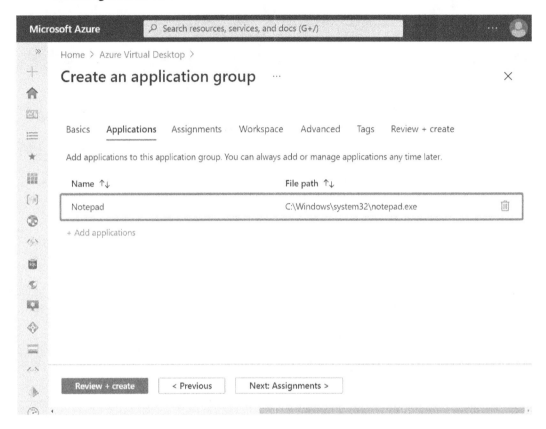

Figure 15.19 – Application added to the Create an application group page

10. Within **Assignments**, add the users/groups you want to have access to the remote application. Once complete, click **Next: Workspace** to move on to the **Workspace** tab:

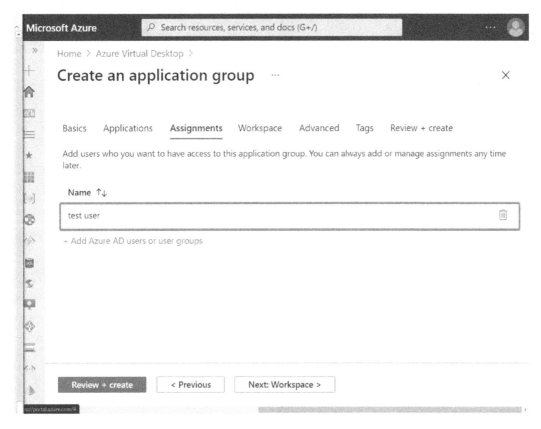

Figure 15.20 – A user account added on the Assignments tab

11. If you want to register the application group to a workspace, select **Yes** to register the application group. If you want to do this later, select **No**. If you have an existing workspace, you can register your application group to it:

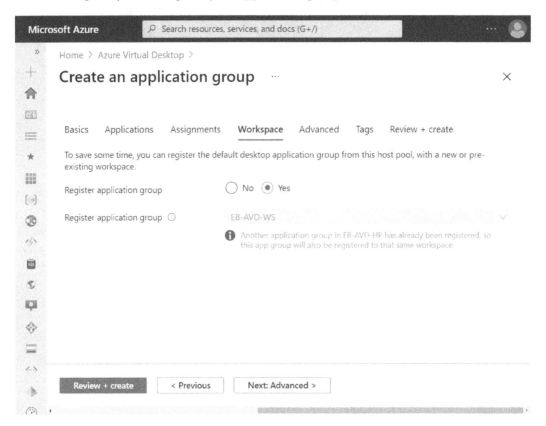

Figure 15.21 – Workspace tab within the Create an application group page

> **Important Note**
>
> Application groups can only be registered to workspaces created in the same region as the host pool. If you've previously registered another app group from the same host pool as your new app group to a workspace, it will be selected, and you won't be able to edit it, as shown in the preceding screenshot. All application groups from a host pool must be registered to the same workspace.

12. Click **Next: Advanced** and configure **Diagnostic** and **Tags**. If **Tags** and diagnostics are not required, then you can click **Review + create** instead.

13. Within the **Review + create** tab, check your configurations, then click **Create**.

14. Once the deployment has been completed, you should see the Notepad application appear as a remote app in the **Remote Desktop** client, as shown in the following screenshot:

Figure 15.22 – Remote Desktop client, displaying the Notepad application we just published as a RemoteApp

This concludes the steps to deploy a RemoteApp. In this section, we looked at the steps required to deploy a RemoteApp. We'll now look at how to implement and manage OneDrive for Business for a multi-session environment.

Implementing and managing OneDrive for Business for a multi-session environment

In this section, we will look at OneDrive for Business and how to deploy for a multi-session environment. A typical OneDrive installation installs per user; this means that the OneDrive client is installed under the `%localappdata%` folder. When deploying OneDrive (sync app) for a multi-session/VDI environment, you need to install the per-machine installation option. This installs OneDrive under the `Program Files (X86)` or `Program Files` directory depending on the operating system architecture. The reason being, if you install per user, you will need to run the OneDrive setup for each user on the session host, which causes issues.

> **Important Note**
>
> To ensure that you can apply sync app updates, you need to ensure that computers in your environment can communicate with the following URLs: `oneclient.sfx.ms` and `g.live.com`. Make sure you don't block these URLs.

To Install OneDrive per machine, please follow these steps:

1. You can download OneDrive from the Microsoft site. The following link is for version 21.150.0725.0001 (August 11, 2021): `https://go.microsoft.com/fwlink/?linkid=844652`.

2. To deploy OneDrive per machine, use the `OneDriveSetup.exe /allusers` cmdlet as shown in the following screenshot:

Figure 15.23 – Installation of OneDrive using the per machine option

3. Once you have installed OneDrive (sync app), you should see the application within `Program Files (x86)` or `Program Files` as shown in the following screenshot:

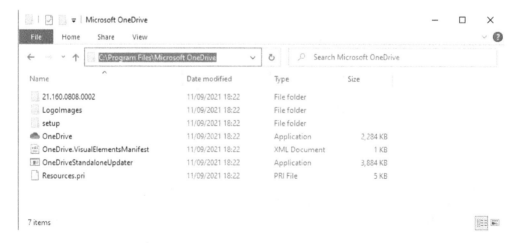

Figure 15.24 – OneDrive program files after installing using the per machine option

> **Important Note**
>
> Using the images provided by Microsoft can save you a lot of time as configurations have already been done by Microsoft.
>
> For more information on OneDrive and controlling its behavior best practice, please see the following link detailing the settings you can configure for OneDrive with Azure Virtual Desktop: `https://docs.microsoft.com/en-us/onedrive/use-group-policy#manage-onedrive-using-group-policy`.

In this section, we looked at how to deploy OneDrive for multi-session deployments. In the next section, we take a look at implementing and managing Microsoft Teams AV redirection.

Implementing and managing Microsoft Teams AV redirection

This section looks at the specific configurations required for Microsoft Teams AV redirection for Azure Virtual Desktop. AV redirection is essentially an optimization for Microsoft Teams. It works by enabling the Windows desktop client to handle audio and video locally for Teams calls and meetings.

You can experience high CPU usage and poor performance when the session host handles audio and video. By redirecting to the local client, you reduce the resources used on the session host virtual machine and improve the overall experience as audio and video is handled by the local client device:

1. The first step is to ensure that you have installed the Teams desktop application on the session host template. This must be installed per device and not per user. If you use the images managed by Microsoft then everything is configured for you.

2. You then need to add the following registry key to `HKEY_LOCAL_MACHINE\SOFTWARE\Microsoft\Teams` as shown in the following table:

Name	Type	Data/Value
IsWVDEnvironment	DWORD	1

You can add the registry key using the following within Command Prompt run as an administrator:

```
reg add"HKLM\SOFTWARE\Microsoft\Teams" /v
IsWVDEnvironment /t REG_DWORD /d 1 /f
```

3. Install the Teams WebSocket Service on the virtual machine image. You can download it from here: `https://query.prod.cms.rt.microsoft.com/cms/api/am/binary/RWFYsj`. If you experience installation issues, you will need to install the latest Microsoft Visual C++ Redistributable. You can find it at this URL: `https://support.microsoft.com/help/2977003/the-latest-supported-visual-c-downloads`.

4. Once you have installed the required components, you will need to reboot the session host image/template.

> **Important Note**
> The configuration for AV redirection is already set up for you when using an image from the gallery, specifically the Windows 10 images with Microsoft 365 Apps in the title.

The following screenshot shows the WebRTC Redirector installed:

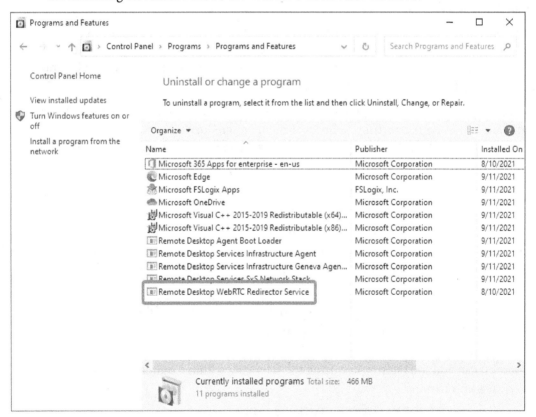

Figure 15.25 – Remote Desktop WebRTC redirector service installed on a templated image

You can also see that the required registry key has been pre-added, as shown in the following screenshot:

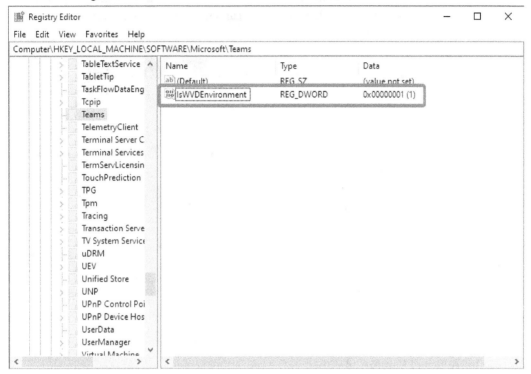

Figure 15.26 – Required registry setting included within the image template

Now that we have configured Teams AV redirection, let's look at the next steps of verifying the configuration is working.

Verifying media optimizations are loaded

We have installed the required components for AV redirection. We now need to verify that teams are configured for AVD redirection. You can check this by navigating to the **Version** button as shown in the following screenshot:

Figure 15.27 – Display the Microsoft Teams version

Once you have clicked **Version** as shown in the preceding screenshot, marked with the number **3**, you should see the version appear as a banner within the Teams app as shown in the following screenshot:

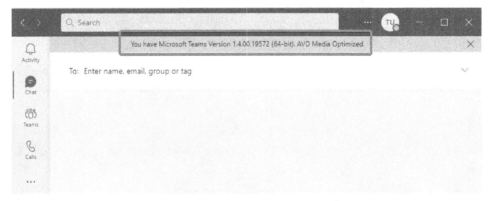

Figure 15.28 – Version output confirming AVD Media Optimized is configured

As shown in the preceding screenshot, you can see that we now have confirmed that Microsoft Teams is configured with Microsoft Teams AV redirection. The version will state **AVD Media Optimized** when configured correctly.

In this section, we looked at how to configure AV redirection for Microsoft Teams within Azure Virtual Desktop. This included how to check whether AV redirection is configured. In the next section, we look at multimedia redirection.

Implementing and managing multimedia redirection

In this section, we take a look at **Multimedia Redirection** (**MMR**) for Azure Virtual Desktop, which at the time of writing is in preview. MMR provides smooth video playback through the Microsoft Edge and Google Chrome web browsers. When MMR is enabled, the media element is remoted to the Remote Desktop client (local machine), reducing resource utilization, specifically the CPU on a session host. This is a feature similar to AV redirection for Microsoft Teams.

> **Important Note**
>
> To use MMR, you need to make sure you use the Remote Desktop client version 1.2.2222 or later. Additionally, you can check if MMR is supported as `MSMmrDVCPlugin.dll` should be present in the Remote Desktop client application installation path.

Getting started with MMR

In this section, we will configure MMR for use with Microsoft Edge and allow `youtube.com` to use MMR. You can add multiple sites or all of them if required.

You firstly need to download and install the **MsMmrHostmri** installer, which installs the MMR extensions for your web browser on the session host. You can download it from here: `https://query.prod.cms.rt.microsoft.com/cms/api/am/binary/RWIzIk`.

Figure 15.29 – The MsMmrhostMsi installation has been completed

Now that we have installed MSMmrHostMsi, we can proceed to the next part of this section, which looks at controlling which websites can use MMR.

Restricting which websites can use MMR

We'll now take a look at how to allow and block websites, configuring Microsoft Edge or Google Chrome for MMR. This example looks at Microsoft Edge only. You can use Group Policy for configuring MMR. Before we can do this, we need to download and install the MS Edge Group Policy administrative template: `https://aka.ms/EdgeEnterpris:`

1. Once you've downloaded the CAB file, extract it to a suitable location on your session host such as `c:\temp`.

2. Copy the ADM and ADMX files to the `PolicyDefinitions` folder. If using the **Group Policy Central Store**, copy to the policy definition path:

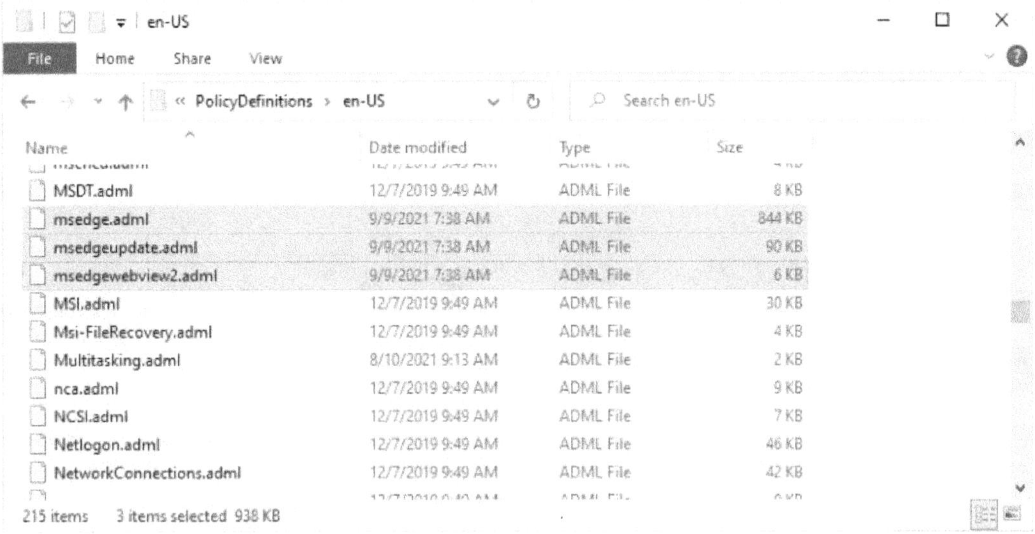

Figure 15.30 – ADML files that have been copied to the PolicyDefinitions folder

3. Create a new policy within **Group Policy Manager | User configuration | Administrative Templates | Microsoft Edge | Extensions | Configure Extensions Management Settings**.

4. Set the policy as enabled and enter the following code in the **Configure Extensions Management Settings policy**:

```
{ "joeclbldhdmoijbaagobkhlpfjglcihd": { "installation_
mode": "force_installed", "runtime_allowed_hosts":
[ "*://*.youtube.com" ], "runtime_blocked_hosts": [
"*://*" ], "update_url": "https://edge.microsoft.com/
extensionwebstorebase/v1/crx" } }
```

You can customize the runtime allowed/blocked hosts. In this example, we are allowing `youtube.com`:

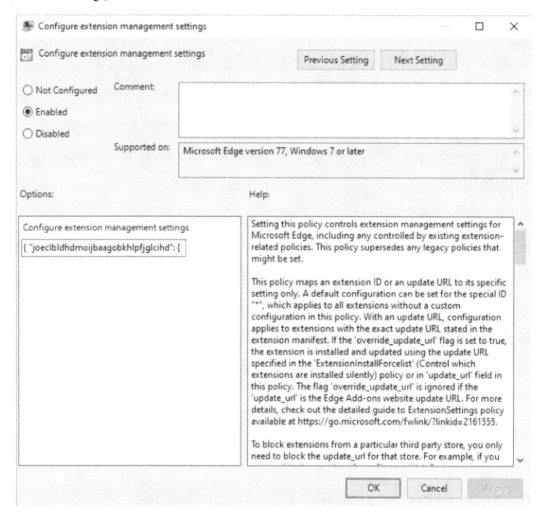

Figure 15.31 – Configure extension management settings policy for Microsoft Edge

5.   Once you have applied the policy, it is recommended that you reboot the session host.

We'll now move on to look at MMR in action.

Testing MMR

When the session host has rebooted, open Microsoft Edge and you will see a Remote Desktop client icon in the menu bar, as shown in the following screenshot. Additionally, when loading an allowed/supported multimedia site, the MMR icon will show a green checkbox if configured correctly, including communicating correctly with the Remote Desktop client:

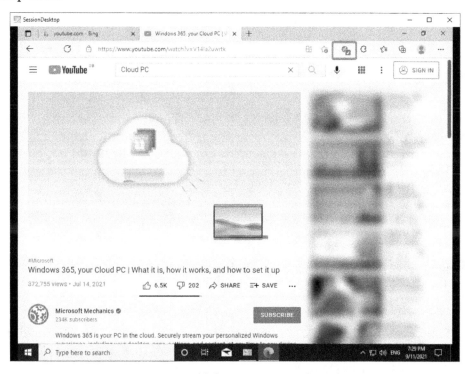

Figure 15.32 – MMR enabled on a Remote Desktop client session

The following table shows the three different icon states that will help you if you need to troubleshoot any issues:

Icon State	Definition
	The default icon appearance with no status applied.
	The red square with an X indicates that the client couldn't connect to multimedia redirection.
	You will see the green square with a check mark indicates the client successfully connected to multimedia redirection.

The preceding table is taken from the Microsoft site; you can find it here: `https://docs.microsoft.com/en-us/azure/virtual-desktop/multimedia-redirection#the-multimedia-redirection-status-icon`.

In this section, we looked at MMR for Azure Virtual Desktop. In the next section, we move on to look at managing internet access for Azure Virtual Desktop sessions.

Managing internet access for Azure Virtual Desktop sessions

In this section, we will take a brief look at controlling internet access for Azure Virtual Desktop.

A typical way to manage access to the internet within Microsoft Azure is by using **Network Security Groups** (**NSGs**). NSGs are used to filter inbound and outbound network traffic from a virtual network subnet. You can filter traffic by IP address, port, and protocol. To restrict internet access for Azure Virtual Desktop users, you can use an NSG to block web traffic.

To block internet access, complete the following steps:

1. Navigate to the session host subnet's NSG.

2. Within the **Settings** menu located on the left-hand side within the NSG, click **Outbound security rules**.

3. Add a new rule.

4. Set **Source** to **Any**; the source port ranges should be the default *. Set **Destination** to **Service Tag** and **Destination service tag** to **Internet**. Then specify **Service** as **HTTPS** and **Action** as **Deny**. You do need to specify a priority and ensure the priority does not impact other services on the virtual network. Please note that you will need to repeat these steps for HTTP traffic to change the service to HTTP. The following screenshot shows an example:

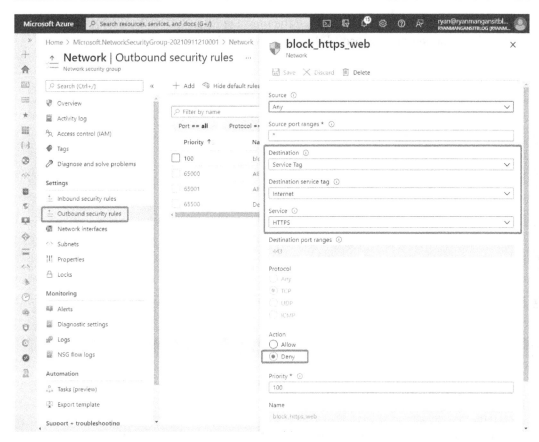

Figure 15.33 – Outbound security rules page of an NSG. What is also shown is the blade for adding a security rule to restrict HTTPS access to the internet

5. Once the policy is set, you should see the message **ERR_CONNECTION_TIMED_OUT** when opening Microsoft Edge, as shown in the following screenshot:

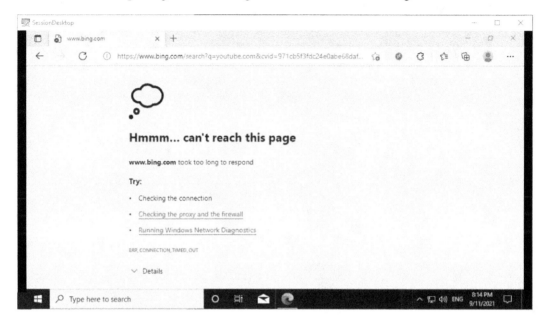

Figure 15.34 – The screen after applying the security rule

> **Tip**
> For more granular control of internet access from the session host, you should look at a third-party **Network Virtual Appliance** (**NVA**) or Azure Firewall. Using an NVA offers advanced third-party features, including content filtering and specific application control policies that take effect at the perimeter.

This section took a summary look at restricting internet access to session hosts without impacting other services and granular control access to specific services using an NSG.

Summary

We started this chapter by looking at Application Masking and hiding applications from users outside the correct security groups, and other assignment options. We then moved on to take a look at the benefits of application file containers and how to redirect application files to a VHD or VHDX. Next, we looked at how to deploy and configure a RemoteApp, and in the example used, we published Notepad as a RemoteApp to the Remote Desktop client.

We then looked at deploying OneDrive for multiple sessions using per-machine installation. Next, we covered both Microsoft Team AV redirection and multimedia redirection. Finally, to finish the chapter, we looked at how to restrict session host internet access using a network security group.

I hope you found this chapter interesting and are looking forward to the next, where we take a look at planning and implementing business continuity and disaster recovery.

Questions

1. What are the four app masking rules you can configure?
2. Can application groups be registered to workspaces in different regions to the host pool?
3. Which DLL should you check for to ensure multimedia redirection has been installed correctly?
4. Which FSLogix App Masking rule would you use to separate applications using virtual disks?

Answers

1. *Specify Value, App Container, Redirection rule, Hiding rule*
2. *No*
3. *MSMmrDVCPlugin.dll*
4. *Application file containers*

Section 6: Monitoring and Maintaining an Azure Virtual Desktop Infrastructure

This section of the book looks at how you design and plan a disaster recovery solution for Azure Virtual Desktop, as well as automate repeat admin tasks, monitor and manage environment health and performance, and use the *Getting started* feature to quickly deploy a full Azure Virtual Desktop environment quickly.

This part of the book comprises the following chapters:

- *Chapter 16, Planning and Implementing Business Continuity and Disaster Recovery*
- *Chapter 17, Automating Azure Virtual Desktop Management Tasks*
- *Chapter 18, Monitoring and Managing Performance and Health*
- *Chapter 19, Azure Virtual Desktop's Getting Started Feature*
- *Appendix, Microsoft Resources and Microsoft Learn*

16
Planning and Implementing Business Continuity and Disaster Recovery

This chapter takes a look at planning and implementing a business continuity and disaster recovery solution for Azure Virtual Desktop. We first take a look at what's required before we can configure a business continuity and disaster recovery solution and then we take a look at the options available to you.

In this chapter, we take a look at the following topics:

- Designing a backup strategy for Azure Virtual Desktop
- Planning and implementing a disaster recovery plan for Azure Virtual Desktop

- Configuring backup and restore for FSLogix user profiles and personal virtual desktops

- Infrastructure and golden images

Designing a backup strategy for Azure Virtual Desktop

Before we get started, I wanted to remind you of the shared responsibilities of using Azure Virtual Desktop. The following illustration details the responsibilities managed by Microsoft and what the customer controls. Within this chapter, we will look at all of the items within the customer section for which you are responsible.

The following screenshot shows the different responsibilities for both the customer and Microsoft. You will note that Microsoft takes care of the management plane, while the customer is responsible for everything inside the subscription.

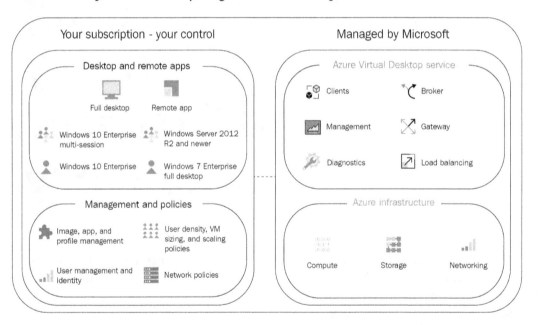

Figure 16.1 – Shared responsibilities of Microsoft and the customer for Azure Virtual Desktop

A robust business continuity and disaster recovery strategy keeps your applications and workloads running during unplanned and planned service outages. For example, when an outage occurs in an Azure region, the Azure Virtual Desktop service infrastructure components will failover to a secondary location and continue to function.

> **Important Note**
> Where required, you should ensure that your business applications that rely on data in the primary region can failover to ensure that all services function correctly.

We'll look at the two types of host pool as each type will have a different backup strategy due to the design and use cases associated with the host pool type:

- **Personal desktops**: These are typically used for those who need admin permissions to the local machine or are completing specific tasks requiring a dedicated virtual machine. A personal desktop commonly has specific user data and operating system customizations that need to be protected.

- **Pooled desktops**: In contrast, pooled desktops are designed to provide users with any desktop in the pool. All the data is typically stored in a central profile store, such as FSLogix profile containers or others. Furthermore, in most environments, a pooled desktop host pool is treated as disposable. This is because personal data is not stored on the virtual machine, and the operating system is typically delivered from an image template.

Depending on your chosen host pool type, you will need to consider the required backup strategy. When using both host pool types, you should design a strategy for both.

The five crucial areas to consider for Azure Virtual Desktop business continuity and disaster recovery strategies are detailed in the following table:

	Azure component	**Description of component**
1	Virtual network	You should consider the design of your network connectivity during an outage.
2	Virtual machines	Dependent on the host pool type and requirement, you may wish to replicate your virtual machines to the second region or replicate an image template using Azure Compute Galleries to deploy new session hosts within the second region.
		Availability zones should also be considered within a local region. Read more here: https://docs.microsoft.com/azure/availability-zones/az-overview.
3	User and app data	For User profile containers, you should set up data replication in the second region, and consider features such as MSIX app attach.
4	User identities	Ensure you can access your user identities within the second region.
5	Application dependencies	Any line-of-business applications will need to be failed over to the secondary region in the event of an outage.

We will take a more detailed look at these five critical components in the next section of this chapter.

Planning and implementing a disaster recovery plan for Azure Virtual Desktop

This section looks at the five critical components for implementing a disaster recovery plan for Azure Virtual Desktop. First, we start with virtual networks, which underpin the Azure Virtual Desktop environment.

Virtual network

In this section, we take a look at the network requirements for disaster recovery in an Azure Virtual Desktop environment.

Connectivity is the first consideration when planning and implementing a disaster recovery plan for Azure Virtual Desktop. Before resources can communicate in a secondary region, you need to ensure that VNet has been set up in your secondary region/location. You may also need to consider connectivity between on-premises and the secondary region.

The most common connectivity type to use between on-premises and the Azure virtual network would be a VPN gateway. The following diagram depicts a simple VPN gateway connecting to an on-premises site:

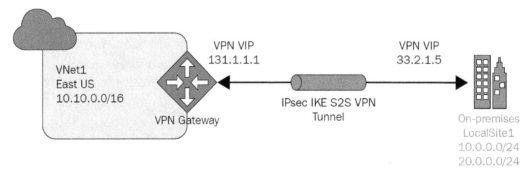

Figure 16.2 – A simple site-to-site VPN connecting an on-premises site to Azure

For smaller Azure Virtual Desktop deployments, you can use **Azure Site Recovery (ASR)** as this can be configured to set up the VNet in a secondary (failover) region. ASR can preserve your primary settings and does not require network peering.

One of the most important things to remember when working with Azure Virtual Desktop and multiple regions is DNS. A common problem customers face in Azure Virtual Desktop is DNS configuration issues relating to the virtual network. Ensure that you have configured the VNet's DNS to communicate with the required domain controller.

One final point within this section is the fact that you need to ensure that all the required URLs are included within the **Network Security Group** or other security technology you may have deployed on the virtual network. For more information on the URL list for Azure Virtual Desktop, please refer to *Chapter 4, Implementing and Managing Networking for Azure Virtual Desktop*.

Virtual machines

When we look at business continuity and disaster recovery options for virtual machines (session hosts) for Azure Virtual Desktop, two specific options are available. The first is **active-active**, and the second is **active-passive**.

Let's first take a look at the active-active option.

The active-active option

When using the active-active option, you can have a single host pool that is stretched across multiple Azure regions. This means creating a single host pool and deploying the virtual machines across a primary and secondary region. You need to use **FSLogix Cloud Cache** to handle profiles to replicate user data between the regions.

> **Important Note**
> This option should only be considered for pooled desktop host pools.

If you choose active-active, you can protect against short storage outages without the user having to log in again. This also means that you can adopt continuous testing of disaster recovery locations as you can use both regions in a normal operating condition. This option does not provide any cost savings and has no benefits in terms of performance; however, as stated, you can continually test disaster recovery.

You can only manage connection using this option via the session host drain stop; otherwise, incoming user connections will be equal. What this means is that user connections could be directed to either the primary region or the secondary region.

We now move on to take a look at the active-passive option.

The active-passive option

The active-passive option should be considered for personal desktop host pools where you need to replicate the dedicated virtual machines over to the second region. You can use the active-passive option for pooled desktops as well if required.

Similar to the active-active option, you can use a single host pool. This is the recommended approach for simplicity. You can also deploy a new host pool in the secondary region with all associated resources turned off. There is still a cost associated with this and you would need to regularly power these virtual machines on to prevent the machine account passwords from expiring. In the event of an outage, you can turn on those resources for the organization to access as a disaster recovery solution. For this method, as with all new host pool configurations, you would need to set up application groups for the required users within the failover region. You can also use an ASR plan to turn on the resources orchestrating the overall process.

> **Important Note**
>
> It is recommended that you use **Azure Site Recovery** (**ASR**) for personal desktop host pools.

Virtual machine availability sets versus availability zones

The default resiliency option for a host pool deployment is **Availability Set**. The resiliency provided by an availability set is at the single Azure data center level. Microsoft provides a 99.5% SLA on an availability set.

The second option would be to use something called an availability zone. This is where virtual machines within a host pool are distributed across different data centers in a region. Again, this offers a higher resiliency, and Microsoft provides a 99.9 SLA on availability zones.

It is recommended that you consider multi-region resilience over availability sets/zones for better coverage. The following link details some of the challenges you may face in larger organizations relating to availability sets and allocation failures: `https://docs.microsoft.com/troubleshoot/azure/virtual-machines/allocation-failure#allocation-failures-for-large-deployments-more-than-500-cores`.

We now move on to take a look at managing user identities.

Managing user identities

In this section, we take a look at managing user identities and some of the different options available to you. The first thing you need to think about when managing user identities is that when you failover to a secondary region, you need to ensure that the domain controller is available so your virtual machines can communicate with it.

I have listed three different options for enabling communication with the domain controller in the secondary region.

Deploying a domain controller in the failover region

Using virtual network peering, you can configure both Region A and Region B virtual networks to communicate using network peering. The following diagram shows how network peering facilities the communication of domain controllers between the two regions:

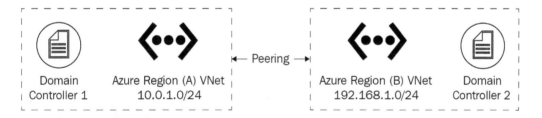

Figure 16.3 – Network peering used to enable domain controllers to communicate across Azure regions

Now that we have looked at deploying a domain controller in the failover region, let's look at how you would use an on-premises domain controller.

Using an on-premises domain controller

Another option would be to use a **virtual network gateway** to connect multiple virtual networks and an on-premises site enabling you to use the on-premises domain controller for multiple regions, as you can see in the following diagram:

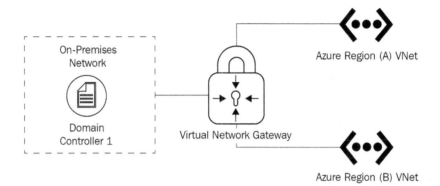

Figure 16.4 – This diagram shows multiple regions connecting
via a VPN gateway to an on-premises site

> **Tip**
> Make sure you configure the DNS settings on the VNet to point to the domain controller. This is quite a common issue.

Let's now take a look at how you would logically use ASR to replicate your domain controller between regions.

Using ASR to replicate your domain controller

One of the most common approaches for ensuring that Azure Virtual Desktop resources can access the domain controller in the failover region is to use Azure Site recovery in a similar manner to what we discussed earlier in the virtual machine part of this section.

The following screenshot shows the use of ASR replication to replicate the domain controller from Azure Region A to Azure Region B:

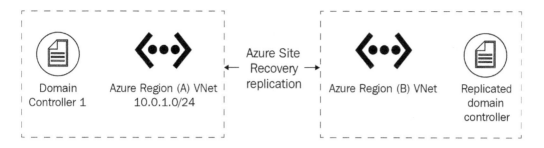

Figure 16.5 – This diagram shows the replication of the domain controller from Region A to Region B

Now that we have taken a look at user identify options, let's move on to learn how best to configure user and app data.

Configuring user and app data

In this section, we take a look at profiles and user data. When using local profiles, it's recommended that you use ASR to replicate user data and the session hosts to the failover region. This is a common approach for those who are using personal host pools.

FSLogix offers the ability to separate both the user profile and office container disks. This also enables you to split user data components into different storage locations. In a typical environment, the office container would consume more disk space than a profile disk. The backup, replication, and user profile disk would be significantly quicker than using office containers as part of the solution.

In most cases, it is typical to expect organizations to use user profile containers only.

The three recommended storage options for storing FSLogix profile containers are as follows:

- Azure files
- Azure NetApp files
- FSLogix Cloud Cache

There are multiple options available in terms of storing your FSLogix profile containers. To find out more about the options available to you and the limitations, please refer to *Chapter 5, Implementing and Managing Storage for Azure Virtual Desktop*.

> **Important Note**
>
> Microsoft recommends storing FSLogix profile containers on Azure files and NetApp files for the majority of scenarios.

When looking to configure disaster recovery for user profiles, you have the following options:

- Use Azure replication (for example, Azure NetApp Replication or Azure Files Sync for file servers).

- Configure FSLogix Cloud Cache for both application and user data.

- Configure app data for disaster recovery only. What this means is that your users would have new user profiles, and the first-time sign-in experience would occur.

- OneDrive is also an option to consider as it can redirect well-known folders, including Desktop, Documents, and Pictures. Again, this offers a level of resilience without any specific business continuity or disaster recovery considerations.

> **Important Note**
>
> When using Cloud Cache, make sure that your session hosts are configured using Premium SSD disks for the local cache file to help with no loss of data.

For more information on Cloud Cache, please refer to the *Configuring Cloud Cache* section in *Chapter 12*, *Implementing and Managing FSLogix*.

Disaster recovery considerations for MSIX app attach

MSIX app attach is a dynamic application delivery feature in Azure Virtual Desktop. MSIX app attach delivers MSIX applications using a virtual disk or CimFS image to pooled and personal desktop host pools within Azure Virtual Desktop.

When implementing a disaster recovery plan, there are two areas of consideration for MSIX app attach. The first is *storage*; you need to ensure that the MSIX images are accessible in the failover region. Similar to FSLogix, MSIX app attach requires network storage for the application disks/images.

The second consideration relates to the *configuration* of MSIX app attach. If the storage path changes in a disaster recovery scenario, you will need to change all the MSIX image paths or reconfigure all applications configured within a host pool.

To avoid the requirement to reconfigure MSIX app attach in a disaster recovery scenario, it is recommended that you use one of the following options:

- Create a separate host pool for the secondary region pre-configured for MSIX app attach.

- Use Azure files with geo-redundant storage.

- Implement Azure NetApp Files cross-region replication.

> **Tip**
> For enterprise deployments, it is recommended that you configure Azure NetApp Files cross-region replication.

To learn more about MSIX app attach, please refer to *Chapter 14, MSIX App Attach*. In the next section, we will take a high-level look at application dependencies.

Application dependencies

When an outage occurs, it may not just impact your Azure Virtual Desktop environment but also any critical business applications that rely on data located in the primary region. This could be web services, SQL databases, and more.

You should also consider any specific settings required for the applications and any additional configurations for these services once you have set up replication or high availability.

You can use ASR plans to model application dependencies, and you could consider configuring the app to use the second region as its default configuration or as part of the failover process.

Please note the following:

- You need to ensure that users can access on-premises applications in the event of a failover. See the *Virtual network* section for more details.

- You need to ensure that you review all dependent applications and any other resources to ensure availability in the disaster recovery location.

In this section, we looked at planning and implementing a disaster recovery plan for Azure Virtual Desktop, looking at the five critical areas: *virtual network, virtual machines, managing user identities, configuring user and app data*, and *application dependencies*.

In the next section, we look at configuring backup and restore for FSLogix user profiles.

Configuring backup and restore for FSLogix user profiles, personal virtual desktop infrastructures (VDIs), and golden images

In this section, we look at backing up and restoring Azure Virtual Desktop components. We first take a look at backup and restore.

Virtual machine backup and restore

When managing personal host pools, you may want to back up the session hosts when local profiles are used. In this section, we'll look at how to take a backup of a session host virtual machine.

We start by creating an Azure Recovery Vault for Azure Virtual Desktop, the steps for which are as follows:

1. First, navigate to the Azure portal.

2. Search for `Backup Center` in the Azure portal and navigate to the **Backup Center** dashboard.

3. Click on **Vault**, located in the main menu of the page.

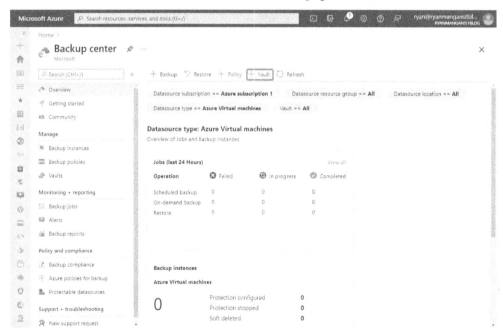

Figure 16.6 – Azure Backup center page

4. Within the **Create Vault** page, select **Recovery Services vault** and then click
Continue:

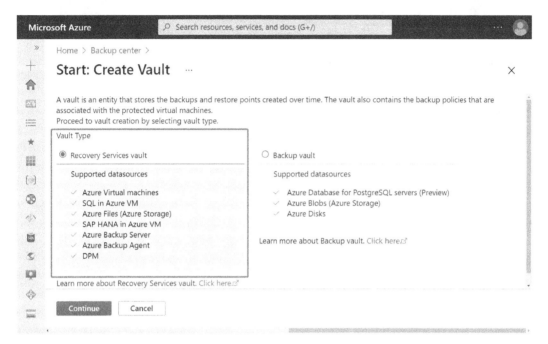

Figure 16.7 – Create Vault page within Backup center

5. You will then see the **Create Recovery Services vault** page.

6.   Select the **Resource group** option or create a new one and specify a vault name and region.

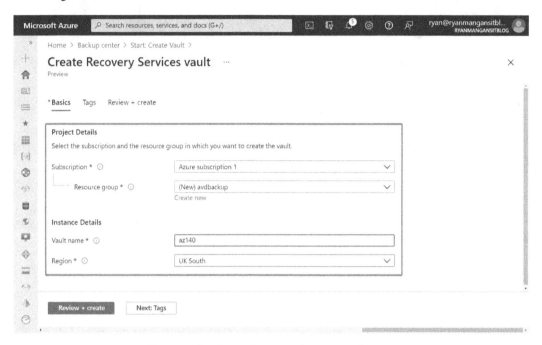

Figure 16.8 – Create Recovery Services vault page

7.   Once configured, proceed to **Review + create**.

8. Once complete, you will see the new **Recovery Services vault** in **Backup center**.

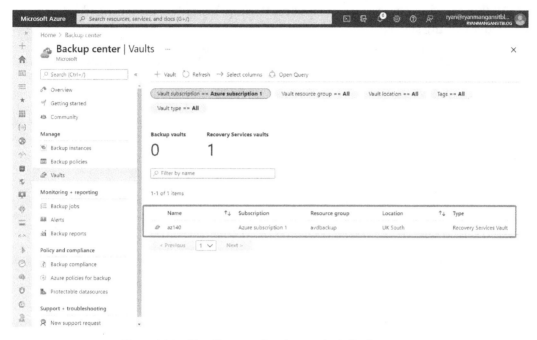

Figure 16.9 – New Recovery Services vaults in Backup center

Now that we have created a recovery services vault, we can progress with backing up a session host virtual machine.

9. Within **Backup center**, select the recently created recovery services vault.

10. Within the recovery services vault, select **Backup**, located on the left-hand side under **Getting started**.

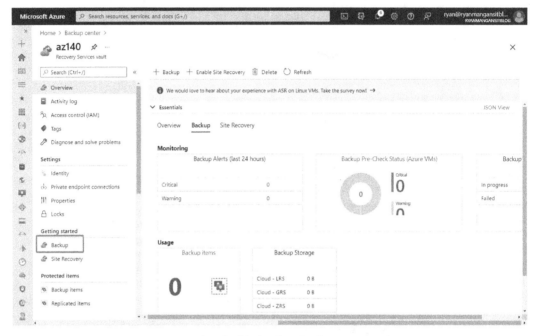

Figure 16.10 – Backup highlighted in the Getting started section

11. Once selected, you will see the **Backup** blade appear. Choose **Azure** for **Where is your workload running**, and **Virtual machine** for **What do you want to backup**, and then click **Backup**.

12. You can use a default policy or create a new policy customized to your specific requirements.

13. Click the **Add** button under the **Virtual Machines** section, choose the virtual machines you wish to back up, and then click **OK**.

14. Once you have selected the backup policy and added the virtual machines, click **Enable Backup**.

15. You should now see the virtual machine listed within backup jobs with the completed **Configure backup** operation. When the scheduled backup runs, you will also see the following within the backup jobs:

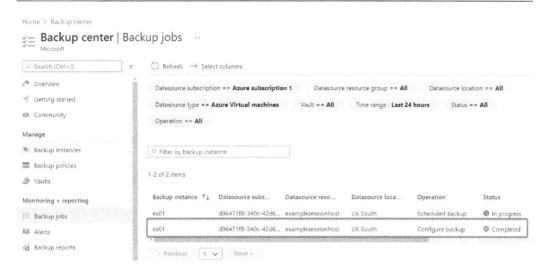

Figure 16.11 – Configuring a backup operation as completed

We now move on to take a look at restoring a virtual machine.

16. To restore a virtual machine, you will first navigate to the Azure **Backup center**.

17. On the main page of the Azure Backup center, click **Restore**, as shown in the
following screenshot:

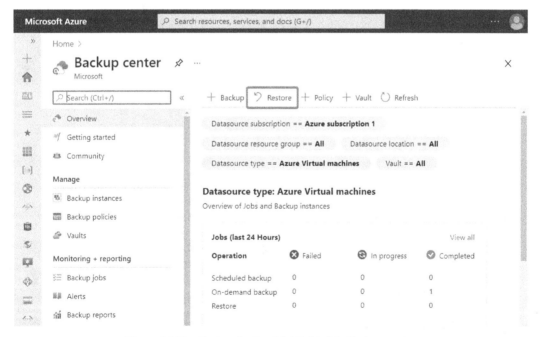

Figure 16.12 – Restore button highlighted in Backup center

18. You will now see the **Start: Restore** page appear. Select the virtual machine backup instance you require to restore.

19. Under the **Restore Region** section, you have a choice of selecting a primary region or a secondary region. In this example, we will select **Primary Region**. Once you have completed the required fields on the page, click **Continue**.

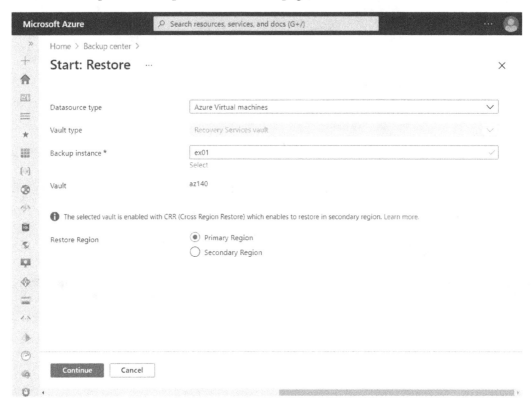

Figure 16.13 – Start: Restore page when restoring a virtual machine within Microsoft Azure

> **Important Note**
>
> You can configure your **Recovery Vault for Cross Region Restore**, allowing the restoration of virtual machines to the secondary region. This is useful for those who are using a single host pool for both a primary and secondary region. In the event of a primary region outage, you can restore the virtual machine to the secondary region. You may want to consider configuring your disaster recovery within a paired region to take advantage of **Cross Region Restore (CRR)**. You can find out more on the region pairs here: `https://docs.microsoft.com/en-us/azure/availability-zones/cross-region-replication-azure#azure-regional-pairs`.

20. You will now see the **Restore Virtual Machine** page appear. Click **Select**, which will
launch the selected **Restore point** blade.

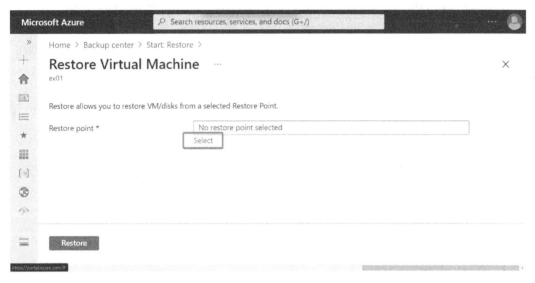

Figure 16.14 – Restore point page within the virtual machine restore wizard

21. Choose the required restore point and then click **Continue**.

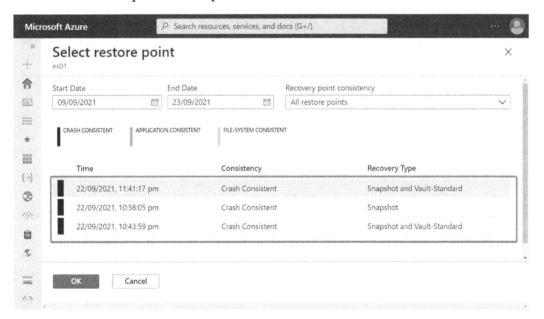

Figure 16.15 – Select restore point blade

22. The final part is to specify whether you want to create a new virtual machine or replace the existing one. In this example, we will select **Create new**.

23. Complete the **Virtual Machine** type fields, **Resource group**, **Virtual network**, and **Subnet**, and select a staging location.

24. Once all the fields have been completed, click **Restore**.

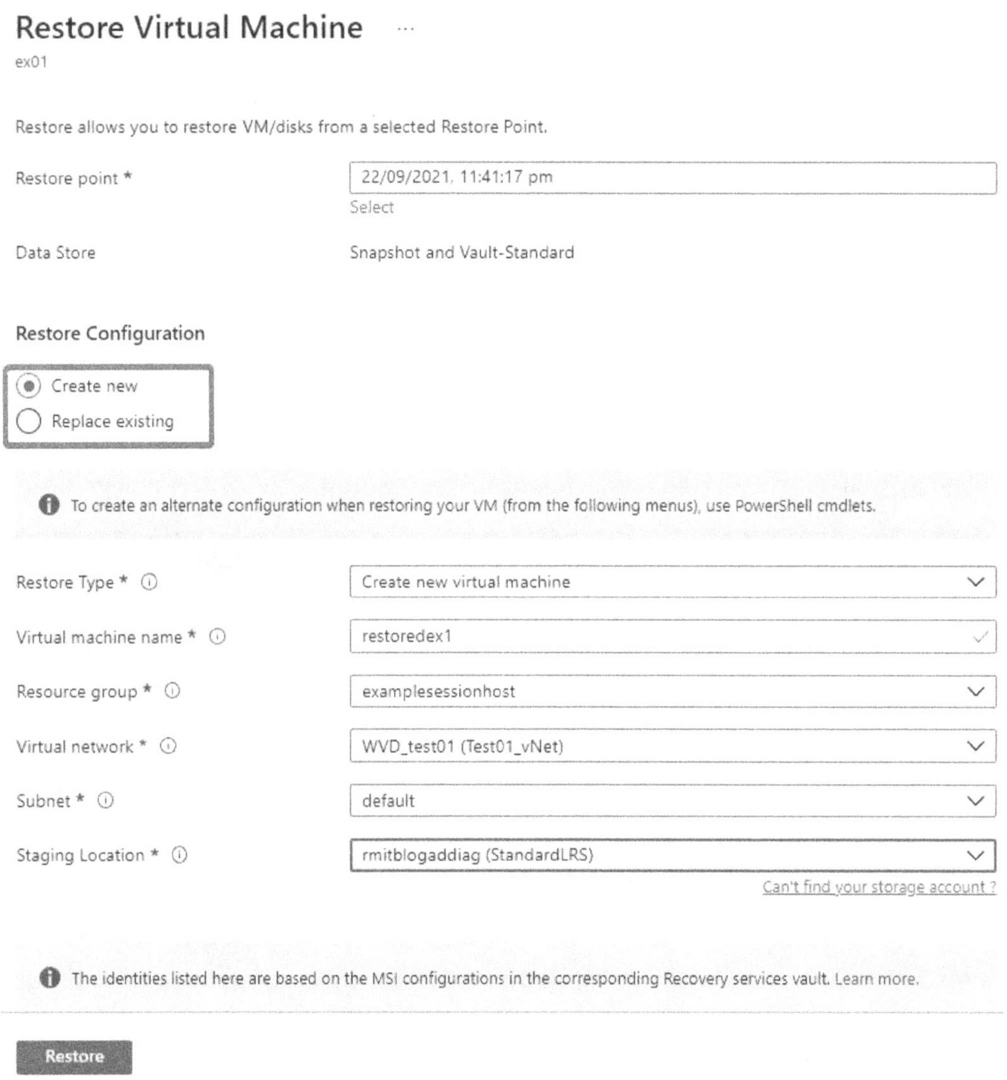

Restore Virtual Machine ···
ex01

Restore allows you to restore VM/disks from a selected Restore Point.

Restore point *	22/09/2021, 11:41:17 pm
	Select
Data Store	Snapshot and Vault-Standard

Restore Configuration

◉ Create new
○ Replace existing

ℹ To create an alternate configuration when restoring your VM (from the following menus), use PowerShell cmdlets.

Restore Type * ⓘ	Create new virtual machine ⌄
Virtual machine name * ⓘ	restoredex1 ✓
Resource group * ⓘ	examplesessionhost ⌄
Virtual network * ⓘ	WVD_test01 (Test01_vNet) ⌄
Subnet * ⓘ	default ⌄
Staging Location * ⓘ	rmitblogaddiag (StandardLRS) ⌄

Can't find your storage account ?

ℹ The identities listed here are based on the MSI configurations in the corresponding Recovery services vault. Learn more.

Restore

Figure 16.16 – Restore Virtual Machine page

25. Once the restore job has been started, you should see the restore operation within
the **Backup jobs** section in **Backup center**:

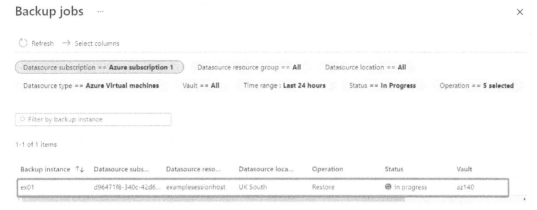

Figure 16.17 – Restore operation in Backup jobs within Backup center

26. Once the restore operation has been completed, you will also see the operation
showing completed from the main page in **Backup center**. This information is
pulled from the **Backup jobs** section of the **Recovery Services vault**.

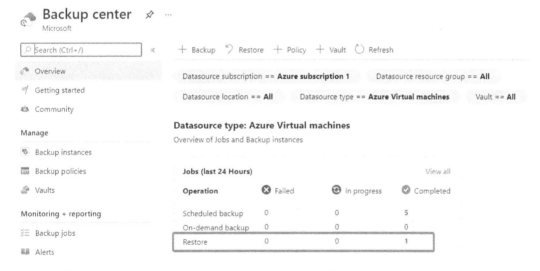

Figure 16.18 – Shows the Restore Operation has completed under jobs (last 24 hours)

Now that we have looked at backing up virtual machines and restoring them, which is
extremely useful for personal desktop host pools, we now move on to backing up Azure
files and restoring them.

Zone-redundant storage

The use of **zone-redundant storage** (**ZRS**) should be regarded as a redundancy option. ZRS essentially replicates your Azure managed disk synchronously over three availability zones within your chosen Azure region.

Read more on ZRS here: `https://docs.microsoft.com/azure/virtual-machines/disks-deploy-zrs`.

Azure file backup and restore

It is recommended that you back up your FSLogix profile containers for Azure Virtual Desktop. You can do this in a similar way to how you would back up a virtual machine. We will now take a look at the steps for backing up FSLogix Profile container stores:

1. Navigate to **Backup center**.
2. Select **Backup** on the main page.

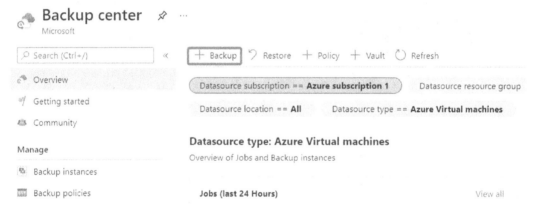

Figure 16.19 – The Backup button in Backup center

3. Within the **Start: Configure Backup** section, choose **Azure Files (Azure Storage)** and the required vault. In this example, we choose **az140** for **Vault**. Once all the fields have been populated, click **Continue**.

Start: Configure Backup   ...

Datasource type	Azure Files (Azure Storage)	∨
Vault type	Recovery Services vault	∨
Vault *	az140	✓
	Select	

Continue   Cancel

Figure 16.20 – Azure Files and the vault when configuring Azure Files for Backup

4. You will now see the **Configure Backup** page. Within this section, you need first to select **Storage Account**. Once it's selected, in the **Select storage account** blade, click **OK**.

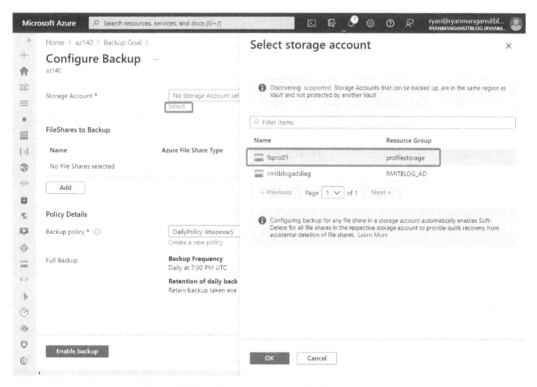

Figure 16.21 – Storage account selection for Backup

5. You will then need to add the required shares on the same page by clicking the **Add** button within the **FileShares to Backup** section. Once you have selected the required file shares, click **OK** within the **Select file shares** blade.

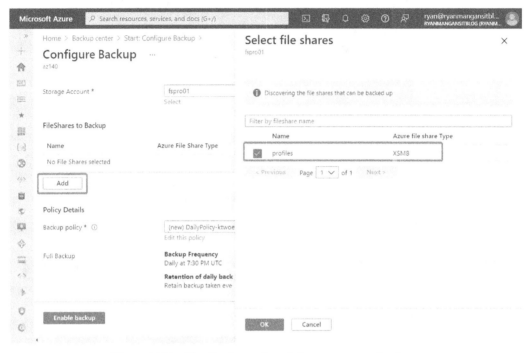

Figure 16.22 – The file share selected that you want to back up

6. Use the **default policy details** section or create a specific backup policy to suit your requirements within the **Policy details** section. Once you are finished, click **Enable** to perform a backup.

7. Once a backup has been taken, you should see the last backup status as being successful. You can find this information by navigating to the recovery vault, selecting **Backup Items** and **Azure Storage (Azure Files)**.

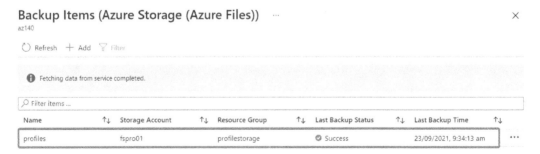

Figure 16.23 – The first backup job has been completed

Now that we have taken a look at backing up an Azure Files share, let's now recover an Azure Files share:

1. Navigate to **Backup center**.

2. Click **Restore** on the main page, as shown in the following screenshot:

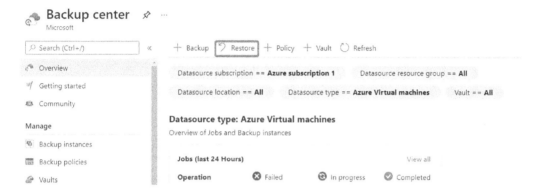

Figure 16.24 – Restore button highlighted within Backup center

3. Select **Azure Files (Azure Storage)** for **Datasource type**.

4. Select the file share you wish to restore.

Figure 16.25 – Start: Restore populated for Azure Files

5. Within the **Restore** page, select a restore point for the backed-up file share.

6. Then you need to select a restore destination. In this example, we will choose **Original Location**; however, you can choose an alternative location if required.

7. In the **In case of Conflicts** section, you can choose to skip or overwrite. In this example, we will skip. Once you have finished, click **Restore**.

Figure 16.26 – Restore page

8. You can then view pending, in progress, and completed restore jobs within the **Recovery services** vault under **Backup Jobs**, as shown in the following screenshot:

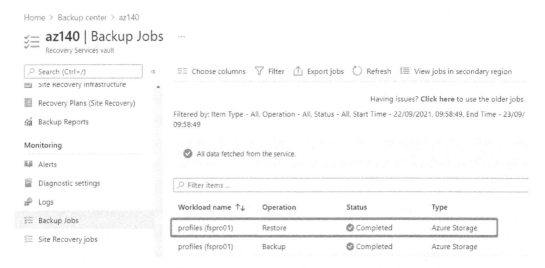

Figure 16.27 – The complete restore job for the Azure Files file share

That concludes backing up and restoring an Azure Files file share. We now move on
to the final section of the chapter, where we briefly look at replicating images across
multiple images.

Replicating virtual machine images between regions

In *Chapter 9, Creating and Managing Session Host Images*, we looked at shared image
galleries. A shared image gallery enables you to replicate across multiple regions. When
working with pooled desktop session host pools, you may want to consider using the
replication feature within shared image galleries to distribute the image template across
multiple regions. In the event of an outage, you can spin up new virtual machines at
the failover.

As shown in the following screenshot, you can see updated image versions target
replications. This enables you to push out a central operating system template image to
multiple regions quickly. You should consider image replication when implementing a
disaster recovery solution:

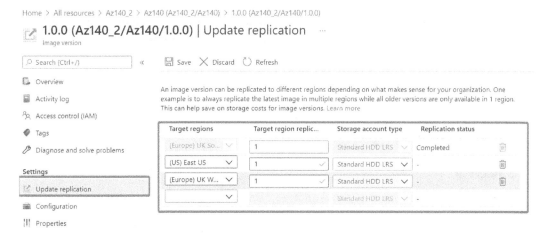

Figure 16.28 – Replication update for an image version within a shared image gallery

This concludes the short section on image replication. For more information on setting
up a shared image gallery and using image versions, please refer to the *Azure Compute
galleries* section in *Chapter 9, Creating and Managing Session Host Images*.

Summary

This chapter looked at planning and implementing business continuity and disaster recovery for Azure Virtual Desktop.

We started by looking at designing a backup strategy for Azure Virtual Desktop. We then moved on to look at the five critical components of an Azure Virtual Desktop environment, which are virtual networks, virtual machines, user identities, configuring user and app data, and application dependencies.

We then looked at how to back up and restore virtual machines and Azure files. We then finished the chapter by reiterating the benefit of using shared image galleries to replicate a gold image/image template across multiple Azure regions.

In the next chapter, we will take a look at automating Azure Virtual Desktop management tasks.

Questions

1. When configuring a VNet for an Azure Virtual Desktop environment, what should you ensure you have checked before deploying virtual machines?

2. Which Azure service would you use to ensure that your Azure Virtual Desktop template/master image is resilient?

3. Which feature within FSLogix can be used to provide resilience if there is a storage failure?

Answers

1. *DNS settings have been configured on the VNet.*

2. *Use Azure Compute Galleries to replicate your virtual machine image across multiple regions.*

3. *FSLogix Cloud Cache.*

17
Automate Azure Virtual Desktop Management Tasks

In this chapter, we take a look at automating Azure Virtual Desktop by taking repeated processes and automating them on a schedule. We will then dive into the automation management of host pools, session hosts, and user sessions using an automation account.

In this chapter, we take a look at the following topics:

- Creating an automation account for Azure Virtual Desktop
- Automating the management of host pools, session hosts, and user sessions using PowerShell
- Implementing autoscaling for host pools
- Scaling plans

Creating an automation account for Azure Virtual Desktop

In this section, we look at creating an automation account for Azure Virtual Desktop. An automation account is used to create runbooks that contain scripts that can automate processes to help you manage your Azure Virtual Desktop environment. Runbooks are extremely useful for automating repetitive tasks and batch processing, which can be quite time-consuming when carrying out such tasks manually.

Let's get started with first creating an automation account:

1. Sign in to the Azure portal: `https://portal.azure.com/`.

2. From the top menu, enter `Automation` in the search bar and click **Automation Accounts**:

Figure 17.1 – Search result showing Automation Accounts

3. On the **Automation Accounts** page, click **Create**:

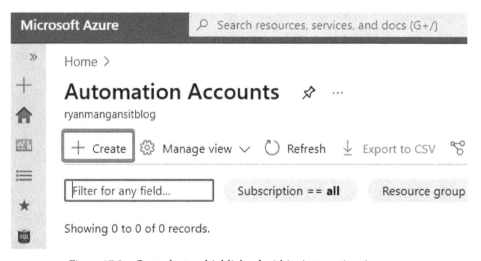

Figure 17.2 – Create button highlighted within Automation Accounts

4. Within the **Add Automation Account** blade, provide a **Name**, select
    a **Subscription**, create a **Resource group** or select an existing one, and choose
    a region. Then click **Create**:

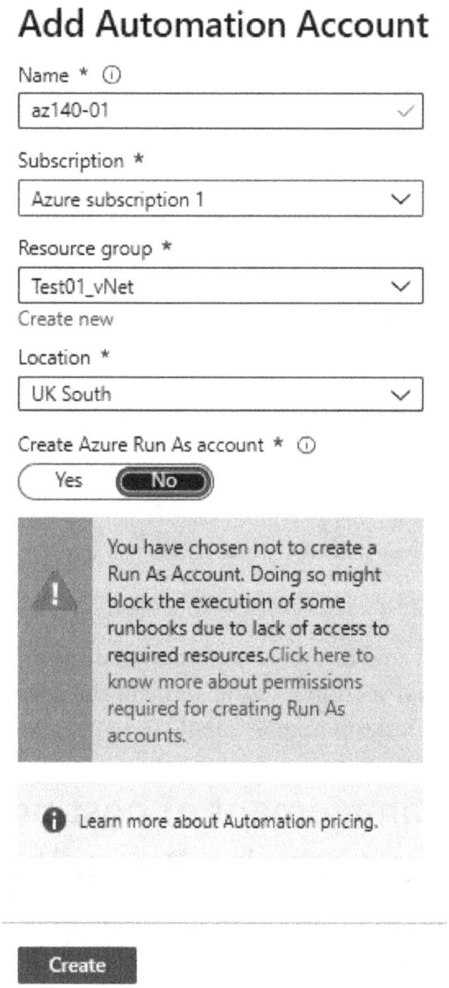

Add Automation Account

Name * ⓘ

| az140-01 | ✓ |

Subscription *

| Azure subscription 1 | ⌄ |

Resource group *

| Test01_vNet | ⌄ |

Create new

Location *

| UK South | ⌄ |

Create Azure Run As account * ⓘ

| Yes | **No** |

⚠ You have chosen not to create a
Run As Account. Doing so might
block the execution of some
runbooks due to lack of access to
required resources.Click here to
know more about permissions
required for creating Run As
accounts.

ⓘ Learn more about Automation pricing.

Create

Figure 17.3 – Add Automation Account blade

5. Once created, you will see the new automation account on the **Automation Accounts** page:

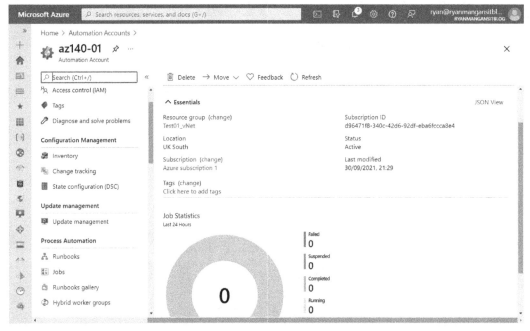

Figure 17.4 – Newly created automation account

There you have it – we have created an Azure automation account ready for use with Azure Virtual Desktop. The next section looks at some of the automation tasks you can use to simplify Azure Virtual Desktop management.

Automating the management of host pools, session hosts, and user sessions using PowerShell

This section looks at using the Azure command-line interface and Azure automation accounts to run repeat tasks and simplify tasks such as logging off multiple users in a batch.

Configuring an Azure automation runbook

This section takes you through creating an Azure automation runbook, configuring the runbook, testing, and configuring a runbook schedule.

Setting up a run as account

This section shows you how to create a simple host pool log-off script using an automation account.

You will need a run as account set up for this example.

You can configure a run as account within the automation account in the **Account Settings | Run as accounts | Create Run As account section**:

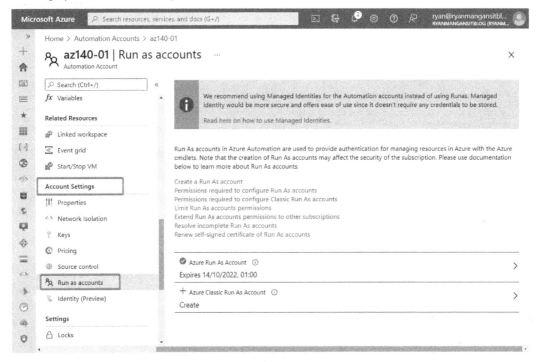

Figure 17.5 – The Run as accounts page within an automation account

Importing PowerShell modules into the automation account

Once you have set up the run as account, you can then progress to preparing the automation account with the correct PowerShell modules, which can be imported using the module gallery.

The following modules need to be imported:

- Nuget
- Az.DesktopVirtualization
- AzureAD

- `Az.Accounts`

- `Az.Resources`

The following screenshot shows the automation account's module gallery, where you would add PowerShell modules for use within runbooks:

Figure 17.6 – PowerShell Modules gallery where you would add the required PowerShell modules

Once you have begun importing the modules, you will see the status is **Importing**. Once importing has finished, you should see the modules shown as available:

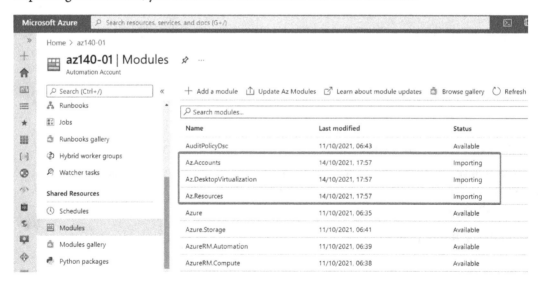

Figure 17.7 – The status of the PowerShell modules in an automation account

The next part of this process is to create a PowerShell runbook within the Azure automation account that we have just created.

Creating a runbook

We'll now take a look at creating a PowerShell runbook within the automation account.

To create a runbook, navigate to the automation account. Under **Process Automation**, click **Runbooks**; once on the **Runbooks** page, click on **Create a runbook**:

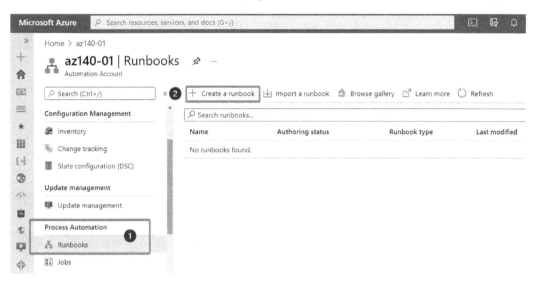

Figure 17.8 – Create a new runbook

You will then see the **Create a runbook** blade appear. Enter a name for the runbook and select the type – in this case, it's a PowerShell runbook. Provide a description:

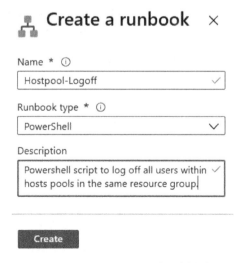

Figure 17.9 – Create a runbook blade

Once the new runbook is created, it will open the runbook page ready for you to start configuring:

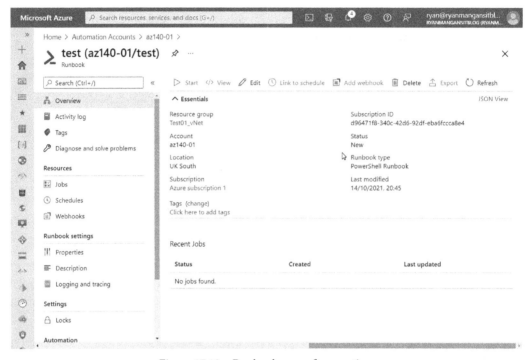

Figure 17.10 – Runbook page after creation

Now that we have created a runbook, we can proceed with configuring it with the required script. In this example, we will be creating a host pool log-off runbook to simplify the logging off of multiple users spread across several session hosts within a host pool.

Adding your PowerShell script to a runbook

Let's take now take a look at adding the PowerShell script to the runbook.

The first thing we need to do is click **Edit** within the runbook page, as shown in the following screenshot:

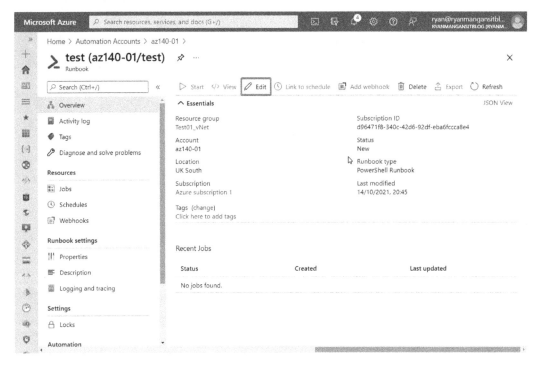

Figure 17.11 – Edit runbook option highlighted

You should now see the runbook scripting interface; this is where you need to enter the PowerShell cmdlets:

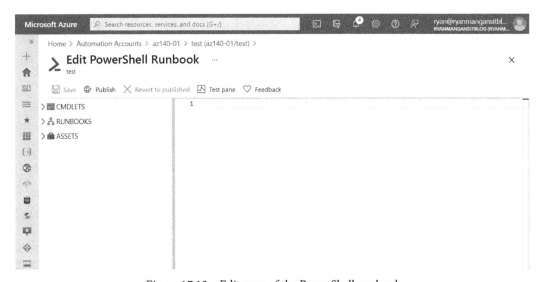

Figure 17.12 – Edit page of the PowerShell runbook

Before entering the scripting and testing, I want to briefly run through the host pool log-off example. This is broken down into multiple sections so that I can discuss the key parts of the script.

The first part of the script is the header, detailing information about the script and any imports you may need for the script:

```
# Mastering Azure Virtual Desktop Log Off User example
import-module az.DesktopVirtualization
import-module AzureAD
```

The next part of the script is the authentication piece. This is needed to ensure the runbook can communicate with the tenant. In this example, we are using the Azure Run as connection to authenticate:

```
# Azure Runbook Auth using RunAsConnection
# Get the connection "AzureRunAsConnection"
$connectionName = "AzureRunAsConnection"
$servicePrincipalConnection = Get-AutomationConnection -Name $connectionName
$logonAttempt = 0
$logonResult = $False
while(!($connectionResult) -And ($logonAttempt -le 10))
{
    $LogonAttempt++
    #Logging in to Azure...
    $connectionResult = Connect-AzAccount '
                        -ServicePrincipal '
                        -Tenant $servicePrincipalConnection.
TenantId '
                        -ApplicationId
$servicePrincipalConnection.ApplicationId '
                        -CertificateThumbprint
$servicePrincipalConnection.CertificateThumbprint
    Start-Sleep -Seconds 30
}
```

Now that we have authenticated with Azure, the next part of the script will call the log-off function. As you will note, the only area you need to specify is the resource group name. Everything else is taken care of for you. This part essentially reads the resource group for Azure Virtual Desktop host pools. The script then counts the user sessions within the host pool and runs `Remove-AzWvdUserSession` for each session. This automates the log-off process for host pools, which in turn simplifies the IT admin's effort to carry out maintenance and so on:

```
# Start AVD Task...
$ResourceGroupName = "avd01-avd" # <<<< enter resource group
$ExistingHostPool = Get-AzResource -ResourceGroupName
$ResourceGroupName | Where-Object ResourceType -eq Microsoft.
DesktopVirtualization/hostpools
if (($ExistingHostPool).count -gt "0") {
# Process to Log off connected Users
foreach($Hostpool in $ExistingHostPool){


$AVDUserSessions = Get-AzWvdUserSession -HostPoolName
$HostPool.Name -ResourceGroupName $ResourceGroupName
$NumberofAVDSessions = ($AVDUserSessions).count # Counts
sessions
if ($NumberofAVDSessions -gt "0") {
    try {
        Write-Host "There are a total of $NumberofAVDSessions
logged on, these user sessions now will be logged off" # Admin
message
        foreach ($AVDUserSession in $AVDUserSessions){
            $InputString = $AVDUserSession.Name
            $AVDUserArray = $InputString.Split("/")
            $AVDUserArray[0]
            $AVDUserArray[1]
            $AVDUserArray[2]
            Remove-AzWvdUserSession -HostPoolName $HostPool.
Name -ResourceGroupName $ResourceGroupName -SessionHostName
$AVDUserArray[1] -Id $AVDUserArray[2]
        }clear # clears PowerShell output
    }

    catch {
```

```
        }
    }
  }
}
```

You can download the full script here: `https://github.com/PacktPublishing/Remote-Productivity-with-Windows-Virtual-Desktop/blob/main/B17392_07/logoff%20AVD%20Users%20Batch.ps1`

Now that we have run through the host pool log-off script structure, we will proceed with configuring the runbook and publishing it:

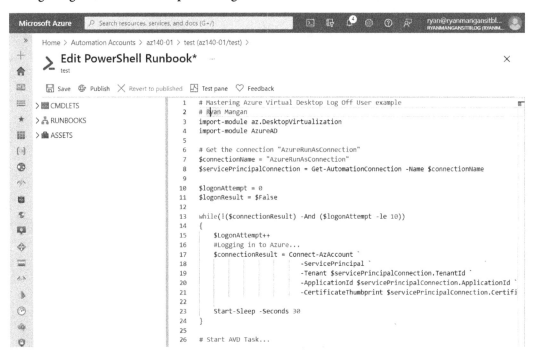

Figure 17.13 – PowerShell scripting added to the PowerShell runbook

Once you have copied the script into the PowerShell runbook, you can proceed with testing by clicking **Test pane**, as shown in the following screenshot:

Figure 17.14 – Location of the Test pane button for testing a PowerShell runbook

In the next section, we take a look at testing the script before publishing.

Testing a PowerShell runbook in Azure

This section runs through the basics of using the test pane to test the script we created for logging off Azure Virtual Desktop users within a host pool.

To test the script, all you need to do is click the **Start** icon as shown in *Figure 17.15*:

1.   Click **Start** on the **Test** page:

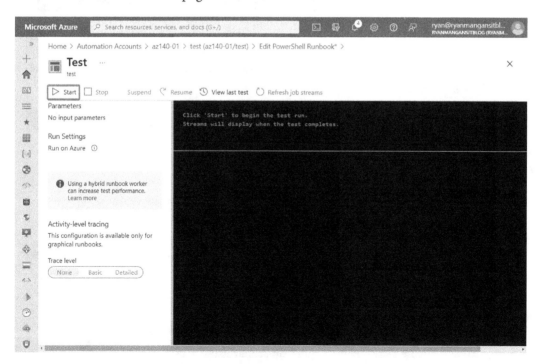

Figure 17.15 – The Test page of a PowerShell runbook

2. The black screen shown in the preceding screenshot shows the script's output and any errors that may occur, requiring you to make the appropriate changes if required.

3. As you can see from the test results, in the following screenshot, the script worked as required and logged off the two user sessions:

Figure 17.16 – Test complete within a PowerShell runbook

4. Once you have finished the test, and you have confirmed the script is working and there are no errors, you can then go ahead and publish the runbook as shown in the following screenshot:

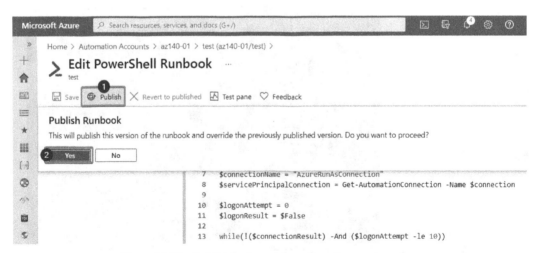

Figure 17.17 – Publish button and confirmation message bar

5. Once the runbook has been published, you will see several previously grayed-out options now shown as accessible. You can find them within the menu bar, including **Link to schedule,** as shown in the following screenshot:

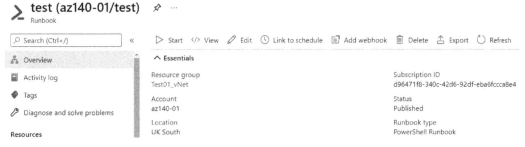

Figure 17.18 – The published runbook

In the next section, we look at creating a schedule and assigning the created runbook to it.

Creating a schedule

Follow these steps to create a schedule:

1. Within the runbook, you can create a schedule. First, you would need to navigate down to the section in the left-hand menu called **Resources**:

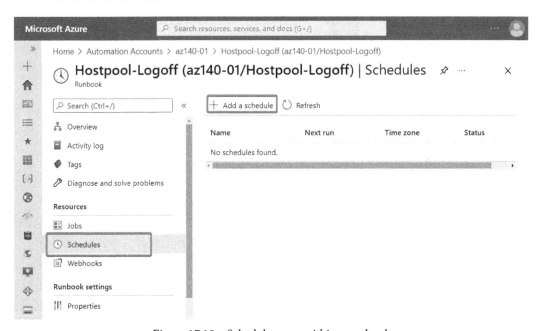

Figure 17.19 – Schedules page within a runbook

2. Click on **Add a schedule** and then click **Link a schedule to your runbook**:

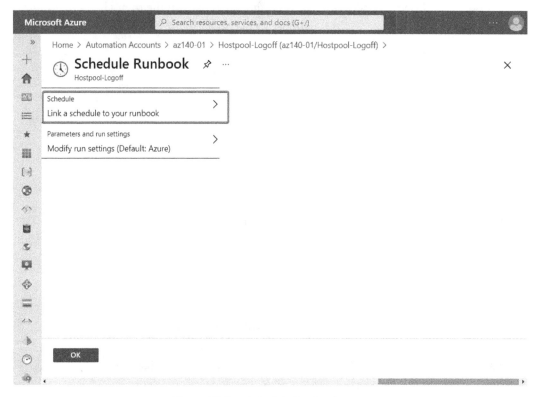

Figure 17.20 – Schedule Runbook page

3. Then click **Add a schedule**, and the **New Schedule** blade will appear:

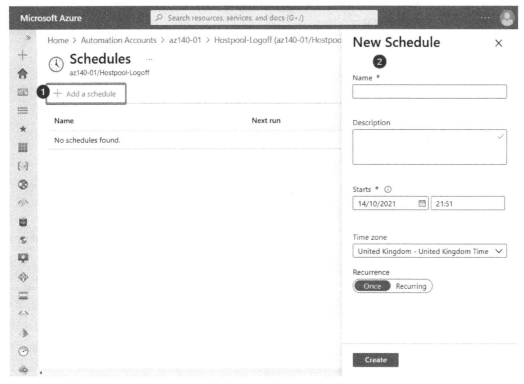

Figure 17.21 – Schedules page and New Schedule blade

4. Provide a name, description, and the **Starts** time and date, ensuring you choose the correct recurrence, either **Once** or **Recurring**. Once you have entered the required information, click **Create**.

5. You will then see the newly created schedule on the **Schedule Runbook** page, as shown in the following screenshot:

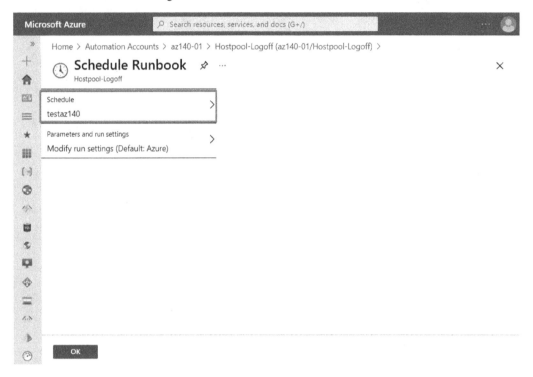

Figure 17.22 – New schedule added to the runbook on the Schedule Runbook page

6. You will now see the runbook is scheduled to run, as shown in the following screenshot:

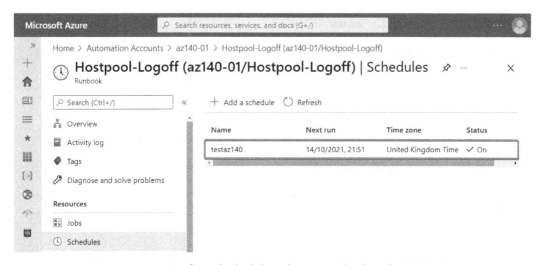

Figure 17.23 – Configured schedule within the runbook under Schedules

In this section, we looked at configuring an Azure automation runbook. First, we covered the setup of a run as account and the importing of required PowerShell modules for an Azure Virtual Desktop PowerShell script to run. We then created the runbook, added the PowerShell script to the runbook, and tested it. We then finished the section by creating an automated schedule for the runbook to run at a specific time.

In the next section, we look at implementing autoscaling in Azure Virtual Desktop using an automation account.

Implementing autoscaling for host pools

In this section, we look at how to configure autoscaling for Azure Virtual Desktop.

The Azure Virtual Desktop autoscale tool optimizes cost and capacity for your Virtual Desktop environment based on time and resource requirements. The tool requires the following Azure components:

- An Azure automation account
- A PowerShell runbook
- A webhook
- Azure Logic Apps

We will take a look at these components in more detail shortly.

The autoscale tool essentially allows you to scale up and scale down resources based on the requirement.

Here are the key features of the autoscale tool:

- Start/stop **Virtual Machines** (**VMs**) based on time criteria such as normal business hours and out-of-hours.

- Deploy additional session host VMs (scale out) based on the number of active sessions on a host pool.

- Reduce the number of VMs (scale in) outside normal business hours.

The tool works based on the following scheduling parameters:

Parameter	Description
`RecurrenceInterval`	How often you'd like the job to run in minutes, for example, 15.
`BeginPeaktime`	The start time for peak hours in local time, for example, 9:00.
`EndPeakTime`	Set the end time for peak hours in local time, for example, 18:00.
`TimeDifference`	Provide a time difference between local time and UTC in hours, for example, +5:30.
`SessionThresholdPerCPU`	Set the maximum number of sessions per CPU that will be used as a threshold to determine when new session host VMs need to be started during peak hours.
`MinimumNumberOfRDSH`	Enter the total minimum number of session host VMs to keep running during off-peak hours.
`MaintenanceTagName`	Provide a tag associated with VMs you don't want to be managed by this scaling tool.
`LimitSecondsToForceLogOffUser`	Set the time in seconds to wait before automatically signing out users. If set to 0, any session host VM that has user sessions will be left untouched.
`LogOffMessageTitle`	Provide a title for the message sent to the user before they are forced to sign out.
`LogOffMessageBody`	Provide the body of the message (text) sent to the user before they are forced to sign out.

The scaling tool works by running a number of jobs to check the current number of user sessions against the total number of VMs running. First, this information is collected, and then a calculation is completed using the parameter `SessionThresholdPerCPU`. Finally, suppose the current resources cannot support the existing active user sessions. In that case, the autoscale tool will start a job to start additional session host VMs within the host pool.

> **Important Note**
>
> It is important to note that the `SessionthresholdPerCPU` parameter only determines when new VMs need to be started. It does not restrict the number of user sessions. The restriction of sessions is completed using the `MaxSessionLimit` parameter.

The out-of-hours usage time, also known as an off-peak job, runs to check how many session host VMs need to be shut down based on the `MinimumNumberOfRDSH` parameter. Suppose you set the `LimitSecondsToForceLogOffUser` parameter to a number greater than zero. In that case, the job will enable drain mode on the session host VMs to prevent new sessions from connecting to the hosts. The job to shut down session hosts sends a message to the users notifying them to save their work. However, once the `LimitSecondsToForceLogOffUser` parameter is reached, all user sessions will be logged off. Once all users have been logged out, the job will then start to shut down the VM. If you leave the `LimitSecondsToForceLogOffUser` parameter as zero, then the job will take no action to force users off a session host; if no users are on the session host, it will shut down the VM.

> **Important Note**
>
> If a session host is already in drain mode, set manually, the job to shut down will ignore the session host in question. Instead, the job will treat the session host as unavailable, making the job start additional VMs to handle the user session load.

The job considers the host pool's `MaxSessionLimit` to calculate if the active number of user sessions is more than 90% of the maximum capacity. If it is, the job will start additional VMs (session hosts).

Here are the autoscale tool's limitations:

- You can only use the autoscale tool for multi-session host VMs.
- The autoscale tool works in all regions; however, you must use the same subscription.
- The maximum time for a job is limited to 3 hours only. If the starting or stopping of VMs hangs or takes longer, then the job will fail.
- You need to ensure at least one VM is turned on for the scaling algorithm to work correctly.
- Autoscaling does not support scaling based on the RAM or CPU of a session host.
- Autoscaling will only work with existing VMs configured in a host pool. The tool does not create new session hosts.

Prerequisites

Before we can get started with setting up the autoscaling tool, you need to make sure you have the following ready:

- An Azure Virtual Desktop environment deployed
- A session host pool with VMs registered and communicating with the Azure Virtual Desktop service
- An Azure admin with contributor access on the required subscription
- Windows Powershell 5.1 or later on the machine where you deploy the autoscale tool

Deploying the auto automation account

In this section, we take a look at deploying an Azure Virtual Desktop autoscale automation account:

1. In the PowerShell console, run `Install-module az` and `Install-Module Az.DesktopVirtualization`:

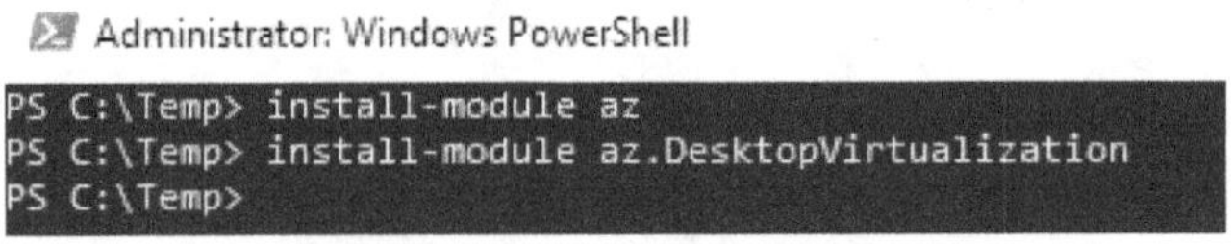

Figure 17.24 – Install module cmdlets for az and az.desktopvirtualization

2. Log in to your Azure account in PowerShell using `Login-AzAccount`.

3. Set the subscription context cmdlet, `Set-AzContext -Subscription xxxx-xxxx-xxxx-xxxx`.

4. Download the required script using the following:

```
New-Item -ItemType Directory -Path "C:\Temp" -Force
Set-Location -Path "C:\Temp"
$Uri = "https://raw.githubusercontent.com/Azure/
RDS-Templates/master/wvd-templates/wvd-scaling-script/
CreateOrUpdateAzAutoAccount.ps1"
# Download the script
Invoke-WebRequest -Uri $Uri -OutFile ".\
CreateOrUpdateAzAutoAccount.ps1"
```

5. Run the script:

Figure 17.25 – Script for downloading the creation of an autoscale automation account

6. Now you have downloaded the required script, you will need to use the configuration script shown in the following screenshot to deploy the automation account:

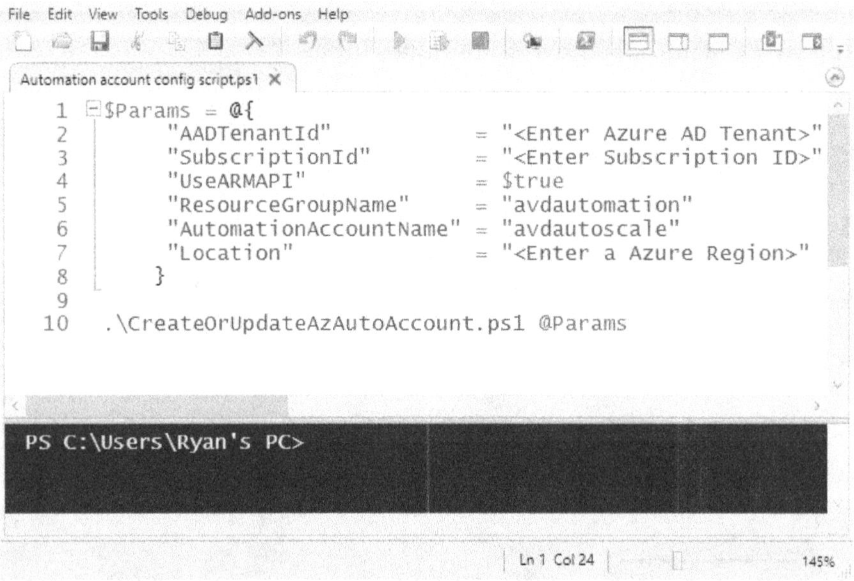

Figure 17.26 – Script for deploying the Azure Virtual Desktop autoscale automation account

You can download the configuration script here: https://github.com/ PacktPublishing/Remote-Productivity-with-Windows-Virtual- Desktop/blob/main/B17392_07/Automation%20account%20config%20 script.ps1.

The following table shows the different parameters you will need to configure for the configuration script:

Parameter	Description	Notes
AADTenantID	Azure Active Directory tenant ID	If not specified, it will use the current Azure context
SubscriptionID	Azure subscription ID	If not specified, it will use the current Azure context
Resourcegroupname	Resource group name	Default: WVDAutoScaleResourceGroup
AutomationAccountName	Automation account	Default: WVDAutoScaleAutomationAccount
Location	Azure region	You must set an Azure region
WorkspaceName	Log Analytics workspace name	Optional

The following screenshot shows the finished output from PowerShell:

```
Administrator: Windows PowerShell                              —    □    ×

AutomationAccountName : avdautoscale
Name                  : OMSIngestionAPI
IsGlobal              : False
Version               :
SizeInBytes           : 0
ActivityCount         : 0
CreationTime          : 10/18/2021 9:47:33 PM +00:00
LastModifiedTime      : 10/18/2021 9:47:34 PM +00:00
ProvisioningState     : Creating

Waiting for module 'OMSIngestionAPI' to get imported into Automation Account Modules ...
Waiting for module 'OMSIngestionAPI' to get imported into Automation Account Modules ...
Waiting for module 'OMSIngestionAPI' to get imported into Automation Account Modules ...
Waiting for module 'OMSIngestionAPI' to get imported into Automation Account Modules ...
Successfully imported module 'OMSIngestionAPI' into Automation Account Modules
Azure Automation Account Name: avdautoscale
Webhook URI: https://36ad7f62-5888-4e46-bca7-561995aa748f.webhook.uks.azure-automation.net/web
hooks?token=9N5P1UObI%2bjwuHntVQkSJZZzYpQzSBVq4fx4oXpoY0s%3d


PS C:\Temp>
```

Figure 17.27 – The process of creating the automation account for autoscale complete

Once the script has finished and your new automation account has been created, you will see the `WVDAutoScaleRunbook` runbook within the automation account.

> **Important Note**
>
> Make sure you configure the run as account as shown in the *Setting up a run as account* section before proceeding to the next section.

Now that we have the required automation account and runbook deployed, we can move on to the final stage of deployment by creating an Azure Logic Apps account and setting the schedule.

Creating an Azure logic app and setting a schedule

We'll now look at deploying an Azure logic app. Like in the previous section, the logic app is deployed using PowerShell, which first downloads the script, and then we use a configuration script for the schedule.

Let's get started:

1. Import the desktop virtualization PowerShell module:

Figure 17.28 – Screenshot showing the import-module cmdlet for Azure Virtual Desktop

2. Log in to your Azure account: `Login-AzAccount`.

3. Set the subscription context cmdlet, `Set-AzContext -Subscription` `"xxxx-xxxx-xxxx-xxxx`.

4. Run the following cmdlets to download the script required for creating the Azure logic app:

```
New-Item -ItemType Directory -Path "C:\Temp" -Force

Set-Location -Path "C:\Temp"

$Uri = "https://raw.githubusercontent.com/Azure/
RDS-Templates/master/wvd-templates/wvd-scaling-script/
CreateOrUpdateAzLogicApp.ps1"

# Download the script

Invoke-WebRequest -Uri $Uri -OutFile ".\
CreateOrUpdateAzLogicApp.ps1"
```

The following screenshot shows the preceding script run, which downloads the `Createorupdateazlogicapp.ps1` script:

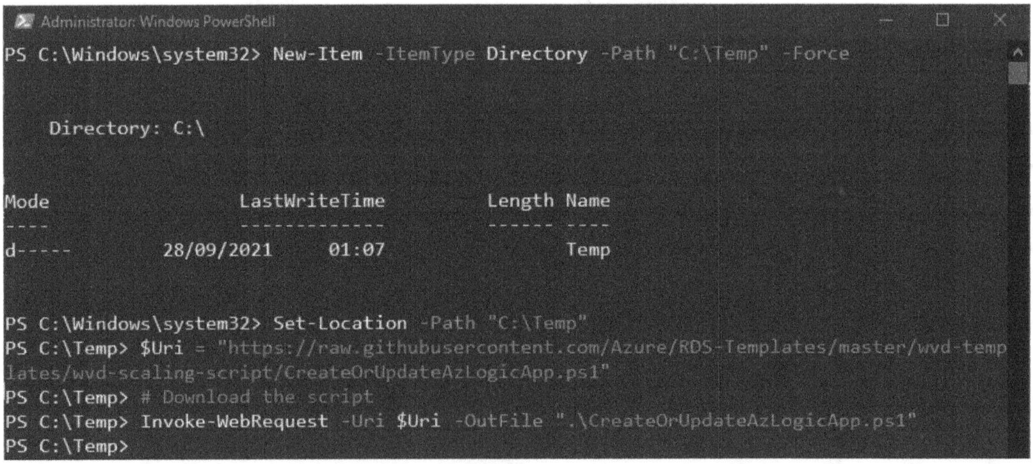

Figure 17.29 – Download of the Azure logic app script for autoscale

Now you have downloaded the script, you will need to configure the configuration script to deploy the logic app. When running the configuration script, you will be asked a series of questions to configure the logic app. Please note you can skip some of the questions as shown in the following table, which has a default setting. You can download the logic app script here: `https://github.com/PacktPublishing/Remote-Productivity-with-Windows-Virtual-Desktop/blob/main/B17392_07/Autoscale_logicapp_config.ps1`.

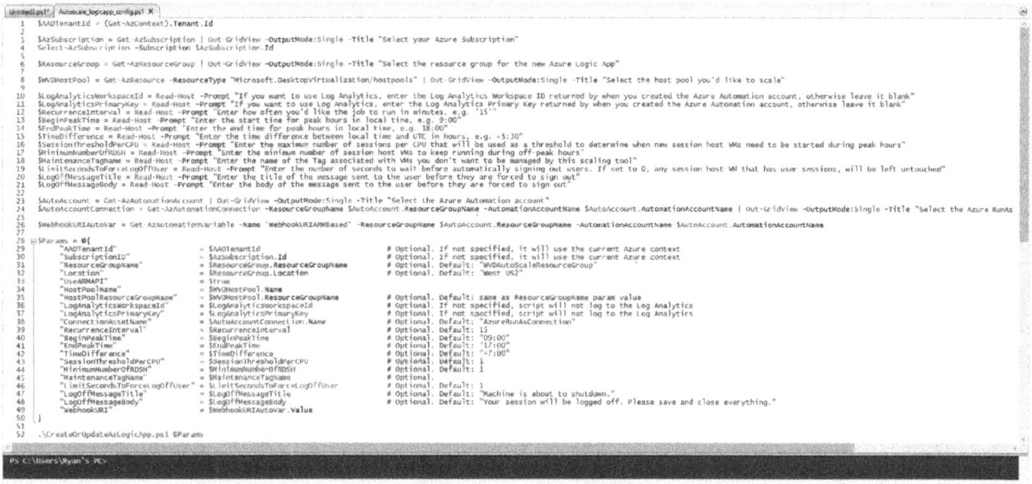

Figure 17.30 – Configuration script for deploying the Azure logic app

Important Note

Make sure you populate all the fields apart from the Log Analytics Workspace ID, as this is optional.

The following table shows the parameters you need to configure to deploy the Azure logic app:

Parameter setting	Question prompt
LogAnalyticsWorkspaceId	If you want to use Log Analytics, enter the Log Analytics workspace ID returned when you created the Azure automation account, otherwise leave it blank
LogAnalyticsPrimaryKey	If you want to use Log Analytics, enter the Log Analytics primary key returned when you created the Azure automation account, otherwise leave it blank
RecurrenceInterval	Enter how often you'd like the job to run in minutes, for example, 15
BeginPeakTime	Enter the start time for peak hours in local time, for example, 9:00
EndPeakTime	Enter the end time for peak hours in local time, for example, 18:00
TimeDifference	Enter the time difference between local time and UTC in hours, for example, +5:30
SessionThresholdPerCPU	Enter the maximum number of sessions per CPU that will be used as a threshold to determine when new session host VMs need to be started during peak hours
MinimumNumberOfRDSH	Enter the minimum number of session host VMs to keep running during off-peak hours
MaintenanceTagName	Enter the name of the tag associated with VMs you don't want to be managed by this scaling tool
LimitSecondsToForceLogOffUser	Enter the number of seconds to wait before automatically signing out users. If set to 0, any session host VM that has user sessions will be left untouched
WebhookURIAutoVar	Enter the PowerShell runbook Webhook URI
LogOffMessageTitle	Provide a title for the message sent to the user before they are forced to sign out
LogOffMessageBody	Enter the text for the body of the message sent to the user before they are forced to sign out

5. Once you have configured the script, you can then run this as an administrator within PowerShell, as shown in the following screenshot:

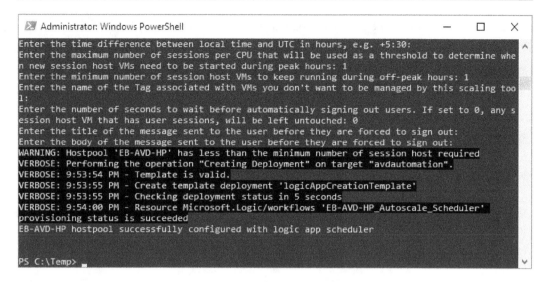

Figure 17.31 – The autoscale deployment successfully completing

Once the deployment has finished, you should now see the Azure logic app appear in the resource group:

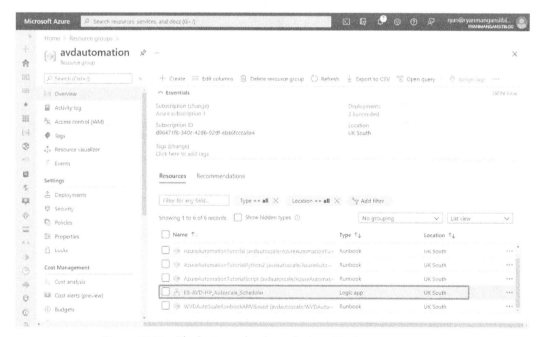

Figure 17.32 – The logic app has been deployed to the resource group

Once complete, you should see the following within the **Jobs** section of the automation account:

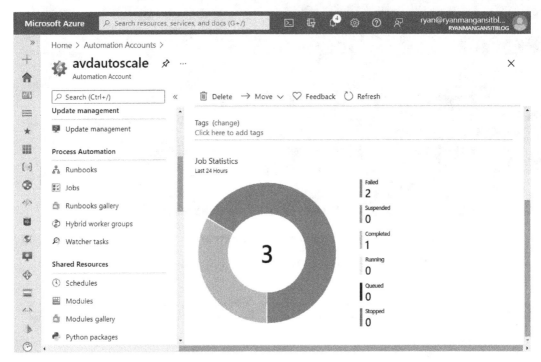

Figure 17.33 – Dashboard view of jobs run in the automation account

The following screenshot shows the jobs under **Process Automation**:

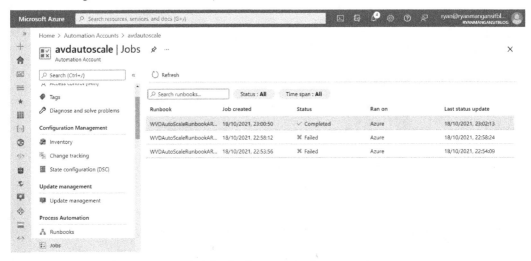

Figure 17.34 – The jobs that have run in the automation account

We have now configured autoscaling for Azure Virtual Desktop. Microsoft has announced a new feature to simplify this at the time of writing, which is in public preview. Scaling plans simplify the configuration and management of autoscale for Azure Virtual Desktop.

We will now progress to the final section of this chapter, where we deploy scaling plans (public preview) for Azure Virtual Desktop.

Managing and updating the autoscale tool

There are two key components used for the autoscaling tool – the automation account that contains the PowerShell runbook and the Azure logic app, which holds the configuration for the autoscaling to work.

To make changes to the autoscaling tool, open the configured logic app. For example, under the **Development Tools** section, you would select **Logic app designer** and expand the HTTP section. Within the HTTP section, you can edit the configuration held in the body section.

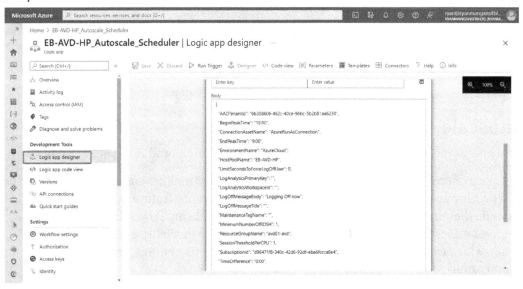

Figure 17.35 – Logic app designer page for the autoscale scheduler

To stop the autoscaling jobs from running, you would simply navigate to the Azure logic app and click **Disable**, located in the logic app page's main menu bar, as shown in the following screenshot:

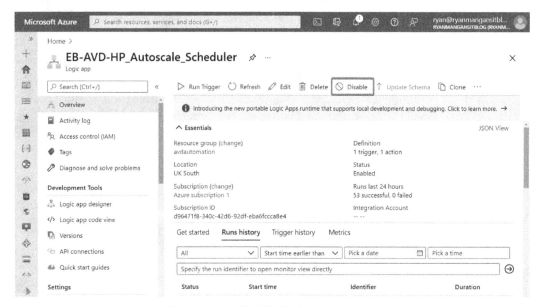

Figure 17.36 – The Disable logic app button

Autoscale – scaling plans

Please note at the time of writing, autoscale within the Azure portal is in public preview.

The built-in autoscale feature with Azure Virtual Desktop simplifies automating scale based on time and session limits per session host. This preview feature is expected to supersede the current autoscale feature, which is deployed using PowerShell. However, it is important to note the scaling plans do not have the same flexibility as the PowerShell version, which can be customized with additional algorithms, settings, and other customisations.

> **Important Note**
> Ephemeral disks are not supported when using the autoscale feature for Azure Virtual Desktop.

Creating a custom role for scaling plans

Before we can start configuring a scaling plan, we first need to configure the required custom role in IAM. To simplify this, I have created a pre-configured JSON file with the correct permissions for the custom role:

1. You first need to log in to the Azure portal.

2. Navigate to the Azure subscription.

3. Under **Access control (IAM)**, select **Add custom role** as shown in the following screenshot:

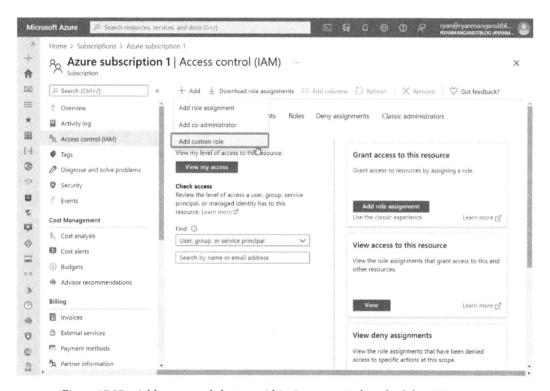

Figure 17.37 – Add custom role button within Access control on the Subscription page

4.   Download the custom role JSON file I configured and upload it on the **Create a custom role** page. You can download the custom role JSON here: `https://github.com/PacktPublishing/Remote-Productivity-with-Windows-Virtual-Desktop/blob/main/B17392_07/autoscale_custom_RBAC.json`

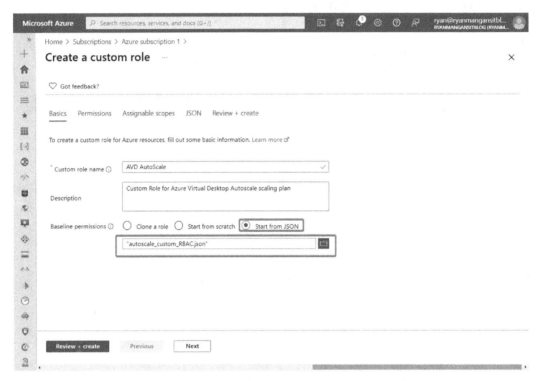

Figure 17.38 – Upload of the Auto_custom_RBAC.json file

5.   Once you have uploaded the required JSON file, `Autoscale_custom_RBAC.json`, click **Review + create**. Check the configuration and create the custom role.

6. Now you have created the custom role, navigate to **Add Role Assignment** within **Subscription | Access control (IAM)**.

7. Click **Add role assignment** and select the custom role **AVD AutoScale**:

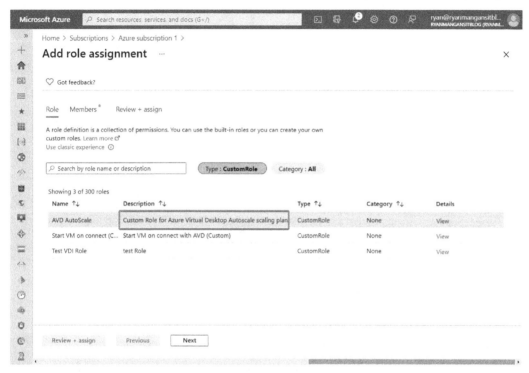

Figure 17.39 – Custom role appearing in Add role assignment

8.   Ensure you assign the Windows Virtual Desktop service as the member:

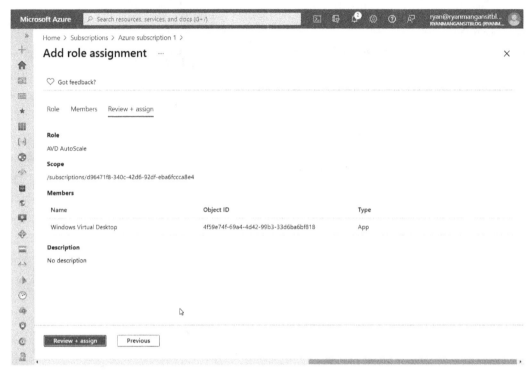

Figure 17.40 – Review + assign page of the Add role assignment page

9.   Once you have reviewed the configuration, proceed with adding the role
     assignment.

Once complete, you should see the custom role with the Windows Virtual Desktop app (service) added:

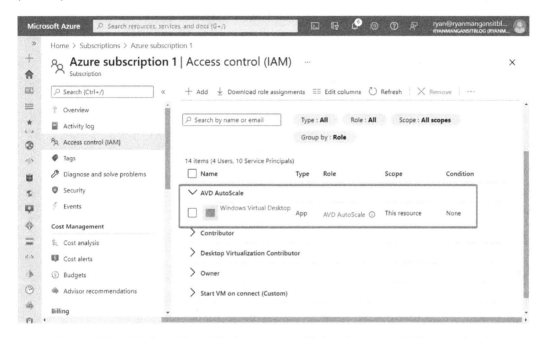

Figure 17.41 – Windows Virtual Desktop service added to the custom AVD autoscale role

> **Important Note**
>
> At the time of writing, the name Windows Virtual Desktop has not changed in some parts of Microsoft Azure. However, this is subject to change, and you should look out for the new Azure Virtual Desktop name.

In this section, we looked at creating a custom role for scaling plans for Azure Virtual Desktop. We can now proceed with looking at creating our first scaling plan.

Creating a scaling plan

Before creating a scaling plan, you first need to ensure you have an existing pooled host pool. All your host pools must have a configured `maxSessionLimit` parameter.

> **Important Note**
>
> You can update the `MaxSessionLimit` parameter using the PowerShell cmdlet `New-AZWvdHostPool` or `Update-AZWvdHostPool`.

Getting started:

1. Log in to the Azure portal.

2. Navigate to the **Azure Virtual Desktop** page.

3. Select **Scaling plans**:

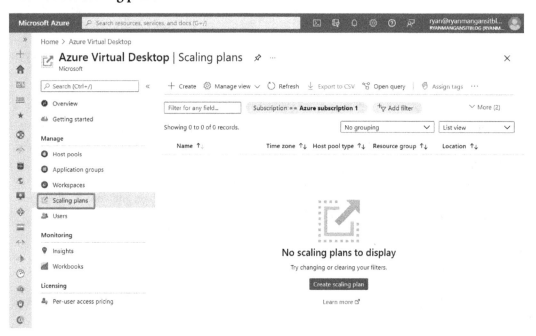

Figure 17.42 – Scaling plans page in Azure Virtual Desktop

4. Within **Scaling plans**, click **Create**.

5. Enter the required resource group or select **Create new** if required.

6. Enter a name for the scaling plan.

7. Select the required Azure region for the scaling plan.

8. Select the required time zone for the scaling plan.

9. Enter a tag for the VMs that you do not want to be included in scaling operations within the **Exclusion tag** section:

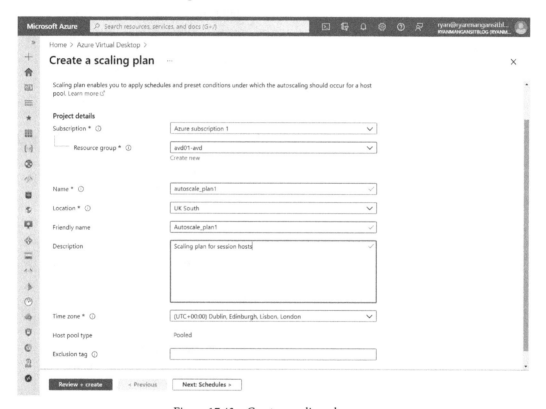

Figure 17.43 – Create a scaling plan page

10. Click **Next: Schedules**.

We'll now move on to look at the configuration of a schedule within a scaling plan.

Configuring a schedule

Schedules are essentially the configuration settings for autoscale. This includes the ramp-up and ramp-down modes, which will activate based on schedules throughout the day.

The following table details the different terms and meanings:

Term	Description
Start time	This is used to start preparing VMs for peak business hours or, as some refer to them, normal working hours.
Load balancing algorithm	The default setting is the breadth-first algorithm. This is recommended as it will distribute user sessions across existing VMs to ensure minimal delay to access times.
Peak hours	The start time for when the usage rate is expected to be the highest during the working day. This is also the same time that is used for the ramp-up phase.
Minimum percentage of session host VMs	You would set the required session host resources required for the ramp-up and peak hours.
Capacity threshold	The capacity threshold is the percentage of host pool usage that triggers the startup of the ramp-up and peak phases.
Load balancing (under peak hours)	This can be set as breadth-first or depth-first load balancing. Breadth-first is recommended for those who want to distribute new sessions across all available sessions within a host pool.

To configure or change a schedule, follow these steps:

1. Within the **Schedules** tab, you can add a schedule. Go ahead and click **Add schedule**:

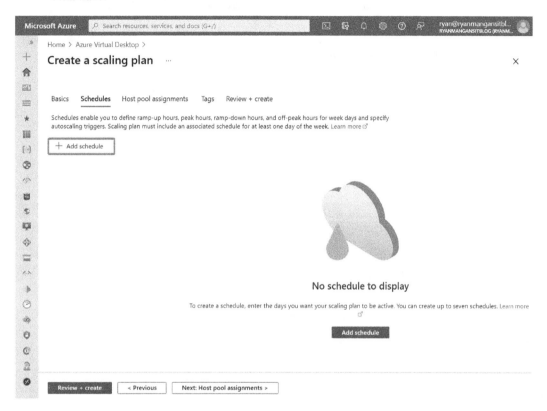

Figure 17.44 – The Schedules tab on the Create a scaling plan page

2. You will then see the **Add a schedule** blade appear with five tabs, including **General**, **Ramp-up**, **Peak hours**, **Ramp-down**, and **Off-peak hours**:

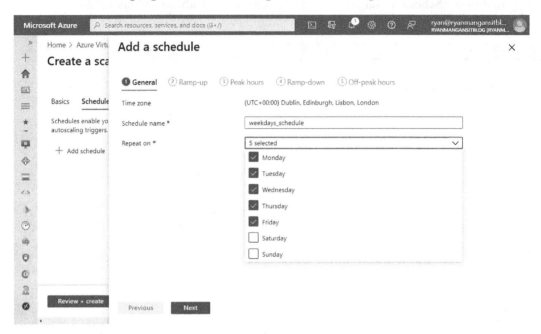

Figure 17.45 – General tab under the Add a schedule blade

3. Enter the schedule name within the **General** tab and set the days you want the schedule to repeat. Then click **Next**.

4. You can set the start time, load balancing algorithm, minimum percentage of hosts, and capacity threshold percentage within the **Ramp-up** tab. Once you have configured the settings you want, click **Next**:

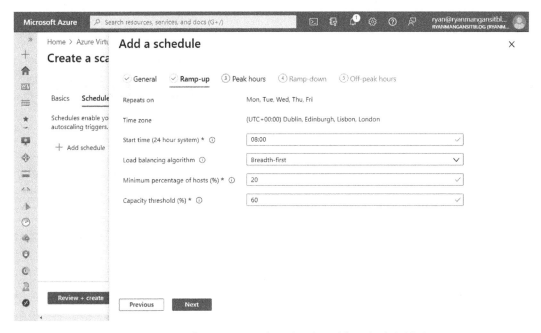

Figure 17.46 – The Ramp-up tab under the Add a schedule blade

5.   You can set the start time for peak hours and the load balancing algorithm within the **Peak hours** tab. Once set, click **Next**:

> **Important Note**
> When applying load balancing preferences within a scale plan schedule, you will override the original host pool load balancing setting.

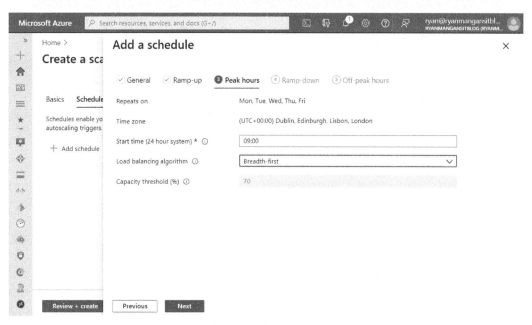

Figure 17.47 – The Peak hours tab under the Add a schedule blade

6.   Within the **Ramp-down** tab, you can specify the start time, load balancing algorithm, minimum number of hosts as a percentage, capacity threshold, and the ability to force logoff users and send a message. Once you have configured this tab, click **Next**.

For **Ramp-down**, you will see similar values to the **Ramp-up** section. It is important to note that in this instance, it will be for reduced host pool usage, also known as drop-offs. The **Ramp-down** section includes the **Force logoff users**, **Delay time before logging out users and shutting down VMs (min)**, and the ability to send a message to the user before they are logged off:

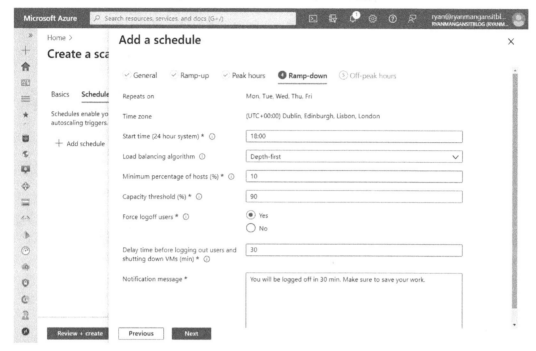

Figure 17.48 – Ramp-down tab on the Add a schedule blade

7. The final tab on the **Add a schedule** page is **Off-peak** hours. You would set the time and the load balancing algorithm. Once configured, click **Add**.

Off-peak hours work in a similar way to peak hours. The difference is that off-peak hours gradually reduce the number of session hosts based on the user sessions on each session host:

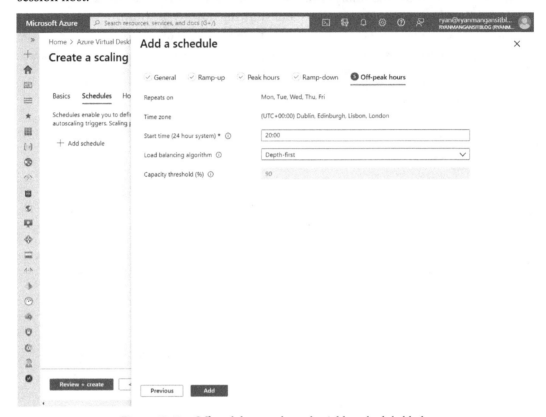

Figure 17.49 – Off-peak hours tab on the Add a schedule blade

Now that we have configured the schedule, we can now assign host pools to the scaling plan.

Assigning host pools

The following steps look at the steps to assign the host pool and complete the creation of the scaling plan:

1. Now that we have created the schedule, we can move on to the host pool assignments. This is where you would select the session host pools you want to assign to the scaling plan.

2. Select the required host pools within the **Host pool assignments** tab and ensure **Enable autoscale** is checked:

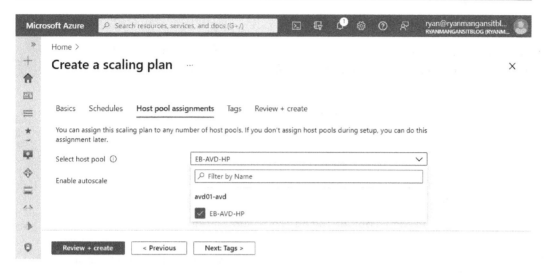

Figure 17.50 – Host pool assignments tab on the Create a scaling plan page

3. Under the **Tags** tab, specify any tags you may want to set, then click **Next**.

4. Review your settings and click **Create**:

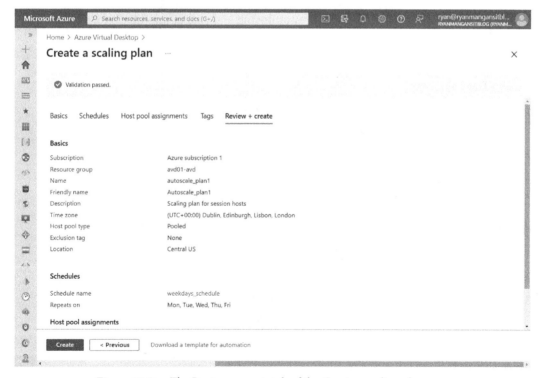

Figure 17.51 – The Review + create tab of the Create a scaling plan page

This concludes the setup process for creating a scaling plan in Azure Virtual Desktop.

There you have it – in this section, we looked at the in-preview Azure portal-based autoscale feature where you can configure scaling plans that meet your specific requirements.

For the latest updates and information on the autoscale tool, see the following Microsoft documentation link: `https://docs.microsoft.com/azure/virtual-desktop/autoscale-scaling-plan`.

Summary

In this chapter, we started by configuring an Azure automation account and then looked at automating Azure Virtual Desktop tasks such as logging multiple sessions of session hosts within a host pool. We then moved on to take a look at the autoscaling feature of Azure Virtual Desktop, which uses a series of PowerShell scripts for deployment. Then we finished off the chapter by looking at a preview feature (at the time of writing) called scaling plans. Finally, we ran through the setup of a scaling plan, configuring a schedule and assigning host pools to a scaling plan.

In the next chapter, we look at the topic of monitoring and managing the performance and health of an Azure Virtual Desktop environment.

Questions

1. You want to automate the logging off of multiple Azure Virtual Desktops users, which Azure service would you use to achieve this objective?

2. Before you can create scaling plans, what must you configure?

3. For custom autoscaling plans, which Azure service should you use?

Answers

1. *An Azure Automation Runbook.*

2. *A custom role with the required permissions.*

3. *For custom autoscale features, it's advised that you use the original PowerShell/Logic Apps solution provided by Microsoft, which you can customize to your specific requirements.*

18
Monitoring and Managing Performance and Health

In this chapter, we look at the monitoring, performance, health, and management of **Azure Virtual Desktop** (**AVD**). Being able to monitor your AVD environment helps you spot issues and optimize the configurations for a good **user experience** (**UX**). In this section, we take a look at the three key areas of monitoring, performance, and health. The key topics we'll cover in this chapter are outlined here:

- Configuring Azure Monitor for AVD
- Using AVD Insights
- Setting up alerts using alert rules
- Introduction to Kusto
- Using Azure Advisor for AVD

Configuring Azure Monitor for AVD

Azure Monitor for AVD is essentially a built-in dashboard built using Azure Monitor workbooks. This helps an **information technology** (**IT**) administrator understand the current environment state and enables the troubleshooting of some of the issues that may occur within an AVD environment.

Before you can get started with Azure Monitor for AVD, you need to make sure of the following:

- One Log Analytics workspace is configured.
- You are using the **Azure Resource Manager** (**ARM**) version of AVD.
- You have enabled the data collection of your AVD environment.

Once you have met the criteria to proceed, we can move on to look at creating a Log Analytics workspace.

Creating a Log Analytics workspace

The first thing to do is deploy Log Analytics to configure it to collect data from AVD. To do this, you will first need to open the **Log Analytics workspaces** page using the Azure search bar, as shown in the following screenshot:

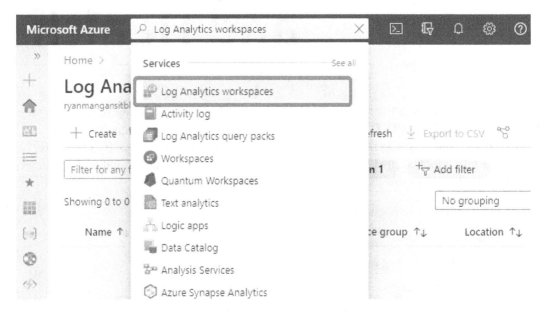

Figure 18.1 – Search bar and the Log Analytics workspaces service

Once we have opened the **Log Analytics workspaces** page, we can progress to creating a new Log Analytics workspace. Here are the steps to do this:

1. Within the **Log Analytics workspaces** page, click **Create**.

2. Select a **Resource group** type within the **Create Log Analytics workspace** page, enter a **Name** value for the instance, and choose an Azure **Region** type. Once complete, click **Review + Create**. The following screenshot provides an overview of this:

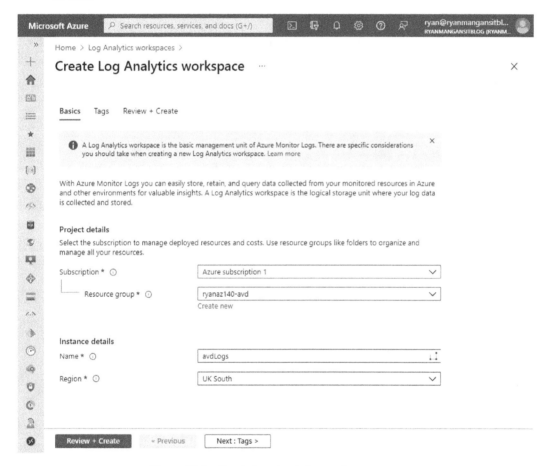

Figure 18.2 – Create Log Analytics workspace page

3.   Review the configuration and click **Create**, as illustrated in the following screenshot:

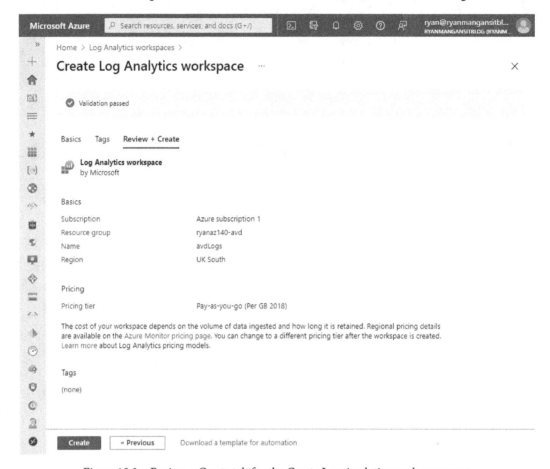

Figure 18.3 – Review + Create tab for the Create Log Analytics workspace page

Once the deployment has finished, you should see the Log Analytics workspace you created in the **Log Analytics workspaces** page, as shown in the following screenshot:

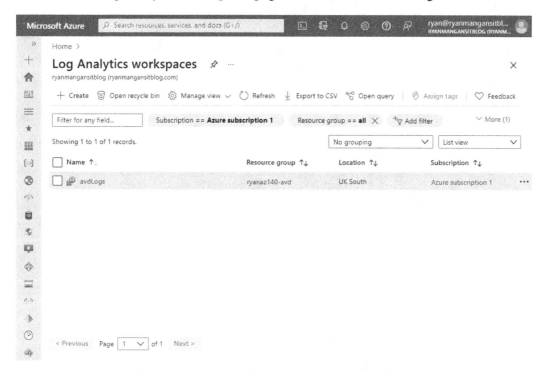

Figure 18.4 – Created Log Analytics workspace avdLogs

Important Note

The default pricing tier for Log Analytics will be configured, as shown in the preceding screenshot. You will not incur any charges until you collect sufficient amounts of data. You can cap data using the **Daily cap** feature located under **Usage and estimated costs** in the **General** menu section.

The following screenshot shows where the **Daily cap** button is located:

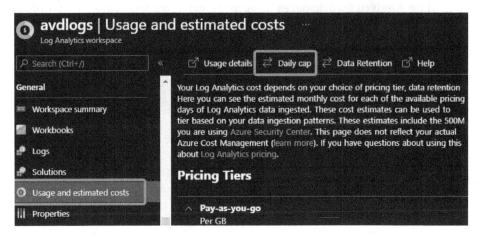

Figure 18.5 – Usage and estimated costs menu within a Log Analytics workspace

The following screenshot shows the **Daily cap** blade, which can be used to control the daily ingestion of data:

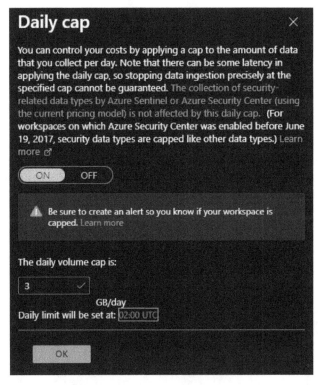

Figure 18.6 – Daily cap blade

Now that we have created our Log Analytics workspace, we can proceed with configuring monitoring in AVD.

Configuring the monitoring of AVD

In this section, we will take a look at setting up the required monitoring components for AVD. To do this, we will navigate to the **Azure Virtual Desktop** page and then click **Insights** under the **Monitoring** section.

There are multiple different ways to configure Azure Monitor for AVD. In this example, we will use **Insights** within the **Azure Virtual Desktop** page. However, we first need to configure the workbook for AVD, as follows:

1. To get started, click **Open Configuration Workbook**, as highlighted in the following screenshot:

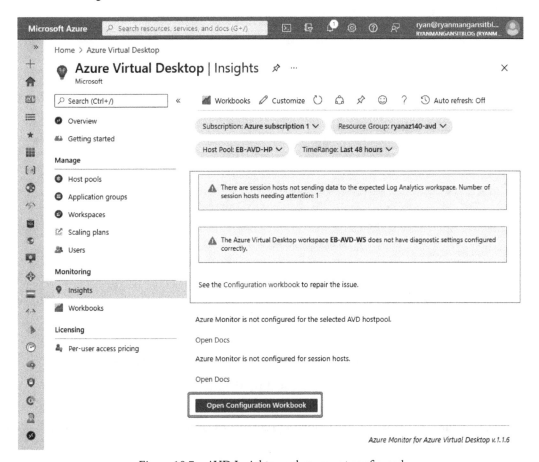

Figure 18.7 – AVD Insights workspace not configured

2. You will now see the **Check Configuration** heading, which has three tabs—
    Resources diagnostic settings, **Session host data settings**, and **Data Generated**.
    You need to ensure that you have configured all the required components within
    Resources diagnostic settings and **Session host data settings**.

    Let's get started.

3. Select the required Log Analytics workspace and then click **Configure host pool**, as
    shown in the following screenshot:

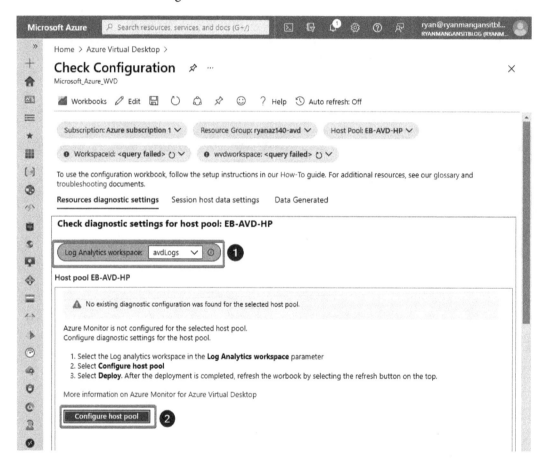

Figure 18.8 – Check Configuration workspace and the Configure host pool button highlighted

4. Once you have clicked the **Configure host pool** button, you will see the **Deploy
    Template** page appear, which is used to configure the host pool diagnostic settings.

5. Click **Deploy**, as shown in the following screenshot, and wait for the deployment
    to finish:

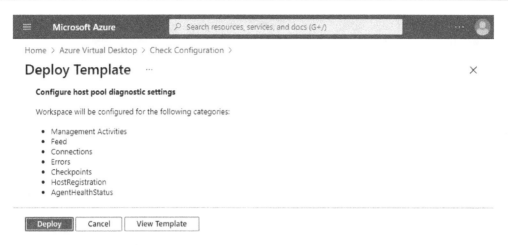

Figure 18.9 – Deploy Template page for configuring host pool diagnostic settings

6. Once deployed, navigate to **Azure Virtual Desktop | Workbooks**, and under **Public Templates**, click **Check Configuration**, as highlighted in the following screenshot:

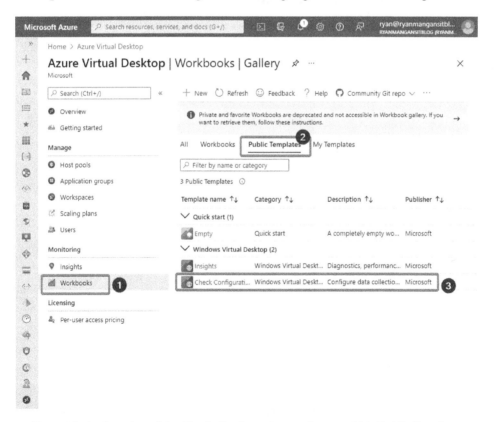

Figure 18.10 – Location of the Check Configuration workspace within Public Templates

7. You should then see that the **Check Configuration** page has changed and the host pool diagnostic settings are now shown.

We now need to configure the workspace by deploying the Log Analytics settings for the AVD workspace. Follow these steps:

1. Click **Configure workspace** to proceed, as illustrated in the following screenshot:

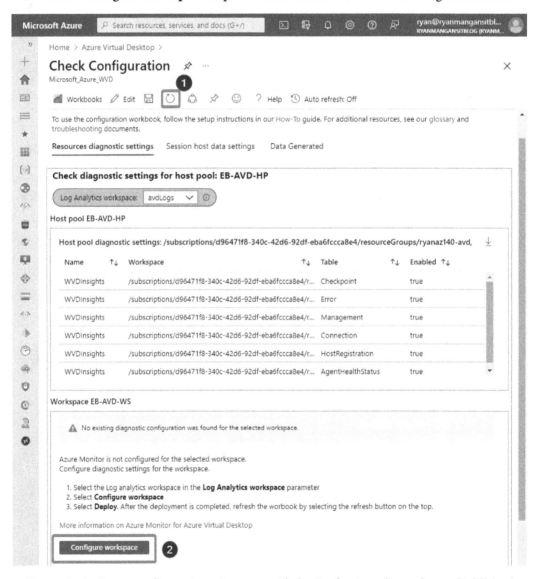

Figure 18.11 – Resources diagnostic settings page with the Configure workspace button highlighted

2. You will then see the **Deploy Template** page appear for configuring the workspace diagnostic settings, as illustrated in the following screenshot. Click **Deploy** to proceed:

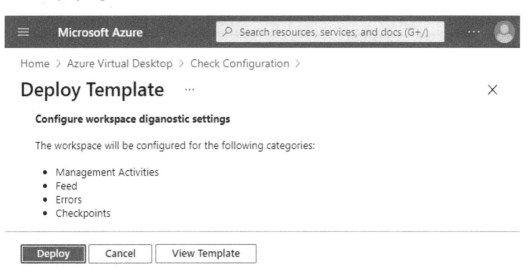

Figure 18.12 – Deploy Template page for configuring workspace diagnostic settings

3. Once you have finished configuring the diagnostics for both host pools and the workspace, we can proceed with **Session host data settings**.

4. Select **Log Analytics Workspace** within the **Session host data settings** page and click **Add hosts to the workspace**, as illustrated in the following screenshot. If you see an error in adding the session hosts, you may need to add them manually:

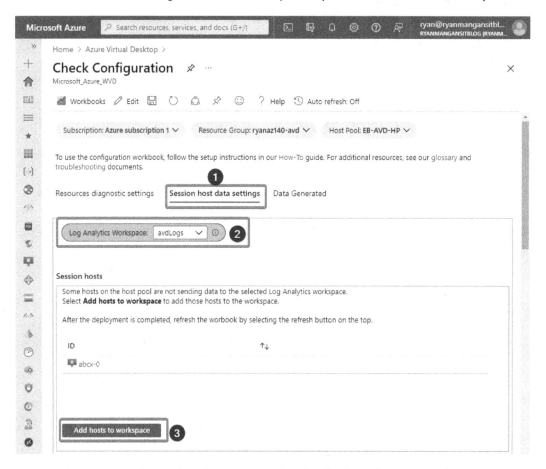

Figure 18.13 – Session host data settings within the Check Configuration workspace

5. Once you have clicked **Add hosts to workspace**, you will see the **Deploy Template** page appear, which will detail the session hosts configured with the workspace. You can see this page in the following screenshot:

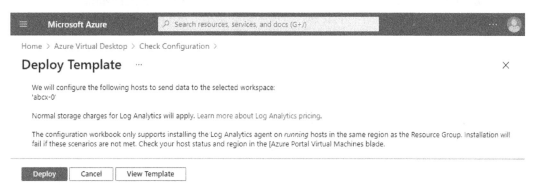

Figure 18.14 – Deploy Template page for configuring session hosts

Once the template is deployed, you can then progress with configuring performance counters.

Configuring performance counters

For the AVD dashboard to display the correct information, we need to ensure that all the correct counters are enabled for each session host. You can enable the counters using configurable performance counters within the **Check Configuration** workbook on the **Session host data settings** tab.

As shown in the previous steps, proceed as follows:

1. Navigate to the **Azure Virtual Desktop** page first and then click **Workbooks** under **Monitoring**. Select **Check Configuration** and click the **Session host data settings** tab. Then, click **Configure performance counters**. The process is illustrated in the following screenshot:

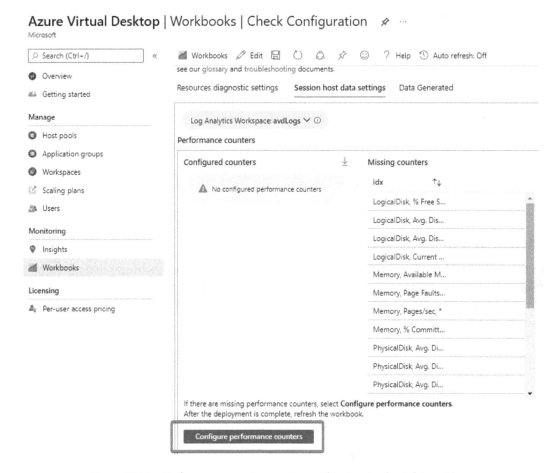

Figure 18.15 – Performance counters section within Session host data settings

2. Similar to the previous **Deploy Template** pages, you will see the following screen. Click **Apply Config** to set the required performance counters:

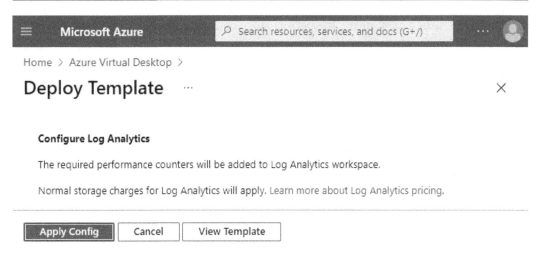

Figure 18.16 – Deploy Template page for configuring the required performance counters

3.   Once the deployment has been completed, you will see **No missing performance counters** within the **Session host data settings** tab, as highlighted in the following screenshot:

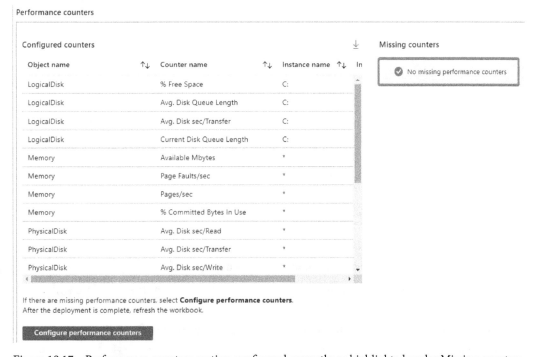

Figure 18.17 – Performance counters section configured correctly, as highlighted under Missing counters

Once you have finished configuring the performance counters, you can then proceed with configuring the event counters.

Configuring events

The final section of configuring Azure Monitor is to configure the event logs. The process is the same as for configuring the performance counters. Scroll down the page to **Configure events** under **Configuration workbook | Session host data settings**, and then proceed as follows:

1. Click **Configure events**, as shown in the following screenshot:

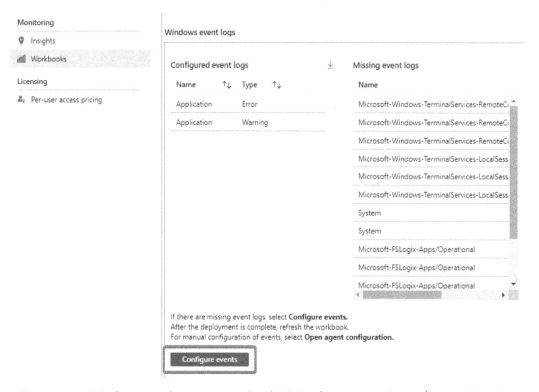

Figure 18.18 – Windows event logs section in the Check Configuration workspace | Session host data settings, with Configure events highlighted

2. You will then see the **Deploy Template** page, which states that the template will deploy the required event logs for the AVD Log Analytics workspace.

3. Click **Deploy** to proceed with the deployment, as illustrated in the following screenshot:

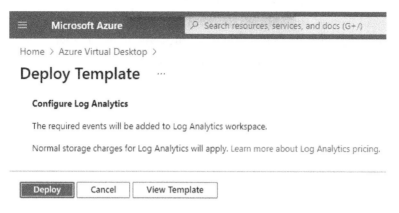

Figure 18.19 – Deploy Template page for configuring the required events logs

4. Once deployed, navigate back to the **Check Configuration** workbook | **Session host data settings**, and scroll down to the **Windows event logs** section.

You should see a **No missing events found** message if the configuration has been done correctly, as highlighted in the following screenshot:

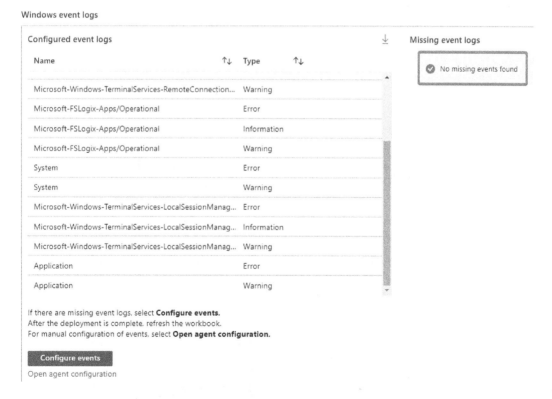

Figure 18.20 – Event logs section has been configured correctly

5. You can now click on **Insights** within the **Azure Virtual Desktop** page and should be able to see data in a dashboard view, as illustrated in the following screenshot:

Figure 18.21 – AVD workspace Insights dashboard

Now that we have finished configuring Azure Monitor for AVD, we can take a look at the different areas of the monitoring workspace for AVD.

Using AVD Insights

In this section, we will take a look at how to use Azure Monitor to spot issues and view the current state of an AVD environment.

> **Important Note**
>
> Log Analytics is essentially the data used when visualizing ingested AVD data. AVD **Insights** is a templated dashboard that uses the configured log analytics and counters to provide IT administrators information about the organization's AVD environment.

Within the AVD **Insights** workspace, there are nine tabs, as follows:

- **Overview**
- **Connection Diagnostics**
- **Connection Performance**
- **Host Diagnostics**
- **Host Performance**
- **Users**
- **Utilization**
- **Clients**
- **Alerts**

The **Overview** tab, as highlighted in the following screenshot, provides an overview of the AVD environment, which looks at the **Host pool** details, **Connection Diagnostics**, **Host Performance**, **Utilization**, and **Alerts**. We can look at the specific workspace tabs to drill down for more detailed information:

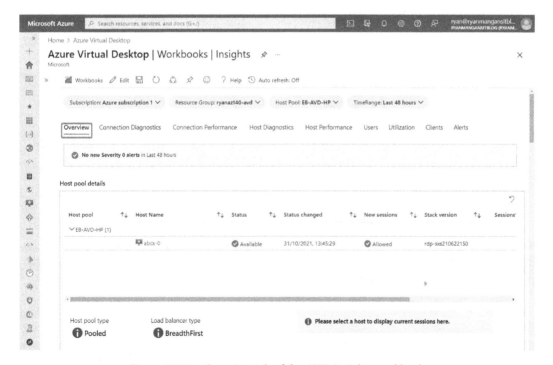

Figure 18.22 – Overview tab of the AVD Insights workbook

The **Connection Diagnostics** tab provides details on connections. This allows you, as the IT administrator, to review any alerts and investigate any problems. In this example, I noticed there was an `FSLogix` error relating to the storage path not being found, which shows up in the **Connection Diagnostics** tab:

Figure 18.23 – List of errors impacting connections

The following screenshot shows a drill-down of errors that provides more granularity:

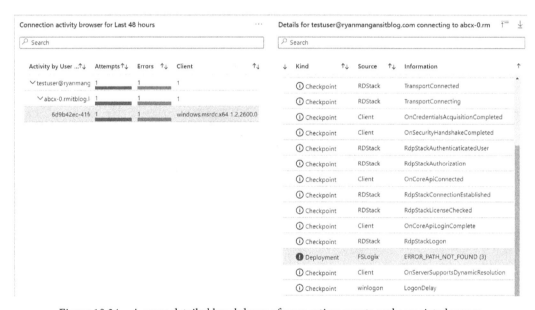

Figure 18.24 – A more detailed breakdown of connection events and associated errors

The **Connection Performance** tab, shown in the following screenshot, provides information on new and existing sessions, which enables IT administrators to review slow sign-in times and diagnose possible login issues:

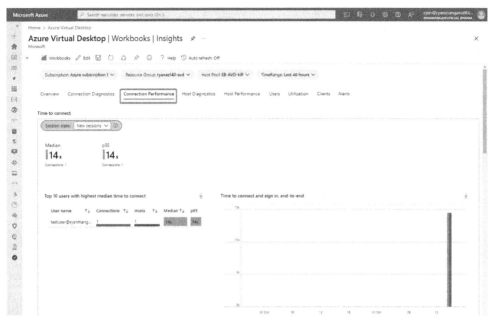

Figure 18.25 – The Connection Performance tab visualizes performance issues/communication issues relating to the user or host

The **Host Diagnostics** tab, shown in the following screenshot, provides information on the host pool configuration, performance counters, events, and any errors. This can help you pinpoint any issues related to a session host and monitor the **central processing unit (CPU)** and memory usage:

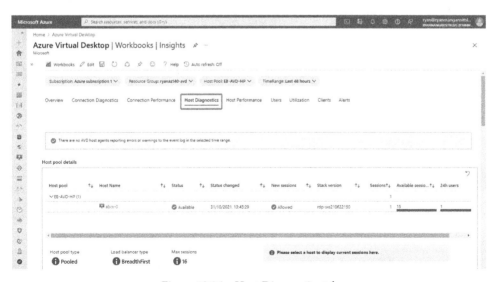

Figure 18.26 – Host Diagnostics tab

The **Host Performance** tab, shown in the following screenshot, provides insights into the overall performance and enables IT administrators to drill down into possible issues with processes, CPU, memory, and disk queuing. This helps to identify the host saturation and any applications that may be consuming a lot of resources:

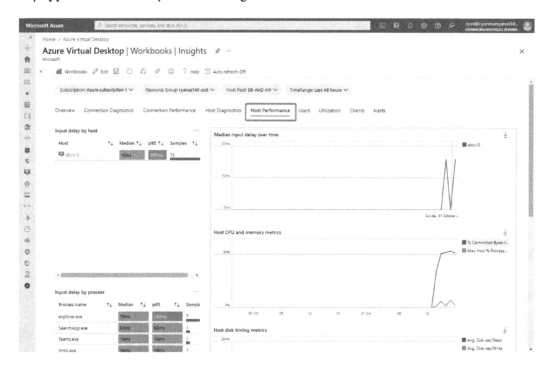

Figure 18.27 – Host Performance tab

The **Users** tab, shown in the following screenshot, provides a detailed output on user performance and any errors relating to a specific user. This tab helps to identify specific user issues and allows IT administrators to quickly understand the client device in use, client version, and any errors during connectivity:

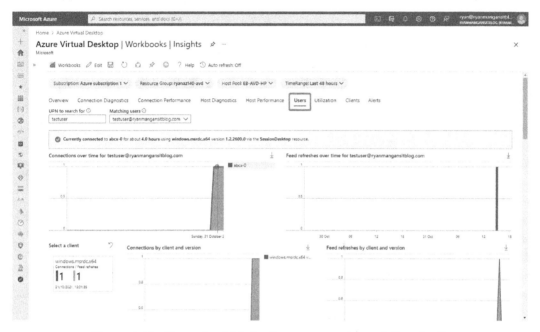

Figure 18.28 – Users tab, which details user connection and client details

The **Utilization** tab shows the current utilization metrics of your AVD environment. This is particularly useful for capacity management and understanding any potential performance degradation of the environment.

The **Clients** tab, illustrated in the following screenshot, shows connections and feed refreshes and the version of the client in use. IT administrators can get a full picture of which clients are being used within the AVD environment from here:

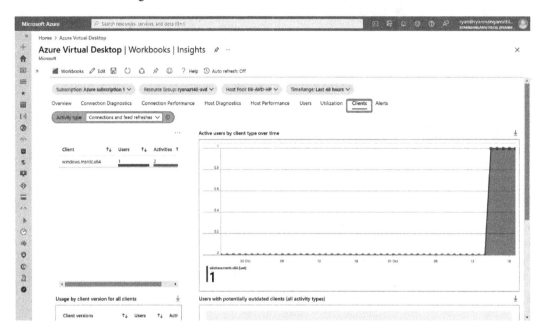

Figure 18.29 – Clients tab, which provides details on client and version usage

The final tab, **Alerts**, is used to show the number of alerts raised over a period of time, and the severity of those alerts. The tab can be seen in the following screenshot. We will cover the configuration of alerts in the *Setting up alerts using alert rules* section:

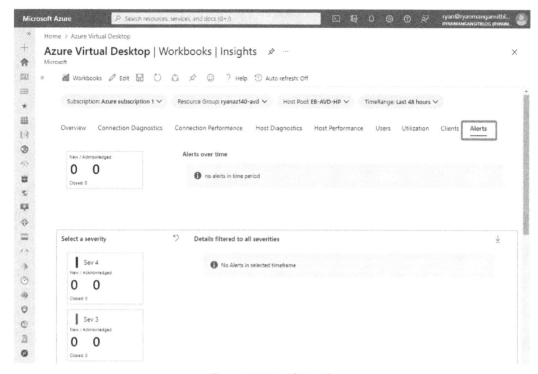

Figure 18.30 – Alerts tab

In this section, we took a quick look at the AVD Insights workspace and the different tabs and learned how IT administrators can use Azure Monitor to quickly diagnose and resolve AVD issues. In the next section, we take a look at setting up alerts based on outputs from a query.

Setting up alerts using alert rules

Within Log Analytics, you can query logs and set a frequency. You can also set an alert based on the output of the query. Rules can be triggered using one or more actions.

> **Tip**
>
> Using alerts to notify administrators or specified users about issues within your AVD environment can be helpful for those who are not continually monitoring the **Insights** page. This can also be useful for IT administrators who may be on-call or need to receive a text message or other notification of a possible issue/failure.

To set up an alert, proceed as follows:

1. Start by typing `monitor` in the Azure search bar and click **Monitor** from the search results that appear, as illustrated in the following screenshot:

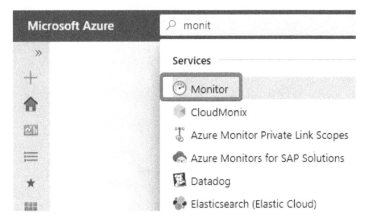

Figure 18.31 – Azure Monitor service within the search bar

2. Once within the Azure **Monitor** page, click on the **Alerts** icon located within the menu on the left, as illustrated in the following screenshot:

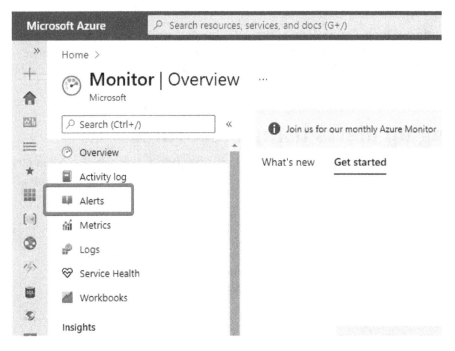

Figure 18.32 – Alerts page icon in Azure Monitor

3. Click the **New alert rule** button, as highlighted in the following screenshot, to load the **Create alert rule** page:

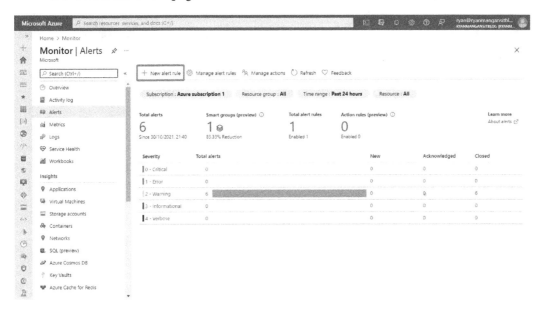

Figure 18.33 – Alerts page and the button to create a new alert rule

4. In this example, we are going to create a simple alert for `FSLogix` disk-related issues. Within the **Create alert rule** page, click on the **Select resource** option, as highlighted in the following screenshot:

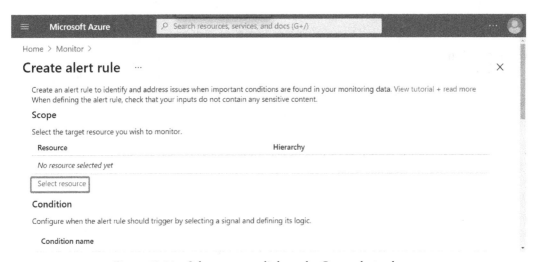

Figure 18.34 – Select resource link on the Create alert rule page

5. Within the **Select a resource** page, click the required subscription and click **Done**, as illustrated in the following screenshot:

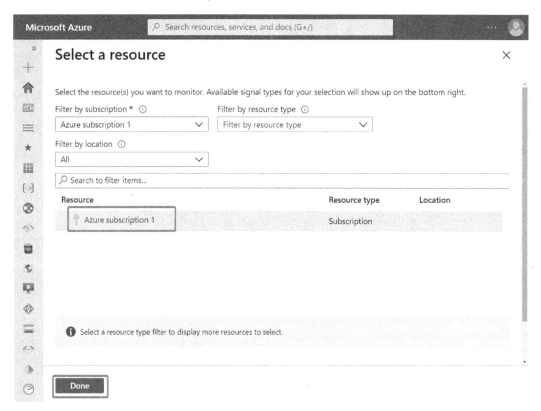

Figure 18.35 – Select a resource page within the Create alert rule section

6. I found that I had to go back in for a second time to select the required Log Analytics workspace. For some reason, it did not apply the first time, so I had to repeat the step. This is shown in the following screenshot:

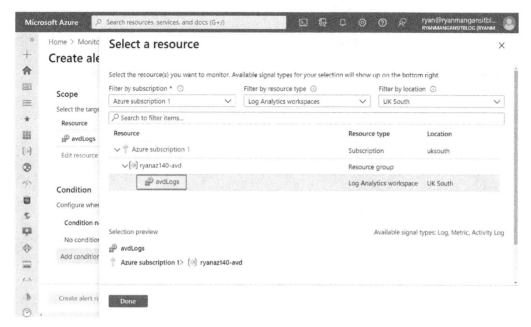

Figure 18.36 – Selection of the Log Analytics workspace

7. Once complete, we need to add a condition. We need to click the **Add condition** option to add a condition, as shown in the following screenshot:

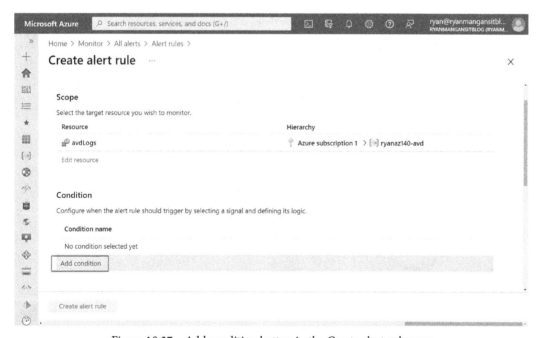

Figure 18.37 – Add condition button in the Create alert rule page

8. Within the **Select a signal** blade, choose the required signal name. In this example, we will select the **Event** signal, as shown in the following screenshot:

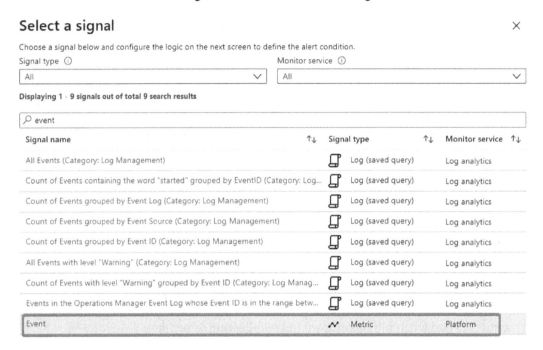

Figure 18.38 – Select a signal page with the signal name metric selected

9. Once you have selected the **Event** signal, you will see the **Configure signal logic** page appear. Within this page, you will set the `Microsoft-FSLogix-Apps/Operational` event log and the `EventID` value as `26`, which is a common event, as shown in the following screenshot.

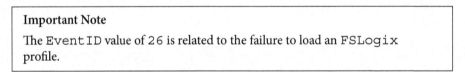

> **Important Note**
> The `EventID` value of `26` is related to the failure to load an `FSLogix` profile.

10. You then need to set the **Alert logic** field to a **Static** threshold, the **Operator** field to **Greater than or equal to**, the **Aggregation type** field to **Total**, the **Threshold value** field to 5, and the **Unit** value to **Count**.

Once complete, click the **Done** button, as illustrated in the following screenshot:

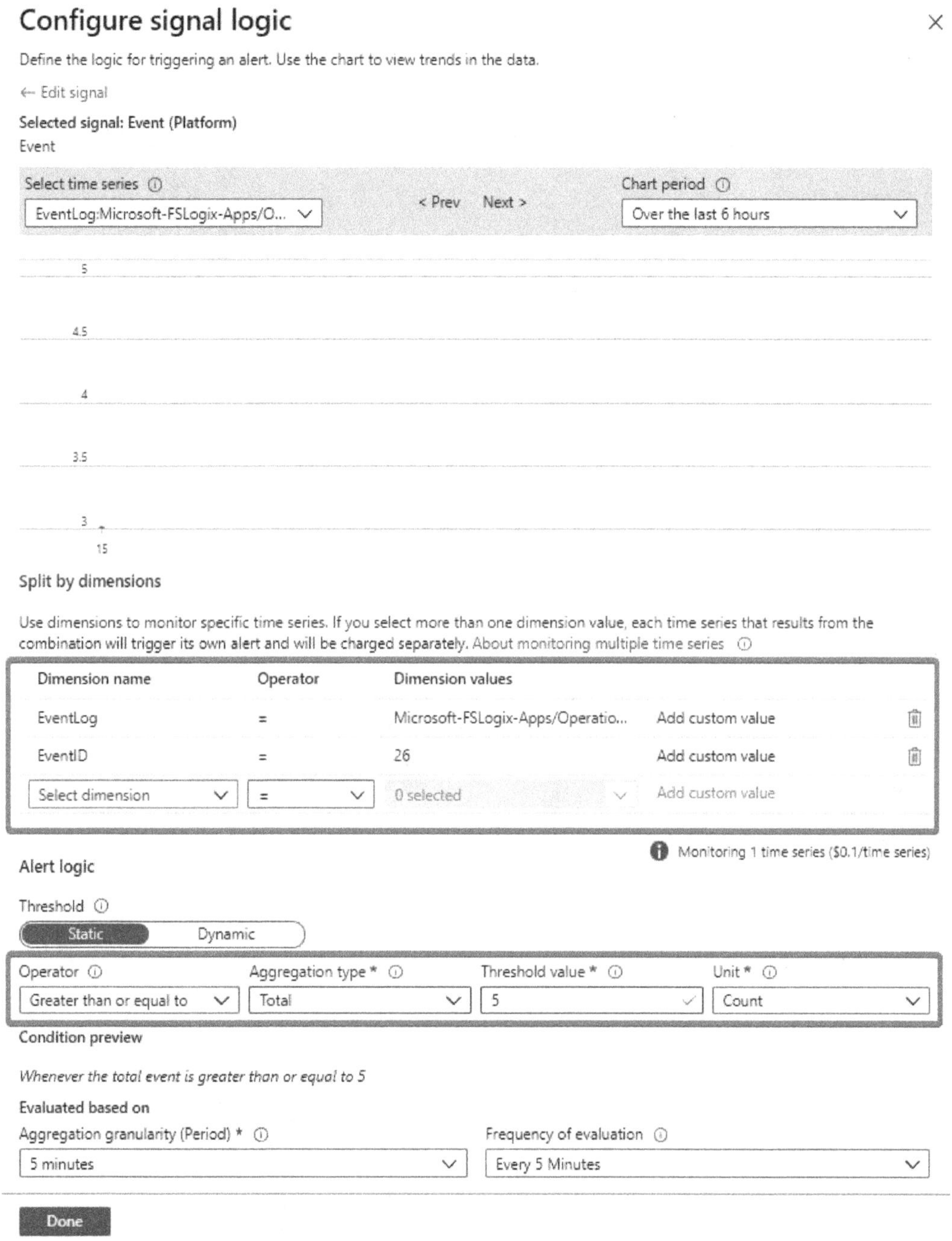

Figure 18.39 – Configure signal logic page

The next step is to create an action group, and in this example, we only need a notification. You can configure actions in more advanced configurations. Proceed as follows:

1. Click on the **Add action groups** button within the **Create alert rule** page, as highlighted in the following screenshot:

Figure 18.40 – Add action groups button

2. In this example, we will create a new action group for notifying IT administrators when an alert is triggered. Click + **Create action group**, as highlighted in the following screenshot:

Figure 18.41 – + Create action group button

3. Once the **Create action group** page appears, select a **Resource group** type, then choose an **Action group name** value and a **Display name** value within the **Instance details** section, as highlighted in the following screenshot:

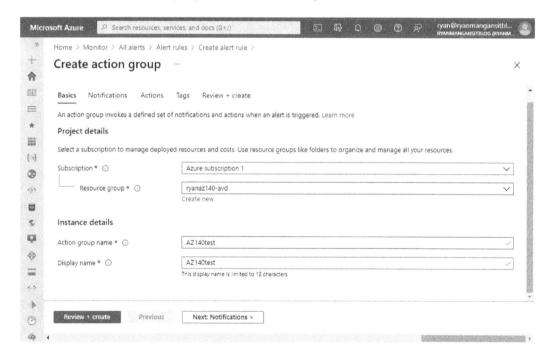

Figure 18.42 – Create action group page

4. Once you have configured all the required fields on the **Basics** tab, click the **Notifications** tab.

5. Within the **Notifications** tab, you can configure a number of different notifications. In this example, we will configure email only. As shown in the following screenshot, we have set the **Notification type** value to **Email/SMS message/Push/Voice** and set the **Name** value to **Admin email**:

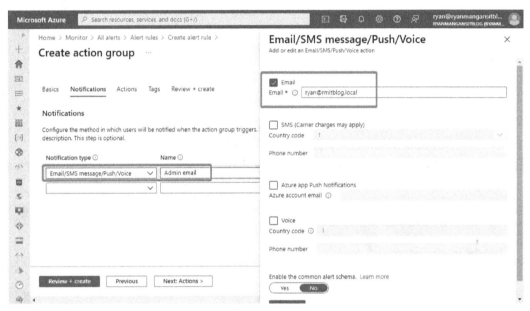

Figure 18.43 – Email configuration within the Notifications tab on the Create action group page

6. Once the notifications have been configured, proceed with the **Review + create** page. Check the configuration and click **Create**, as illustrated in the following screenshot:

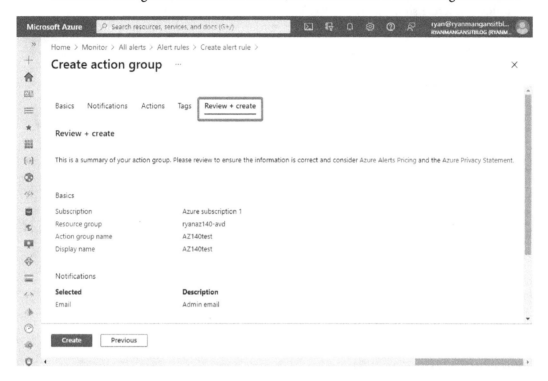

Figure 18.44 – Review + create tab

7. You should now be able to see the new action group name we just created under the **Actions** section within the **Create alert rule** page, as highlighted in the following screenshot:

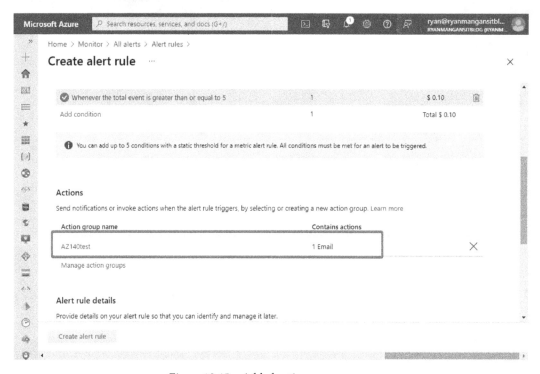

Figure 18.45 – Added action group name

8. The last action on the **Create alert rule** page is to complete the alert rule details located at the bottom of the page. Enter values in the **Alert rule name**, **Description**, and **Resource group** fields, and enter a **Severity** ranking, as shown in the following screenshot. Once finished, click **Create alert rule**:

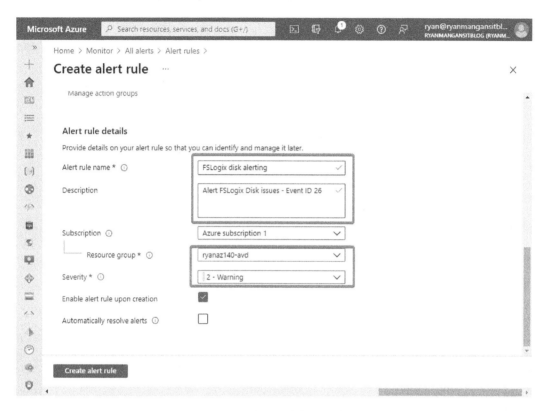

Figure 18.46 – Alert rule details within the Create alert rule page

9. You will now be able to see the new alert within **Monitor | All alerts**, as shown in the following screenshot:

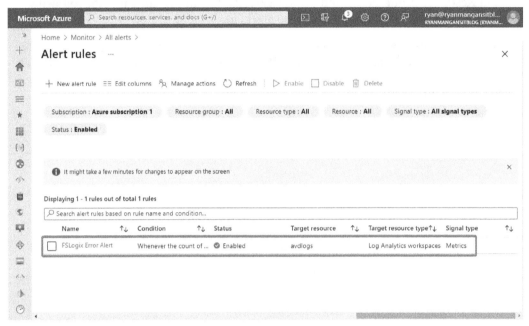

Figure 18.47 – Newly created FSLogix alert rule

This section looked at creating an alert rule to notify IT administrators of a specific issue or problem with the AVD environment. The example I showed was a simple `FSLogix` alert using event logs; however, you can create custom and customized alerts specific to your environment.

In the next section, we take a look at Kusto and how you can use this query language to query AVD to diagnose issues and pull useful information specific to your environment.

Introduction to Kusto

Kusto Query Language (**KQL**) is a *read-only* language used to query datasets within Microsoft Azure. Similar to **Structured Query Language** (**SQL**), Kusto can be used to query data, but it can't update or delete, as SQL can. Kusto can be used when querying AVD services and other related components, and you can create custom queries to output information that is important to you.

You can use Kusto with the following Azure services:

- Azure Application Insights
- Azure Log Analytics
- Azure Monitor Logs
- Azure Data Explorer
- Microsoft Defender for Endpoint
- Microsoft Sentinel

> **Fun Fact**
>
> It is understood that the name *Kusto* was an internal code name named after Jacques Cousteau, as a reference to *exploring the ocean of data*. You may notice that reference when launching the Kusto Explorer tool, which we will look at shortly. The development of Kusto was focused on addressing the need for fast and scalable logs analytics.

Connecting Log Analytics to Kusto Explorer

Before we start writing a basic query for AVD, we first need to look at how to use Kusto Explorer. Kusto Explorer is a free tool you can download from the **Microsoft Docs** page here: `https://aka.ms/ke`.

Once you have downloaded and installed Kusto Explorer, you'll need to connect to your Azure Log Analytics workspace using the following (cluster connection):

```
https://ade.loganalytics.io/subscriptions/<subscription-id>/
resourcegroups/<resource-group-name>/providers/microsoft.
operationalinsights/workspaces/<workspace-name>
```

Remember to change the subscription **identifier** (**ID**), resource group name, and workspace name within the preceding string (cluster connection).

To connect your Log Analytics workspace to Kusto Explorer, you will need to add a connection, as shown in the following screenshot:

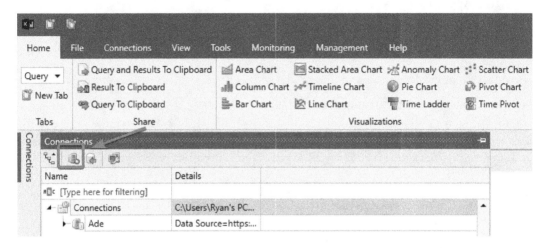

Figure 18.48 – Add connection icon within Kusto Explorer

Enter the cluster connection (the **Uniform Resource Locator** (**URL**) for Log Analytics), as illustrated in the following screenshot:

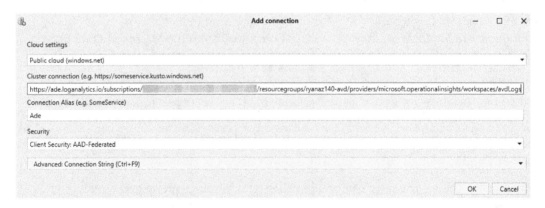

Figure 18.49 – Adding a cluster connection within Kusto Explorer

Once connected, you should be able to see the **Connections** tab and a list of tables within the tree, as shown in the following screenshot:

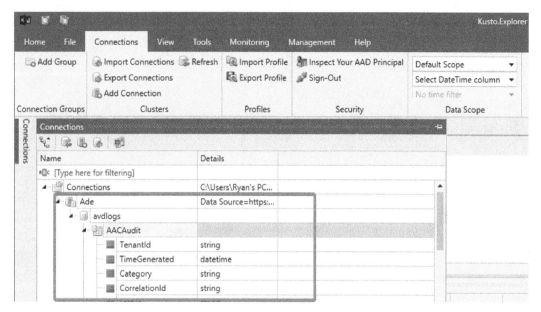

Figure 18.50 – Connection to the Log Analytics workspace

Now that we have configured Kusto Explorer, we can proceed with creating queries for AVD.

Creating queries for AVD using Kusto Explorer

In this section, we will take a look at a few quick queries you can build using Kusto Explorer. You can create and customize queries within Azure; however, Kusto Explorer allows you to work on them in a nice client application and produce graphs as well.

Let's get started with a basic AVD error query.

Within the **Connections** tab, right-click on **Connections** and select **Open in New tab**, as highlighted in the following screenshot:

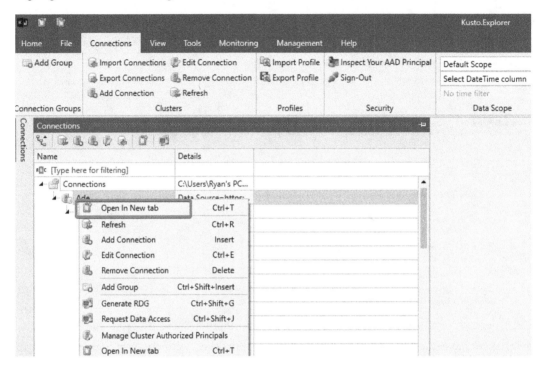

Figure 18.51 – New tab (Ctrl + T) used for creating a new query tab

Once you have clicked the new tab, you should be able to see a new tab created, as shown in the following screenshot:

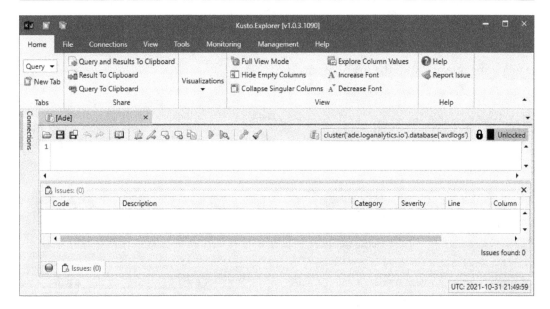

Figure 18.52 – New tab

A straightforward query with no filtering would be WVDErrors—this will collect any recorded errors within the WVDErrors table and display them within the output panel, as shown in the following screenshot:

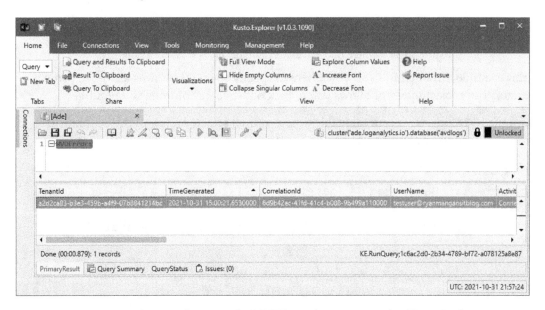

Figure 18.53 – Output of running the WVDErrors basic query within Kusto Explorer

You can then add a filter by using the `where` *Boolean expression* to pull a specific time or time range, which may be helpful when reviewing the logs for a specific issue.

The following query shows the usage of `where`:

```
WVDErrors
| where TimeGenerated > (datetime(2021-10-31T20:02:18.0000000Z)
- 24h)
```

Here's the output:

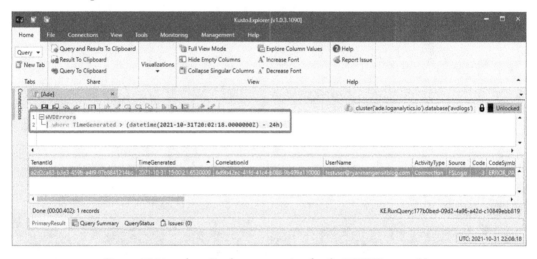

Figure 18.54 – where Boolean expression for the WVDErrors table

In this example, I wanted to show you where to specify specific columns using the **project** operator. The project operator allows you to pick out specific columns you require.

I used the `WVDConnections` table this time and then selected a few of the columns to provide an easy-to-read output. Here's an example:

```
WVDConnections
| where TimeGenerated > (datetime(2021-10-31T20:18:18.0000000Z)
- 24h)
| project UserName, State, SessionHostName, TimeGenerated,
ConnectionType
```

The following screenshot shows the usage of Kusto Explorer, using the preceding query, which uses the project operator:

Figure 18.55 – WVDConnections query using project operator to select a few columns

In this final example, I wanted to show you how to filter using CodeSymbolic, which allows you to filter on a specific message. In this example, I have shut the session host down without logging a user off. I wanted to find out which users did not successfully log off before host shutdown. To do this, I used the following Kusto query:

```
| where CodeSymbolic ==
"ConnectionFailedReverseUngracefulClose"
```

The following screenshot shows the results of the preceding query:

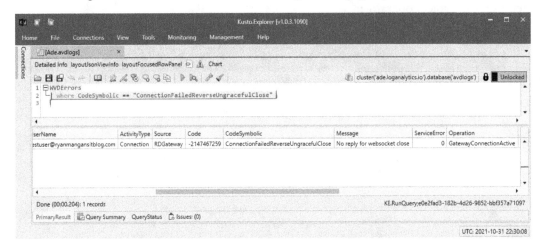

Figure 18.56 – Use of CodeSymbolic filtering

In this section, we looked at querying a Log Analytics workspace using Kusto Explorer. We also looked at a couple of examples to help you get started with querying your own AVD environment.

In the next section, we will take a look at using Azure Advisor for AVD.

Using Azure Advisor for AVD

Azure Advisor can be used to help resolve common issues, and it also provides recommendations. Azure Advisor's recommendations include resource reliability, security, operational excellence, performance, and cost.

To get started with Azure Advisor, simply enter `advisor` into the Azure search bar and select the service that appears, as illustrated in the following screenshot:

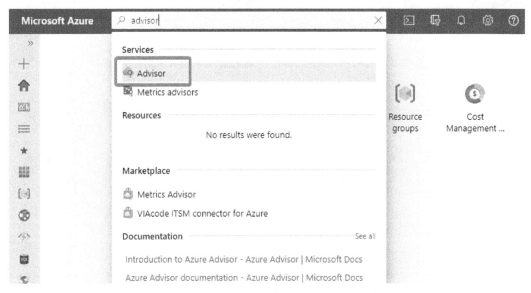

Figure 18.57 – Advisor service within the Azure portal search bar

You will then be presented with several advisories within five categories, as follows:

- **Cost**
- **Security**
- **Reliability**
- **Operation excellence**
- **Performance**

The following screenshot shows the Azure Advisor **Overview** page:

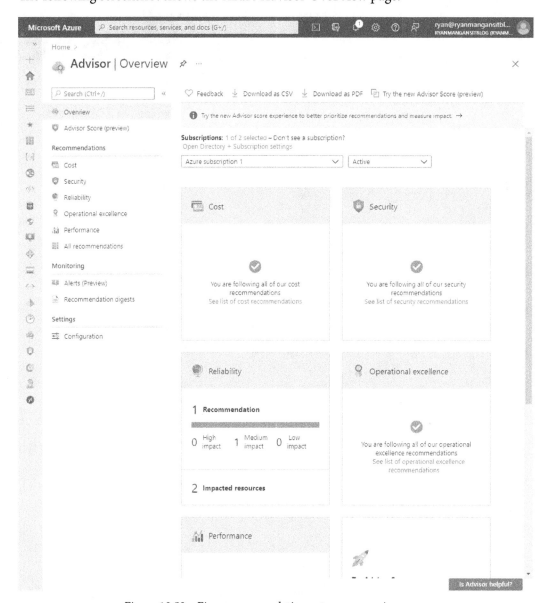

Figure 18.58 – Five-recommendation category overview page

Use the recommendations to enhance your configuration and relatability and reduce the cost.

We looked at Azure Advisor in this section and briefly looked at the value it can bring to your AVD environment.

Summary

This chapter looked at setting up and configuring Azure Monitor for AVD and using the AVD Insights workspace. We then moved on to setting up custom alerts using alert rules, which will notify IT administrators of a specific error or issue. We then looked at KQL and a few examples of querying a Log Analytics workspace. We then finished off the chapter, briefly looking at Azure Advisor for AVD.

Questions

Here are a few questions to test your understanding of this chapter:

1. How can a user limit the ingestion of data to Log Analytics?
2. What is Kusto?
3. What does the `EventID` value `26` commonly refer to when reviewing `FSLogix` profile logs?
4. What is the name of the feature used for viewing metrics and troubleshooting issues with AVD?

Answers

1. *Configure the Daily cap setting found under the usage and estimated costs page within the Log Analytics workspace*
2. *A read-only language used to query datasets*
3. *The failure to load an FSLogix profile*
4. *AVD Insights*

19
Azure Virtual Desktop's Getting Started Feature

In this chapter, we'll look at using the **Getting Started** feature to deploy Azure Virtual Desktop. This feature provides an easy way to deploy and configure an Azure Virtual Desktop environment.

By the end of this chapter, you should be able to use the Azure Virtual Desktop Getting Started feature to deploy Azure Virtual Desktop environments.

In this chapter, we will cover the following topics:

- How the Getting starting feature works
- Using the Getting started feature with Azure AD DS and AD DS
- Using the Getting started feature without an identity provider
- Post-deployment cleanup
- Troubleshooting the Getting started feature

How the Getting started feature works

The purpose of the Getting started feature is to address the challenges associated with deploying Azure Virtual Desktop environments.

The Getting started feature removes the multi-step processes and makes deploying Azure Virtual Desktop simple.

Two key benefits of using the Getting started feature are as follows:

- You can remove complex multi-step processes, including FSLogix profile container setup and configuration, which includes Azure Files and permissions.

- You can create session hosts and configure Azure Virtual Desktop core components, including host pools, workspaces, application groups, and validation user accounts.

There are two options you can choose from:

- **Existing Setup**: This is for organizations who already have an Azure Tenant and Subscription, including Active Directory or **Azure Active Directory Domain Services (Azure AD DS)**.

- **New Subscription (Empty)**: This is tailored for subscriptions that have no Active Directory or Azure AD DS).

The Getting started feature is essentially a wizard that enables you to deploy an Azure Virtual Desktop environment within a matter of hours. It lets you rapidly deploy small environments that can be used in production, testing, or lab environments.

The Getting started feature uses nested templates to deploy the required Azure resources for validation and to automate the deployment of Azure Virtual Desktop. The Getting started feature creates two or three resource groups that are dependent on the identity provider option that's selected within the wizard, which we will cover shortly.

Prerequisites

Before you get started, you need to ensure that you have an Azure Active Directory tenant. You will also need to ensure that the account you are using has global admin permissions on the subscription being used within Azure Active Directory.

> **Important Note**
>
> At the time of writing, the Getting started feature does not support the use of accounts with **multi-factor authentication** (**MFA**). You need to make sure the account that's being used has MFA turned off. Also, **managed service accounts** (**MSA**), **business-to-business** (**B2B**), and guest accounts are not supported at the time of writing.

For those who are using an environment with **Active Directory Domain Services** (**AD DS**), take note of the following:

- You need to have the AD DS domain admin credentials to hand.

- You must configure Azure AD connect on your subscription and make sure the USERS container is syncing with Azure Active Directory. You can check this by viewing the Azure Active Directory page within the Azure portal.

- You need to ensure you have a Domain Controller deployed within the required region you plan to deploy Azure Virtual Desktop.

- The domain controller that you deploy to Azure must not have DSC extensions of the Microsoft.Powershell.DSC type.

For those who plan to deploy Azure Virtual Desktop without an identity provider, take note of the following:

- You need to ensure that the AD domain join's **user principal name** (**UPN**) does not include specific keywords such as admin, server, or support. The full list can be found here: https://docs.microsoft.com/azure/virtual-machines/windows/faq#what-are-the-username-requirements-when-creating-a-vm-.

- You must create a new host pool to add session hosts when using the Getting started feature while using the **without an identity provider** option; if you're trying to deploy a session host in an existing host pool, it will fail.

Now, let's look at using the Getting started feature wizard.

Using the Getting started feature with Azure AD DS and AD DS

This section details how to use the Getting started feature to deploy an Azure Virtual Desktop environment in a subscription that already has **Azure Active Directory Domain Services (Azure AD DS)** or **Active Directory Domain Services (AD DS)**:

1. First, you need to open the Azure portal.

2. Once you have signed into Azure, open the **Azure Virtual Desktop** page using the search bar or navigate through the services.

3. Within the **Azure Virtual Desktop** page, select the **Getting started** tab:

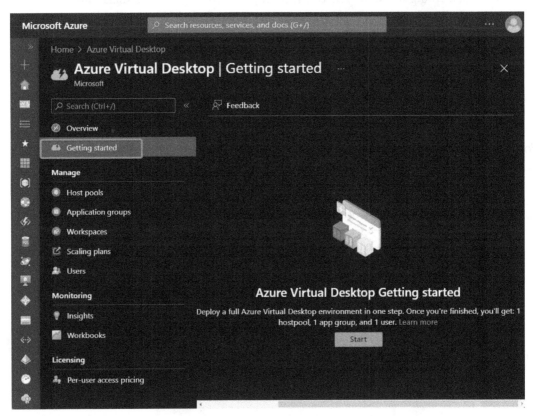

Figure 19.1 – The Getting Started tab within the Azure Virtual Desktop page of Azure

4. Click the **Start** button.

5. Select the required **Subscription** the select **Existing Active Directory** in the **Identity provider** section.

6. For **Identity Service type**, select **Active Directory** or **Azure Active Directory Domain Services**. For this example, we will choose **Active Directory**.

7. Enter a **Resource group** name:

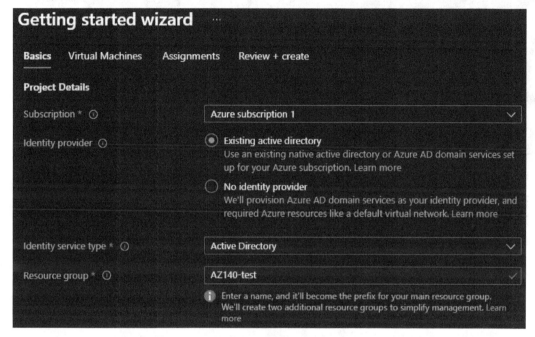

Figure 19.2 – The Getting started wizard using an existing active directory identity provider

8. For **Location**, select the Azure region you wish to deploy your Azure Virtual Desktop resources to. This example uses **UK South**.

9. Select the required **Virtual network** and **Subnet**:

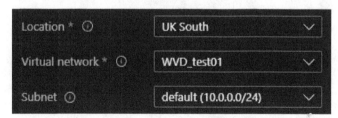

Figure 19.3 – The Location, Virtual network, and Subnet options within the Getting started wizard page

10. Enter the required **Azure User credentials**. This is the full user principal name and ensures the account has the owner permissions on the Azure tenant.

11. Enter the required **Domain administrator credentials**. You will need to ensure you enter the full user principal name:

Figure 19.4 – Both the Azure user credentials and Domain administrator sections within the Getting started wizard

12. Click **Next: Virtual Machines** to continue to the **Virtual Machines** tab.

13. Within the **Virtual Machines** tab, select the required option for **users per virtual machine**. For this example, we will choose **multiple users**.

14. Select an **Image type**, and then an **Image**. In this example, we will use the default of **Gallery** for **Image type** and **Windows 11 Enterprise multi-session + Microsoft 365 Apps** for **Image**.

15. Select the required **Virtual machine size** and **SKU** you would like to deploy:

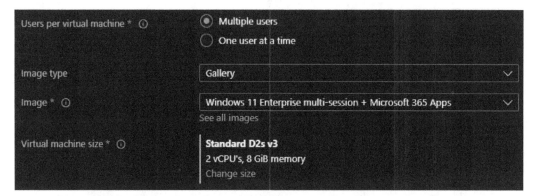

Figure 19.5 – The first four fields within the Virtual Machines tab within the Getting started wizard

16. Enter a **Name prefix** for naming the session hosts that will be deployed.

17. Under **Number of virtual machines**, specify the number of virtual machines you would like to deploy:

Figure 19.6 – The Name prefix and Number of virtual machines fields

18. **Specify domain or unit**. This option enables you to specify a domain to join and the organizational unit path you wish to use. For this example, we will select **No**:

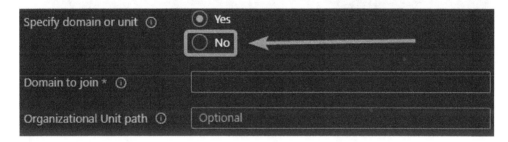

Figure 19.7 – The Specify domain or unit section

19. Select a **Domain controller resource group**. This is the resource group where the domain controller will reside.

20. Select a **Domain controller virtual machine**:

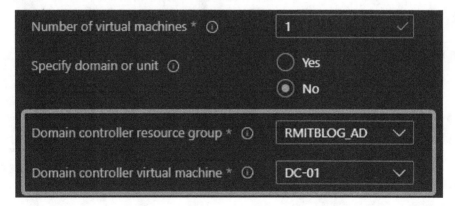

Figure 19.8 – The Domain controller resource group and Domain controller virtual machine fields

21. You can also chain a custom **Azure Resource Manager (ARM)** template. This allows you to insert specific customizations into the deployment process. You can download an example template customization here: `https://github.com/Azure/RDS-Templates/tree/master/wvd-sh/arm-template-customization`. In this example, we will skip linking to the Azure template:

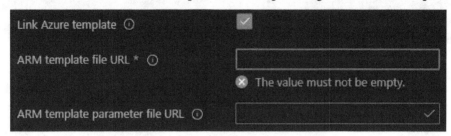

Figure 19.9 – The Link Azure template section within the Virtual Machines tab when using the Getting started wizard

22. Click **Next: Assignments** to move on to the **Assignments** tab.

23. Within the **Assignments** tab, you can create a test user account. This will be used as a validation user account to test your deployment. In this example, we will skip the **Create test user account** section. Uncheck the box for **Create test user account**:

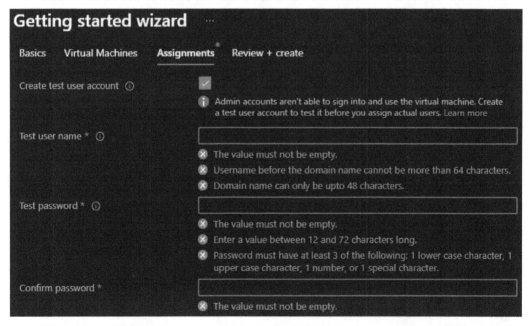

Figure 19.10 – The Create test user account fields within the Assignments tab in the Getting started wizard

24. Within the **Assign existing users or groups** field, add the users or groups you wish to add to this Azure Virtual Desktop deployment:

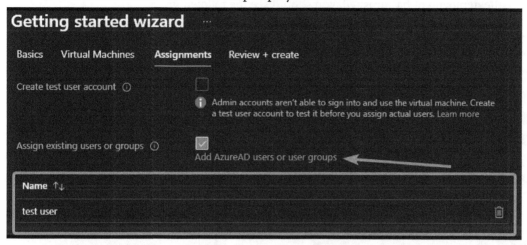

Figure 19.11 – Button to add users and groups to the Getting started wizard deployment

25. Once you've finished adding users and groups, click **Review + Create** to progress to the **Review + create** tab:

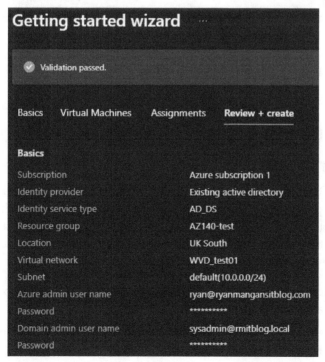

Figure 19.12 – The Getting Started wizard – validation has passed

26. Once validation has passed, click **Create**.

Once the deployment has finished, you should see the following:

Figure 19.13 – Your deployment is complete

In the next section, we will look at using the Getting started feature without an identity provider.

Using the Getting started feature without an identity provider

Interestingly, when deploying Azure Virtual Desktop using the Getting started feature without an identity provider, the wizard has fewer options. The reason for this is that the Getting started wizard will deploy the Azure Active Directory Services infrastructure as part of the wizard and will take care of the majority of the configurations. Let's take a look at using this feature without the identity provider settings:

1. Within the Getting started wizard, in the **Basics** tab, under **Identity provider**, you will need to select **No identity provider**.

2. Under the **Identity service type** section, you will see that the only option you have is **Azure AD Domain Services**; select it:

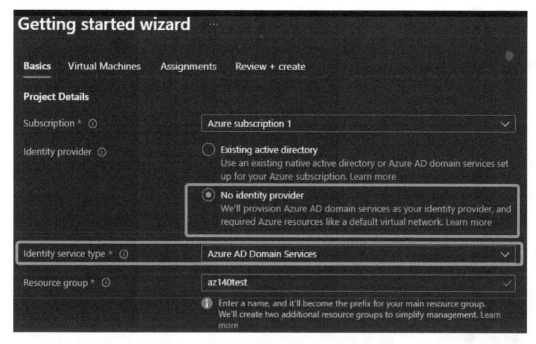

Figure 19.14 – Setting the No identity provider option

3. You need to make sure that you set a **Domain admin user name** and **Password** as these credentials will be used with the deployed Azure Active Directory Domain Services resource:

Figure 19.15 – The Domain administrator credentials section within the Getting started wizard

4. You may also note that there is less to configure within the **Virtual Machines** tab:

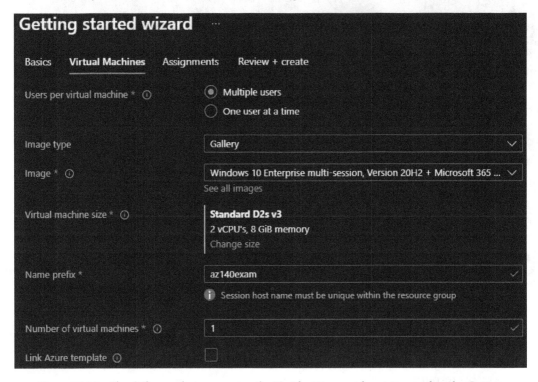

Figure 19.16 – The difference between using the No identity provider option within the Getting started wizard

Now, let's look at the post-deployment cleanup.

Post-deployment cleanup

Once you have deployed Azure Virtual Desktop, you will see that two resource groups have been created – one marked with a prefix of -avd, which specifies all the resources you require for Azure Virtual Desktop to function, and another marked with a prefix of -deployment, which specifies all the resources that will be used to automate the deployment of the Azure Virtual Desktop environment within your subscription:

Figure 19.17 – Two resource groups created by the Getting started feature

If you have used the Getting started feature to deploy an Azure Virtual Desktop environment without an identity, such as when using a new Azure AD DS, then you will see three resource groups marked with the `-deployment`, `-avd`, and `-Prerequisite` prefixes.

In the following screenshot, you can see the resources that have been used to deploy the Azure Virtual Desktop environment:

Figure 19.18 – The -deployment resource group's contents

The resource group marked with the prefix of prerequisite contains the virtual network, network security group, and the Azure AD DS resource. The following screenshot shows what you will find within this resource group:

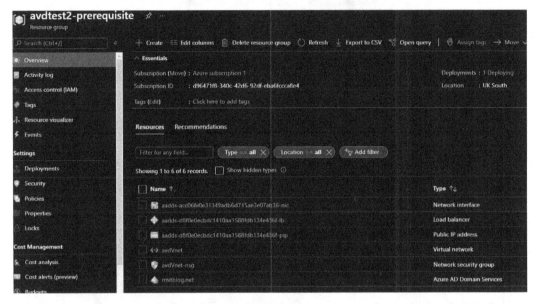

Figure 19.19 – The resource group deployed as part of the Getting started wizard when the No identity provider option is selected

You can go ahead and delete the resource group marked as -deployment as it's no longer required. If you have finished with the deployment, you can remove the two/three resource groups to safely delete the deployed Azure Virtual Desktop environment.

Now, let's look at some of the errors you may see and how to solve them while troubleshooting the Getting started feature.

Troubleshooting the Getting started feature

In this section, we'll look at some of the issues and errors you may come across when using the Getting started wizard.

The following table details some of the most common issues:

Error	Description
No subscriptions.	When opening the Getting started feature wizard, you will see an error message stating *no subscriptions*. This is because you need to activate the Azure subscription. You should also ensure that the user account that's being used has the *Owner* **role-based access control (RBAC)** applied to the subscription.
The username must not include reserved words.	Make sure that you are not using any of the words that have been reserved by Microsoft. The following link lists these reserved words: `https://docs.microsoft.com/azure/azure-resource-manager/templates/error-reserved-resource-name`.
The value must be between 12 and 72 characters long.	This error message occurs when you have a password less than 12 or more than 72 characters long. You also need to ensure that the password will comply with Azure's password length and complexity requirements.
You don't have permission.	This issue is related to the user account not having the owner permissions applied to the active Azure subscription.
The `Microsoft.Powershell.DSC` extension is installed on the Active Directory Domain controller **VM has reported a failure when processing extension Microsoft.Powershell.DSC.**	Uninstall the `Microsoft.powershell.DSC` extension.

You can read more about troubleshooting the Azure Virtual Desktop Getting started feature here: `https://docs.microsoft.com/azure/virtual-desktop/troubleshoot-getting-started?`.

Summary

In this chapter, we looked at using the Getting started feature to simplify the deployment of Azure Virtual Desktop. We started by looking at the benefits before looking at the prerequisites. We then ran through the full Getting started wizard and looked at the subtle differences between using an existing identity provider and no identity provider. Finally, we learned how to troubleshoot deployment errors when using the Getting started wizard feature.

Questions

Answer the following questions to test your knowledge of this chapter:

1. How many resource groups are created when deploying an Azure Virtual Desktop environment when creating an Azure AD DS environment as a part of the deployment?

2. When you're deploying an Azure Virtual Desktop environment using the Getting started feature, what is the required RBAC role for the user account?

3. Which resource group should you delete once you've deployed using the Getting started wizard?

4. If the resource group with the `-prerequisites` prefix is present, which resources would you expect to find in there?

Answers

1. *-prerequisites, -deployment, and -avd*

2. *Owner*

3. *-deployment*

4. *Azure Active Directory, virtual network, network security group*

Appendix
Microsoft Resources and Microsoft Learn

The following table details a number of additional resources that you may find useful. The links provided include technical information, new releases, and information relating to fixes and implementing new features for Azure Virtual Desktop:

Name	Website
Virtual Desktops Community	`https://virtualdesktops.community/`
MS Learn – Azure Virtual Desktop	`https://docs.microsoft.com/learn/paths/m365-wvd/`
Azure Virtual Desktop forum	`https://techcommunity.microsoft.com/t5/azure-virtual-desktop/bd-p/AzureVirtualDesktopForum`
Microsoft Docs – Azure Virtual Desktop	`https://docs.microsoft.com/azure/virtual-desktop/`
Azure Virtual Desktop ebooks	`https://azure.microsoft.com/en-gb/resources/whitepapers/search/?term=Azure+Virtual+Desktop&type=EBookResource`
Azure Virtual Desktop Feedback	`https://techcommunity.microsoft.com/t5/azure-virtual-desktop-feedback/idb-p/AzureVirtualDesktop`

Azure Virtual Desktop Community shout-outs!

The IT industry is full of very smart people who spend their own time solving problems and creating software, scripts, and other solutions for the community that is free for all. The following list features some of the community members you should check out for information on Azure Virtual Desktop:

Name	Social channel / website
Simon Binder	www.kneedeepintech.com
Freek Berson	https://microsoftplatform.blogspot.com/
Christiaan Brinkhoff	www.christiaanbrinkhoff.com
Marcel Meurer	https://blog.itprocloud.de/
Neil McLoughlin	www.virtualmanc.co.uk
Anoop Chandran	www.howtomanagedevices.com
Bas van Kaam	www.bassvankaam.com
Patrick Köhler	https://avdlogix.com/
Shabaz Darr	https://iamitgeek.com/
Stefan Dingemase	https://stefandingemanse.com/
Sander Rozemuller	https://rozemuller.com/
Niels Kok	https://www.nielskok.tech/
Travis Roberts	https://www.ciraltos.com/
Ryan Mangan	https://Ryanmangansitblog.com
Johan Vanneuville	https://johanvanneuville.com/
James Kindon	https://jkindon.com/
Esther Barthel	https://www.virtues.it/
Donna Ryan	http://www.thenotoriousdrr.com/
Tom Hickling	https://xenithit.blogspot.com/
Jim Moyle	https://www.youtube.com/jimmoyle
Jen Sheerin	https://www.jensheerin.com/
Denis Gundarev	https://twitter.com/fdwl
Dean Cefola	https://www.youtube.com/AzureAcademy
Peter Wigleven	https://twitter.com/PieterWigleven
Marco Moioli	https://twitter.com/marco_moioli
Ryan Mangan (GitHub)	https://github.com/RMITBLOG

Cool vendors

Here is a list of cool vendors that you can use with Azure Virtual Desktop:

Vendor name	Description	Link
appCURE	appCURE helps customers with the migration of legacy apps to Windows 10 and Windows 11. appCURE uses unique packaging technologies and methodoligys to help customers move quickly from a to b. appCURE also rovides a full MSIX app attach packaging portfolio to assist with delivering MSIX images to Azure Virtual Desktop.	www.appcure.io
LoginVSI	Understand the impact of change in your production environment.	www.loginvsi.com
IGEL	Edge operating system for cloud workspaces	www.igel.com
Rimo3	Analyze, modernize, and manage applications at scale and quickly in any Windows environment.	www.rimo3.com
Nerdio	Quickly and easily deploy Azure Virtual Desktop and Windows 365, manage all environments from one simple platform, and optimize costs by saving up to 75% on Azure compute and storage.	https://getnerdio.com/
AppVentiX	Deployment and application life cycle management for Microsoft Application Virtualization (App-V) and MSIX.	https://appventix.com/
Parallels Remote Application Server	Extend Azure Virtual Desktop capabilities by integrating, configuring, and unifying all virtual workloads and resources from a centralized console.	www.parallels.com
VMware	Get more value from your existing VMware investments by modernizing your **Virtual Desktop Infrastructure (VDI)** with Azure Virtual Desktop.	www.vmware.com
Citrix	Get more value from your existing Citrix investments by modernizing your VDI with Azure Virtual Desktop.	www.citrix.com

Other resources written by Ryan Mangan

You can read more from Ryan on Azure Virtual Desktop here:

Title	Link
A introduction to MSIX App attach	`https://www.amazon.co.uk/Introduction-MSIX-App-attach-Application-ebook/dp/B08L43M6KM/ref=sr_1_1?keywords=ryan+mangan&qid=1639484968&sr=8-1`
Quickstart Guide to Azure Virtual Desktop	`https://azure.microsoft.com/en-gb/resources/quickstart-guide-to-azure-virtual-desktop/`
Azure Virtual Desktop Handbook: Disaster Recovery	`https://azure.microsoft.com/en-gb/resources/azure-virtual-desktop-handbook-disaster-recovery/`
Migration guide: Citrix Cloud with Azure Virtual Desktop	`https://azure.microsoft.com/en-gb/resources/migration-guide-citrix-cloud-with-azure-virtual-desktop/`
Azure Virtual Desktop: Application Management	`https://azure.microsoft.com/en-gb/resources/azure-virtual-desktop-handbook-application-management/`

Summary

This short chapter provided you with a number of Microsoft and community resources that you can turn to for further reading. I hope you enjoyed this book and found it useful, and I want to say a big thank you for buying a copy.

Final Assessment

Welcome to the study guide assessment test. The test questions are designed to resemble real-world **AZ-140** exam questions. To make the test as realistic as possible, you should attempt the questions *closed book* and allocate the time accurately. You can use notepaper or a sketchpad to jot down notes, although this will be different in a real test environment as you will be using an approved Microsoft software-based testing solution. To take a look at the Microsoft Learn site for the AZ-140 exam, check out the following URL: `https://docs.microsoft.com/learn/certifications/exams/az-140`.

Number of questions: 53

Length of test: 90 minutes

Passing score: 75% (estimated)

Questions

1. What is Azure Virtual Desktop?

    A. An Azure service that provides both a desktop and app virtualization service in the cloud

    B. A service that provides desktop virtualization for on-premises users

    C. A Windows Server role that provides both desktop and app virtualization similar to Remote Desktop Services

2. What subscription is required before you can set up Azure Virtual Desktop?

    A. Windows 10/11 subscription

    B. Microsoft 365 subscription

    C. Azure subscription

3. Which of the following options is not a method to synchronize Active Directory with AD DS?

   A. Password hash sync

   B. Pass-through authentication

   C. Windows Hello for Business

   D. AD replication

4. You have a group of internal software developers that require virtual desktops that they can manage. What type of host pool would you create for them?

   A. Personal

   B. Pooled

   C. Standalone

5. If you create a pooled host pool, which **virtual machine (VM)** image should you use?

   A. A Windows 11 or Windows 10 multi-session image

   B. A VM image that can support Windows Server or Windows 7

   C. Windows 10

6. You need to ensure your users can access both apps and a remote desktop. How do you give your users the required access?

   A. Not possible. Users can only belong to one application group type at a time.

   B. Create a RemoteApp application group and assign it to the required Azure AD users or groups.

   C. Assign the RemoteApp and desktop application groups to the required users.

7. Which of the following steps is not part of creating an FSLogix profile?

   A. Create an Azure Storage account with a file share.

   B. Create a new role in Azure AD to read from and write to Azure Storage.

   C. Install FSLogix on the Azure Virtual Desktop gallery image.

8. What's one of the key reasons you would use automated scaling in Azure Virtual Desktop?

   A. To increase virtual disk storage when users get close to reaching the limits in a VM

   B. To increase service uptime and overall availability

   C. To save costs by matching the required number of running VMs to user demand

9. Which of these steps is not part of testing MSIX app attach?

   A. Destage

   B. Deregister

   C. Stage

   D. Enable

10. Which of the following Windows operating systems can you use MSIX app attach with? Choose the correct three.

    A. Windows 10 version 2004 and later

    B. Windows 11

    C. Server 2022

    D. Windows 8.1

    E. Windows 7 Enterprise

11. How does Azure Firewall help protect network traffic for Azure Virtual Desktop?

    A. Only allows network traffic that's routed to the Azure Virtual Desktop service

    B. Denies all network traffic to the internet

    C. Denies all network traffic routed to the firewall except traffic explicitly allowed by firewall rules or policies

12. Your company is preparing a **Business Continuity Disaster Recovery (BCDR)** strategy for an Azure Virtual Desktop environment. You need to configure your host pool to failover to another region in case of a major outage in the Azure region that you operate. What service should you include in the BCDR plan for Azure Virtual Desktop?

   A. Use ExpressRoute to establish connectivity with the virtual network that's used by Azure Virtual Desktop.

   B. Azure Backup.

   C. Azure Site Recovery.

   D. Virtual network peering.

13. You want to implement a disaster recovery plan for your domain controllers, which are used in your Azure Virtual Desktop deployment. Currently, these domain controllers are deployed in the North Europe region.

   Your design must provide a region failure solution. What do you need to include in the disaster recovery plan?

   A. Implement two domain controllers in the West Europe region.

   B. Create a site-to-site VPN with your on-premises network.

   C. Implement two domain controllers in an availability zone.

   D. Use Azure AD.

14. Which of the following services or components should you include in your BCDR plan for Azure Virtual Desktop?

   A. FSLogix Profile Container

   B. Connection broker

   C. Roaming profiles

   D. Mandatory profiles

15. Why is Conditional Access recommended as a security control for Azure Virtual Desktop deployments?

   A. It allows for the management of risk before access is granted.

   B. Enabling Conditional Access lets you manage risk before you grant users access to your Azure Virtual Desktop environment.

   C. You simplify users' access to **multifactor authentication (MFA)** using Conditional Access.

16. Which of the following services should an administrator enable in a secure Azure Virtual Desktop deployment?

    A. A generic administration password to limit complexity for users and admins

    B. Reduced logging for performance reasons

    C. Azure MFA

17. What is the recommended tool to understand the connection **round-trip time (RTT)** from a specific location through the Azure Virtual Desktop service to an Azure region?

    A. Azure Virtual Desktop Experience Estimator

    B. Azure Pricing Calculator

    C. Remote Desktop Services Diagnostic tool

18. What Desktop Virtualization role should be assigned to allow a user to manage all aspects of Azure Virtual Desktop host pools, including access to resources?

    A. Desktop Virtualization Host Pool Contributor

    B. Desktop Virtualization Reader

    C. Desktop Virtualization Workspace Contributor

    D. Desktop Virtualization User Session Operator

19. You have an on-premises network with an Azure subscription containing a virtual network, an Azure Virtual Desktop host pool, and Azure Firewall. The virtual network connects the on-premises network using a typical site-to-site VPN. You have been asked by management to make sure that only users within the on-premises network connect to the Azure Virtual Desktop in the host pool. What should they do?

    A. Run the `New-AzRoleAssignment` cmdlet.

    B. Run `mstsc.exe`.

    C. Conditional Access policy assignments.

20. Your organization wants you to enable security posture management for VMs that includes a secure configuration assessment and Secure Score. What should you do?

    A. Utilize Microsoft Defender for Cloud.

    B. Configure automatic assignment.

    C. Enable **network security groups (NSGs)**.

21. Your organization deploys Azure Virtual Desktop using the Start/Stop VMs during off-hours solution in Azure. You want to isolate VMs that should never be stopped by the solution. What should you configure?

    A. Remote Desktop Services Diagnostic

    B. Remote connection gateway service

    C. An Azure Automation account variable

22. Your organization wants to monitor Azure Virtual Desktop with Azure Virtual Desktop Insights (included with Azure Monitor). Which diagnostic destination setting should you use for configuring the host pool?

    A. Azure Resource Mover

    B. Azure Queue Storage

    C. Log Analytics workspace

23. What should you configure for FSLogix in the event of a primary location shutdown?

    A. Configure FileStorage storage accounts.

    B. Configure the FSLogix agent with a path to the secondary location within the main Azure region.

24. What should be used to enable VM image sharing between regions?

    A. Azure VM Image Builder

    B. Azure Marketplace

    C. Azure Compute Gallery

25. What is the recommended method to manage the language requirements for users of a Windows 10/11 Enterprise multi-session image?

    A. Build dedicated host pools with a customized image for each language.

    B. Provide access to Azure Compute Gallery images.

    C. Customize the images to ensure all the required languages are installed on the image, enabling the user to select the most appropriate language.

26. What does Azure Virtual Desktop use for establishing remote sessions and streaming **Remote Desktop Protocol (RDP)** traffic?

    A. Session host communication channel

    B. RDP

    C. Reverse connect transport

    D. Azure Bastion

27. What is used to ensure secure connectivity and prevent exposing **Remote Desktop Protocol Secure Shell (RDP/SSH)** ports being opened externally to all VMs in a virtual network?

    A. NSGs

    B. Azure Load Balancer

    C. Azure Bastion

    D. HTML5

28. Which of the following is the recommended Azure Virtual Desktop user profile solution?

    A. FSLogix Profile Container

    B. Azure Disk Storage

    C. User Profile Disks

    D. Roaming profiles

29. Which storage solution is used to deploy Azure file shares on Premium/**solid-state disk-based (SSD-based)** hardware?

    A. FileStorage storage account

    B. **General-purpose version 2 (GPv2)** storage account

    C. Premium block blobs

    D. Azure NetApp Files

30. What should be used to register VMs to the Azure Virtual Desktop host pool?

    A. Azure Virtual Desktop agent.

    B. Create a VM from a managed image.

    C. Azure Compute Gallery image.

    D. Azure portal.

31. Your organization has an Azure Virtual Desktop host pool with ten Windows 11 Enterprise multi-session hosts. The users connect to the Azure Virtual Desktop deployment from Windows 11 computers.

    You plan on using FSLogix Application Masking to deploy Application Masking rule sets. Where should these rule sets be copied to?

    A. `C:\Program Files\FSLogix\Apps\Rules` on every session host

    B. Azure Storage account

    C. Office Container

    D. The FSLogix Profile Container of each user

32. Which container solution is recommended and most appropriate in non-persistent, virtual environments, such as Azure Virtual Desktop?

    A. Office Container

    B. Cloud Cache

    C. Profile Container

33. Your organization has an Azure Virtual Desktop host pool named `HostPool1a`. You are investigating an issue for a Remote Desktop client that is no longer responding.

    You want the default Remote Desktop client settings restored and unsubscribed for workspaces. What should be done to restore the settings?

    A. Run `msrdcw.exe`.

    B. Install the FSLogix agent on all session hosts in `HostPool1a`.

    C. Use the Azure Guest Agent service.

    D. Configure a workspace.

34. Your organization has an Azure Virtual Desktop host pool named `HostPool1a` and two session hosts named `AVDSH1a` and `AVDSH2a`. Additionally, they have app groups named `AppRGR1a` and `AppRGR2a` with a RemoteApp named `UserRA1a`. You have been asked to configure a policy to prevent users from copying and pasting content from `UserRA1` to a local computer or device. What should you do to configure this?

    A. Modify the RDP properties of `HostPool1a`.

    B. Require MFA.

    C. Re-register the `AppRGR1a` and `AppRGR2a` app groups.

35. What format should MSIX packages be in for a file share using MSIX app attach?

    A. Azure Compute Gallery

    B. MSIX images

    C. MSIX packages

    D. ZIP files

36. You receive requests for chat, calling, and meeting functionalities from users within your Azure Virtual Desktop environment. What should you configure?

    A. Microsoft Teams on Azure Virtual Desktop

    B. Go to meeting

    C. Skype for Business

37. Your organization has an Azure AD tenant named `rmitblog.com` and an Azure virtual network named `VNET2`.

    You deploy a new Azure AD DS managed domain named `rmitblog2.com` on `VNET2` within your Azure subscription.

    You have been asked to deploy an Azure Virtual Desktop host pool named `Pool1` on `VNET2`.

    You must ensure that you can deploy Windows 11 Enterprise host pools to `Pool1`.

    What should you do first?

    A. Modify the settings of the `rmitblog2.com` DNS zone.

    B. Modify the DNS settings of `VNET2`.

    C. Add a custom domain name to `rmitblog1.com`.

    D. Configure Azure AD Connect cloud sync.

38. You have the local client devices shown in the following table:

Name	Operating System
Device_a	Windows 10 Home
Device_b	Windows 8.1 Professional
Device_c	Windows 10 IoT Enterprise
Device_d	Windows 11

You plan to deploy Azure Virtual Desktop for client access to remove virtualized apps. Which devices support the Remote Desktop client?

A. Device_a, Device_b, and Device_d

B. Device_a, Device_c, and Device_d

C. Device_a, Device_b, and Device_c

D. Device_a and Device_d

E. Device_a

39. You plan to deploy Azure Virtual Desktop. The deployment will use existing VMs. You create an Azure Virtual Desktop host pool.

You must ensure that you can add the VMs to the host pool. What should you do first?

A. Register the Microsoft.DesktopVirtualization provider.

B. Generate a token.

C. Run the Invoke-AzVMRunCommand cmdlet.

D. Create a role assignment.

40. You have an Azure Compute Gallery that contains the Windows 11 images shown in the following table:

Name	Location	Operating System State
Image_a	UK South	Generalized
Image_b	UK South	Specialized
Image_c	North Europe	Generalized
Image_d	North Europe	Specialized

You create an Azure Virtual Desktop deployment that has the following settings:

- Host pool name: `Pool1`
- Host pool type: Pooled
- Location: UK South

Which of the images listed can you use for the session hosts?

A. `Image_a`

B. All listed images

C. `Image_b`

D. `Image_a` and `Image_b`

E. `Image_a` and `Image_c`

41. Your organization has an Azure Virtual Desktop host pool named `Pool1a` that contains the following:

- A linked workspace named `Workspace1a`
- An application group named `Default Desktop`
- A session host named `Host1a`

You have been asked to add a new data disk. What should you modify?

A. `Host1a`

B. `Workspace1a`

C. `Pool1a`

D. `Default Desktop`

42. You deploy a new Azure Virtual Desktop session host named `pool1a`.

You have been asked to provide a small group of pilot users access to the VMs in the new host, `pool1a`.

What should you do to provide access?

A. Add the required users to the local Administrators group on the VMs.

B. Add the required users to a Remote Desktop Users group on the VMs.

C. Create a role definition.

D. Create a role assignment.

43. You have an Azure Virtual Desktop deployment. You publish a RemoteApp named `App1`. You need `App1` to appear in the Remote Desktop client as Sales Contact Application. Which PowerShell cmdlet should you use?

    A. `New-AzADApplication`

    B. `Update-AzWvdApplicationGroup`

    C. `Register-AzWvdApplicationGroup`

    D. `Update-AzWvdApplication`

44. Your organization has an Azure Virtual Desktop host pool that contains four session hosts. The Microsoft Teams client has been installed on each session host.

    You discover that only the Microsoft Teams chat and collaboration features work on this host pool. The calling and meeting features are disabled.

    You have been asked to configure the following features:

    • Teams calling

    • Meetings

    What should you do?

    A. Install the Remote Desktop WebRTC Redirector Service.

    B. Configure remote audio mode in the host pool's RDP properties.

    C. Install the Teams Meeting add-in for Outlook.

    D. Configure audio input redirection.

45. Your organization's network contains an on-premises AD domain and an Azure Virtual Desktop deployment. All the session host computer accounts are stored in an **organizational unit (OU)** named `AVDHostOU`. All user accounts are stored in an OU named `ORGUsers`.

    A colleague creates a **Group Policy Object (GPO)** named `Policy1` that only contains user settings. Your colleague links `Policy1` to `AVDHostOU`.

    During testing, you discover that when users sign in to the session hosts, none of the settings from `Policy1` are being applied.

    What must you configure to apply GPO settings to users when they sign in to the session hosts?

    A. Loopback processing

    B. FSLogix profiles

C. Mandatory Roaming User Profiles

D. Restricted groups

46. Your organization has built a basic Azure Virtual Desktop deployment.

    You have been asked to make a recommendation to run containerized applications without installing the applications on the master session host image.

    What should you include in your recommendation?

    A. EXE applications

    B. MSI packages

    C. App-V app packages

    D. MSIX images (MSIX app packages)

47. Your organization has an Azure Virtual Desktop host pool named `Pool1a`, an application named `App1a`, and an Azure file share named `Share1a`.

    You must ensure that you can publish `App1a` to `Pool1a` using MSIX app attach.

    Which five of the following actions should you perform and in which order before you publish `App1a`?

    List out the required five actions in sequence:

Actions	Answer area
Create an MSIX image.	
Generate a code-signing certificate.	
Upload the MSIX package to Share1a.	
Create an MSIX package.	
Upload an MSIX image to share1a.	
Configure the required storage permissions for MSIX app attach.	

48. Your organization has an Azure Virtual Desktop host pool that runs Windows 11 Enterprise multi-session. You have been asked to configure automatic scaling of the host pool that meets the following requirements (Preview feature):

    ▪ Distribute new user sessions across all running session hosts.

    ▪ Automatically start a new session host when concurrent user sessions exceed 30 users per host.

What should you include in the solution?

A.   Scaling plan and the depth-first load balancing algorithm

B.   Scaling plan and the breadth-first load balancing algorithm

C.   The breadth-first load balancing algorithm

D.   The depth-first load balancing algorithm

49.   Your organization has an Azure Virtual Desktop host pool in the UK West
Azure region. You must ensure that the host pool can failover to the UK South
Azure region.

What should you configure to ensure the host pool can failover?

A.   Create a Recovery Services vault.

B.   Create VM snapshots for each session host in the pool.

C.   Create an Azure Storage account that uses **geo-redundant storage** (**GRS**).

D.   Configure Cloud Cache.

50.   Your organization has an Azure Virtual Desktop host pool named `Pool1a` in the
West Europe region. You have a storage account named `storage1a` that contains
FSLogix Profile Containers.

In the West Europe region, you have an Azure Compute Gallery named `ACG1a` that
contains a VM image named `Image1a`. `Image1a` is used to deploy new session
hosts in `Pool1`.

You have been asked to deploy a new Azure Virtual Desktop host pool named
`Pool2a` to the UK South Azure region.

You have been asked to implement a session host deployment solution for `Pool2a`
that meets the following requirements:

- `Image1a` must replicate in the West Europe region.

- The session hosts in `Pool2a` must be based on `Image1a`.

- Changes made to `Image1a` must be available in the UK South and West
Europe regions.

What should you do?

A.   Create a new Azure Compute Gallery named `ACG2a` in the UK South region.
Upload a copy of `Image1a` to `ACG2a`.

B.   Create a new Azure Storage account named `storage2a` in the UK South
region. Copy `Image1a` to a shared folder in `storage2a`.

C. Using `ACG1a`, update the replication configuration for the latest image version of `Image1`.

D. Configure GRS replication for `storage1a`. Copy the VHD file of `Image1a` to the FSLogix Profile Container.

51. You have deployed an Azure Virtual Desktop host pool named `Pool1b`. You have an Azure Storage account named `store1a` that FSLogix Profile Container in a share named `fslprofiles`.

    You have been asked to configure the path to the storage containers for the session hosts.

    Which path should you use?

    A. `\\store1a.blob.core.windows.net\fslprofiles`

    B. `https://store1a.file.core.windows.net/fslprofiles`

    C. `\\store1a.file.core.windows.net\fslprofiles`

    D. `https://store1a.blob.core.windows.net/fslprofiles`

52. You have been asked to deploy Azure Virtual Desktop session host VMs based on a preconfigured master (gold) image. The master image will be stored in Azure Compute Gallery.

    You create a VM named `Image1a` to use as the master image. You install applications and apply all the required configuration changes to `Image1a`.

    You must ensure that the new session host VMs created based on `Image1a` have unique names and security identifiers.

    What should you do on `Image1a` before you add the image to Azure Compute Gallery?

    A. At a command prompt, run the `sysprep` command.

    B. From PowerShell, run the `rename-computer` cmdlet.

53. You have an Azure Virtual Desktop host pool named `Pool1a` and an Azure Storage account named `Storage1a`. `Storage1a` stores FSLogix Profile Containers in a shared folder named `share1a`.

    You have completed the following:

    • You create a new group named `Group1a`.

    • You provide `Group1a` with permission to sign in to `Pool1a`.

You must now ensure that the members of `Group1a` can store the FSLogix Profile Containers in `share1a`. The solution must also use the principle of least privilege.

Which two privileges should you assign to `Group1a`? Please ensure you select two answers.

A. The Storage Blob Data Contributor role for `storage1a`

B. The List Folder/Read Data NTFS permissions for `share1a`

C. The Storage File Data SMB Share Reader role for `storage1a`

D. The Storage File Data SMB Share Elevated Contributorrole for `storage1a`

E. The Storage File Data SMB Share Contributor role for `storage1a`

Answers

1. **A**. Azure Virtual Desktop, previously known as Windows Virtual Desktop, is a cloud-based desktop and app virtualization service offered by Microsoft within Microsoft Azure.

    External reference: `https://docs.microsoft.com/azure/virtual-desktop/overview`

    See *Chapter 1, Introduction to Azure Virtual Desktop*, for more information.

2. **C**. Before you can start to set up and configure an Azure Virtual Desktop environment, you need to ensure you have an Azure subscription.

    External reference: `https://docs.microsoft.com/azure/virtual-desktop/overview#requirements`

    See *Chapter 2, Design Azure Virtual Desktop Architecture*, for more information.

3. **C**. Azure Virtual Desktop requires the on-premises AD to be synchronized to Azure AD. Both password hash sync and pass-through authentication are two features of AD sync. See *Chapter 3, Designing for User Identities and Profiles*.

    External reference: `https://docs.microsoft.com/azure/virtual-desktop/authentication#on-premise-identity`

4. **A.** Typically, software developers use applications that require local administration permissions to run as well as the requirement of downloading and installing extensions and software libraries. Using a pooled desktop would not be suitable for this type of use case. See *Chapter 7, Configure Azure Virtual Desktop Host Pools.*

   External reference: https://docs.microsoft.com/azure/architecture/example-scenario/wvd/windows-virtual-desktop#personal-and-pooled-desktops

5. **A.** Pooled desktops are for use with multiple users sharing the same session host. Using either Windows 10 multi-session or Windows 11 multi-session is a cost-effective way of delivering a Virtual Desktop environment as well as a similar user experience to what a user would expect using a traditional physical device. See *Chapter 2, Designing Azure Virtual Desktop Architecture.*

   External reference: https://docs.microsoft.com/azure/virtual-desktop/windows-10-multisession-faq#what-is-windows-10-enterprise-multi-session

6. **C.** You would need to assign users to both the desktop and RemoteApp application groups to ensure access. See *Chapter 15, Configuring Apps on a Session Host.*

   External reference: https://docs.microsoft.com/azure/virtual-desktop/environment-setup#app-groups

7. **C.** FSLogix is pre-installed on all Windows 10 Enterprise multi-session images, this removes the need to install FSLogix apps on the master image. However, for the few that use a custom blank image, you would need to ensure that you have installed the FSLogix software on the master image. See *Chapter 12, Implementing and Managing FSLogix.*

   External reference: https://docs.microsoft.com/azure/virtual-desktop/windows-10-multisession-faq#which-profile-management-solution-should-i-use-for-windows-10-enterprise-multi-session

8. **C.** The purpose of automated scaling is to help customers reduce the overall cost of Azure Virtual Desktop using scaling. See *Chapter 17, Automate Azure Virtual Desktop Management Tasks.*

   External reference: https://docs.microsoft.com/azure/virtual-desktop/set-up-scaling-script

9. **D**. MSIX app attach has six possible phases for application provision and registration. These are Stage, Register (regular and delayed), Deregister, and Destage. Read more in *Chapter 14, MSIX App Attach*.

    External reference: `https://docs.microsoft.com/azure/virtual-desktop/app-attach-glossary`

10. **A**, **B**, and **C**. MSIX app attach is supported on Windows 10 build 2004 onward, Windows 11, and Server 2022. All other operating systems do not have the required operating system APIs. Please note that for this exam, you may only be given Windows 10 build 2004 as a supported option. Read more in *Chapter 14, MSIX App Attach*.

    External reference: `https://ryanmangansitblog.com/2021/01/29/understanding-whats-general-release-and-whats-supported-for-msix-and-msix-app-attach` and `https://docs.microsoft.com/en-us/azure/virtual-desktop/app-attach-faq#which-operating-systems-support-msix-app-attach-`

11. **C**. Like most firewall vendors, Azure Firewall denies all network traffic to the firewall except traffic that has been allowed using firewall rules or policies. See *Chapter 3, Designing for User Identities and Profiles*, *Chapter 15, Configuring Apps on a Session Host*, *Chapter 13, Configuring User Experience Settings*, *Chapter 2, Designing the Azure Virtual Desktop Architecture*, and *Chapter 4, Implementing and Managing Networking for Azure Virtual Desktop*.

    External reference: `https://docs.microsoft.com/azure/firewall/rule-processing`

12. **C**. To replicate VMs between regions, you would need to use Azure Site Recovery. Read more in *Chapter 16, Planning and Implementing Business Continuity and Disaster Recovery*.

    External reference: `https://docs.microsoft.com/azure/cloud-adoption-framework/scenarios/wvd/eslz-business-continuity-and-disaster-recovery#host-pool-active-active-vs-active-passive`

13. **A**. If there is a regional failure leading to network outage in the North Europe region, services could fail over or be spun up within the West Europe region as the identity servers are present. See more in *Chapter 16, Planning and Implementing Business Continuity and Disaster Recovery*.

External reference: `https://docs.microsoft.com/azure/cloud-adoption-framework/scenarios/wvd/eslz-business-continuity-and-disaster-recovery#design-recommendations`

14. **A.** FSLogix Profile Container, Office Container, and Cloud Cache should be reviewed for any Azure Virtual Desktop BCDR plan. See more in *Chapter 12, Implement and Manage FSLogix.*

   External reference: `https://docs.microsoft.com/azure/cloud-adoption-framework/scenarios/wvd/eslz-business-continuity-and-disaster-recovery#optimal-storage-for-profile-and-office-containers`

15. **A.** Conditional Access enables you to build a set of conditions that must be met to grant access. This enables improved risk management. See more in *Chapter 11, Managing Security.*

   External reference: `https://docs.microsoft.com/azure/virtual-desktop/set-up-mfa#create-a-conditional-access-policy`

16. **C.** It is recommended that Azure MFA is configured and enabled to improve the user sign-in security posture. Read more in *Chapter 11, Managing Security.*

   External reference: `https://docs.microsoft.com/azure/virtual-desktop/authentication#multifactor-authentication`

17. **A.** Azure Virtual Desktop Experience Estimator provides an estimated connection RTT. See *Chapter 2, Designing the Azure Virtual Desktop Architecture.*

   External reference: `https://azure.microsoft.com/services/virtual-desktop/assessment/#estimation-tool`

18. **A.** The Host Pool Contributor role enables the management of all aspects of host pools including access to resources. See *Chapter 10, Managing Access,* for more information.

   External reference: `https://docs.microsoft.com/azure/virtual-desktop/rbac#desktop-virtualization-host-pool-contributor`

19. **C.** You can use trusted IP address ranges to control user access to Azure Virtual Desktop. See *Chapter 11, Manage Security,* for more information.

   External reference: `https://docs.microsoft.com/azure/active-directory/conditional-access/overview`

20. **A**. Microsoft Defender for Cloud, previously known as Azure Security Center, is used for security posture management and security assessments. Read more in *Chapter 11, Managing Security*.

    External reference: `https://docs.microsoft.com/azure/defender-for-cloud/defender-for-cloud-introduction`.

21. **C**. You would use the `External_ExcludeVMNames` variable for those VMs you want to exclude. Please note that the limit is 140 VMs. Read more in *Chapter 17, Automate Azure Virtual Desktop Management Tasks*.

    External reference: `https://docs.microsoft.com/azure/automation/automation-solution-vm-management`

22. **C**. You would configure a Log Analytics workspace. See *Chapter 18, Monitoring and Managing Performance and Health*.

    External reference: `https://docs.microsoft.com/azure/virtual-desktop/azure-monitor`

23. **B**. You would add the secondary region to the FSLogix Profile Container VHDLocations path. See *Chapter 12, Implement and Manage FSLogix*.

    External reference: `https://docs.microsoft.com/fslogix/configure-profile-container-tutorial#configure-profile-container-registry-settings`

24. **C**. Azure Compute Galleries are used to share images. The previous name was **Shared Image Gallery** (**SIG**). Watch out for the old name within the exam. Read more in *Chapter 9, Creating and Managing Session Host Images*.

    External reference: `https://docs.microsoft.com/azure/virtual-machines/shared-image-galleries`

25. **C**. You can add language packs to a Windows 10 multi-session image. Read more in *Chapter 9, Creating and Managing Session Host Images*.

    External reference: `https://docs.microsoft.com/azure/virtual-desktop/language-packs`

26. **C**. Reverse connect is the technology used for Azure Virtual Desktop. Read more in *Chapter 4, Implementing and Managing Networking for Azure Virtual Desktop*.

    External reference: `https://docs.microsoft.com/azure/virtual-desktop/network-connectivity#reverse-connect-transport`

27. **C.** Azure Bastion is used to provide a secure connection to VMs using an HTML5 browser. Read more in *Chapter 4, Implementing and Managing Networking for Azure Virtual Desktop.*

    External reference: `https://docs.microsoft.com/azure/bastion/bastion-overview`

28. **A.** FSLogix Profile Container is the recommended user profile solution of choice. Read more in *Chapter 12, Implement and Manage FSLogix.*

    External reference: `https://docs.microsoft.com/fslogix/overview`

29. **A.** A FileStorage storage account is required. Read more in *Chapter 12, Implement and Manage FSLogix.*

    External reference: `https://docs.microsoft.com/azure/storage/files/storage-files-scale-targets#azure-files-scale-targets`

30. **A.** The Azure Virtual Desktop agent is used to register Azure VMs with the Azure Virtual Desktop service. Read more in *Chapter 13, Configuring User Experience Settings.*

    External reference: `https://docs.microsoft.com/azure/virtual-desktop/troubleshoot-agent`

31. **A.** The app Masking rules need to be deployed to `C:\Program Files\FSLogix\Apps\Rules`. Read more in *Chapter 15, Configuring Apps on Session Host.*

    External reference: `https://docs.microsoft.com/fslogix/application-masking-rules-ht#deploying-rule-sets`

32. **C.** FSLogix Profile Container is the recommended profile container technology. Read more in *Chapter 12, Implement and Manage FSLogix.*

    External reference: `https://docs.microsoft.com/fslogix/configure-profile-container-tutorial`

33. **A.** Running `msrdcw.exe` resets the Remote Desktop client. Read more in *Chapter 13, Configuring User Experience Settings.*

    External reference: `https://docs.microsoft.com/azure/virtual-desktop/troubleshoot-client#remote-desktop-client-for-windows-7-or-windows-10-stops-responding-or-cannot-be-opened`

34. **A.** You can restrict user access to items such as USB redirect and the clipboard using custom RDP properties. Read more in *Chapter 7, Configure Azure Virtual Desktop Host Pools.*

    External reference: `https://docs.microsoft.com/azure/virtual-desktop/customize-rdp-properties#default-rdp-file-properties`

35. **B.** MSIX image is a term used for an MSIX package that has been expanded into a VHD/VHDX image or a CIM image. Read more in *Chapter 14, MSIX App Attach.*

    External reference: `https://docs.microsoft.com/azure/virtual-desktop/app-attach-image-prep`

36. **A.** When using Microsoft Teams in an Azure Virtual Desktop environment, make sure you configure **Audio/Video** (**AV**) redirection to ensure that you don't impact session host performance. You can read more in *Chapter 15, Configuring Apps on a Session Host.*

    External reference: `https://docs.microsoft.com/azure/virtual-desktop/teams-on-avd`

37. **B.** The virtual network DNS must point to the AD or functions such as domain join will fail. Read more in *Chapter 4, Implement and Manage Networking for Azure Virtual Desktop.*

    External reference: `https://docs.microsoft.com/azure/virtual-network/virtual-networks-faq#can-i-specify-dns-servers-for-a-vnet`

38. **B.** Windows 10 and 11 are fully supported. Read more in *Chapter 2, Designing the Azure Virtual Desktop Architecture.*

    External reference: `https://docs.microsoft.com/azure/virtual-desktop/overview#requirements`

39. **B**. Previously known as a registration key, you would generate a token for the host pool to deploy VMs to the specified host pool. Read more in *Chapter 6, Creating Host Pools and Session Hosts*.

    External reference: `https://docs.microsoft.com/azure/virtual-desktop/create-host-pools-powershell?tabs=azure-powershell#create-a-host-pool`

40. **E**. You would need to use generalized images. Read more in *Chapter 9, Creating and Managing Session Host Images*.

    External reference: `https://docs.microsoft.com/windows-hardware/manufacture/desktop/sysprep-process-overview`

41. **A**. You would add a data disk to the image or session host. Read more in *Chapter 9, Creating and Managing Session Host Images*.

    External reference: `https://docs.microsoft.com/azure/virtual-machines/windows/attach-managed-disk-portal#add-a-data-disk`

42. **D**. You would assign specific users or a group as an assignment within the host pool. Read more in *Chapter 7, Configure Azure Virtual Desktop Host Pools*.

    External reference: `https://docs.microsoft.com/azure/virtual-desktop/configure-host-pool-personal-desktop-assignment-type#configure-automatic-assignment`

43. **D**. To update the RemoteApp, you can use the PowerShell `Update-AzWvdApplication` cmdlet.

    See *Chapter 15, Configuring Apps on a Session Host*.

    External reference: `https://docs.microsoft.com/powershell/module/az.desktopvirtualization/update-azwvdapplication?view=azps-7.1.0#example-1--update-a-windows-virtual-desktop-application`

44. **A**. To ensure optimum performance and a good user experience, AV redirection should be used. Read more in *Chapter 15, Configuring Apps on a Session Host*.

    External reference: `https://docs.microsoft.com/azure/virtual-desktop/teams-on-avd`

45. **A.** You should use loopback processing to ensure all the required policies linked to computer objects are applied to the users. Be aware that loopback processing can slow the user logon process. Read more in *Chapter 10, Managing Access.*

    External reference: `https://docs.microsoft.com/troubleshoot/windows-server/group-policy/loopback-processing-of-group-policy`

46. **D.** MSIX app attach provides the administrator the ability to configure MSIX apps in an MSIX image that attach on user logon. This provides a simple way of delivering apps to a session host without having to install the apps on the master image. Read more in *Chapter 14, MSIX App Attach.*

    External reference: `https://docs.microsoft.com/azure/virtual-desktop/what-is-app-attach`

47.

Actions	Answer area
	Configure the required storage permissions for MSIX app attach.
	Generate a code-signing certificate.
Upload the MSIX package to the Share1a.	Create an MSIX package.
	Upload the MSIX image to the share1a.

Read more in *Chapter 14, MSIX App Attach.*

External reference: `https://docs.microsoft.com/azure/virtual-desktop/app-attach-file-share`

48. **A.** You would use a scaling plan and the depth-first load balancing algorithm as depth-first spreads the sessions across all running session hosts. It is important to note that scaling plans are currently in preview and you would need to use an Azure Automation account if you wanted to use the traditional PowerShell method. Read more in *Chapter 17, Automate Azure Virtual Desktop Management Tasks.*

    External reference: `https://docs.microsoft.com/azure/virtual-desktop/autoscale-scaling-plan`

49. **A.** You can use Azure Site Recovery to replicate VMs from one region to another. Read more in *Chapter 16, Planning and Implementing Business Continuity and Disaster Recovery.*

    External reference: `https://docs.microsoft.com/azure/virtual-desktop/disaster-recovery#vm-replication`

50. **C.** You would use Azure Compute Gallery to replicate your master images between the required Azure regions. Read more in *Chapter 9, Creating and Managing Session Host Images*.

External reference: `https://docs.microsoft.com/en-us/azure/virtual-machines/shared-image-galleries#replication`

51. **C.** Azure Files should use the path `\\*.file.core.windows.net\fslprofiles` . `*` denotes the Azure Storage account name. Read more in *Chapter 12, Implementing and Managing FSLogix*, and *Chapter 5, Implement and Manage Storage for Azure Virtual Desktop*.

External reference: `https://docs.microsoft.com/azure/virtual-desktop/create-profile-container-adds`

52. **A.** You would use `sysprep` to generalize the image so that you can upload it to Azure Compute Gallery. You can read more in *Chapter 9, Creating and Managing Session Host Images*.

External reference: `https://docs.microsoft.com/windows-hardware/manufacture/desktop/sysprep-process-overview`

53. **C and F.** You need to ensure that the required NTFS permissions are set: Modify permissions for users, and Modify for creator/owner and full control for administrator. You also need to ensure the File Data SMB Share Contributor role is configured on the Azure Storage account. You can read more in *Chapter 12, Implement and Manage FSLogix*, and *Chapter 5, Implement and Manage Storage for Azure Virtual Desktop*.

External reference: `https://docs.microsoft.com/azure/virtual-desktop/create-profile-container-adds`

Index

N

O

R

S

`Packt.com`

Subscribe to our online digital library for full access to over 7,000 books and videos, as well as industry leading tools to help you plan your personal development and advance your career. For more information, please visit our website.

Why subscribe?

- Spend less time learning and more time coding with practical eBooks and Videos from over 4,000 industry professionals

- Improve your learning with Skill Plans built especially for you

- Get a free eBook or video every month

- Fully searchable for easy access to vital information

- Copy and paste, print, and bookmark content

Did you know that Packt offers eBook versions of every book published, with PDF and ePub files available? You can upgrade to the eBook version at `packt.com` and as a print book customer, you are entitled to a discount on the eBook copy. Get in touch with us at `customercare@packtpub.com` for more details.

At `www.packt.com`, you can also read a collection of free technical articles, sign up for a range of free newsletters, and receive exclusive discounts and offers on Packt books and eBooks.

Other Books You May Enjoy

If you enjoyed this book, you may be interested in these other books by Packt:

Mastering Microsoft Endpoint Manager

Christiaan Brinkhoff, Per Larsen

ISBN: 9781801078993

- Understand how Windows 365 Cloud PC makes the deployment of Windows in the cloud easy
- Configure advanced policy management within MEM
- Discover modern profile management and migration options for physical and cloud PCs
- Harden security with baseline settings and other security best practices
- Find troubleshooting tips and tricks for MEM, Windows 365 Cloud PC, and more
- Discover deployment best practices for physical and cloud-managed endpoints
- Keep up with the Microsoft community and discover a list of MVPs to follow

Hands-On Microsoft Teams - Second Edition

João Ferreira

ISBN: 9781801075275

- Perform scheduling and manage meetings, live events, and webinars
- Create and manage Microsoft Teams templates to streamline company processes
- Deal with permissions and security issues in managing private and public teams and channels
- Extend Microsoft Teams using custom apps, Microsoft 365, and PowerShell automation
- Build your own Teams app with The Developer Portal without writing any code
- Deploy helpful chatbots using QnA Maker and Power Virtual Agents
- Explore Teams use cases for education, frontline work, and personal life
- Bring together knowledge, learning, resources, and insights with the new employee experience platform, Microsoft Viva

Packt is searching for authors like you

If you're interested in becoming an author for Packt, please visit `authors.packtpub.com` and apply today. We have worked with thousands of developers and tech professionals, just like you, to help them share their insight with the global tech community. You can make a general application, apply for a specific hot topic that we are recruiting an author for, or submit your own idea.

Share Your Thoughts

Now you've finished *Mastering Azure Virtual Desktop*, we'd love to hear your thoughts! Scan the QR code below to go straight to the Amazon review page for this book and share your feedback or leave a review on the site that you purchased it from.

`https://packt.link/r/1801075026`

Your review is important to us and the tech community and will help us make sure we're delivering excellent quality content.

Printed in the USA
CPSIA information can be obtained
at www.ICGtesting.com
JSHW061131301023
50973JS00006B/25